Soldier's Paradise

Samuel Fury Childs Daly

Soldier's Paradise

Militarism
in Africa
after Empire

Duke University Press   *Durham and London*   2024

© 2024 Duke University Press
This work is licensed under a Creative Commons Attribution-
NonCommercial-NoDerivatives 4.0 International License,
available at https://creativecommons.org/licenses/by-nc-nd/4.0/.
Printed in the United States of America on acid-free paper ∞
Project Editor: Ihsan Taylor
Designed by Courtney Leigh Richardson
Typeset in Warnock Pro and Helvetica Neue
by Westchester Publishing Services

Library of Congress Cataloging-in-Publication Data
Names: Daly, Samuel Fury Childs, [date] author.
Title: Soldier's paradise : militarism in Africa after empire /
    Samuel Fury Childs Daly.
Description: Durham : Duke University Press, 2024. | Includes
    bibliographical references and index.
Identifiers: LCCN 2023050704 (print)
LCCN 2023050705 (ebook)
ISBN 9781478030836 (paperback)
ISBN 9781478026594 (hardcover)
ISBN 9781478059820 (ebook)
ISBN 9781478094180 (ebook/other)
Subjects: LCSH: Postcolonialism—Nigeria. | Dictatorship—
    Africa—History—20th century. | Military government—
    Africa—History—20th century. | Postcolonialism—Africa.
    | Nigeria—History—1960- | Nigeria—History, Military—
    20th century. | Nigeria—Politics and government—1960- |
    BISAC: POLITICAL SCIENCE / Colonialism & Post-
    Colonialism | LAW / Legal History
Classification: LCC DT515.8 .D24 2024 (print) | LCC DT515.8
    (ebook) | DDC 320.966909/04—dc23/eng/20240405
LC record available at https://lccn.loc.gov/2023050704
LC ebook record available at https://lccn.loc.gov/2023050705

Cover art: Ghana, 1982. Courtesy A. Abbas/Magnum Photos.

THE MOST EXQUISITE PLEASURE IS
DOMINATION. NOTHING CAN COMPARE
WITH THE FEELING. THE MENTAL
SENSATIONS ARE EVEN BETTER THAN
THE PHYSICAL ONES. KNOWING YOU
HAVE POWER HAS TO BE THE BIGGEST
HIGH, THE GREATEST COMFORT.
IT IS COMPLETE SECURITY,
PROTECTION FROM HURT. WHEN
YOU DOMINATE SOMEBODY YOU'RE
DOING HIM A FAVOR. HE PRAYS
SOMEONE WILL CONTROL HIM, TAKE
HIS MIND OFF HIS TROUBLES. YOU'RE
HELPING HIM WHILE HELPING
YOURSELF. EVEN WHEN YOU GET
MEAN HE LIKES IT. SOMETIMES
HE'S ANGRY AND FIGHTS BACK BUT
YOU CAN HANDLE IT. HE ALWAYS
REMEMBERS WHAT HE NEEDS. YOU
ALWAYS GET WHAT YOU WANT.

—Jenny Holzer, untitled
(*Inflammatory Essays*), 1979–1982

"Why have you come here?" a law professor asked me over a beer. We were sitting on a patio at the faculty club of the University of Lagos, overlooking the lagoon that is slowly but surely eroding the spit of land the campus stands on. The vast Third Mainland Bridge crossed the water in the distance, choked with traffic even though it was late at night. I had been telling him about a document I found earlier that day in a library across town. It was an account of a public execution on a Lagos beach from the early 1970s, full of fire and brimstone: "When the military vehicle arrived," a spectator described, "I expected a ragged, brutish man to appear for execution. Instead, I saw a handsome, swishy young man, impeccably clad in a pink shirt and trousers. It was almost unbelievable that that day was going to be his last."[1] Finding a document like this is like striking gold. The suspense, the pathos, the "swishy" bandit dressed in pink—these are things I know I can polish into a good story. I handed a photocopy to my drinking partner, and he looked at it for a while. He held his hands in front of him in a gesture that was both inquiring and supplicating.

"Why do you worry about these old things?" he asked, sounding exasperated but not wanting to offend me. I replayed his question over and over, each time putting the accent on a different word until I no longer remembered where he had actually put it. Why do *you* worry? Why *these* things? I didn't have an answer for him then, and I still don't. But I have an inkling why this grim story of lost freedoms and thwarted plans is the one I chose to tell. Acknowledgments are typically about the people and institutions that give a book form, but the past few years have taught me that context matters too. I wrote *Soldier's Paradise* at a time of intense personal turmoil. What did my unraveling life let me see in this history? What did it *keep* me from seeing? These are vain questions—ones that put the historian too close to the action for my taste. But this is a book about vanity (one raconteur called soldiers "narcissuses in uniform"), so perhaps it's fair to ask them.[2]

Historians bring people back to a shadowy kind of life by digging them out of archives and putting them in our books. I suspect the wraiths we create often look more like *ourselves* than the people we base them on. When we're happy, we make them happy too. When the world around us seems crooked, we tell a crooked tale about them. This book was shaped, I admit, by what was happening in my own life. When my marriage ended, every document that passed through my hands seemed like evidence of failure, as if the only kind of historical change I could register was *decline*. The isolation of the pandemic showed me how the army's camaraderie appealed to loners—I knew because I craved it myself. When, later, I was jilted by a charismatic musician, I could suddenly see why so many people hated Fela Kuti (see chapter 5). I suspect other historians have these solipsistic streaks too, but propriety discourages us from owning up to them. We're more introspective than we used to be about how race, sex, and nationality shape the study of the past. We're less attuned to how other factors—psychology, circumstances—might also be in play. I acknowledge the fury and solitude that helped me write this book. You can probably see it peeking between the lines.

None of this is to say that people and institutions aren't important. An army of friends helped me through this hard time, and many colleagues have contributed to this book through reading, talking, and arguing (and to be clear, no one has agreed with all of it). Whatever interpretive crimes committed here were my work alone, but Neil Agarwal, Nima Bassiri, Nishant Batsha, Mark Drury, James Clinton Francis, Sara Katz, Vivian Chenxue Lu, Gregory Mann, Elizabeth Jacqueline Marcus, Nana Osei-Opare, Mairi Shepherd, Nicholas W. Stephenson Smith, Titilola Halimat Somotan, Luise White, and Thomas Wilson Williams left fingerprints at the scene. At the University of Chicago, my new academic home, I'm grateful to Adom Getachew, Adrian Johns, Kenneth Moss, Emily Osborn, Steve Pincus, Danielle Roper, Amy Dru Stanley, Thuto Thipe, and others for making my transition to Chicago so seamless. I look forward to many years of working together. At Duke, where I started this book, I'm grateful to my beloved colleagues in the Department of African and African American Studies (AAAS). Mark Anthony Neal gave me the kind of freedom our department was built for. Adriane Lentz-Smith, Anne-Maria Makhulu, and Charles Piot have been constant sources of inspiration, and they gave me more of their time than I had any right to ask them for. So did Lee Baker, Jasmine Cobb, Michaeline Crichlow, Sandy Darity, Kerry Haynie, Tsitsi Jaji, Wahneema Lubiano, Rick Powell, Charmaine Royal, Karin Shapiro, Stephen Smith, Javier Wallace, and Joseph Winters. I also thank Heather Martin, Tyra Dixon, Wilhelmina Green, and Mian Wu. Beyond AAAS, I'm grateful to Anne Allison, Sarah Balakrishnan, Siobhan Barco, Juliana Barr, Nathaniel Berndt, James Chappel, Leo Ching, Prasenjit

Duara, Janet Ewald, John French, Thavolia Glymph, Michael Hardt, Ranjana Khanna, Mbaye Lo, Justin Leroy, Jehangir Malegam, John Martin, Kathryn Mathers, Cecilia Márquez, Adam Mestyan, Eric Mvukiyehe, Barbara Ofosu-Somuah, Jolie Olcott, Simon Partner, Sumathi Ramaswamy, Renée Ragin Randall, Carlos Rojas, Adam Rosenblatt, Giulia Riccò, Felwine Sarr, Orin Starn, Dubie Toa-Kwarpong, Ellie Vilakazi, Yun Emily Wang, Kathi Weeks, Kelsey Zavelo, and the much missed Diane Nelson. I look forward to many more transcendent Sundays with Gabriel Rosenberg and Harris Solomon. Ben Grunwald, Jessica Namakkal, Eli Meyerhoff, Mike Blank, and Tara Hopkins made Durham home, and Nima Bassiri made its gyms and dive bars the center of my intellectual life. At Duke University Press, Elizabeth Ault has been a peerless editor and a prized friend, and I'm grateful to her in more ways than I can count. I also thank the three anonymous readers who prepared thoughtful, constructive reports on this manuscript, and Ben Kossak, Ihsan Taylor, Christopher Hellwig, and Matthew John Phillips.

I'm grateful to Wale Adebanwi, Saheed Aderinto, Rabiat Akande, Simon Allen, Jean Allman, David Anderson, Victoria Barnes, Taiwo Bello, Lauren Benton, Fahad Bishara, Binyamin Blum, Jane Burbank, Arudra Burra, Erin Braatz, Katherine Bruce-Lockhart, Emily Burrill, Pedro Cantisano, Frederick Cooper, Amy Chazkel, Robyn d'Avignon, Rohit De, Mamadou Diouf, Roy Doron, Laura Fair, Elisabeth Fink, Katherine Franke, Abosede George, Ariela Gross, Bruce Hall, Emily Hamilton, Vincent Hiribarren, Trina Hogg, Irvin Hunt, Stacey Hynd, Anthony Idigbe, Larissa Kopytoff, David Kruger, Egor Lazarev, Dan Lee, Lisa Lindsay, Louisa Lombard, Dan Magaziner, Enrique Martino, Daniel McCracken, Naomi Mezey, Andrew Miller, Ben Miller, Dirk Moses, Michelle Moyd, Kenda Mutongi, Stephanie Newell, Cyril Obi, Toja Okoh, Philip Olayoku, Jimoh Oluwasegun, Mariana Dias Paes, Derek Peterson, Nana Quarshie, Reynolds Richter, Sarah Runcie, Teemu Ruskola, Chetana Sabnis, Paul Sant-Amour, Lynn Schler, Rebecca Scott, Mitra Sharafi, Anooradha Iyer Siddiqi, Raquel Sirotti, Daniel Jordan Smith, Nicholas Rush Smith, Jonny Steinberg, Rhiannon Stephens, Scott Straus, Trey Straussberger, Judith Surkis, Matt Swagler, Rob Tendy, Madina Thiam, Lynn Thomas, Elizabeth Thornberry, Geoff Traugh, Egodi Uchendu, Martha Umphreys, Inge Van Hulle, Megan Vaughan, Stefan Vogenauer, Kim Wagner, Charlotte Walker-Said, and Natasha Wheatley. Jonathan Gillard Daly and Gale Fury Childs read every word, and they, along with Emily Fury, are the ones I thank last, and loudest.

Financial support was provided by the University of Chicago, Duke University, the Max Planck Institute for Legal History and Legal Theory, the Columbia

University Seminars, and the Josiah Charles Trent Memorial Foundation. A generous grant from the University of Chicago's Center for International Social Science Research, under the leadership of Jenny Trinitapoli, allowed this book to be published open access. A version of chapter 3 was published as "The Portable Coup: The Jurisprudence of 'Revolution' in Uganda and Nigeria," *Law and History Review* 39, no. 4 (November 2021): 737–64.

* * *

What follows is an allegory about people trying to build a new civilization with broken tools and mismeasured plans. I offer no pieties about what they constructed. Chroniclers of independent Africa are at an impasse about how contentious stories like this one should be told.[3] At one extreme, there are cynics who revel in spectacles of decay that they pass off as tell-it-like-it-is empiricism. At the other, there are gatekeepers who police what's said about the continent and who says it, as if a billion people's history is a family secret that shouldn't be talked about in mixed company. What defines the sides is not nationality, race, or generation. Most scholars fall somewhere in the middle, and I have played on both teams. In this book, I take neither side— both inhibit historical understanding. A true-to-life portrait of Africa's military dictatorships can't leave out their ugliness. But it also can't ignore their charisma, connivance, and *splendor*.

A group of men crowds around the news anchor's desk looking ready for a fight. They wear full combat gear—camouflage, helmets, bulletproof vests. All of them are young and big, seemingly chosen for this task on the basis of size rather than seniority. Their drab uniforms contrast with the cheerful lighting of the TV station, which is better suited to weather reports than coup announcements. They pose like actors in an action movie, and they've cast themselves in the leading roles. These soldiers have taken over their government, and they're not the first of their kind to do so.

After the end of colonialism, dozens of African countries experienced military coups. Across the continent, societies that had just won their independence from Europe became military dictatorships. Once soldiers were in charge, politics shifted course. Promises of liberty were replaced by a vision of *discipline*, and military principles like rank, readiness, and obedience supplanted the softer political values—equality, nondomination—that civilians had preached.[1] Politics became a war of position between men in uniform, and in some countries that war raged for decades. Eventually most armies returned to the barracks, and for a while it seemed like Africa had left military rule in the twentieth century.

It has not. From 2020 to the time of writing, soldiers have brought an end to civilian government in Guinea, Mali, Sudan, Niger, Burkina Faso, and Gabon. The journalists and diplomats who didn't see them coming have fumbled around for an explanation, usually landing on shortsighted theories involving Russian meddling or foreign mercenaries. But these coups didn't come out of nowhere. The soldiers in the TV studios are building on a deep political tradition: for much of the late twentieth century, Africa's most pervasive ideology was *militarism*.[2]

From the 1960s to the 1990s, African politics revolved around soldiers' blood feuds and power grabs.[3] The men who staged them were intoxicated by their own strength, brimming with ambition and nervous energy. "It has proved infectious, this seizure of government by armed men, and so effortless," wrote the South African sociologist Ruth First in 1970. "Get the keys of

FIGURE I.1. Soldiers announcing the January 2022 coup in Burkina Faso.

the armoury; turn out the barracks; take the radio station, the post office and the airport; arrest the person of the president, and you arrest the state."[4] On the surface, their coups were about corruption, or bad behavior by politicians, or low pay. But militarism was not always reactive, or reactionary. Nearly all militaries wanted to transform their countries, even though they didn't always spell out exactly what they wanted them to become. Coups also came with *ideas*, and militarism—the ideology of rule by soldiers—aimed to make a new kind of society.

Soldiers run countries like they fight wars. Combat is their metaphor for politics. They approach political problems like battles to be won or lost, even when it isn't clear what winning or losing would mean. They treat their rivals like enemies—not people who see things differently but adversaries who have to be defeated. They divvy up the population into friends and foes and treat them accordingly. They enforce conformity, and they try to make everyone think like they do. They put up a united front, but behind the scenes they plot against one another—each wants to be the alpha. Not every military regime fits this description, at least not perfectly. But this is what military government often looks like to the governed. To civilians, military rule can be hard to distinguish from an occupation. The difference is that in a homegrown militocracy, the commands don't come from a foreign army. They come from your own sons and brothers.

The years covered by this book are sometimes referred to as Africa's "lost decades"—a time when the continent's future was mortgaged and its spirit was smothered under a uniform.[5] But they didn't feel "lost" in the moment. Militarism promised to channel Africa into the flow of modernity, and many civilians rallied to that cause (at least at first). Soldiers offered an attractive vision of the future, and force wasn't the only arrow they had in their quivers. They promised to make a bountiful, orderly world. They would bring a second, deeper, more lasting freedom than the disappointing one formal independence had brought. The army would repair the dignity colonialism had broken, and it would strengthen the nation so foreigners could never conquer it again. Everyone would march to the same cadence, their differences hidden underneath their uniforms. Soldiers would provide for the poor (the class most of them came from), and they would help the weak become strong—something the British and the lackeys they left in charge would never have allowed. Militarism offered Africans a heroic view of themselves: not the "whimpering football of humanity at large," as a Liberian militarist put it, but a civilization of honorable, upright people who followed no orders but their own.[6] These promises were appealing to soldiers and civilians alike, and they remained seductive even as military regimes broke them over and over again.

"In Africa since decolonization," wrote a Nigerian general-*cum*-statesman with a certain pride, "military rule has been the rule of the day rather than the exception."[7] Militarism touched states in every part of Africa and from every former empire. Even the two countries that avoided European colonization, Ethiopia and Liberia, didn't sidestep militarism—both became military dictatorships. Militarism was a continent-wide phenomenon, and many new countries came under the spell of their armies in this era. This book doesn't describe them all. I focus on one important subset: the former British colonies (sometimes glossed as Commonwealth Africa).[8] Militarism also took root in countries that had been colonized by France, Italy, Portugal, and Belgium, but arguably it was in the Commonwealth where it flourished the most. Not every British ex-colony in Africa was taken over by its military, and it was a West African phenomenon most of all. There, Nigeria, Ghana, Sierra Leone, and Gambia were ruled by their armed forces for extended periods. Elsewhere on the continent, Uganda, Sudan, and Lesotho were the former British territories that had military regimes.[9] But even states that weren't taken over by their militaries were touched by militarism. The fear of coups shaped how civilian politicians governed, and autocrats of all stripes took pages from the military playbook.

The argument of this book passes through all these countries, but it lingers in the one with the longest experience of army rule. Nigeria was ruled by soldiers from 1966 to 1999 with only two brief interruptions—over thirty years in total. Over those years militarism became a mature ideology there, which makes it an obvious place to set this story. Nigeria is also important because of its scale. It has Africa's largest population—more than double the next largest, Ethiopia—and more people reside in Nigeria than in West Africa's fifteen other states *combined*. It's a rich country, but it doesn't feel like it. Nigeria is a major producer of oil, and from the 1960s onward most government revenue came from oil and gas. Oil made Nigeria more economically self-reliant than most other African states, but it also made it more unequal, and more volatile.[10] Thanks to oil, military governments could raise revenue without taxing people much. When oil prices were high in the 1960s and 1970s (and stratospheric during the OPEC oil embargo), the military could make grand plans without worrying about how to pay for them. When they were low in the 1980s and 1990s, soldiers' ambitions shrunk accordingly.[11] Those soldiers made up the largest and most domineering military in this part of the world, and they exported some aspects of their martial culture to the rest of Africa. Nigeria was closely tied to other former British colonies in this era, and it went from being a model for them to a cautionary tale.

For all these reasons Nigeria looms large in this book. I admit to a certain amount of chauvinism here. Foreign historians like me can be just as prideful about a place as patriots—I know other fellow travelers who describe the small island or obscure corner of a vanished empire they study as if it were the center of the universe. Writing about a country, one becomes a sort of ambassador for it. When that country is a backwater, an ex-colony, or a "shithole," as Donald Trump described Nigeria, it's hard not to overcorrect.[12] So be it. Histories from Africa can offer as much insight into human behavior as those from anywhere else. This one is a parable about the visions and vanities of soldiers.

Freedom Comes Dressed in a Uniform

On 1 October 1960 the British left Nigeria under cover of night. At a midnight ceremony, the Union Jack that flew over the Lagos Racecourse was lowered. "In that darkness, the Nigerian Flag was unfurled over our country," a witness described.[13] "The dark tropical sky was at once set ablaze by the spontaneous detonation of thousands of fireworks, which turned the sky into a fantastic riot of glorious rainbow colours," recalled another. "Thus was born amidst this glittering spectacle the country containing the largest concentration of black peoples the world has ever known."[14] Within a few years, that racecourse had been converted into a parade ground, and the country had become a military dictatorship. How did this happen?

African militaries were not popular at independence. Armies were the most English-accented parts of the state. They were tainted by the memory of colonial conquest, which everyone knew couldn't have been done without them. At Ghana's independence ceremony, Ralph Bunche, there representing the United Nations, took notice of how people reacted to the soldiers marching in the procession. Two units with British officers were greeted with silence. The third, commanded by a Ghanaian, received applause, but even the most "indigenised" armies were not fully trusted by the public.[15] Soldiers were aloof from politics. In the runup to independence they stayed "in their barracks," as the political scientist Claude Welch observed, "cut off from direct participation in nationalist activities, and occasionally [fighting] against guerilla groups favoring self-government."[16] They sharply contrasted with civilian politicians, who got the credit for independence while promising huge improvements in public welfare. Soldiers, with their pith helmets and defense pacts with Europeans, seemed like the dregs of imperialism.[17]

Almost immediately after independence, the stock of civilian politicians began to fall. It was hard to implement the transformations they had promised, and the legacy of colonial underdevelopment proved more intractable than anyone had hoped. Once they were in power, the nationalists seemed frustratingly similar to the British administrators they had replaced. They were corrupt and acquisitive, and there was a large gap between them and the farmers and traders who had voted them into office. Malcontents began to grumble that the "independence" Africa had won was meaningless. This false decolonization had kept the structures of imperialism in place, merely replacing the Europeans at the top of the heap with local "compradors," as social critics of the time called the Africans who managed the continent's dealings with the wider world. African elites carried on the extraction that had defined colonialism, only now they did it to serve themselves. Ordinary people, who saw their lives improve less than the politicians had promised, started to feel like they'd been sold a bill of goods. True decolonization, radicals like Walter Rodney and Samir Amin argued, was yet to come.[18]

Soldiers saw an opportunity. No longer the stooges of the British, they would be the saviors of their new countries. They presented themselves as the *true* bearers of decolonization—the ones who would deliver a second, more authentic independence that actually broke with the British way of doing things. They contrasted themselves to the civilian elite, beguiled by

Europe, who had lost touch with the common people. As men of humble birth, soldiers would bring freedom to everyone, not just the rich. For some this was just rhetoric, but most of them genuinely believed themselves to be liberators.

Soldiers disdained how nonsoldiers governed. They saw British civilians as pale shadows of the decisive officers who had trained them, and the African civilians who took over from them at independence were just as bad. They squandered money left and right. They violated the old ways—patriarchy, tradition—in the name of their own trivial "freedom" to do what they wanted. Soldiers saw civilian government as a pathetic mimicry of colonialism, and they weren't the only ones. The same critique came from the left. The civilian elite "adored [the] image of itself in the shape of its colonial predecessor, and worked avidly to enhance it," Ruth First wrote. "The imitation was a parody not of twentieth century society but of the nineteenth, the age of colonialism."[19] The South African communist shared soldiers' contempt for the politicians who had taken over from the British, even though she didn't agree that the solution was to let the army run things.

Soldiers invariably spoke of their coups as "revolutions," and in some respects militarism really was revolutionary. It turned things upside down. "This is a military regime, and *every* soldier has power," testified a teenaged critic of the Nigerian Army in 1977.[20] He put his finger on one of military rule's most radical characteristics: coups upended the class order. When the military was in charge, the lowest soldier outranked the highest civilian. The military's hierarchy became the only one that really mattered, and powerful civilians who were usually insulated from the state's violence might find themselves harassed by a soldier at a checkpoint or hauled before a military tribunal. The poor, who were never shielded from those humiliations, welcomed military coups because they offered a different way of ordering rank: you might still be at the bottom, but at least the rich are down there with you. Those who had something to lose saw it differently. To the middle classes, military rule felt more like dragging everyone down to the level of the army—an institution that most civilians with degrees or savings accounts saw as a reservoir for the talentless. Military rule worked by "idiotizing" society, the Nigerian intellectual Wole Soyinka argued. "It is the dregs who, against all natural laws, appear to rise to the top."[21]

Military coups often came from below. Their leaders were usually young, and few of them took the helm naturally. A military president was not a "head of state" but a "*foot* of state," as witty Sierra Leoneans called Major Johnny Paul Koroma, who clawed his way to power for one tumultuous year in the 1990s.[22] Writing in the wake of General Idi Amin's coup in Uganda, the Kenyan scholar Ali Mazrui argued that the putsch constituted a real revolution. It marked the ascendance of a new class—a "lumpen militariat" who came from a much lower social position than the civilians they overthrew. They were "semi-organized, rugged, and semi-literate" men, whose authority came not from merit but from physical strength and access to guns.[23] Amin, like most soldiers, came from "the womb of the countryside," not the city, corrupted by capital. The political awakening of the soldier class would be something to celebrate if they could break the stranglehold Western-educated elites had over politics.[24] Most observers followed Mazrui's lead in seeing soldiers as lumpen—plebeian, tinged with backwardness, and, in the Marxian sense, ideologically unsophisticated. In fact, soldiers did have an ideology. It just wasn't one Mazrui was looking for.

* * *

Militarism is the most neglected of the modern era's isms, but we ignore it at our peril. Like communism or capitalism, wars were fought in its name and societies were made in its image. Nigeria was one of them. So were Brazil, Pakistan, Indonesia, and wide swaths of southern Europe, Latin America, and the South Pacific. A large share of the world's population lived under the jackboot in the late twentieth century, and for this reason alone soldiers' political philosophies are worth our attention. So too are their psychologies. "One function of authoritarianism is to lock an entire people in a single man's mind," Patricia Lockwood writes.[25] In this era, millions of people were locked in the "military mind," as Samuel P. Huntington called soldiers' mentality—a mind that was cynical, nationalistic, and obsessed with discipline.[26] In Africa, the conservative realism of the *military* mind met the liberatory spirit of the *decolonizing* mind, and some strange ideas were born.

Many military leaders wanted to remake their societies in their own image—as colossal armies, real or figurative. Some believed that making their countries into vast open-air barracks was what would make them truly *free*. This wasn't a contradiction to them. Soldiers equated freedom with self-control, and they argued that true freedom came only from the mastery of one's own instincts. They saw civilians as a chaotic rabble who needed to be brought to heel. They valued discipline as an end in itself, and they saw no reason why this principle, which structured *their* lives, might not serve as a philosophy for everyone. With the reckless confidence of young men, they believed they could bend Africa into a shape resembling themselves.

Officers had total faith in the military way of doing things. If a factory owner ran his business more like an army, he would produce more and waste less. If a woman selling produce on the roadside could be made to think like a warrior, then she would become free—no longer a slave to her own impulses, discipline would allow her to "self-actualize" (officers swore by pop psychology). If everyone did this, they argued, Africa would become a well-ordered Arcadia. To be clear from the outset: they were wrong, and my description of their martial philosophy is not an endorsement of it. The idea that *discipline is freedom*, beloved of drill sergeants and self-help books for men, makes for a very illiberal kind of politics. The "freedom" of rigorous discipline feels like no freedom at all.

Militarism's true believers hoped to make military values *public* values. Rules would be followed, authority figures would command universal respect, and everyone would be ready when the battle came—which was the telos that all soldiers trained for and many of them longed for. They were vague about exactly what that battle would be, but that wasn't the point. Militarism was a way of life, an ethos, and a design for living. Its champions called it a "revolution." It had a procreative logic. The army would pluck promising young men from the countryside and induct them into the ranks. Those men would marry wives who would be partners in the military revolution. Their children would be raised to be good soldiers or good wives to soldiers, and the cycle would continue until the revolution was complete. If the colonizers came knocking again, this time Africa would be ready for them. To militarists, building a strong army and building a strong society were one and the same. Making the state into a war machine was what would make it *work*.[27]

Soldiers believed they were building a paradise, and that belief is critical to Africa's modern history. But this was a *soldier's* vision of paradise, which was not a place most civilians wanted to live. "Everyone looks to government to lead the country into the paradise that was promised during the period of agitation for Independence," wrote the Ghanaian coup-plotter General Albert Kwesi Ocran. But paradise meant more than one thing in independent Africa. To the poor, "the promised paradise is more and cheaper food to eat, cheap clothes, . . . shelter, soap, kerosene, drink." To the rich, "paradise means more high offices and better pay for themselves, improved living conditions, higher education (if possible free), improved roads, more industries, more imports of foreign goods."[28] In public, military officers insisted they were creating a paradise for the downtrodden.[29] Behind closed doors, they reassured the bourgeoisie that they were building a different kind of society—one designed for them, where contracts would be juicy and capital would flow freely. But what they ended up creating was a paradise for neither the rich nor the poor. They built a ramshackle utopia *for themselves*, at the expense of everyone else.

As one military regime gave way to another, the distance between soldiers and civilians grew. Officers began to see themselves as a caste apart, cut off from the public they ostensibly served. They were different from the ordinary people who milled around outside their parade grounds, ill-mannered and unwashed. Soldiers had their own rituals and values, their own lingo and dress. They lived together in barracks or on bases with their families, and they saw those bases as islands of order in seas of chaos. The military depended on civilians for less and less as time went on, and officers began to speak of "taming" people, as if they were wild animals.[30]

During militarism's bloody denouement in the 1990s, Nigeria's military would abandon its goal of transforming society. Under the dictatorship of General Sani Abacha, soldiers no longer spoke of military rule as a mission; it was an opportunity to loot the state, which they did brazenly. They still compared civilians to animals, only now the goal wasn't to "tame" them— it was to *cage* them. A Lagos businesswoman looked back on these final years of dictatorship with undiminished fury. The "jackboots" who ran the country into the ground were "hot-blooded young lions with no respect for human life," Nkem Liliwhite-Nwosu wrote. "Blue-blooded aristocrats who spoke with authority through the nozzle of the gun; ignorant greenhorns who claimed to have the solution to problems which their refined, erudite, old fathers could not solve, and who ended up compounding the problems for us all."[31] Many civilians shared her rage about what soldiers had done to their own countries.

* * *

The global history of military rule in the late twentieth century might lead one to believe Africa's coups were driven by forces from abroad, and it's true that some military rulers threw in their lots with Europeans.[32] Even the ones who didn't seemed suspiciously colonial, with their stiff-upper-lip mannerisms and their imperious attitudes. Many observers of the coups that swept the continent saw them as neocolonial in one way or another. Coups certainly had that quality elsewhere. In Latin America, the United States was often behind military takeovers from the right. In eastern Europe and Asia, Soviet interference had the same effect from the other ideological direction. Across the postcolonial world, European diplomats quietly encouraged coups when populist movements threatened their interests.

The most infamous meddling in the affairs of an African country was in the Democratic Republic of the Congo, where Belgium and the United States conspired to kill Prime Minister Patrice Lumumba and put General Mobutu Sese Seko in his place. France also orchestrated politics in its former colonies in Africa. The Élysée was notorious for supporting dictators (many of them soldiers) if they aided French political or commercial interests—a dynamic cleverly captured by the term *Françafric, fric* being French slang for money. French mercenaries meddled in African politics to benefit both France and themselves. The most outrageous of them was Bob Denard, who staged no fewer than four coup attempts in the Comoros. There, he fancied himself "a warrior king out of Homer," as a toady admirer called him.[33] Across Africa, coup-plotters who had good intentions were painted as "placeholders" or "custodians" who would clean things up and hand power back to civilians. When they didn't relinquish the reins they were called other things—"big men" if you found them tolerable, "tyrants" if you didn't. Some were the "running dogs of imperialism," as a Maoist epithet of the time went, exemplified by Jean-Bédel Bokassa's Napoleonic affectations or Idi Amin's embarrassing love of Scotland.

But military rule was not just an extension of colonial rule—look closely and you'll see breaks in the line that connects them. Soldiers had mixed feelings about the Europeans who had trained them, and they tarred *civilians* as the ones in the pocket of the British. Most Commonwealth armies used English as their language of command, but this didn't mean they were English in character. Quite a few military regimes were explicitly anticolonial, both in rhetoric and in practice. Nigeria's coups were not planned by outsiders, and no one was pulling the strings from abroad. To be sure, soldiers had friends and enemies in foreign capitals. American diplomats disliked General Murtala Muhammed, for example, and they quietly celebrated when General Olusegun Obasanjo replaced him. But Nigeria's coups were not obviously Cold War maneuvers. Like most conspiracy theories, whispers of foreign plots often said more about the whisperer's fears (or hopes) than the reality of the situation.

The world powers watched what was going on in Nigeria, but they seldom dirtied their hands in the coups and countercoups that constituted national politics. British and American diplomats occasionally bragged in their memoirs about one soldier or another being "his man," but this reflected vanity more than wire pulling. They exaggerated how much sway they had, and to conclude that foreign ambassadors were the kingmakers of *all* African politics buys into their mythmaking—this is exactly what they wanted people to believe. Unlike in Congo or the Comoros, in Nigeria foreign governments kept their distance from national politics. They did so not out of any respect for Nigeria's sovereignty, but because they saw no reason to risk much there. Both the military and the government at large leaned to the right ideologically, and there was no communist threat that might have worried the United States. The absence of a viable left meant the Soviet Union didn't see much point in getting involved either. The oil kept flowing whether soldiers or civilians were in charge, and so Nigeria was mostly left to its own devices. It may be tempting to say that military rule was orchestrated somewhere else, or imposed from afar, but the truth is more complicated.

Law and Decolonization

On a visit to West Africa's jazz clubs in the mid-1980s, the American music critic Stanley Crouch kept getting distracted by men in uniform. Soldiers "walked about with the vicious arrogance of pit bulls," he wrote, and dressed him down whenever he tried to talk to them. "The Reign of Terror is almost always a few seconds away in Africa, the distance only as far as the gathering of enough guns to wrest control."[34] Many shared Crouch's belief that guns were the only thing that mattered in African politics, but he was wrong. Laws mattered too, and for that reason this book takes the form of a legal history. One of the driving forces of Africa's postcolonial politics was the struggle between soldiers and judges—the executive and the judiciary—about who made the rules and what they should be. Military regimes venerated "law and order," and many soldiers thought law could be a bridge between the army and society at large. Criminal codes rhymed with their culture of obedience, and rules-based structures spoke to their love of discipline. They treated judges like their deputies, and they put law at the center of their political strategies. But soldiers and judges were not natural allies.

Law didn't work the way the military thought it did. As a disciplinary tool, the courts were unreliable. A judge might acquit someone the army wanted to make an example of, or a decision might limit what kinds of punishment it could mete out.[35] Military governments found that civilians could turn law back on them, just as they had turned it against Europeans in the days before independence. It was hard to avoid getting tripped up by doctrinal complexities (including ones of their own making). Military dictators thought law was all stick, no carrot, and they were disappointed when they realized it wasn't always punitive. Nonetheless, they needed law, even though they grew wary of it as they learned more about how it worked. They had no problem dissolving legislatures or disemboweling bureaucracies when they thought they were working against them. It was much harder to do without a judiciary. Without the courts, Nigeria's Major General Ibrahim Haruna admitted, "we would be in a hell of anarchy with nobody to piece us together."[36]

Society couldn't function without law, and officers couldn't implement their disciplinary "revolutions" without magistrates, courts, and jails. For this reason, judges had the ear of the military. They could criticize executive power, or shape it to their own ends, when no other civilians could.

At first glance, courts in a dictatorship might seem merely ornamental. In many single-party states, whatever happens in a courtroom—in a show trial, for example—endorses the party's dictates. In absolute monarchies, the judge and the king might be fused, making any kind of separation of powers unthinkable. But not all authoritarian governments are like this. Many twentieth-century dictatorships, from Pakistan to Chile, had vigorous and combative legal cultures.[37] Even the sternest legal orders could be turned against those who made them. If you make a rope to tie someone's hands, you have to be prepared that *your* hands might get tied with it, as many dictators learn. There are judges who push back against the army's vision for society, legal decisions that undermine its decrees, and lawyers who scheme quietly in the background. Legal institutions can be tools of repression, but it would be wrong to think this is *all* they are, even in a dictatorship.

The lesson of this is not that Africa's military dictatorships were softer than we thought they were, or more bound by law. Rather, it is that *judicial independence does not foreclose repression.* The rule of law is not necessarily antithetical to authoritarianism, and a government can delicately hold out legalism with one hand while it cracks a whip with the other. Legal scholars who work in the democratic vein have been slow to see this—to appreciate the fact that lawyers can be just as irksome to an authoritarian state as to an "open" one. Military regimes had many reasons for maintaining some semblance of judicial independence.[38] Legalism helped them perform accountability at home, and it placated meddling do-gooders from abroad. It painted a gloss on their dictates, and it gave them a scapegoat to blame when things didn't go according to plan. Law can cast a "legitimizing glow" over authoritarian institutions, as Mark Fathi Massoud writes.[39] Soldiers relied on the courts to make their visions stick, and as law-and-order ideologues they saw judges as partners in discipline even when they disagreed with them.

Soldiers needed public accountability, which law could give them. But they wanted that accountability to be on their own terms, so the laws they made were looser and more pliable than the rigid ones the British had left behind. Africa's legal systems had been created by Europeans, soldiers pointed out, so they called their attempts to change them "decolonization." In practice, decolonizing law often meant gutting the rules that might limit the military's powers and replacing them with something more pliable—all done in the name of freedom. Some version of this played out all over the postcolonial world, and the legal history of how it happened—dry and technical as it sometimes is—shows us something broader: Decolonization had a thick militaristic streak, even in countries where independence hadn't required an armed struggle.

This isn't the liberation story most people want to hear. The end of empire was not a morality play of doomed revolutionaries and the scheming elites who sold them out—this was a time of strange bedfellows and surprising ideological commitments. Law reveals its ironies starkly, if not always clearly. In courtrooms, unexpected stands were taken and puzzling alliances were made. We find British-trained military strongmen borrowing radical language from Frantz Fanon or Ngũgĩ wa Thiong'o and committed anticolonialists arguing that English law was the only thing that could hold off tyranny.[40] Judges and soldiers shared a rhetorical commitment to "freedom," but they seldom agreed about what it meant. Bright moral lines became hazy in court.

In this history, we find a long debate over what law fundamentally *was*. Was it a weapon or a shield? Was it a remnant of colonialism, or a tool that could *dismantle* what colonialism had left behind? As legal historians are fond of pointing out, law could be all these things at once, and it would be wrong to conclude that militarism and its legal contrivances only worked one way, or only did one thing. I don't celebrate the soldiers who ruled in the late twentieth century, but I don't vilify them either. Not every military regime was led by a power-hungry madman, and not every civilian president was a saint. The same goes for judges, who sometimes reined tyrants in and at other times egged them on. The heroes had a dark streak, and the villains sometimes spoke the truth. Look elsewhere for moral clarity.

* * *

Militarism had a maverick side that looked radical from some angles. Soldiers pledged to rid their countries of colonialism's remnants, starting with the ones they found most inconvenient. The constitutional model hastily foisted on them by the British at independence was their first target, followed by the rowdy legislatures those constitutions had created. The English common law, with its fusty traditions and powdered wigs, was next on the chopping block. Soldiers were perplexed by law's jargon, and they found the civilian legal system's hierarchy baffling—not least because it ran counter to their own system of rank. Even though they liked the order that law offered, they agreed with the more radical factions of the nationalist movement that there was something shameful about still using the colonizers' laws after they had packed up and left.

"Colonization," General Ibrahim Babangida of Nigeria would proclaim, "brought with it a legal twist. The indigenous legal system became traumatised, following the importation of foreign legal concepts and experiences. [The fact] that our indigenous concepts of justice were supplanted not only by foreign laws but also by alien notions of justice is sad."[41] What irked Babangida about law was not really that it was foreign or colonial. After all, militaries owed their structure to colonialism too, and soldiers weren't in a position to criticize anyone for being too attached to British things. Babangida, like General Idi Amin of Uganda before him and Colonel Yahya Jammeh of Gambia after, condemned neocolonialism while revering Britain's military culture. What actually perturbed Babangida about colonial law was that it could undermine him. To keep that from happening, he turned a powerful rhetorical weapon against it—"decolonization."

It wasn't a paradox that soldiers pitched themselves as decolonizers, and Babangida's words were not just doublespeak (though he was known for his silver tongue). There was an affinity between militarism and more seemingly radical forms of anticolonialism; they were two ends of a horseshoe, closer to one another than they were to the points in between them. As an example of this, we might look to Nigeria's first president, Nnamdi Azikiwe. Zik, as he is known, was the paradigmatic radical-turned-militarist—an anticolonial freedom fighter who came to embrace the army's vision for society. Nigerians remember Zik as a father of the nation, not a military apologist, and his portrait adorns the thousand-naira banknote.[42] Zik never wore a uniform—he was a muckraking activist who rose to fame as a newspaper impresario. He was elected president in 1960, and he remained in office until he was ousted in Nigeria's first military coup six years later. During the civil war he initially sided with the Biafran secessionists but then returned to the Nigerian fold midway through (the army garlanded him with honors for switching sides). As military rule continued, he became one of its most respectable defenders. Zik argued that civilians had squandered independence, which meant something coming from the country's first, and for a long time only, civilian president. "I, for one, know that I did not stick out my neck opposing the mighty British lion," he admonished, "only to have the independence that we paid dearly for subjected to ridicule and contempt by the shameless method adopted by some politicians."[43]

Zik was a lifelong civilian whose time in power was cut short by a military coup. It may seem strange that he would ever endorse military rule—and yet he did, heartily. "Military leadership, anywhere in the civilised world, is a highly educated and skilled caste of human beings," he declared in 1974,

FIGURE I.2. Ibrahim Babangida in his office, 1986.

eight years into the military dictatorship. "It would be imprudent to over-look the constructive role the armed forces can play in stabilising a nation that has just emerged from colonialism and a bloody civil war." The idea that militaries should answer to civilians was a foreign concept, he argued, and the principle that soldiers should stay out of politics was a holdover from colonialism. "We have imitated Europe long enough."[44] Military rule would allow Nigeria to beat its own path to the future.

Zik's embrace of militarism wouldn't have surprised anyone who had fol-lowed the evolution of his thought. Long before independence, Zik espoused a radical anticolonial philosophy that came to be known as "Zikism."[45] It was an ideology of renascence, and it was national, rather than ethnic, in scope. It was also decidedly militant. Zik parted ways with more moderate na-tionalists to argue that some measure of violence was necessary to kick the British out.[46] In Zik, we can see what anticolonialism and militarism shared. Soldiers and anticolonial radicals shared a conviction that violence could blast through political problems. Both believed that emancipation required *discipline*—tellingly, Zik's rallies began with marches and drills, as if he was training his followers for battle. Like the military regimes that would come later, Zik wanted to make civilians more like soldiers. Anticolonialism and militarism could live in one person's mind, and sometimes it was hard to tell them apart.

* * *

For those unfamiliar with Nigeria's political history, here is a breakneck summary. After independence from Britain in 1960, Nigeria had six years of democracy under President Nnamdi Azikiwe and Prime Minister Abubakar Tafawa Balewa. These were years of growth and optimism, but they were also years of political rancor. In January 1966 a group of five army majors staged a coup, allegedly over the nepotism and dysfunction of the Nigerian First Republic. Their coup failed, but not before they assassinated Balewa and several other prominent politicians. Major General Johnson Aguiyi-Ironsi, who had not participated in the coup, became head of state as the highest-ranking surviving officer (though his rank was disputed). Six months later he was assassinated, and General Yakubu Gowon became head of state. The Eastern Region of Nigeria seceded nine months into Gowon's administration, claiming that the federal government's failure to protect Igbos in a series of pogroms in northern Nigeria was tantamount to genocide. A civil war followed, pitting the Nigerian military government against the secessionist Republic of Biafra.[47] Biafra lost the war and was reintegrated into Nigeria in January 1970, and Gowon remained in office for another five years. On 29 July 1975 he was deposed by General Murtala Muhammed, who accused Gowon of corruption. Muhammed was assassinated seven months later, on 13 February 1976, by Lieutenant Colonel Buka Suka Dimka, who had accused Muhammed of corruption. Dimka failed to take the statehouse and was captured by a group of loyalists, who executed him. Lieutenant General Olusegun Obasanjo became head of state. Obasanjo ruled for the next three and a half years, and in 1979 he made the unprecedented decision to hand over power to civilians.

Elections were held, a new constitution was written (Nigeria had gone without one since the first military coup), and a teacher-turned-politician named Shehu Shagari was elected president of the so-called Second Republic. Shagari was reelected in 1983 (both elections were disputed), but on 31 December 1983 Major General Muhammadu Buhari staged a coup overthrowing Shagari's democratically elected government. Buhari was in power for an eventful year and a half, although many suspected that his powerful deputy, Tunde Idiagbon, was really in charge. On 27 August 1985, General Ibrahim Babangida overthrew Buhari. Babangida ruled Nigeria for the next eight years, during which he fought off several coup attempts. After much pressure from the rest of the world and many false starts, Babangida agreed to hold an election, which took place on 12 June 1993. A businessman named Moshood Abiola won the election, which international observers deemed free and fair. Abiola would have led the Third Republic, but he was never allowed to take office. Babangida annulled the results, claiming electoral irregularities. The international community turned against Babangida over the annulment, as did some of his fellow officers. In August 1993 he resigned from office, handing over power to an interim civilian government led by Ernest Shonekan, who had weak support from everyone except Babangida's faction of the military. Less than three months later, on 17 November 1993, Shonekan was deposed by General Sani Abacha. Abacha pitilessly looted the country for the next four and a half years, making it into a prison as he did so. Many dissidents were killed or jailed, and Nigeria became a pariah state. On 8 June 1998 Abacha died suddenly of a heart attack, though some believe he was poisoned. After his death, General Abdulsalami Abubakar came to power. Abubakar had no appetite to continue military rule, and he initiated an electoral process to transfer power to civilians. A presidential election was held on 27 February 1999, and the winner was Olusegun Obasanjo of the People's Democratic Party, now retired from his military career and standing for election as a civilian. When Obasanjo took office later that year, the Fourth Republic began. This one stuck, and Nigeria has been governed by civilians ever since.

Nigerian history turned on the minute-to-minute drama of this pageant of coups, assassinations, and double crosses. Who ruled the country was determined less by ideology or geopolitics than by tiny contingencies—how many guns were in the arsenal, who was in the barracks when the coup started, who could get to the radio station first to broadcast a victory message. These were the factors that decided which *specific* officer came to power, but militarism can't be boiled down to the rivalries of trifling generals. When this story is told, it usually looks like a bloody family feud among the army's commanders.[48] Here, I try to take a wider view of military rule and its spirit. Once each coup was finished, the officers who were still standing mopped up the blood in the barracks and set about *governing*. How? What did they believe about human nature, and how did they try to change it? Plenty of the civilians they ruled liked them. Why?

The Promise of Militarism

The National Museum of Nigeria is disappointing in most respects. Dusty ethnographic displays fill its sprawling building, which sits in a quiet corner of Lagos Island.[49] There are some bronzes from the archaeological site at Igbo-Ukwu, and a few ancient Nok figurines sit in a small room cooled by a rattling air conditioner (the only one consistently guarded). One hall shows work by Nigeria's twentieth-century modernist painters, but it's usually empty. The most popular gallery is a low-ceilinged room dominated by a black Mercedes-Benz limousine, pockmarked with bullet holes. This was the car that General Murtala Muhammed was riding in when he was assassinated in the failed coup of 1976. Muhammed was a popular dictator who became a martyr after his death, and the gallery feels like a shrine to him even when it's full of rambunctious school groups.

This is the Hall of Nigerian Government. On its walls hang portraits of Nigeria's heads of state, each apparently chosen to illustrate his reputation. Handsome Gowon smiles beatifically. Buhari rigidly stands at attention. Babangida looks slyly to the side like he has a secret. A blurry photograph of Abacha looks more like a mugshot than an official portrait. I've visited many times, but I'm still not sure whether the portraits are supposed to be an indictment of the military's role in Nigerian politics or a celebration of it. The hall is the closest thing the country has to a political pantheon: a parade of men, most of them in uniform, marching around a bloodstained status symbol.

Nigeria was ruled by these men for most of the late twentieth century. Many other African countries were ruled by men like them. Some generalizations can be made about them, even though they were a more varied group than their uniforms might suggest. Born in the 1930s or 1940s, they were among the first to be commissioned as officers in their national militaries, usually within a few years on either side of independence. They were the pride of their families—they came from rural backgrounds, and most (though not all) of them grew up poor. They learned their vocation in the West African Frontier Force and other colonial outfits, or, starting in the early 1960s, their national armies.[50] The best of them went on to officer training in England or India. They were young, at least at the beginning of military rule. Major General Yakubu Gowon was thirty-three when he came to power in 1966. Wole Soyinka, whom Gowon put in prison, called him "the boy scout dictator."[51] In Ghana, Flight Lieutenant Jerry Rawlings was thirty-two when he took the helm, and in Sierra Leone Captain Valentine Strasser was only twenty-five, making him one of the youngest nonhereditary heads of state in modern history.

Officers thought they could train their societies like they themselves had been drilled and molded in boot camp. Their hubris about military training came from the fact that most of them had just finished it—nobody is as confident about a regimen as someone who doesn't know it very well. Africa's military leaders were not staid professionals whose arrogance had been drummed out of them by experience. They were fledgling, impetuous officers who were convinced that their brief military experience let them see the world clearly and their weapons allowed them to change it. "As a soldier, I was taught to dominate a situation either by observation or superior fire," Babangida once remarked.[52] This was also how he approached politics. Some were wildly optimistic about how much civilians supported their plans to transform their countries, and about human nature in general. Others had the opposite problem, believing that people were irredeemable except through force.

One of the most perceptive observers of Africa's militaries was the American sociologist Morris Janowitz. African soldiers were "puritans," he argued, who saw modesty and self-restraint as political values. "The desire to be strong and unyielding is reinforced by the rigors and routines of daily existence. But the military demands these qualities not only for itself but for society as a whole, and it sets itself up as a standard-bearer of hard work and unflinching dedication."[53] They were also collectivists, of a sort. Soldiers were trained to work as a team and to think of themselves as a collective fighting toward a common purpose. This primed them for a distinctly communal approach to governance, even among those who leaned to the right. Babangida had a warm relationship with Margaret Thatcher, for instance, but it would be hard to imagine her famous diktat "there is no such thing as society" coming out of his mouth.[54]

In military regimes, the interests of individuals were subordinate to the well-being of the collectivity, just like in a military unit. This dovetailed with the bread-and-butter ideas of African politics in this era—African socialism, neotraditional collectivism, and certain strands of Pan-Africanism. Militarism didn't always sit easily with these ideas, but it shared their spirit of cooperation. As First Lady Maryam Babangida observed, soldiers were all alike, even across the national borders they defended: "The military have acquired a common corpus of traditions which is practiced from one country to another with minor variations dictated, as in dialectal differences within a language, by individual local circumstances. An amusing irony, considering that the armies of different countries are potential enemies of one another. . . . United by profession, yet divided by cause."[55] Soldiers worked together in some circumstances but not others, and the fact that the military elite was a kind of a fraternity (or, in its final years, more of a cult) didn't mean there was solidarity between its members. They fought bitterly among themselves, and they seldom passed up an opportunity to unseat a rival if they got the chance. Officers did not practice the discipline they preached.

In this book, I use the term *soldier* to refer to men at all levels of the military hierarchy. This follows a pattern of West African speech—in everyday parlance, all military personnel, officers and enlisted men alike, were *soja* ("soldiers," in pidgin). To civilians, *soja* were all more or less the same. This shorthand tells us something about how the public understood militaries, but it doesn't tell us how soldiers saw themselves. It obscures the subtleties of rank that structured military life. Officers and enlisted men were cut from different cloths. They had different origins and self-conceptions. They shared a culture, but those at the top of that culture had total power over those at the bottom. Nonetheless, from privates to generals, *all* men in uniform saw themselves as different from civilians. Those uniforms were a reminder that whatever divided them against one another—rank, religion, ethnicity—they had a common cause.[56]

Most of the men in this book were in the top brass or were vying for it from somewhere in the middle. It was officers who put the ideology of militarism to paper, and I rely heavily on them as sources. They presented militarism as an egalitarian project, but there was an obvious irony there. No one is more obsessed with the pecking order than an ambitious officer, and their insistence that everyone *pull their weight* in no way implied that everyone was *equal*. Nonetheless, the men at the bottom of the military pyramid were indispensable to militarism's mission, and they knew it. Ordinary soldiers were its muscle. They were the ones who modeled discipline to civilians, enforced it, and cracked skulls when necessary. Subalterns were also militarism's objects. This was an ideology *for them*, but their perspective on it—the "worm's eye view," so to speak—was often less optimistic than the austere, gleaming visions their superiors prophesied.[57]

* * *

Military officers insisted they were the only ones who could transform Africa's made-up, fractious ex-colonies into strong, united countries. They believed themselves to be the most Nigerian of the Nigerians (or the most Gambian of the Gambians, etc.), and there was some merit to this belief. Soldiers had patriotism hammered into them in ways that civilians didn't. They traveled the length and width of their countries, and they fraternized with comrades who spoke other languages and believed in other gods. They were among the few people for whom allegiances like ethnicity and religion came second to their citizenship. Major Chukwuma Nzeogwu, one of the five junior officers whose 1966 coup started Nigeria down its martial path, was a "fanatical nationalist," as one of his admirers described. "His hatred of tribalism and corruption was pathological."[58] "My loyalty does not go to any government," proclaimed Flight Lieutenant Jerry Rawlings as he staged his second coup in Ghana. "It goes to the state, the constitution."[59] This was more radical than it might sound. In pluralistic countries like Ghana, where chieftaincies competed with the state for people's allegiances, the loyalty that Rawlings proclaimed was not something everyone felt.[60] At least in their own minds, soldiers were the heart and soul of their new countries.

Soldiers prescribed militarism as a tonic for ethnic discord. Mozambique's Samora Machel famously put this promise best: "For the Nation to live, the tribe must die." Soldiers like Machel believed they could kill it—though others came to appreciate that ethnic divisions could be useful in politics. Even militarism's critics hoped some charismatic general might succeed at nation building where the civilians had failed. "What we need is a Napoleon Bonaparte," the dissident Nigerian lawyer Olu Onagoruwa wrote, "who will bring the country together."[61] In any African society, argued a Liberian fellow traveler to the military cause, "there are the Epicureans, the Bohemians, the hooligans (armed robbers, thieves, roughnecks, etc.), the moralists, the frauds, the zealots, the politicians and the security forces." The only people who had the "organizational solidarity" to bring all these factions in line were soldiers. The "military ethic," he wrote, demanded "austerity, valor, chivalry, composure, sharpness of intellect, discipline, physical prowess and patriotism. These are virtues that are indispensable to the struggle against neocolonialism, to the African Renaissance. They are the virtues relevant to the African cultural revolution."[62] "The place of the Army in governance is comparable to the place of the engine in a motor car," declared a Nigerian officer.[63] It powered everything else. This self-regard started the day they joined up, and it was reiterated throughout their careers in ways both subtle and overt. It made them think they had a monopoly on honor.[64]

At their best, soldiers were down-to-earth but worldly, righteous but not smug. A Nigerian political scientist begrudgingly admired General Idi Amin of Uganda for his common touch, at once commanding and unpretentious. Amin seemed "messianic, as though he possessed mystical warranty." His pronouncements were indeed visionary—his decision to expel Uganda's South Asian minority allegedly came to him in a dream from God.[65] This kind of vision was unusual. Many soldiers presented themselves as saviors of the

FIGURE I.3. Soldiers in the streets of Accra, 1982. Photo by A. Abbas.

nation, but few went so far as to say they were divinely ordained. Even in pious Nigeria, military leaders were conspicuously nonsectarian—a fact that has been forgotten by a public that remembers them as more uniformly Muslim than they actually were. Their secularism was part of their mission.[66] Whether it was religion, ethnicity, or less obvious lines of division like caste or clan, soldiers insisted that they were the only people who could bring everyone together under the same flag. They promised their governments would be efficient and forward-thinking. Everyone would be treated equally. Military regimes wouldn't have elections, but this didn't mean they couldn't be democratic. Soldiers constantly gauged "the feelings and aspirations of the people—even more so than a civilian regime," Major General David Jemibewon wrote. "While a civilian government can feel complacent because it is elected and therefore representative of the people, a military regime [must] feel the pulse of the people all the time."[67]

This was what they promised, but it wasn't necessarily what they did. Soldiers grew out of touch with "the people" the longer they stayed in power. They favored their kin just like civilians did, and some spilled blood in the name of putting their friends in power. They weren't perfect mirrors of their countries. The long-standing colonial practice of recruiting from certain "martial races" meant that most armies were lopsided in their composition.[68] In West Africa, enlisted men were more likely to come from the Sahelian regions of the north than from anywhere else, and in East Africa, Acholi and Kamba men filled the ranks because the British had preferred them over their shorter and allegedly less soldierly neighbors. The colonial decision to tap "warlike" peoples for the army had fundamentally changed how those peoples saw themselves; military service wasn't something you did—it became *who you were* as, for example, a Hausa or Acholi man. In this way, militarism had tightened ethnic loyalties instead of loosening them. Moreover, military rule didn't actually make civilians identify less with their "tribes" or regions. Sometimes it did the opposite; people built walls around themselves, withdrawing into their families or villages while soldiers occupied the public sphere.

Cutting off one sense makes the others sharper. What does African history look like if you bind the sense that social scientists rely on most—ethnicity? Here, I will tell you relatively little about tribalism in the ranks, the balance of ethnic politics in government, and other questions that have long preoccupied Africanists. These questions were not the wrong ones to ask, but they sucked the air out of the room; they obscured the *other* ways African societies were organized, and they reduced the continent's politics to ethnic horse trading and monistic identitarianism. In Nigerian historiography, sidelining ethnicity puts me at odds with many, and writing a history of the armed forces without putting it front and center will seem absurd to some readers. In some places, I admit, African history can't be understood without it. But ethnicity is not a lens that sharpens every image. When it comes to these armies—institutions that consistently described themselves as *nonethnic*—it is more likely to blur the picture.[69] Fixating on the gritty details of who was what, and how many of them there were, obscures how militarism could transcend all that. It often did. Armies remade people in their own cool, groomed, perfectly uniform image, and officers rose above the grotty mud pit of ethnic politics. Or so they told themselves.

Not all soldiers loved militarism, and not all civilians hated it. Some officers were uncomfortable among civilians, demurring that they should have no place in government. In their humbler moments, they could admit that "the problems of society, especially of the nature and magnitude that confront us, cannot be commanded away," as one wrote.[70] "Military rule is not the answer to Africa's perennial political and economic problems," allowed a repentant Ghanaian coup plotter. Moreover, governing civilians was bad for *soldiers*. "Military involvement ruins the military," he went on. "It creates a politically-orientated force which is not good for war." It was disheartening to see a promising young officer come back from a stint in a civilian ministry "pot-bellied and shabby, with his military cap resting precariously over his nose."[71] Too much proximity to civilians made soldiers effeminate and weak-willed, and this alone was reason to keep out of politics. Military officers who "meddled" in government "adopted civilian characteristics," General Sani Abacha complained, a year before he himself meddled his way right into the statehouse. "This is sad, as the new change of behavior is contrary to military ethics and traditions."[72]

Some civilians, on the other hand, were optimistic about military rule. "There is nothing inherently sacred about civilian governments, and there is nothing inherently evil about military governments," wrote President Julius Nyerere of Tanzania—hardly someone remembered as a militarist.[73] It was also possible to dislike military rule in general but appreciate the virtues of one dictator or another. "Military regimes, by their very nature and structure, are generally aggressive to human rights," contended Niki Tobi, a prominent judge. "But surprisingly, the Nigerian situation under President Ibrahim Babangida is reasonably different." "The current military regime is the most benevolent that Nigerians have seen and experienced. I salute the regime."[74] Tobi didn't want his country to be a garrison state forever, but he stood by his man.

The Charms of Soldiers

"The leader of men in warfare can show himself to his followers only through a mask," wrote the military historian John Keegan, "a mask that he must make for himself, but a mask made in such a form as will mark him to men of his time and place as the leader they want and need."[75] Even though they generally did not lead *in warfare*, Africa's military leaders cultivated personalities people wanted to follow. What were the masks they made? Chidi Amuta sketched a portrait of Babangida that would fit many of his comrades: he was "a brave soldier and a gentleman officer, a committed patriot and a friend of the West, a benevolent friend and a ruthless foe, a black godfather who would reward loyalty with abiding solidarity and punish dissidence with precise ferocity, a talented statesman in uniform with an imperial disposition.

A smiling enigma, but above all a visionary and a survivalist."[76] The military taught men qualities that made them good political leaders, wrote Major General James Oluleye. Their training gave them decisiveness, courage, intelligence, fitness, tact, honesty, and "personal magnetism." "It is possible to have a person who can combine both roles of a soldier and a politician," he insisted, and a smart soldier could "conveniently manage" the tasks of politics if he set his mind to it.[77] But this didn't work both ways. No civilian, no matter how capable, could command men in battle. Nearly all soldiers shared this chauvinism about their profession. They used it as license to take power whenever they wanted to.

Guns weren't the only weapons soldiers had at their disposal. They also had charm. As I bore deeper into the archives of Africa's military regimes, I realized that part of their appeal lay in their *glamour*, which I mean in the archaic sense: their allure was heavily dosed with deception. They were bumbling administrators and unpopular populists. They weren't even good at tyranny—a police state requires planning, and most soldiers were not well organized. But what they did have was charisma. Reading through their papers I sometimes found myself nodding along—not because I agreed with what they said, but because I was seduced by how they said it. If I feel this half a century on from when they were in power, it's fair to assume that people did at the time too. Soldiers may have come to power through force, but they kept it through panache.

Some soldiers were people one wanted to know. There was General Yakubu Gowon, the jaunty war hero who discreetly flexed his biceps whenever he posed for a state photograph, or Major Emmanuel Ifeajuna, the Olympic athlete with a flashing smile. There was Colonel Mobolaji Johnson, the jocular governor of Lagos State, who baked chocolate cakes for his rivals to win them over to his side.[78] Johnson was modest and moderate, and he was known for his generous spirit. "It is only by coming out and seeing how and where other fellow Nigerians live, how they work, how they dress and generally their way of life, that we can truly claim to understand ourselves," he wrote in a greeting card to the governor of the defeated eastern region after the civil war.[79] When many Nigerians pictured a soldier, they pictured somebody like Johnson—dashing, conscientious, and upright. This was "military government with a human face," as an attorney general described it.[80]

To its adherents, militarism was not just powerful—it was *beautiful*. It dazzled the eye with polished brass and billowing flags, straight backs and strong muscles. Many of Africa's military leaders were young and attractive, and some of their popularity lay in their sex appeal; Babangida's "rock solid physique," Gowon's boyish charm, Rawlings's swagger, and of course the famous handsomeness of Captain Thomas Sankara, who ruled Burkina Faso in the 1980s.[81] "I will never forget how crazy in love I fell with a newspaper photograph," quipped a student, reflecting a continent-wide infatuation with the tall, dashing coup plotter.[82] First Lady Maryam Babangida described the hold officers had on "the hearts of the ladies." "There is this strong impression that the life of an Army Officer's wife is one of glamour, prestige and plenty; the world is at her feet, hers to command with just a snap of her fingers." "The parades, the uniform, the tough-guy look and smart 'turn-out' of officers leave a deep impression in the heart of many a young bride."[83] Soldiers had a vitality that made the elderly civilians they replaced seem like waxworks. Their wives were equally captivating, and the press reported on them as if they were movie stars.

Throughout this book, I use the general pronoun *he* to refer to soldiers in the abstract. This is intentional. It is not an accidental elision of women—it is a reminder about the sex of militaries in this time and place. Not all who have been called "soldiers" in history have been men, but here militaries were overwhelmingly male in their composition, culture, and self-regard.[84] Military governments were assemblages of men, and this explains certain things about how they worked. Readers who find this essentializing would not be wrong, but militarism cannot be fully understood without acknowledging the overwhelming maleness of African armies. What does an ideology that comes from a determinedly masculine place like a barracks look like? How did soldiers' sex shape their political visions? Masculinity could have more than one meaning, and it wasn't always what one might expect—more than one veteran told me that homosexuality was quietly tolerated in the ranks, which hints at something mottled underneath militarism's macho veneer.[85] Ideas about gender were themselves a product of militarism. The "war system" produces gender difference in many settings, and Africa is no exception.[86] War makes men, as the adage goes, but war also makes maleness itself.

In the 1980s the historian Nina Mba reported that, as far as the military was concerned, "women were just not there."[87] Mba was right that soldiers had an androcentric view of the world, but African armies didn't ignore women. Officers realized that women commanded a "reserve army of labor," as Amina Mama recalled, and the state couldn't function without them.[88] Although women's votes were irrelevant in nondemocratic military regimes, their labor and capital were indispensable. Soldiers had strict ideas about what women should and should not be doing, but they also knew they *needed* women, so they actively courted their support (arguably more than civilians did).[89]

In armies where soldiers were fed by their wives, as had been the colonial convention, women were never seen as unimportant.[90] Women would also raise the next generation of soldiers, and for this reason a pronatal thread ran through military ideology. "The hand that rocks the cradle rules the nation," General Murtala Muhammed told an assembly of prominent women. But, he went on, "this does not mean that the Government expects the women only to help in raising families. Surely, we want our women to contribute their quota in *all* aspects of our national activities."[91] They did indeed contribute, especially to the military's auxiliary functions. For many years the highest-ranking woman in the Nigerian armed forces was Major General Aderonke Kale, a psychiatrist who commanded the Army Medical Corps. Women's roles in a military society may have been limited to healing, cooking, and sex, but no soldier thought those things were unimportant.

Wearing a uniform was not the only way to participate in militarism. Civilian women had a prominent place in military administrations, and they had a stake in the coups that shook up national politics every few years. The wives of high-ranking officers were especially powerful, and the first lady became a quasi-official office in Nigeria.[92] First ladies maneuvered behind the scenes, whispered in their husbands' ears, and exerted influence through their charities. "Every queen can choose the way she lives," declared First Lady Maryam Abacha. "She can eat bread and honey and sleep on and on in her palace. Or she can come out and toil with the people. I have chosen to come out and toil with the people."[93] Nigeria's "queen" shared this sense of noblesse oblige with many military wives, who saw themselves as "visionary mothers" of the nation.[94] They were the gentle, giving complement to their stern husbands. "The milk of kindness which flows in Hajiya Hauwa Lawal Ningi Haruna knows no bound," gushed a profile of Borno State's first lady.[95] Their good works were often cover for politics—Maryam Babangida's Better Life for Rural Women program was largely about sanitizing her husband's reputation abroad, for example.[96] Women weren't above barracks intrigue. "Chief (Mrs) Modupe Adebayo was a first class intelligence officer for her husband," noted a biographer, "a principal vessel used by God to provide the indispensable emotional and political wherewithal with which all obstacles were firmly confronted and surmounted."[97] Subtlety wasn't a military virtue—the army's propaganda almost always had this overbearing tone. The bluster was a symptom of something larger.

Soldiers believed they had a world-historical mission, and to see it as anything less than that is to sell it short. They were confident they could change their societies, and they had no qualms about using tyranny to make them "free." Some had good intentions. But to admit that not all of them were mad-men, crooks, or sadists is not to defend militarism. The soldiers who ruled Nigeria failed by virtually every measure. They bungled their revolution-ary mission, and they maimed millions of lives in the process. Nonetheless, credit should go where credit is due: It is largely thanks to them that Nigeria survived the twentieth century intact. If the goal of a state is to preserve itself, then the soldiers who shepherded their country through a civil war and maybe a dozen existential challenges *succeeded*. Of course, not every-one agreed that Nigeria's survival was a good thing. Then as now, this is not a country that endears itself to its citizens. Many Nigerians—dissidents, free thinkers, secessionists—felt incarcerated in its borders. For them, the mili-tary's motto of "One Nigeria" was not a promise, but a *threat*.

Sources and Methods

When I first went to Nigeria, what caught my eye were the uniforms—starched, improbably pristine, in every shade of camouflage, in bright green, electric blue (for a youth brigade called Man o' War), or hot pink (for a paramilitary group called Àmòtékùn). Students my age wore the less martial but no less immac-ulate khaki uniforms of the National Youth Service Corps (a public service draft for civilians). My first lesson in their power came when a policeman tried to confiscate the shirt off my back—a fast-fashion button-down with epau-lets, which he deemed too close to a uniform. Over the years that followed I wrote a book about the Biafra War, also known as the Nigerian Civil War, which took place during the military dictatorship. Sometimes, I came across documents from the Nigerian Army. They were striking—plainer than the baroque bureaucratese of civilians but full of saber-rattling and misspelled bombast. Some bore seals of skulls and hand grenades, and once, memora-bly, an emblem of a menacing red octopus. I made copies and put them in a folder, which grew to a crate, and eventually a hard drive. Those documents became the basis of this book. This was a scattershot way to do research, but it was the approach that scattered archives required.[98]

Military dictatorships aren't the easiest governments to know about. Soldiers were poor recordkeepers, and it is mostly their fault that Africa's first decades of independence are so thinly documented. They loved secrets. Their training primed them to think that all information was privileged in-formation, and they thrived on cloak-and-dagger intrigue. When they went into politics, their omertà came with them. Even when they kept records, they seldom handed them over to archivists. This fact makes researching them difficult, but it is also a piece of historical evidence in and of itself.[99] Their thin archives reflect how they thought about time. "Soldiering is not a sentimental profession," remarks an officer in Chinua Achebe's novel of military rule. "The first thing we learn is: Soja come, soja gwo."[100] Soldiers didn't record their activities for the same reason they didn't make long-term plans: most military regimes believed themselves to be temporary. They acted like this even as their forays into politics stretched from months, to years, to decades. Posterity was not something they worried about. In Nigeria—a country where autobiography is a kind of national pastime—it's striking that many officers never wrote a word about themselves.[101] Those who did seldom showed much self-reflection. "A soldier is never sorry for what he has done," Major General David Jemibewon wrote in his own impenitent memoir. "He may be wrong or he may be right in his action, but there is no room for regret or expression of sorrow."[102]

Soldiers could be vain, but their vanity was seldom about their historical legacies. Unlike civilian politicians, who memorialized themselves constantly, soldiers emphasized their modesty. They cared about how they looked in their uniforms, but they wanted to look "ready" and "smart" rather than rich or suave. They saw themselves not as patriarchs who deserved veneration but dutiful elder brothers who would do their jobs humbly, without the need for public recognition (although a few liked the spotlight). The eye they felt judging them was not they eye of the public, but the eye of *other soldiers*. A chest full of medals meant more to them than a shelf full of memoirs. There was also a more basic explanation for their halting paper trail—they were wary about writing. Theirs was a world of shouted commands, and although no officer was illiterate, some struggled to express themselves in print. They mistrusted the written word, preferring the radio or the television when they felt the need to address the public. The ephemeral nature of those broadcasts makes some of postcolonial Africa's most important figures seem curiously silent. Despite spending years in Nigeria's archives, the number of documents I've seen written in the hand of any of its military dictators wouldn't fill a single folder.

Conspicuously absent in the bibliography for this book is the National Archives of Nigeria, which has few documents from the period after the first military coup in 1966 (or at least few I've ever managed to cajole my way into seeing).[103] The archives have failed in their mission to preserve Nigeria's state records, but not all blame lays on the archivists. Soldiers were reluctant to leave behind evidence of what they were doing, and I suspect that most papers only left their barracks as clouds of smoke. I may be proven wrong, and if someday those records turn up this story might have to be rewritten. But in the meantime, I had to triangulate military rule's plot from other places.

Oral history could have been one of them, but I decided early on that this book would be written from documents rather than interviews. To decline the oral-historical approach is a kind of blasphemy among historians of Africa, but I quickly found that what I wanted to capture—the attributes of militarism as an ideology—couldn't be found in people's partial and often regretful memories of that time.[104] Rather, I found it on paper. This book is about *how militarism worked* more than *how people felt about it*, and that question was best answered with sources from the era. They include decrees, speeches, government gazettes, and court cases.[105] In them, we can see the state talking to itself. Soldiers try out different voices and affects. They fret over their foibles and missteps, and they pump themselves up like a nervous date in front of a bathroom mirror. These are mostly documents of *intent*, not evidence about how things turned out. Taking them seriously widens the scope of political theory to include the people who wrote them—officers who are remembered as men of action, but seldom as men of thought.

* * *

African history's power lies in its capacity to unsettle. When it's at its best it is uncouth and obtuse, probing things that are unseen, unexpected, or uncanny. How colonial liberation slunk into martial tyranny is one of them. Social scientists have given us many accounts of the decline of the state in postcolonial Africa. Few have tried to understand why it's still with us. For a long time, their primary task seemed to be not *interpreting* African states but *cataloging their deterioration*. One didn't have to mentally deconstruct countries like Somalia or Liberia to see how they worked—you could watch them crumble right before your eyes. Something was gained by observing the machinery of state fall apart; with each piece that failed, it became easier to see how it was supposed to work.[106] But there was also something perverse about this entropic method. It made it hard to see that even broken structures can mean something to people. Bacchic revelry and violence drew the eye away from everything else that was going on in Africa's statehouses, and a fixation on corruption blinded observers to any function a state might serve besides channeling money or shielding the powerful.

States are not just protection rackets run by their elites. They contain multitudes, and even the most hollowed-out ones are full of conflicting impulses and countervailing forces. An apt corrective comes from the unlikely source of David Foster Wallace: a state is "not a team or a code, but a sort of sloppy intersection of desires and fears."[107] This may sound pedantic, but it isn't obvious from reading social science about postcolonial Africa. Scholars have no problem describing African states, even "the" African state, as if it only works one way, or only does one thing—theft, for example, or punishment, or protecting foreign capital. We have come up with overwrought metaphors of bellies and phalluses to explain African politics, and we have allowed those metaphors to stand in for empirical description.[108] Contingency and causation seem irrelevant when all you can see is *rot*. *Soldier's Paradise* tries to see Africa's militocracies in the fullness of political life—it catalogs their tensions, strengths, and flaws, and it asks what made them that way. It takes seriously their visions of the future. Even the harshest dictatorships had philosophies, and even seemingly reactionary soldiers were trying to create something new.

This is hard to see in African history as it has been written. Intentionally or not, what journalists and scholars like me have produced is a *postcolonial gothic*. The story as we've told it is full of dark magic, surreal cruelties, and crimes committed behind barbed-wire fences. We use the language of haunting constantly, often letting it do the work of explanation. Dead bodies are our objects of study more often than one might imagine, and the most well-traveled concept to come from postcolonial Africa, coined by its most celebrated intellectual—Achille Mbembe—is something called *necropolitics*.[109] There are so many ethnographies of garbage dumps and toilets that one could be forgiven for thinking that *waste* is the defining feature of African life. None of this is inherently a problem. There are good reasons to use a dead body or an overflowing latrine to make a point, and sometimes the gothic style of storytelling is the one that fits the tale.[110] The question is whether modern Africa—a place of bright sunshine and deafening noise—is best described using a language of whispers and shadows. This is not just a representational problem. The failure to capture the feel of African life is a symptom of other, larger misapprehensions.

Militarism had a distinct sensibility. Its sounds were martial: Marches on the radio announcing that a coup was underway, orders shouted by drill sergeants commanding the public in displays of physical fitness. Or else silence, which soldiers tried to impose in cities, where itinerant preachers with megaphones, sidewalk stereos, and traffic otherwise made for a constant din. It smelled of diesel fumes (armored vehicles were everywhere), and Kiwi, the Australian shoeshine used by soldiers throughout the Commonwealth. Food didn't taste different when the military was in charge, except that there was somewhat less of it—most military governments imposed high tariffs for imported grain and rice to protect local agriculture.[111] Men in uniform could be seen everywhere, especially in cities. The Nigerian journalist Christine Any-anwu described "the bravado of the military boys; the reefer-soaked soldiers dressed in camouflage uniforms, heads clad in green helmets covered with tattered camouflage fabric. It made them look like they were wearing tattered rags on their heads—*jungle men* engaged in *jungle warfare* in the very heart of Lagos. Those red-eyed, stone-faced men hanging atop open trucks, looking menacing as they caressed their sub-machine guns, were something to see."[112]

These sensations are important in understanding military rule as a form of politics. Militarism's ambience—what it felt like, the emotions it evoked—was part of what made it work. The sun wasn't dimmer when the army was in charge, and certain quarters of society felt fairly free. Sitting in a combative university seminar or dancing in a raucous Lagos nightclub, one could forget that this was a dictatorship. But a military checkpoint was never far away, and crackdowns were harsh when they came. The press was free, until a journalist mysteriously disappeared. Universities were places of dissent, but a campus might abruptly shut down if student politics got out of line. Even in relatively open periods of military rule, freedoms could only be enjoyed knowing they might vanish at any minute. Nigeria's domestic intelligence branch, the Security Organization, was no Stasi. It was famously inept, and dissidents had more reason to fear the impulsive soldiers patrolling the streets than the military's klutzy spies. Even so, one could never be quite sure who was listening.[113] Unpredictability was a strategy, and the element of surprise was useful to military regimes that had neither the reach nor the resources to monitor everyone.

Militarism had many ironies, and looking for consistency in it is a fool's errand. An officer could be a poetic humanist and a petty martinet at the same time. He could ardently preach "freedom" while locking up scores of people in the name of defending it. He could describe his regime as temporary while also insisting it was a "revolution" that had transformed society permanently. "Each regime intends to stay briefly in power, pilot the democratic experience and hand-over to civilians," a Nigerian Marxist described. But once soldiers took the statehouse, they almost always wanted to stay there. Each coup "vomits a contagion which courses quietly and slowly through the arteries of the armed forces," he averred. Few soldiers were immune to the "venom of power."[114] Even as they promised that democracy was right around the corner, they spent fortunes on monuments glorifying themselves. In Lagos, they built the National Theatre in the shape of an enormous officer's cap, literally hanging their hat on the capital city. It remains there long after they left. These contradictions aren't something to be explained away—they were immanent to militarism as a system of thought. *Soldier's Paradise* is devoted to describing the most important of them: soldiers ruled by the gun, but they also had a deep, sometimes delusional, faith in the *law*.

Militarism's contradictions didn't mean it was an ideological free-for-all, and its internal flaws didn't make it incoherent. It had an intelligible meaning, especially in its legal form. A legal system is like an ecosystem, and like in nature, the different flora and fauna work together even as they compete. Each organism—courts, judges, bodies of law—has its own traits. Each occupies a distinct niche. In modern Africa, we find common-law courts, customary law, commissions of inquiry, and military tribunals, all growing side by side. They interact in complicated ways, winding their tendrils around one another, sometimes competing and sometimes cooperating. Their seeds may have come from Europe, but they grew differently in African soils. *Soldier's Paradise* describes this intricate ecology. Chapter 1 asks where militarism came from: What parts of it were repurposed from colonialism, and what parts were new? Chapter 2 asks where it was going: What destination were soldiers aiming for, and what moral compass did they use to get there? Chapter 3 describes why military regimes were wedded to the idea of "revolution" and how its jurisprudence moved across the continent. Chapters 4, 5, and 6 show law in action. Each describes a legal form that was important to soldiers—customary law, commissions of inquiry, and martial law, respectively—and how civilians got caught up in it.

* * *

In the criminal courtroom, judges sometimes use the concept *cui bono*—who benefits?—to understand the evidence in front of them. Crimes are usually committed to profit their perpetrators, so in narrowing down the suspects there is some value in asking who gained from, say, the death of a murder victim. Social scientists ask this question too, and it can be useful for understanding history. Repeatedly over the course of this research, I tried to ask it about the documents in front of me: Who benefited from the crimes of Africa's military dictatorships?

The answer is often nobody. Militarism did not work for soldiers, or for civilians, for men, or for women. It didn't work for the rich, who lived in fearful alienation, or the poor, who lived in conditions that were among the most degrading on the planet. It didn't work for people with skill or ambition, who found themselves stymied at every turn (many of them eventually emigrated). Nor did it work for those *without* talent or drive, who found that if they stumbled, there was no safety net to break their fall, and no bottom they would eventually hit. Perhaps it worked for individual officers when they were in power, but few of them stayed there for long. Every officer who ruled Nigeria, tyrant or moderate, ended his reign in humiliation—or in a coffin.[115] Military rule brutalized *all* Nigerians in one way or another. Some managed to profit from it for a while, but no one did forever. A handful of kleptocrats got rich stealing from the government, but most of them met a bad end too. No amount of money or power could insulate you from the state's worst failures: the crime, the chaos of the roads, and the ever-present danger of being smacked around by a teenager in a baggy uniform.

So why did people put up with military rule? It was because it gave them a *plan*—or at least the illusion of one. Militarism offered the promise of security and order, which soldiers tried to deliver through law. Law wasn't actually very useful for making an orderly society, but people learned they could turn the military's law-and-order vision to their own ends. Many saw something appealing in militarism's aggression, austerity, and independent-mindedness. Some found weapons they could turn against their rivals. Another cold truth: some found pleasure in submission. Patrick Wilmot, a Jamaican-Nigerian sociologist who made a career out of needling the military, argued that his adopted country secretly longed to be dominated. "Naïve liberals thought people whose noses you rubbed in shit would rise up and try to fuck you," he addressed soldiers in a thinly fictionalized polemic, "but the truth was they dunked their heads even deeper in it to hide from the source of their pain before lining up to kiss your dick or crawling away to die."[116] Wilmot's vulgarity landed him in court constantly, and eventually it got him kicked out of the country. But there was a grain of truth in what he said. Militarism was humiliating, but soldiers' ability to shame and humble people was part of their appeal.

Part I.

Militarism as a Civilization

1

THE MASTER'S TOOLS

The Inheritance of Colonialism

When the British Empire died, Africans inherited a basket of odds and ends. There were some useful items in it, but most of it was rusty scrap that the British had stopped using at home long ago. Dusty heirlooms, old medals, and moth-eaten uniforms had meant something to people once, but now they embarrassed their inheritors. Sharp objects that might draw blood were mixed into the chattel. The first task of independence was to pick through and see what, if anything, was worth keeping. It took a long time. Two parts of the colonial bequest were especially important in Africa—the culture of the military and the institutions of law. To understand Africa's military dictatorships, we must hold two countervailing ideas in our minds at once. First, militarism's violence was a colonial legacy, and second, that same colonial legacy gave people tools to fight *against* militarism's violence. To the civilians who squirmed under soldiers' thumbs, this was not a paradox. Colonialism's jumbled estate was both the wound and the remedy. The challenge, both for militarism's supporters and its opponents, was figuring out which items in the basket were which.

What did Africans see when they looked back at colonialism from the vantage point of military dictatorships? And which of those dictatorships' characteristics came from colonialism? The answer is *many*, but to say that countries like Nigeria, Ghana, Uganda, or Sudan were British inventions doesn't tell us all we need to know about them. It wasn't just that their borders had been drawn in London.[1] After independence, Africa's leaders adapted colonial governmentality to their own purposes. They didn't abandon the colonial model, even though many of them publicly promised they would. They often turned to the colonial library for guidance, but they had no interest in the books in that library that had been written specifically for them—paeans to European civilization, parables about soap or the baby Jesus. Rather, they read the architects of empire—Rudyard Kipling, Frederick Lugard—to learn *how to rule others.*

Then as now, governing Nigeria was a tall order. If you're trying to rule a quarter of a billion people who speak over seven hundred languages, worship many different gods, and follow irreconcilable customs, it is an empire, not a nation, that offers the closest template for administration. Many of Nigeria's leaders have understood this, even though few have said it in public.[2] "Nearly all of our military leaders have displayed imperial tendencies," wrote Chidi Amuta, not entirely disapprovingly. "They have ruled by decree, and generally tended to regard and run the affairs of Nigeria like one vast empire."[3] When Nigerians decided to keep certain features of colonialism, it wasn't out of any love for the British. It was because they were practical. The English language, for example, had a certain value. English had no intrinsic advantage over African languages, but it served a purpose. In a country with many mother tongues, a lingua franca that was local to nowhere had its uses, as many Nigerian intellectuals came to appreciate.[4] Soldiers reasoned in a similarly pragmatic way. As they learned, the imperial toolkit was useful for managing a vast, mixed, and divided society like Nigeria. After all, governing difference is what empires do.

Soldiers learned to fight in colonial armies, but force wasn't the only thing the British taught their African cadets. The British Empire didn't work through violence alone, nor would the military regimes that followed it.[5] Violence was expensive, and the colonial government was cheap—it was a "frugal gourmet," and it practiced "hegemony on a shoestring," to cite two well-known metaphors for imperialism's political economy.[6] Britain's goal was to make money, not to destroy the people who would make it for them, and the example of other empires (notably King Leopold's excesses in the Congo Free State) had taught them that too much violence might hurt the bottom line.

After the initial shock of conquest, they had little interest in propping up colonies if the only way to keep them standing was through constant warfare. Calling their rule the Pax Britannica was an ironic boast, but there was an evil genius to it. War was costlier than peace, and it was cheaper to rule subject populations by luring them in or buying them off than constantly subjugating them through force.

The British also worried about the moral cost of colonial violence—not to Africans but to themselves. Joseph Conrad was not the only European to fret about the psychic effects of brutality *to the brutalizer*. Like Conrad, British officials worried about what license to commit unhinged violence in the colonies would do to their young men.[7] For this reason and others, they decided to rule their African colonies by subtler means. In the twentieth century, colonial administration became a pseudoscience, with manuals, experiments, and an entire school in London devoted to honing its methods.[8] Colonialism worked by manufacturing consent, co-opting allies, and making vague promises about freedom, prosperity, and "fair play" (sometimes glossed as liberalism).[9] And if these tactics failed, violence was still an option: "Whatever happens, we have got the Maxim Gun, and they have not," went a satirical British poem of the late nineteenth century.[10] What made colonialism insidious was not just the rubble left in the wake of conquest. It was its capacity to co-opt people, rewire their brains, and bind them to a cause that was definitively *not in their interests*.

The African soldiers who ruled in Europeans' stead had learned these lessons well. They governed much like their predecessors. They would be harsh one day and gentle the next. They alternatively baited their critics, bought them off, and obliterated them. They conditioned their subjects to think like they did, and they created new, chillingly effective forms of extraction and repression that they successfully passed off as "traditions." Violence might seem like the most obvious characteristic of both colonial rule and the military dictatorships that followed it, but both these forms of tyranny also had more delicate mechanisms. Law was one of them.

Nigeria's history after 1960 was shaped by what came before, but this book is not another attempt to measure continuity and change across the moment when empires broke apart into nation-states.[11] Historians have expended much energy assigning blame for African states' failures or credit for their successes. Which aspects of postcolonial governance came from Europe? Which were innovated in Africa, for good or for bad? The purpose of this line of questioning is usually to account for a defect ("why is this country so corrupt?") or less often to recognize an achievement, sometimes in a backhanded way ("how has this country survived, even though its composition makes no sense?"). Most who pursue it arrive at some version of the same answer, even if they quibble about where to put the accent: some things changed at independence, others didn't. A certain idea or practice might originate with colonialism, but how it evolved after independence isn't answered by looking at the colonial archive. British institutions were transubstantiated into Nigerian ones after 1960, but this didn't mean they were magically transformed. This is true of both subjects of this chapter—law and martial culture—and readers satisfied by this lukewarm observation should skip to chapter 2. Those who need more convincing—who believe that independence was a real, total revolution that undid colonization from the ground up or alternatively think it meant nothing and that Britain continued to pull all the strings—should read on. Africans made their own futures, but they did not make them as they pleased.[12]

* * *

Nearly six years passed between independence in October 1960 and the military coup that set Nigeria on its martial path in 1966. What happened during those first years of freedom? If one reads the radicals of the era, the answer appears to be "not much." Nigerians got a new flag and a seat at the United Nations, new stamps and passports. But the state they built was hard to distinguish from the Nigeria of the 1950s. The British pulled out of Nigeria "so surreptitiously that many of us became suspicious," wrote Tai Solarin.[13] Not all of them had actually left. British administrators stayed on in the employ of the Nigerian government, some at high levels. Their presence embarrassed nationalist politicians, but it was hard to get rid of them. They were protected by their contracts, and at any rate the government needed them—the managerial class the British had failed to train couldn't be created overnight. The economy continued to be an awkward mix of free-market liberalism and state-led development. British curricula remained in the schools, and tastemakers still looked to London. Nigeria wasn't changing fast enough for some people.

As for the elected civilian government, its most obvious feature seemed to be its corruption. Most social scientists described the sleaze and left it at that.[14] It is hard to say how corrupt the First Republic actually was, but the best way to understand its apparent vice is from Steven Pierce: "corruption" was a discursive language of politics and public morality, not something that could be objectively measured.[15] Landmark events from these first years of independence would be overshadowed by everything that happened later.

Nigeria became a republic in 1963, moving it a level out from the British monarchy (but still in the orbital of the Commonwealth). The army's mettle was tested in a United Nations peacekeeping mission in the Democratic Republic of the Congo—a test that the officers declared they passed.[16] A crisis in the Western Region wracked the political elite, and the country nearly came to blows over a contested census. It was a time of disappointments and growing pains. But critics—high and low, left and right—began to talk as if it was all-out anarchy.[17]

The First Republic was less of a failure than the soldiers who ended it made it out to be. Civilian politicians faced a difficult task, and they did the best they could with the meager resources at their disposal. They had some successes. They expanded primary education and medical care, bringing basic public services to millions who had never had them. Nigeria's economy performed well, and the state built new factories, refineries, ports, and roads. But all this was left out of the story soldiers told later. All you needed to know, they insisted, was that Nigeria's brief experiment with democracy had failed. The country was still poor, but a suspicious number of politicians had gotten rich. The flush of colonial humiliation hadn't faded, and civilians hadn't created a strong, unified national identity. Those who wanted these things started to see their government as defective, and soldiers and radicals converged in their condemnation of civilian politicians.[18] "Life became uncertain and fearful," General Ibrahim Babangida would later maintain. "The political system was vandalised, the Constitution was abused and individual citizens who exercised the legitimate right of dissent were brutalised." These forms of repression, he insisted, compelled the military to take over. "Those who had a religious frame of mind pleaded with God to intervene in the affairs of Nigeria. As a consequence, the military intervened."[19]

Critics of the First Republic were right about one thing: Nigeria was deeply divided. During the civil war of 1967–1970 it had come to the brink of dissolution. The federal side won the war, and at the end of it the secessionist Republic of Biafra was reintegrated into the federation. Nigeria was still intact, and the military took credit for saving the country—even though it had leveled the eastern region and killed over a million of its citizens to save it. Although the war was over, the military didn't relinquish the power it had grown accustomed to. Soldiers were convinced they were the only ones who could hold Nigeria together, and they came to fear that if they allowed democracy to come back, ethnic discord would return with it (never mind that this problem plagued military governments too). For decades, they justified their coups by invoking the possibility of another civil war.[20] They never tired of reminding the public of civilian democracy's failures. They did this even after they had failed many times, and failed just as hard.

The civil war had nourished militarism. The Federal Military Government had built a war machine to defeat Biafra, and once it was built, soldiers were reluctant to take it apart. Even after the conscripts had been sent home, the army remained much larger than it had been before 1967. Many officers had been promoted during the fighting, bloating the ranks of the leadership. Nigeria had bought (and been given) a huge amount of hardware to use against Biafra's homemade artillery. This became a self-fulfilling prophecy. If you have tanks, you need tank crews, and if you have bombers, you need an air force to fly them. Whole units of technicians were kept on to keep the machines in working order, even though they had no clear purpose once the war was over. The legacies of the civil war helped the military keep a stranglehold on politics, but this explanation for why militarism set in wasn't portable beyond Nigeria. Many African states that didn't have civil wars also became military dictatorships, and an army didn't have to be on a war footing for its officers to covet political power. What they *did* share was that they were former colonies.

Independence meant different things to different people, and when African politicians and intellectuals talked about "decolonization," they were not all talking about the same thing. Some saw political independence as the condition that would make everything else possible: "Seek ye first the political kingdom," Kwame Nkrumah advised his fellow nationalists.[21] To others, decolonization was a mindset rather than a politics: Ngũgĩ wa Thiong'o enjoined Africans to decolonize their minds by "re-membering" the knowledge lost through colonialism's linguistic violence, and Wamba-dia-Wamba and Kwame Gyekye made the case for epistemologies that emerged organically from African life. To these philosophers, decolonization was an act of repair; it was about suturing a dismembered political body back together and healing over the scars. Others called for "de-linking" from the West, believing that true decolonization required economic isolation from the First World (a minority view in capitalist Nigeria). To some, it demanded purging society of colonial institutions or expelling the foreigners who staffed them.

In its most basic sense, decolonization was a process—an entropic shift from one political form (an empire) to another (a nation-state), neither of which was more or less inherently good, just, or humane than the other. When Nigeria's soldier elite called for decolonization, they typically meant it as shorthand for two things: discipline for civilians and unfettered power for themselves. Decolonization was capacious enough to hold all of this.

Then as now, the injunction to decolonize camouflaged the workings of power. Behind every call to overthrow a colonial system (real or metaphorical) was a bid by someone to take power themselves. Rarely was there only one person vying for it. The language of decolonization displaced the local struggle over who was in charge onto outsiders—all the better if they were no longer around to defend themselves. In postcolonies like Nigeria, invoking decolonization as an ongoing process papered over differences among "the colonized"—a vast, heterogeneous group of people with wildly divergent interests (and a wide range of experiences under colonialism itself). The specter of neocolonialism gave all Nigerians a common enemy, which was useful for building a national consensus.[22]

"In each case where there has been counter-revolutionary armed action," Kwame Nkrumah wrote from exile after the Ghanaian military deposed him, "there has been a link-up between foreign-trained army officers, local reactionary opposition elements and imperialists and neocolonialists." "The neo-colonialists smile: the peoples of Africa suffer." "These men trained in various English military establishments prided themselves on being more 'English' than Ghanaian," he wrote, "and tended to frown on everything in our Ghanaian way of life which did not conform with English customs and traditions. They gradually became more British than the British as they slavishly tried to imitate the traditional English army officer. Ankrah [who overthrew Nkrumah] is a typical example with his enthusiasm for the Turf Club, his love of ceremonial, and his sense of caste." What soldiers learned in "imperialist countries," Nkrumah argued, made them "easy game for those plotting the overthrow of progressive governments."[23]

Nkrumah was right that a web of connections tied countries like his to London. There were defense pacts, university scholarships, training schemes for government officials, and aid projects.[24] The Commonwealth of Nations gained many new members as the empire ended, and by 1965 it had outgrown its London headquarters. The secretariat moved into Marlborough House, a shabbily genteel palace a few doors down from Lancaster House, where many African nationalists had negotiated their countries' independence. But this wasn't where the plot against Nkrumah was hatched. That happened in the officer's mess of the Second Infantry Brigade in Kumasi, where lieutenant generals Emmanuel Kwasi Kotoka and Akwasi Amankwaa Afrifa made the plan that sealed his fate.[25] If soldiers took power it was because they wanted it, not because they were strong-armed by the British, who had neither the will nor the credibility to influence them that way. But conspiracy theories can be comforting, and the argument that military rule was orchestrated from London still gets a hearing today.

Ensconced in their comfortable retirements in the home counties, the departed colonial rulers tutted over "tribalism" as if that explained why Britain's ex-colonies were erupting into civil wars or spiraling into dictatorship. Few of them took any responsibility for what was happening. But if their goal was to hide their role in it, they did a poor job. At independence British administrators sent documents home by the shipload. The manor house where they hid the most incriminating ones has obsessed people since it was discovered, but the documents they kept in plain sight were just as damning—look at any Colonial Office series at the National Archives at Kew and you'll find evidence of mischief and violence right up until the moment they left. But after independence, the British stayed less involved in African affairs than one might expect. Conservatives defended the legacy of colonialism in the abstract, but the British government kept the messy politics of its ex-colonies at arm's length. The Foreign and Commonwealth Office watched countries like Nigeria closely, but it wasn't willing to risk much there.

This became blatantly obvious during the Nigerian Civil War. Although the United Kingdom gave the Nigerian side some tepid military assistance, British officials were surprisingly ambivalent about whether or not the country survived. The Nigerian leadership was scandalized—not by neocolonial meddling but by how *little* the British seemed to care that their most important ex-colony in Africa was on the brink of dissolution. Kenya received significant military aid after independence, but assistance for other former colonies was paltry: secondhand uniforms for the Gambian army, ropes and nets for "adventure" training for Ghana. When the UK Ministry of Defence sent some instructors to the Nigerian Army Staff College in the 1980s, the scandal that followed wasn't about the fact that Nigerian officers were receiving British training, but that Britain sent Nigeria a bill for it—to the tune of £400,000 per instructor.[26]

What the British actually did was the opposite of the string-pulling and kingmaking that conspiracy theories trafficked in: they cut ties, shut the gates, and declared the ledger of colonialism closed. Once the United Kingdom had thrown in its lot with Europe, the Commonwealth came to seem like a burden—an embarrassing assortment of backwaters and dictatorships, not a resource to be exploited. Some Britons mourned the empire, but more forgot it had ever existed.[27] Except for a few areas that directly affected life in the United Kingdom, like immigration and drug trafficking, most British governments couldn't have cared less what countries like Nigeria did. To make this point is not to absolve Britain of responsibility for Africa's militaristic turn. Neglect is not necessarily benign, and it is just as damning to say that Britain forgot its former colonies as that it remembered them too well. There is also a deeper history here; the fact that African soldiers were the architects of their countries' military dictatorships does not mean they built them from the ground up. Their foundations had been laid by the jingoists, conquerors, and teeth-gnashing "men on the spot" who built the British Empire. I am not here to lay blame, but Whitehall would be a good place to put it.[28]

There is a custom of comparing modern states to monsters—to leviathans and behemoths, or ogres that eat their own children. The monster usually summoned to explain Nigeria is the "Zombie," as Fela Kuti sang in an immortal 1976 song of that name. This metaphor implied that Nigeria's leaders carried on in the British way long after the empire itself was dead, like a zombie doing a master's bidding. There is some truth to this, but the better metaphorical monster for this era might be the golem of Jewish mythology, as the political theorist Nicholas Rush Smith has described.[29] A golem is a creature made of earth or ash that comes to life when the right incantations are said. People make golems to protect themselves—much like they make armies. But like an army, a golem's "protection" can feel more like menace. Roughly made, imperfectly obedient, and stuporific until it becomes violent, the golem is a monster that can turn on its makers. In Africa, the British formed their soldiers from the soil of rural villages. They mixed in some gravel from English parade grounds and some poisoned mud from the battlefields of the world wars. Once these golems-in-uniform came to life, they had minds of their own.

Militarism

Where did late twentieth-century Africa's militarism come from? Those who think over the *longue durée* explain it as a return of old military traditions that had been interrupted by colonialism. Others see it as a belated effect of the nineteenth century's continent-wide military "revolution," as Richard Reid calls the flurry of wars that attended the end of the slave trade.[30] But soldiers themselves rejected the long view of their origins. To be sure, they thought about what had happened before the British came along and conscripted their grandfathers. They found precolonial traditions useful as tools of control, discipline, and punishment. For this reason they studied history—or, at least, the conservative version of it they got from the British, who had construed the past in as authoritarian a way as possible.

But men in uniform didn't find some version of themselves in the deep past. When asked to describe where their philosophies came from, they pointed back to the British or Indian military academies they had attended, but no further. The regimental histories they wrote about themselves started with colonialism, not before.[31] Soldiers did not romanticize the warrior-kings and queens of the past, and it would have been awkward to do so knowing who had done the dirty work of colonial conquest—*them*. Africa's warrior states had been crushed by British firepower, after all, and the armies that had done the crushing were the predecessors of the armies that now held power.

If anyone, it was *civilians* who tended to lionize precolonial military heroes—Yaa Asantewaa in Ghana, Uthman dan Fodio and Jaja of Opobo in Nigeria, and others. In the 1980s, the Ghanaian scholar Maxwell Owusu argued that coups were "rituals of rebellion" that built on precolonial political traditions. Coups echoed how people had deposed bad chiefs in the past—except that today the "chiefs" being overthrown were heads of state. Precolonial military forms like the militias called *asafo* hadn't disappeared, he argued. They had morphed and changed, but their basic shapes could be traced in modern society.[32] Owusu wasn't wrong to find an affinity between chiefs and soldiers, and maybe he was right that Ghanaians could see some shadow of the soldier-kings of their past in General Ignatius Acheampong or Flight Lieutenant Jerry Rawlings. But the real appeal of militarism was that it was *modern*.

There was nothing primordial about military rule. When an Irish journalist tried to account for Africa's militarism as a natural response to a "forest world inhabited by savage reptiles, great cats and disease bearing insects, where one's very existence was the most desperate struggle to survive," a Nigerian military governor scoffed. Hadn't Ireland been a backwater too? Would it not be absurd, he asked, to explain the rise of the IRA by evoking Ireland's ancient, primeval darkness?[33] Nigeria's militarism, like Ireland's, responded to the challenges of the moment. There was nothing mysterious about it, he insisted, and soldiers were pragmatic and forward-thinking leaders. One of their virtues, in fact, was that they were *not* beholden to the past. Africa's young officers kept their sights trained on the future. It was a clean slate. "The colonial situation was a total revolution which destroyed the very life of the colonized African leaving him confused and often demoralized," wrote General Albert Kwesi Ocran in his apologia for the military's takeover of Ghana. "The situation can only be abolished by a counter-revolution."[34] Men like him would lead it.

Among other things, colonialism had been a military occupation. The armies the British built in Africa, like the King's African Rifles and the West African Frontier Force, had been the leading edge of colonial conquest. Once that conquest was done, African soldiers were given a prominent place in colonial administration.[35] In Nigeria and elsewhere, the British used soldiers for imperialism's most important tasks—collecting taxes, suppressing revolts, and fighting encroachment by other European empires. They wanted African soldiers to be "black mirrors" of their white counterparts, and a host of military institutions were created to achieve that effect, all replicas of British ones.[36] Like most colonial copies, however, the imitation was not supposed to be perfect. Homi Bhabha's famous description of colonial mimicry—"white but not quite"—captures what the British hoped for from African troops.[37] They were expected to be loyal and disciplined and to hop to the same commands as their European comrades. But there was no illusion that they were their equals. They were commanded to do things that Europeans weren't, and to do them for lower pay and fewer privileges. The discrimination that had always been embedded in colonial soldiering became obvious during the world wars, when Africans fought alongside Europeans but got only a fraction of the recognition.[38] The armed forces were the colonial institution par excellence, right down to the racism.

One of a colonial army's main functions was to put down local resistance. For this reason, the British designed them to be as far removed from civilian society as possible; when a rebellion came, they wanted to make sure that African soldiers didn't join in. This made for armies that were profoundly alienated from the civilians they ostensibly served. There had been no concept of the "citizen-soldier" in the empire. The colonial military, a major wrote in the Nigerian Army's official magazine, had been "a place for the illiterates and criminals whose duties were to kill and be generally brutal."[39] Colonial militarism proved durable, and it would long outlast the empire itself. After independence, soldiers had few illusions about the chauvinism of British officers, and those who served before they left had firsthand experience of it.

But none of this stopped them from feeling proud to wear their uniforms. The fact that the armed forces' origins were British did not mean that they were *still* British, and there was no inherent contradiction in being anticolonial but promilitary. Soldiers had an unwavering faith in the martial tradition they had been trained in. Just as African Christians could love the gospel but hate the narrow-minded Victorian missionaries who had brought it, African soldiers could revere the British military way but dislike imperialism.[40] As Terence Ranger described, Britain's imperial military tradition was invented hastily and done on the cheap, but it worked chillingly well.[41] It was seductive, and its charms worked on all kinds of people. Militarism had an appeal that soldiers could disaggregate from colonial subjugation. It's debatable whether they were right to see it this way, but this is why British-trained soldiers like Idi Amin and Ibrahim Babangida could speak of themselves as decolonizers or freedom fighters without blushing.

After independence, "Africanizing" the officer class was the first order of business. Although the rank and file of the colonial military was entirely African, most officers were Europeans; as of 1954, there were a mere nine African commissioned officers in the entire West African Frontier Force. It was embarrassing for independent countries to have Britons commanding African soldiers, so talented subalterns were promoted quickly (and somewhat haphazardly) to replace them. They were promoted for being good soldiers, not necessarily good administrators. One private was put on a path to leadership when his marksmanship impressed a visiting dignitary at a weekend shooting trip.[42] Within a few years, he would be the military governor of his entire region. Change was slower to come at the very top. It was only in 1965, five years after independence, that a Nigerian, Major General Johnson Aguiyi-Ironsi, was appointed commander of the Nigerian Army. After the January 1966 coup that toppled the First Republic, Aguiyi-Ironsi became Nigeria's first military head of state. Like all top officers, Ironsi had a target on his back, and he would only rule Nigeria for six months before being killed by a rival. Where did officers get their ideas about politics? And where did they learn this bloody kind of careerism? Part of the answer lies in a bleak garrison town thirty miles south of London.

For Nigerians of a certain generation, the name Mons conjures an image of military prestige—sharply pressed khaki, sober discussions of strategy made less so by the port in the officers' mess. Knowing of it only from Nigeria, I assumed that the Mons Cadet Training School was what its graduates made it out to be—an elite institution of the British Army, on par with Sandhurst. Mons was in fact no such thing. Tucked away on the outskirts of Aldershot, what remains of Mons today is a parking lot and a few modest buildings, but even at its height it wasn't much more than that. The military academy that existed there from 1961 to 1972 is barely a footnote in the history of the British Army, but it was much more than that for the countries of the Commonwealth. From Guyana to Fiji, this obscure training school was the crucible of a particular form of militarism.

Mons graduates would become military strongmen all over the world, but it left its deepest mark on Nigeria. More members of Nigeria's military elite were trained at Mons than at any other institution, and its alumni constitute a who's who of Nigerian politics. Its graduates included future heads of state Muhammadu Buhari, Olusegun Obasanjo, and Sani Abacha.[43] Coup plotters including Theophilus Danjuma and Joe Garba passed through Mons, as did too many state governors and ministers to count. Most of the leaders of the 1966 coups trained there, including Emmanuel Ifeajuna and Adewale Ademoyega. Military leaders on both sides of the civil war did too, including Hassan Katsina and Chukwuemeka Odumegwu Ojukwu. Since the courses were short, not all these men overlapped during the time when Mons was training Nigerian officers, but they thought of themselves as "old boys" of the place when they returned home. Nigeria has been in the stranglehold of these men for its entire independence.

Named for a battle in the First World War, the Mons Barracks were constructed in 1926 as an outpost for training army signalers. It was hastily reconfigured as an officer-training school during the Second World War. In the 1950s it trained men for leadership positions in the reservist Territorial Army (greatly expanded through the universal male draft), although it commissioned regular army officers too. Mons was a shortcut to a military career; one could get a commission in just six months, compared to two years at Sandhurst. It attracted a mix of British reservists, logistics specialists, and, increasingly, soldiers from the colonies. After 1960, when compulsory national service ended in Britain, Mons underwent a crisis of purpose. With the size of the standing army at a century-long low, it struggled to fill its training courses. The swell of new countries created by the empire's dissolution presented an opportunity. African militaries relished the opportunity to send their cadets on training courses in Britain. Mons, long a backwater of the army, rebranded itself as a keeper of Britain's elite military tradition.[44] There, African cadets learned a particular version of that tradition—one stripped down and sharpened for the empire, now available for use in the independent states of the Commonwealth. Training programs for reservists to learn logistics (cooking, signaling) were repackaged as courses in strategy and generalship, now offered to former colonial subjects who would soon lead their national militaries. It was cheaper to send officers to Mons than the larger, more established academies, and for this reason African governments preferred it to Sandhurst, where Britain trained its own military elite.

At Mons, cadets learned the rudiments of military leadership. The curriculum included lectures on military law, civilian relations, and constant parading.[45] It emphasized the peacetime functions of the military. This included "duties in aid of the civil power," as a former cadet recalled, such as controlling a hostile crowd: "Before opening fire, select a specific trouble-maker as a target. Order a specific soldier to fire one round at that particular individual to kill him: a living martyr was not desirable. Collect the cartridge cases of the rounds fired, to provide evidence at the Court of Enquiry that inevitably would ensue."[46] This was not the way soldiers controlled a crowd in Britain. It was, however, how they had done so in the colonies, and it would become the norm in Nigeria under military rule (right down to the enquiry).

There was hardly a year in the 1960s and 1970s that Mons didn't graduate a future head of state, which makes it an easy scapegoat for the Commonwealth's epidemic of coups. To what degree was that Britain's intent? Unlike similar training schools in the United States, Mons had not been established to project military influence, and unlike in France, few in the British government believed that Britain's place in the world depended on its former colonies in Africa.[47] The courses had a certain value for keeping ties to the Commonwealth, but this was not the main way Britain profited from Mons. Rather, it profited more literally. Mons charged tuition, and like the foreign students being recruited to British universities, foreign cadets became part of the institution's funding model. For their part, most Nigerian soldiers jumped at the chance to go to England for a training course. However they felt about colonialism, learning from the army that had conquered half the world had a certain appeal.

Soldiers knew that "colonialism" was not just one thing, and they saw no contradiction in being nationalists—true nationalists, unlike the decadent civilians they disdained—while also having something to learn from their British instructors. They worshipped the rituals of the barracks, and they coveted the awards that were handed out to the best cadets. They took pride in the fact that their uniforms were just as smart, their boots just as polished, and their weapons just as deadly as the white men training them. But none of this meant they revered colonialism. It was one thing to uphold the ethos that had been drummed into them in the British military. It was quite another to love Britain in general. They knew from experience that the colonial administration had been racist, violent, and corrupt. Their view of history was nuanced enough to know there had been many types of people involved in the colonial enterprise, and the ones they liked were their fellow soldiers. The British people they held in lowest esteem were the civilians who had administered the empire—weak-willed men who exhibited all the stubbornness and pettiness of their national culture but none of its honor or brio. When they went home after their training courses, they took what they had learned at Mons with them. Emboldened by their British pedigrees, they came to believe they were destined to lead.

Legalism

The other part of the colonial bequest was law. What was true of militarism was true of legalism: Like soldiers, lawyers and judges did not see what they had inherited from Britain as a single, indivisible package. They were selective about what parts of it they wanted to preserve and what they didn't. Historians now know a lot about colonial legal systems.[48] We understand their coercive powers, their cultures, their function in buttressing the imperial project, and their uses to colonial critics and reformers. Law served the task of conquest, but it would also serve the cause of liberation. Much less has been said about African law after independence. What happened when colonial law was untethered from colonialism? How did it change when it served not a foreign occupation but a *nation*? The answer involves both continuity and change. New laws were drafted, and old ones found new purposes. Others remained exactly the same.

The enduring power of colonial law was evident whenever soldiers dispersed a crowd, detained a troublemaker, or bulldozed a shantytown.[49] When they arrested a dissident, for example, they usually did so under section 52 of the Nigerian penal code, which criminalized sedition. This code had been written by British draftsmen in the late nineteenth century, and they modeled it on similar codes in Queensland and Calcutta. It remained in force after independence, basically unchanged. Nobody was very interested in "decolonizing" it. It worked perfectly well, at least from the state's perspective, and a whole forest of institutions had grown up around it that would have to be uprooted if it was altered. As the code's longevity shows, there was some continuity between colonialism's tyranny and what came after.

But law cut both ways; the dissident could use it too. If a Nigerian civilian (or her lawyer) wanted to challenge her arrest, she *also* might reach for a legal principle associated with colonialism—habeas corpus, which came to Nigeria via English law. When a farmer sued the state, a magistrate investigated a property dispute, or a judge summoned a witness to his courtroom, those actions mobilized English laws, now made Nigerian through the alchemy of independence.[50] All kinds of people used legal tools one might call "colonial." What those tools did depended on who was using them and how.

Just as soldiers learned their vocation in British military academies, lawyers learned theirs in British universities. Legal education was not available in

Nigeria until 1962, which meant that anyone who wanted to practice law had to go abroad to study. Most went to England, though a few went to Ireland, India, and other places in the common-law world (followed by a stint at one of the inns of court in London for those who wanted to become barristers). There, they learned the ins and outs of English law, and most came to believe in it. Legal education was grueling, and law was a guild. Those who successfully joined it felt pride at their accomplishment, even if they opposed the broader project of colonialism (as many of them did). In this respect, they were not unlike the soldiers down the road at Mons, who were being steeped in Britain's martial culture—while also getting to see the underside of British society up close.

What budding lawyers learned was important, but so were the circumstances in which they learned it. In London, there were unusually close ties between law students (who would later become judges) and cadets (who would lead independent militaries). The barriers that typically cordoned off the future judges from the future generals were absent in this small group of young men. As black colonial subjects in the metropole, they were a conspicuous presence wherever they lived. Some had formative experiences with racism, and this galvanized their relationships with one another.[51] Their friendships were fostered by organizations like the West African Students Union (wasu), which drew members from across British Africa.[52] The cadets studying at military institutes joined them, spending their holidays at wasu's large house in Camden Square or with friends from home.[53] In this way, the small circle of men who would become the presidents, judges, and generals of independent African states came to know one another from a young age. They would take the beliefs, friendships, and rivalries they made in Britain back to Africa with them.[54]

Those rivalries played out in intricate and sometimes bloody ways over the rest of the twentieth century. Independence, wrote chief justice of the Nigerian Supreme Court Taslim Elias in 1978, had been like a hastily arranged marriage between soldiers and civilians. "Like the proverbial wedding bells, which, when they ring, make the prospective couple dreamy and starry eyed, the advent of independence carries with it a certain euphoria bordering on delirium." In the first flush of independence, Africans could fantasize about what was possible. But like in a marriage, "it is living together thereafter that causes all the troubles."[55] As chief justice, Elias was well placed to see how hard it was for soldiers and civilians to live together. He fretted about the erosion of judicial independence under military rule—something that he and others had fought for in the leadup to independence and during the First Republic.

The military's boosters insisted that there was no reason a military regime could not have an independent judiciary, one "as effective and free as that of any civilian regime which equally observes and applies the Rule of Law," as one contended. It could even be *more* independent, they argued, since in a military regime judges could perform their judicial "duty" (a native concept for soldiers), without having to worry about pleasing the public or placating politicians.[56] Judges like Elias tacked back and forth about this. In theory, there was no reason a military regime couldn't have an independent judiciary. But in practice, it was hard to maintain the rule of law when the judiciary was armed with law books and the executive had guns.

Executive power was strong almost everywhere in postcolonial Africa. In military regimes the head of state's commands trumped everything, and his lawmaking authority was "limitless," as a Nigerian jurist argued.[57] The laws soldiers made varied from one country to another, but they had some common characteristics. They were usually retroactive such that actions committed in the past could be punishable in the present. Most had ouster clauses that prohibited the courts from examining the validity of the decrees that made them. Decrees were legislative in that they made general laws, but they could also be ad hominem when they targeted individuals. There were decrees that banned specific newspapers, seized property from specific companies or institutions, or sent specific people to jail. The structure of the presidency changed constantly. Sometimes there was a Supreme Military Council made up of high-ranking officers, sometimes it was just the head of state—but the executive branch was always at the top.[58] Nigeria was hardly alone in this. Nearly all African states had lopsided political systems. Why?

Africa's presidents, prime ministers, juntas, kings, "emperors," and soldier-statesmen were strong because Europeans had designed the executive to be strong. During colonial rule, the governor was by far the most powerful person in any given colony. He was an unmistakably martial figure; even when a civilian held office, his starched white uniform and plumed helmet reminded the public that he was backed by military force. Colonies like Nigeria had legislatures, but they were feeble by design. Most lacked the power of the purse, which meant they were little more than debating chambers.

British colonial administration had been an uneven pastiche of liberal ideas and domineering ones. Some measure of liberalism was necessary for the colonial economy to work; encouraging private property ownership meant recognizing Africans' land claims in court, for example. But law could not be *too* liberal. Colonialism was fundamentally a rule of might, and the right to own things could not be allowed to blur into, say, the right to speak freely or to vote. When the British enumerated what they had "given" Africans, law was always toward the top of the list. Colonialism promised a just and equitable system of law, but there had always been a danger to that promise: If law was actually equitable, colonial subjects might turn it against the colonial state. Judges constantly balanced the liberal spirit of "fair play" embedded in English law against colonialism's fundamental tyranny.

Like legislatures, colonial judiciaries were designed to be weak. But in places like the Atlantic ports of Lagos and Accra, they broke out of that mold. African judges proved to be more independent-minded than colonial officials expected them to be, and African litigants often managed to *capture* colonial law, adapting it to their own purposes or wielding it against the government. Law could hold the British to account—even if only partially and only some of the time.[59] The British had trained African lawyers because they needed people who could draw up contracts, arbitrate disputes, and help keep the peace colonialism promised. They had *not* trained those lawyers to defend African interests against the government, but that was often what they ended up doing. This mismatch of intention and outcome was a mainstay of colonial law nearly everywhere.

The courts sometimes undermined the colonial government, most famously in the cases *Amodu Tijani v. Secretary, Southern Provinces of Nigeria* from 1921 and *Esugbayi Eleko v. Officer Administering the Government of Nigeria* from 1931, both of which were decided by the Privy Council in London in favor of the Nigerian appellants. These decisions put the colonial state on notice and emboldened nationalists across the empire. To be sure, the rights that African subjects could win in the colonial courtroom were limited, and there was no slippery slope that led from *Tijani* and *Eleko* to the unraveling of the British Empire. But it meant something that Africans could win at all. "The important thing," Adewoye wrote, "was the visual impression created in the minds of the masses: that Africans could stand up to their white overlords."[60] "Power in the courts," worried a British administrator, "leads to power outside the courts."[61]

For these reasons, the British treated the legal order they had created with some trepidation. Far from seeing African lawyers as allies in the colonial project, colonial officials distrusted the people who had studied "their" law in Britain.[62] After independence, military rulers would have the same worries about the subversive potential of law. For their part, the military's critics valued law for the same reasons as the anticolonial activists who came before them. Adewoye, who was one of those critics, argued that "whether or not English common law is itself good for Nigeria is beside the point." The "social revolution" of colonialism had "swept Nigeria irreversibly into the common law world, and it is from that viewpoint that one must argue."[63]

In their briefs and courtroom statements, lawyers mimicked the macho bravado of soldiers. Unlike the military, the legal profession included a small number of women in this era—but one would never know it from how male lawyers talked about themselves. They used the language of romance to describe their relationship with law, casting law as a woman and themselves as its husbands, suitors, or lovers. Anywhere in the world that tyranny reigned, a handbook for attorneys described, the judiciary must have been "emasculated and reduced to unenviable impotence." The duty of the bar and the bench was to "enthrone Justice on her proud and lofty Seat and keep her there." Like knights in a chivalric drama, lawyers had to protect "her" at all costs—to be "a chilling terror to the malignant and the vile."[64] Just as soldiers claimed they were defending the honor of the nation, judges insisted that their task was defensive. "To win public affection, we, the judges, must do our jobs well," Tanzania's chief justice told his biographer. "It is really the quality of justice that determines whether we remain independent."[65] Perhaps. But no amount of evenhandedness or artful reasoning would protect a judiciary from a military regime that wanted to gut it. Even the most upright judges bent before soldiers.

After the fact, many people blamed civilian elites—like lawyers and judges—for the disappointments of independence. Those elites could have dismantled colonialism's institutions, critics opined, but instead they used them to get rich. The critics were partially right, but it is wrong to think that anything was *supposed* to be dismantled. Lawyers took a pragmatic view of the laws the British left behind. They had spent years learning how they worked, and most had come to see them as useful. The liberals among them argued that they would need law to constrain presidents and generals, just as they had used it against the British. Those with a disciplinarian bent valued it as a tool to reform society. Even those who wanted to transform law radically didn't question its basic validity. Jurists reminded the public that the common law had been useful in the fight against colonialism—it wasn't some foreign thing. Africans had made it their own, and there was no sense in abandoning it now. "Above all," wrote the historian Isaac Okonjo, "the greatest legacy which British rule has bequeathed to Nigerians must be the principle of the rule of law."[66] Okonjo was a committed nationalist, and his words would not have struck his comrades as accommodating, apologist, or treasonous.

For most Africans, the decision to oppose colonialism hadn't been a hard one. Britain was an alien power, and the tide of history had turned decisively against imperialism. There was moral clarity in independence, even if not everyone wanted *the same* independence—or for the same reasons. What happened next was murkier. After freedom had been won, lawyers who had spent their careers using law to poke and prod the empire now found themselves citizens of their own countries. The bright moral lines dimmed. Self-rule meant that there was no longer a common enemy, and dissident judges found themselves part of a government that beat people down in the same ways the British had. It hadn't been ethically fraught to criticize imperialism (even though it might get you thrown in jail). It was much harder to complain about a military regime that loudly proclaimed its nationalist bona fides as it held a gun to your back. Compromises had to be made, and judges began to make Faustian bargains. Some of those bargains were with soldiers, and others were with the principles of justice they had sworn to defend.

* * *

To this day, Nigerian lawyers adopt the dress of their colonial predecessors, including heavy robes and an elaborate white horsehair wig. Most African judiciaries have done away with this costume, but Nigeria and a few other countries haven't. Outsiders to the legal profession often mock the wigs. To critics, they are a reminder that the legal system is of foreign origin—tangible proof that it was made by and for white men several centuries ago. "I wish someone would tell me why our lawyers [and] judges would want to hood themselves in wigs and gowns other than the fact that they want to be British," complained a military lawyer who had done his training in the United States. "They look like baboons, not to talk of the personal pain and suffering they have to endure in a nation as hot as ours."[67] The fact that he chose this comparison to describe his colleagues reveals something about the bar's internal tensions: Not all lawyers saw the colonial legal tradition as something to defend. But most legal practitioners were attached to their wigs. To them, the wig stood for continuity, not colonial backwardness. It was part of law's pageantry, and they cherished it as a marker of their membership in a professional guild. Radical ideas could come from the minds underneath them, and it is important not to confuse the *trappings* of law with its substance.

The robes and wigs were part of a larger reckoning going on all over independent Africa. How could colonial legal systems be adapted to the needs of independent countries? Could law be rewired to deliver the things that civilians wanted—development, prosperity, dignity—*and* what the military wanted—discipline, order, honor? Were these desires compatible with one another? At a ceremony to lay the foundation for the Ghana Law School in 1959, Kwame Nkrumah warned that Ghana's law had been "made for ap-

FIGURE 1.1. Members of the Sierra Leone judiciary, 1984. Photo by J. Gaumy.

plication to an imperialist and colonial purpose" and that it was "entirely unsuited to a free nation evolving new methods of social relations in a democratic society."[68] A new nation needed new laws and new legal institutions. To many nationalist politicians, this process "involved disentangling it from colonial state structures and imperial systems that were built upon racial inequality and administrative dominance," as Ellen Feingold writes of Tanzania.[69] Soldiers saw the task differently. Most of them had no interest in giving up the power that rested with the executive (first with British governors, now with them), even as they preached the need to "decolonize" law.

Judges saw their task as world-historical. The establishment of the Ghanaian Supreme Court, Chief Justice Samuel Azu Crabbe remarked, "may be truly said to have its counterparts in such landmarks in world history as the reception of Roman law in continental Europe."[70] "Never before in the long history of human thought has law had to face a more challenging situation than that in contemporary Nigeria," claimed Justice Taslim Elias in 1969. "The prevailing social and economic forces call for a type of lawyer who is at once a social engineer and an analyst, a Pericles and a plumber, capable of appreciating the values of existing institutions and mores and yet ever ready to make a dynamic contribution to [maintaining] the balance between the need for stability and the need for change."[71] Elias overstated the particularity of Nigeria's situation—all African states were buffeted by these forces, and all leaders have to weigh priorities like this. But he was right that Nigeria's lawyers faced a difficult task.

Independence presented new challenges that demanded new forms of law. Some judges argued that the judiciary had to pull its weight in Nigeria's decolonization, which meant letting go of certain principles—especially liberal ones—that the British had left behind. "The source of justice must be pure and unpolluted," wrote Justice Kuti of the Abuja High Court, "like the Ikogosi springs."[72] The implication was clear: African law had to come from an African source. Nigeria's "archaic laws," Justice Ayo Irikefe argued, were "an assault on the nation's dignity." Another enjoined the judiciary to "discard all English law books" and "evolve" laws that fit the needs of the times. The military couldn't agree more. It was "absurd," General Ibrahim Babangida responded, that English statutes were still in force a quarter century after independence.[73] The more liberal-minded members of the judiciary looked on nervously.

One combative judge, Justice Chukwudifu Oputa of the Nigerian Supreme Court, exemplified the tensions of this era particularly well. Most judges keep their cards close to the vest, but Oputa preferred to lay his on the table. In his decisions, he always pointed out the ironies of using English law in a decolonizing society. Oputa was full of contradictions. He was an anti-imperialist who knew the colonial legal tradition backward and forward, and an architect of military dictatorship who personally disliked soldiers.[74] He had a prophetic streak. Those who broke laws, he wrote, broke the rules of nature: "Nature keeps her books relentlessly and pitilessly. Your credit is good for her, but she collects all her debts. There is no land you can flee to and escape her bailiffs. Every day her bloodhounds track down the men and women who owe her. Every generation a new crop of fools come in. *They think they can beat the orderly universe. They are wrong.*"[75]

Oputa saw himself and his fellow judges as nature's proxies. The arc of history bent toward order, he argued, and the judge's job was to reform or sweep aside those who dissented. If lawyers didn't appreciate how the times were changing, they might end up hoisted on their own petards. "We lawyers inured in the status quo, worshipping at the altar of precedence, may not easily discern the reality of the changes that are taking place around us," he wrote in 1985. A static system of law might become the "government of the living by the dead."[76] If military law was the way to avoid this, so be it. A decolonized law would have to balance many different influences—custom, statute, common law, and now martial law. The challenge, Elias added, was how to achieve "a synthesis, or, if you like, a symbiosis" of all of these different sources of law into something that was stable, elegant, and functional—a law that didn't ditch the English model altogether (which lawyers had sweated away their youths studying) but adapted it to Nigeria's needs.[77]

The legal profession was divided between those who wanted to tie the military's hands through law and those who wanted to make law more "dynamic"— which, many came to realize, played right into those hands. One reform that most African jurists agreed on was the need to end appeals to the Judicial Committee of the Privy Council, the final court of appeal for the empire. Some jurists hoped to reinvent it after independence as an international court that would serve commonwealth jurisdictions.[78] But more saw it as irredeemable. As Bonny Ibhawoh writes, the Privy Council was "a 'court' located overseas, made up mostly of English judges who were sometimes considered out of tune with local values."[79]

Few people mourned its end. But other attempts to "decolonize" law met more mixed reactions. One example is the elimination of the Judicial Service Commissions, the colonial-era bodies that had overseen the appointment of judges and magistrates. These commissions had ensured some measure of judicial independence. They placed staffing decisions in the hands of the judiciary itself, which made it difficult for a governor (or, after independence, an officer) to fire a judge he disagreed with or appoint one he liked. Reformers saw these commissions, not without reason, as guilds that shielded European judges from public accountability. Most were dissolved at independence, or their powers were reduced to merely "advisory" roles.[80] But once they were gone, their absence was felt. Direct appointments of judges by the executive became the norm, with no mechanism for ensuring that appointees were impartial, let alone competent. In Nigeria, judges were appointed by the Supreme Military Council, which also reserved the right to dismiss a judge "for any reason."[81] Cronyism flourished, and bar associations began to call for the return of the service commissions, even if they were colonial relics.[82]

The content of the laws themselves was also contentious. In 1968, the teacher Tai Solarin asked why the local alcohol known as "Ogogoro" or "Push-me-I-push-you," which the British had banned to protect the English gin industry, was still illegal after independence. "Why not throw out the anachronistic law made by the British, who have long departed, but whose malignant spirit goes marching on in our country?" What was true about alcohol was true about people. "The British are still ruling us," he continued, pivoting from gin to personal status, "for he who rules your mind is the more powerful and, in this case, the more dangerous man than your physical ruler."[83] A few judges agreed that independence demanded this kind of radical reform. In one of his speeches defending the military government, Oputa claimed that the law Britain had left to Nigeria had no moral center. It was "empty of God, swept clean of common decency and garnished with glittering notions and ill-conceived philosophies—the type of law that had led to two world wars with a third in the pipeline." It was European law, he wrote, "which produced Dachau and Auschwitz."[84] Oputa's bombast was unfair; continental Europe's legal tradition was distinct from England's, as he well knew, and it was misleading to lump them together. But he was right that laws made by imperialism didn't sit on moral high ground.

Some jurists hoped to renovate law so that, eventually, it would no longer be recognizably English. Drawing on the Prussian jurist Friedrich Carl von Savigny, Akinola Aguda argued that Nigeria's law should reflect its *volkgeist*—its organic, national spirit—which, in the long run, meant creating a legal system that bore no trace of its English origins. Nigerians should remember that they had their own "ideas and concepts of justice before the imposition of foreign values, foreign concepts of morals, and foreign concepts of justice."[85] He decried the "extreme legalism" of Nigerian judges and lawyers, who were keen to prove themselves against British standards that they would always fall short of—by design, he argued, since the British had rigged the system against them.[86] Aguda was also disappointed by the meekness of his fellow judges. "Unfortunately it does not appear that any of the African states has produced a moving and irresistible force such as Savigny was in Germany; nor has any jurist in Africa been able to kindle the flame of national consciousness."[87] Aguda found defect in many areas of colonial law, especially those governing sexuality. Plural marriage, which was common in many African societies, should be given statutory recognition (not just in customary law). Adultery and prostitution, which the public generally tolerated, should be treated more permissively than the law currently allowed. There were good reasons to keep homosexuality and child marriage out of bounds, he argued, but the military government should ease most other "vice" laws. "I see no justification whatsoever in using the big stick of the criminal law to punish those who practice what is morally and socially acceptable and accepted by the vast majority of the people of this country."[88]

In some military regimes, judges were tasked with making laws more "African" in character. During the regime of General Olusegun Obasanjo, Nigeria's Supreme Military Council gave a law reform commission the mandate to study Nigeria's colonial-era laws and recommend which ones should be preserved, which abolished, and which reworked. In 1979, the Ministry of Justice staged a lavish conference to discuss "modernising" and "decolonising" the law.[89] It was chaired by Sir Darnley Alexander, and its goal was to identify which "inadequate, obsolete, and even vindicative" laws still on the books should be struck off. Of course, the most "vindicative" laws were arguably the military's, but its decrees weren't up for debate. An obsequious jurist called the conference "yet another golden feather" for the military's "already well-decorated cap of achievements."[90] But critics recognized that these commissions did little besides endorse the military's rulemaking. If anything, the reforms would make it easier for soldiers to hold onto power.

This is what politics looked like during military rule: the judiciary and the military haggled over the colonial inheritance, cooperating when they shared a goal and checking one another when they didn't. Ordinary civilians found themselves caught between a man with a gavel and a bigger man with a gun. Judges promised aggressive reform when soldiers were listening, but among themselves they were more cautious. The reform commissions didn't get very far. Even if judges could agree on which laws were good and which bad, it wasn't straightforward how to change them. There was no legislature to make laws, and judge-made law accounted for only part of the legal system. They could only advise the military about how it might make or improve laws by executive decree—and the only "improvements" that soldiers were interested in were those that strengthened their hand. Judges often accommodated them. Thus, judicial reform commissions "advised" things like prohibiting civilians from wearing camouflage or banning people from painting their cars green (lest they be confused with the army's), and the military happily obliged with a decree. But if they advised, say, scaling back colonial-era prohibitions on free assembly, that recommendation would be ignored. Only some kinds of decolonization appealed to military governments.

Colonial law cast a long shadow in Africa, but it also created light and heat. Priya Satia writes that the "rule of law" was a "Trojan horse" that the British used to smuggle in the violence, abasement, and larceny of imperialism, all disguised as a gift.[91] This is a powerful metaphor, but it obscures something important. Some Nigerians found the weapons that had been smuggled in useful, both in their fight against colonialism and in the political contests that followed independence. To extend Satia's metaphor, it is as if the people of Troy wrestled away the soldiers' spears and turned them against their conquerors.[92] Once the invaders were gone, those weapons fell into the hands of all kinds of people. Both the state and its critics could use them. Law was such a weapon. It was not necessarily an *effective* weapon, and there were limits to what could be done with it. Nonetheless, critics of militarism did not choose what they had at their disposal. They made do with what was available—often, dusty tools from the English common law. They felt no compunction about turning those tools against military regimes. Liberal opponents of the military valued the rule of law, but they did not value it because it came from Britain. They valued it *despite* its colonial provenance. It wasn't evidence of good intentions, and it wasn't something to thank their conquerors for.

It was possible to like colonialism's fixings without liking colonialism itself, and this was true beyond law. One could be culturally Anglophile without feeling any love lost for the empire—drinking Guinness or reading Agatha Christie wasn't the same as wanting the British to come back. Some Nigerians rued that the streets had been cleaner before 1960 or mourned that a certain shine was lost after independence. But this line of complaint petered out quickly. Those clean streets had come at the price of liberty, and everyone knew it. Many Nigerians hoped that somebody might clean them up, but nobody except a handful of eccentrics wanted the British to be the ones to do it. The types of people who *might* have wanted them to weren't around in West Africa. There were no European settlers who would fear losing their privileges under majority rule.[93] There were few racial outsiders who had been brought from elsewhere to make the colonial apparatus tick (like South Asians in East Africa) or groups that had been created by imperialism (like the Anglo-Irish) who might be anxious about what would happen to them once the British packed up and left. There were not many Nigerian mourners at the British Empire's wake.

But you don't have to mourn the dead to claim your share of the estate. Many African jurists saw English law as a resource—their birthright as British subjects—not something to be discarded. "Courts manned by upright Judges and Magistrates and assisted by an honest, responsible and trustworthy Bar," Oputa described. "This is the British tradition. It is also our common inheritance, our heritage."[94] Under both colonialism and military rule, law was one of the few tools ordinary people had to criticize the state. Lawyers defended British law from encroachment by soldiers because it was valuable, not because they were stuck in a colonial trance. My objective here is to convey a point that is uncontroversial among most legal historians—that law is neither naturally aligned *with* power nor *against* it—into the history of decolonization, which has been told in a much more black-and-white way. "The fascists played the tune," Mahmood Mamdani wrote of Uganda's military dictatorship, "and the judges danced."[95] It was not nearly so simple. There were few ideological purists in the courtroom. Everyone made compromises, and there is no point in trying to pigeonhole people as radicals or reactionaries, saviors or sellouts.[96]

Conclusion

In 1980, a law professor at the University of Ibadan declared that the military had destroyed the rule of law in Nigeria. General Olusegun Obasanjo, who had recently handed over power to the short-lived civilian government of Shehu Shagari, felt compelled to respond. The jurist and the general had a public debate. The jurist, Folarin Shyllon, described the many ways military rule had maimed the legal system, including arbitrarily enforcing the death penalty, imposing cruel punishments, and violating habeas corpus. "They passed Decree after Decree," Shyllon remarked. "They set up special tribunal after special tribunal[,] the composition of which offends against the rule of law and fundamental rights of the Constitution of the Federation. The exercise of arbitrary power is neither law nor justice."[97] Obasanjo responded:

> I believe that it is necessary to refresh our minds of the political, security, and law and order situation in the country before the advent

of the Military in the political arena in 1966. There was arson, murder, robbery and general insecurity of life and property. There was in effect a total breakdown of law and order. . . . Mr Shyllon also criticised the reversal of the onus of proof or burden of proof and the acceptance of the evidence of accomplices. He described this as *the travesty of legal process*. I ask whose legal process? How relevant is this received legal process and system to our own society and situation today? Is the totality of our legal system and process keeping pace with the economic, social and political changes within our society, or is it sufficiently dynamic to bring about the assured change within the society? I doubt it very much.[98]

Their angry exchange mirrored a quarrel that was going on all over Africa in the 1970s. Elite civilians like Shyllon had been led to believe they would inherit power when the British left, and losing it to soldiers made them angry and bitter. Obasanjo defended the military's record by invoking decolonization. When he asked "whose legal process?" the answer was so obvious he didn't need to say it: *Britain's*. Soldiers like Obasanjo used law to advance their own interests, calling it "colonial" when they wanted to undermine it and touting how they had "decolonized" it when they didn't. Their critics did the same thing. Obasanjo was right that law was derivative, archaic, and out of touch with Nigeria's realities. But law was also a powerful tool, and he had good reason to fear what people might do with it.

Audre Lorde's truism that "the master's tools will never dismantle the master's house" doesn't get us very far in the history of decolonization.[99] Some people had no interest in dismantling the house the British built. Others didn't see it as a house, but a "mansion with many rooms," to use a biblical metaphor more readily to hand in Lagos than *Sister Outsider*. And among those who *did* want to tear it down, there was no reason to believe tools like colonial law couldn't come in handy. Even the most creative revolutionaries often find themselves using the tools of the ancien régime, and sometimes what surprises them most is just how well those tools work.

2

THE SOLDIER'S CREED

Discipline as an Ideology

At first glance, Africa's soldier-kings look like an unthinking rabble: men with guns but no plans, only "ideological" in the barest sense. Most foreign journalists who had dealings with them arrived at this conclusion, and historians have followed their lead. One can search in vain for an account of what they believed. This is not just a problem of African history; beyond Europe, few authoritarians are studied for their political philosophies. When a dictator is profiled, the portrait that results is often some version of the "oriental despot"—childlike, petulant, beholden only to his perverse desires and scatological impulses. Any creed vanishes behind his larger-than-life personality.[1]

This isn't because they haven't left us something to read. Not only did the twentieth century's tyrants have ideologies, many published them in convenient pocket size. These include Mao Zedong's famous *Red Book* but also the lesser-known *Green Book* of Muammar Gaddafi, Kim Il-Sung's *On the Juche Idea*, and Saparmurat Niyazov's *Ruhnama*.[2] These treatises are easily mocked, with their folk platitudes and watered-down blends of other philosophies (of the left or the right). They swing between the grandiose and the ridiculous, and some would almost be comic if not for the violence done in their names. But authoritarian ideologies are worth taking seriously. Like their better-loved civilian counterparts—Nyerere, Nkrumah, Senghor—Africa's military leaders grappled with the big questions of the twentieth century. How should a country be? What is freedom? Who gets what, and how much? Only a few of Africa's military leaders wrote little books, but all of them had plans for their societies.[3] We can find them in their actions, their words, and the laws they made.

Pinning soldiers down to a single philosophy is a difficult task. Take, for example, the Liberian Pan-Africanist Muhammed Kamil's admiring description of Nigeria's Murtala Muhammed—a military leader whose regime lasted just six months and is best known for a purge of the civil service. Kamil argued that Muhammed had a "Khaldunian philosophy of history," both secular and pious, with a broad-minded sense of Africa's unity. His thought fused Quranic principles, Marxism by way of Nkrumah and Sékou Touré, the "jihadist spirit" of Usman dan Fodio and the Mahdi of Khartoum, and the culture of discipline and duty cultivated in "highbrow British schools." These were odd pieces to fit together, but the appeal of military ideology was not consistency—it was the opposite.[4]

Soldiers and their accomplices offered rough and ready philosophies, agile enough to meet the needs of their quickly changing societies. First Lady Maryam Abacha, her official biographer wrote, was "the ensemble of social relations." "The words of the German philosopher Karl Marx best describe the quiet but revolutionary leader of our time, a woman who has risen from humble beginnings to devote her time and energy to the poverty alleviation of Nigerian families."[5] There wasn't anything very Marxist about Maryam Abacha (or her husband, General Sani Abacha), but this wasn't the point. Soldiers saw themselves as pragmatists who weren't wedded to any single worldview, especially one that came from abroad. What mattered to them was that their paradise arrived. "I will deliver to the Gambian people," Colonel Yahya Jammeh promised, "and if I have to rule this country for one billion years, I will."[6]

Why did soldiers covet political power? Most observers at the time explained coups as responses to working conditions in the armed forces rather than acts born of conviction. Militaries were, as Ruth First described, "the best organized trade unions in African states."[7] Low pay was often first among soldiers' grievances, and they staged "strikes" just like stevedores or rail workers. Of course, in an army, standing up to your boss is not a strike but a mutiny.[8] In Kenya, Uganda, and Tanganyika, a series of coordinated mutinies took place shortly after independence, mostly over pay.[9] But it soon became clear that money was not the only thing at play—soldiers started to think they could run things better than civilians. The first full military takeover of a civilian government was in Togo in 1963, where a tiny army (some 250 men in total) overthrew the government of Sylvanus Olympio.[10] It was followed by dozens of others across the continent. Some believed soldiers took power simply because they could; they controlled the means of producing violence, and the novelty of democratic institutions in ex-colonies made them easy to topple.[11] Others saw the hand of foreigners, citing the fact that men like Mobutu Sese Seko in Zaire and General Siad Barre in Somalia parroted the Cold War powers bankrolling them. Soldiers themselves often claimed they had no ideology. They insisted they were nonpolitical, but this meant they would not broker political *parties*—not that they had no political beliefs. Most claimed to be temporary, promising to hand back power to civilians as soon as they had cleaned things up.[12] Few of them actually did.

Today, most prefer to remember Africa's military dictatorships as mistakes or aberrations. Those on the left present them as an embarrassing symptom of neocolonialism. Those on the right treat them as evidence of Africans' inability to govern themselves. Both these perspectives are wrong. Not all military regimes were imposed by nefarious foreigners against the will of African publics. Nor were they expressions of some elemental despotism embedded in African societies. Instead, the turn to militarism was a calculated response to a set of problems that existed in the moment. This doesn't change the fact that military coups were power grabs. The men who staged them were paranoid and cynical, always looking over their shoulder for the next putsch—they knew that what goes around comes around.[13] Their doctrines often boiled down to unbridled power for themselves and their friends. But military rule had real ambitions, and in all their squabbling soldiers had a vision. In many places, militarism was an ideological *end in itself*.

* * *

Something of soldiers' plans for their societies can be seen in how they built the environment around them. I have to steel myself to enter government offices in Nigeria. Crowded, loud, and confusing, they make finding a court record or getting a driver's license a gauntlet of pushing, begging, and waiting. These buildings all have the same feel, whether they serve high or low functions of the state (or rich or poor citizens of it). They are down-at-heel, and most have a pong of mildew that mixes with the nervous sweat of the people who come to them in need of something. These are utilitarian places, but even the humblest of them reveal something about the values of the governments that built them—better, in some ways, than the monuments that are designed with that purpose in mind.

In the offices, schools, and courts they constructed, Nigeria's leaders recorded their commitments in stone. Those from the colonial era are crumbling imitations of the British public buildings of the day—neoclassicism on the cheap, with breeze walls and air conditioners tacked on in deference to the climate. The ones built in the burst of development just after independence are in the high international style, some by Nigerian architects like Demas Nwoko, who adapted what they learned in the modernist ateliers of Europe to their booming home countries. These are the buildings I least dread visiting. They are light and cool even when the electricity is out, and they still feel like places of optimism even though the glass louvers in the windows have been replaced with bits of wood. Nigeria's federal universities date from this era, as do most of its old-guard cultural institutions.[14]

The buildings the army built feel very different. They made architecture for giants; everything is oversized, and their public spaces are cavernous and bare. Dark and poorly ventilated, many of them are only habitable with air conditioning and electric lights. Every military regime promised to generate enough steady electricity to make them usable, but none succeeded (to be fair, neither did the democratic governments that followed them). They built enormous parade grounds in the cities, where soldiers could show off to the public and to one another.[15] The one in Lagos, erected on the site of a colonial-era racecourse, is an architectural oddity that perfectly captures the aesthetics of the armed forces. An overwhelming expanse of asphalt that can hold fifty thousand spectators, it is adorned with folkloric designs rendered in poured concrete, guarded by four enormous white horses rearing up at the entrance.[16] Its carillons, covered with spikes and metal protuberances, can be seen from all over the city. It's easy to feel like they're watching you.

The facilities soldiers used for themselves were austere and simple, at least in the early years of military rule. The seat of government was the Dodan Barracks in Lagos, an inconspicuous complex of clapboard buildings named for a Burmese battlefield where the 82nd West African Division distinguished itself during the Second World War. This was where they received visiting dignitaries, impressing upon them how humble and parsimonious they were. The military's great achievement of urban planning was Abuja, the gleaming, orderly new capital where the federal government moved from Lagos in 1991. An anticity of shopping malls and subdivisions, parts of Abuja might be mistaken for a Houston suburb. There, a showier aesthetic prevailed, favored by the Saudi contractors who built much of the city's initial infrastructure.

This architecture showed that soldiers could be just as avaricious as the civilians they deposed. Abuja's courts and ministries have flourishes that seem lifted from an episode of *Dallas*—gilt, dark mirrors, enormous chandeliers. They're grand and gaudy in a way that only an arriviste officer would find tasteful. They announced what the military wanted Nigeria to be: rich, lush, larger than life. Like the broader project of military rule, it was indifferent to how people actually wanted to live.

Ideology from the Barracks

From a distance, African politics from the 1960s to the 1990s looks like an endless parade of khaki. The uniforms military presidents wore made it seem like they were all alike, but up close each was distinct. None was loved or hated universally, and even the most reviled of them had their defenders. Some exercised restraint in their dealings with civilians, while others took a hard line. Many used their authority for personal gain. In Nigeria, public memory has settled on thumbnail sketches about what they were like. Murtala Muhammed was a noble reformer cut down in his prime. Obasanjo was the one who put the country first by giving up power. Buhari was a sanctimonious dunce who surrounded himself with smart people. Babangida was an evil genius. Abacha was a con man. These vignettes capture an important truth: not all military leaders were the same.

Nonetheless, military life had a rhythm that carried on regardless of which specific officer was in power. Militarism was an ideology of stability, even though it didn't always look like it (especially to outsiders). There was a certain predictability to military rule, despite all the coups. A man who enlisted in 2000 was inducted into the same military tradition as his father would have been in 1980 and his grandfather in 1960 (and indeed, soldiers' sons often became soldiers themselves). There were other commonalities too. Order and discipline were the lodestars of every military regime, and all of them were patriarchal—even when they gave high status to certain types of women, like patriotic mothers and dutiful wives.

Officers called each other "brother" even as they murdered one another to take power. They had romantic ideas about comradeship, and they believed they had a common purpose. They shared a social and professional world. Some had served in the Second World War, which had been galvanizing. Their relationships crossed borders, since soldiers from across the British Empire had trained together (so had those in French colonies). For this reason, they had a funny tendency to cooperate better with soldiers in other countries than with civilians in their own. They generally avoided public displays of international cooperation (it smacked of communism), but exceptions could be made in the name of Pan-Africanism, to which leaders across the political spectrum paid lip service. Behind the scenes, they came to one another's aid when threatened by rebel movements or internal enemies.[17] They could present a unified front when they had to; all of them opposed white minority rule in southern Africa, for example, even though they sometimes disagreed about strategy. Their shared interest in broader struggles—against apartheid, for African dignity—trumped some of their differences. "We talk about issues as brothers and friends," Robert Mugabe remarked of Babangida. This friendship might be surprising given how far apart they were on the political spectrum, but it makes sense when we understand that they saw one another as brothers *in arms*.[18]

If we assume that an army's purpose is to wage war, we quickly find a paradox: Africa's military regimes were strangely peaceable. War was the metaphor they used for policymaking, but most military regimes weren't very warlike in the day-to-day.[19] Many African countries had *civil* wars in this era, but they were noticeably cordial in their relationships with one another. There were hardly any interstate wars in Africa in the second half of the twentieth century, and countries led by professional soldiers rarely went to war with one another. Military regimes had plenty of disagreements with their neighbors, but few of them boiled over into armed conflict. Of the few interstate conflicts that did take place between 1960 and 2000, most were between military regimes and civilian governments.[20] Wars waged by nonprofessional soldiers, like those in the Mano River Basin or the Great Lakes Region, blurred these distinctions. There, warriors like the infamous General Butt Naked (the nom de guerre of Joshua Milton Blahyi) in Liberia, or Alice Lakwena, the prostitute-turned-warlord who raised an army in Uganda, were not part of a formal military and never had been.[21] Their wars were regional in scale, but even these transnational conflicts did not take place between *states*—they were conflicts among militias and other nonstate actors that spilled over borders but did not take the form of one country declaring war on another. There are reasons to quibble with all this. For one thing, there was no clear line between *civil war* and *interstate conflict*, and many wars had characteristics of both.[22] But the point remains that waging war against foreign enemies was not what Africa's militaries were doing most of the time.[23]

Aside from its own civil war, Nigeria was at peace for the duration of military rule. It participated in several conflicts, but not as a belligerent. When Nigerian soldiers saw combat, it was usually as part of international peacekeeping missions. Their first postindependence test was in the Democratic Republic of the Congo, where Nigerian troops supported the United Nations mission during the Katanga crisis. Major General Johnson Aguiyi-Ironsi, who would briefly lead Nigeria after the January 1966 coup, cut his teeth there, as did many officers of his generation. They learned certain lessons from it. Katanga taught them that politicians were useless and that the only good answers to questions of state were answers involving guns.[24]

After Katanga came the Nigerian Civil War, which started when Nigeria's eastern region seceded as the Republic of Biafra in 1967. The Nigerian Federal Military Government starved and pummeled Biafra until the rebel government surrendered in 1970. The fallout from the civil war made Nigeria *feel* like it was still at war for many years, but after Biafra's defeat there were no more actual battles to fight. Other crises unfolded within Nigeria's borders, like the insurgency led by the Movement for the Emancipation of the Niger Delta (MEND) and the Islamic revival movement called Maitatsine. These threatened to become civil wars, but they never came close to the level of Biafra's carnage.

In the 1990s, Nigerian troops participated in the Economic Community of West African States Monitoring Group (ECOMOG) mission in Liberia, pejoratively called "Every Car Or Moving Object Gone" by Liberians who deplored the bad behavior of the Nigerian peacekeepers. Nigerians also joined UN missions in Haiti, Somalia, and Bosnia, where they carved out a niche for themselves as medics and dentists. But these were distant conflicts involving small numbers of troops, and none entailed mass mobilization.

Making war is not the only, or even primary, thing soldiers do, and there is a whole range of other functions that militaries can serve. But soldiers are trained to believe that warfare is their first, and highest, purpose. What do they do when they don't have a war to fight? They fight among themselves. When they grow bored of barracks intrigue, they start looking for other distractions. Politics is a good one.[25]

A useful guide to how this can happen is the unjustly forgotten soldier-turned-scholar Alfred Vagts. In 1930s Germany, Vagts identified a difference between the "military way"—the way that armies wage war—and militarism, a sociological phenomenon which, he argued, explained the Nazi ideology sprouting up around him. Militaries focused on winning battles, but *militarism* constituted something else. It had its own "customs, interests, prestige, actions, and thoughts" that transcended the narrower tactical goals of armies and sometimes actually worked *against* the abstemious thinking that warfare demands. "Militarism flourishes more in peacetime than in war," he wrote. Modern militaries, which are not fighting all (or even most) of the time, "are more likely to forget their true purpose, war, and the maintenance of the state to which they belong. Becoming narcissistic, they dream that they exist for themselves alone."[26] This is what happened in Nigeria. There reached a point when the military no longer served the state—it *was* the state, and the men who constituted it came to think of themselves as such.

* * *

Militarism is a system of thought and action. It has an ethos, an institutional culture, and a political economy (consider the "military-industrial complex"). It has an aesthetic, and it has a libidinal side. What made Nigeria's strain of militarism particular? Was it closer to the left or the right? What was its relationship to other African military regimes, including those in countries that had *not* been colonized by Britain? The Nigerian Federal Military Government bore a family resemblance to military regimes in Uganda, Ghana, and elsewhere. But Nigeria's assignation with militarism lasted longer than any of theirs. It had its own character. Its juntas were more sedate than the flamboyant dictatorships of Mobutu in Zaire or Jean-Bédel Bokassa in the Central African Republic, where martial showmanship and grotesque pageantry stood in for governance.[27] With the possible exception of Babangida, none of Nigeria's leaders fit the "strongman" type Ruth Ben-Ghiat describes, obsessed with his own virility.[28] Unlike in Spain or Portugal, militarism was not embodied in a single long-serving patriarch. And unlike the geriatric colonels of Greece and Egypt, Nigeria's upstarts flashed with youth and vitality.

There were more Muslims in the armed forces than Christians, but militarism did not have a strong religious orientation. Unlike in South America, where military rule was grounded in Catholic thought, the Nigerian military kept religion at arm's length.[29] Most soldiers were committed to secularism, and faith didn't determine national politics when they were in charge (this would change dramatically after 1999, when Nigeria became, as Ebenezer Obadare describes it, a "Pentecostal republic").[30] Most leaned to the right, but they also had an egalitarian streak. Babangida expressed a desire to replace "the fraternity of the horse and its rider with the fraternity of equals and colleagues." He admitted that this "levelling act" would provoke resistance, but it would be worth it: "We know that the equality and collegiality that we strive for is the hope for a stable polity."[31] Unlike other twentieth-century authoritarians, Nigeria's military regimes did not close ranks against a minority, and there was no fundamental rule of difference that they governed through. Military leaders put little stock in ethnicity or in other ways of defining people by blood or lineage.

In fact, soldiers consistently spoke *against* ethnicity, and they presented the military as Nigeria's only truly national institution. They constantly reminded their fellow citizens that the country belonged to "All Of Us," which became a political slogan after the civil war. So did "One Nigeria," which went from being a federal battle cry to a reminder that all Nigerians had the right to live in whatever part of the country they wanted. Military regimes were not big on rights, but one right they consistently supported was the right of free movement within Nigeria's borders.[32] "Every Nigerian must be free to settle and work wherever he chooses to reside, irrespective of his ethnic origins. This is why we fought a long war to preserve the unity of this country," General Yakubu Gowon declared on the tenth anniversary of independence.[33] Soldiers wanted Nigerians to be patriotic, to respect one another's differences, and to break bread together, as they themselves did on their bases.

To this end they built monumental federal museums in regional capitals, where people could learn about how Nigerians lived in other parts of the country and sample their cuisines in affordable cafeterias. They established a public service draft, which was an explicit attempt to make public culture more like the culture of the army. From 1973 onward, all university graduates had to spend a year in the National Youth Service Corps (NYSC), where they would teach, build, or serve the public in regions far from home. NYSC cadres wore uniforms and did stints in military-style camps, where patriotism was drummed into them. There, they were reminded of what they owed the nation in return for their subsidized degrees.[34] Later, both Ghana and Uganda would conduct similar experiments in military training for civilians, in the hope of making them "active agents of the new epoch," as a Ugandan skeptic described. "It is fair to say that in both Ghana and Uganda, the experiment with offering military training to the general population was dictated by political imperatives," wrote Amii Omara-Otunnu. If militarism ruled the day, as it did in Uganda, the way to expand political participation was to make *everyone* into a soldier or at least something like it.[35]

To the extent that there was a Homo Nigerianus, he was a man in uniform. Militaries drew recruits from all over, and the top brass bragged that every corner of the country was represented in the armed forces.[36] This was only a partial truth—some corners sent more men than others. Across West Africa, the Sahelian regions of the north were overrepresented in the ranks. This was largely due to the colonial belief, still intact at independence, that northerners (especially Hausa) were naturally a "martial race." Southern critics cited this as proof that military rule was a cover for northern domination, and the case can be made that it had a northern accent. Nonetheless, there was no single ethnic group or region that fully dominated the military, and the national feeling that soldiers evinced was often genuine. It wasn't actually the case that the army was an exclusively northern institution, as many in southern Nigeria feared, or that militarism was a Muslim conspiracy, as Christian Ugandans sometimes suspected. After independence, militaries had gone out of their way to recruit from places where the British had not. The officer class tended to be more diverse the higher one went up the ranks, even though there were ethnic divisions of labor (in Nigeria, for example, Igbos performed most of the army's technical functions).

Soldiers had an unflagging faith in their ability to make a harmonious society—if only civilians would get out of the way. First Lady Maryam Babangida put this belief best:

> If by some divine intervention all existing geographical boundaries were suddenly erased and the world were scrambled into a real global village, the armies of the former countries would be one of the first to form a truly cohesive, unified and all-embracing brotherhood. Faster than brigands, journalists, writers, prostitutes, gays and lesbians and even transvestites. Least of all, politicians and religious fanatics. Faster because the military, more than any other group in the modern world, has developed a stronger code of intra-professional discipline.[37]

Everything else—tribe, religion, class, gender—came second to the uniform. For Babangida as for many others who joined the army (or married into it), this was what entitled them to rule. Not all soldiers were actually above the "tribalism" their leaders criticized. But there was some truth to the idea that they were the people with the strongest connection to their national governments—which, after all, were colonial artifacts that didn't inspire much patriotic feeling.

If neither religion nor blood-and-soil nationalism animated military rule in Nigeria, what did? Nigerian militarism was a chimera, born with two distinct sets of genes. The first was the stiff-upper-lip martial tradition of the British. This was the culture of the post–World War II British military—a form of militarism that respected soldiers but did not worship them, unlike the extremist Nazi strain Britain had confronted in the war. In this model, the armed forces were there to help civilians and to defend liberal values. Staid and unadventurous, the military should be a force of defense rather than conquest (which, of course, is what it had been when Africa was conquered a generation before—an awkward truth that most Britons preferred not to think about).

The other side of the family tree was something more radical—the militarism of anticolonial liberation movements. This lineage stretched from Steve Biko in South Africa to Frantz Fanon in Algeria, with stops along the way in figures like Amilcar Cabral and Albert Memmi. Nigeria's officers did not agree with everything these radical thinkers wanted. They had no interest in communism, for example, and they took a pragmatic approach to their relationship with Britain that would have scandalized the likes of Fanon. Nonetheless, the Nigerian military elite had much in common with their comrades in Umkhonto we Sizwe or the FLN. They treated respect and dignity as political values, and they promised to restore the wholeness of societies dismembered by colonialism. They would shore up the institutions it had weakened (the family, the village) and exorcise the colonial spirit from the African body politic. Like the radicals who theorized the armed struggle against colonialism, soldiers believed that men with guns held the key to liberation.

These two countervailing forces shaped how they reasoned: the colonial militarism of their training and the martial anticolonialism of their times—a culture of "armed wings" and "freedom fighters." If one loitered around a parade ground in Commonwealth Africa in the 1980s, one might have heard soldiers marching to "The British Grenadiers" followed by "Umshini wami" (Bring me my machine gun), the anti-apartheid military anthem. There was no inherent contradiction in this to the men who were marching. Soldiers were at home in both these martial traditions in a way that they never were in civilian society. There was less distance between a "freedom fighter" and a colonial soldier than there was between a soldier—*any* soldier—and a civilian.

* * *

These subtleties have vanished in the telling and retelling of African history. Historians have an unfortunate tendency to write about the monsters we abhor or the heroes we admire, but seldom the people in between. Studying monsters allows us to bask in gore, which we render respectable by asking *what went wrong here?* or appending tart judgments to our accounts of depravity. In African studies, the fixation on "monsters" is fundamentally a product of racism, although it also reflects an impulse to plumb the depths of evil that many historians feel—myself included.[38] Cruelty is a natural source of narrative drama, and all but the most abstemious of us crave a good story to tell. On the other hand, we also pay attention to those we admire. We uplift leaders whose politics aligned with our own in some way, plucking from historical obscurity people we can recognize—a sensibility that appeals to us, or a private life we could see ourselves living.

So, in twentieth-century Africa, we know about a few rogues (Mobutu, Bokassa, and Amin among them), and a few supermen (Mandela, Nkrumah, Nyerere), and not much in between. This latter group is the "Heroes' Acre of African nationalist thinkers," as Daniel Magaziner has called them.[39] Their writings have become the canon of twentieth-century political theory in Africa, and the fact that many of them led their countries makes them noteworthy examples of the philosopher-king.[40] The heroes have their detractors and the villains their defenders, but generally this good-and-evil view of African politics still holds. It leaves out the middling figures—despots who weren't as flashy as Mobutu, radicals less visionary than Nyerere, leaders who lacked Senghor's élan or Nkrumah's éclat. The workaday soldiers who governed much of the continent figure only faintly in the story of African decolonization as it has been told. They are seldom discussed as "thinkers," but of course they did think, and they played at least as much a role in making Africa's political culture as the more beloved civilians—Modibo Keïta, Patrice Lumumba, Sékou Touré—they deposed.

Frantz Fanon looms large in this story, even though he never set foot in Nigeria. Fanon was a psychiatrist from Martinique who joined the anticolonial struggle in Algeria in the 1950s. He was a firebrand who wrote absorbing accounts of how colonialism shaped the minds of the colonized; his books offered a formula for how to understand it, defeat it, and then clear the wreckage that was left behind.[41] His theories of colonial racism and armed struggle were influential from the 1960s onward, and African soldiers and intellectuals alike read him enthusiastically.

One of Nigeria's most important thinkers described an almost religious encounter with Fanon's work as a student in London. Finding a copy of *Black Skin, White Masks* forgotten on a train platform, Yusufu Bala Usman started idly reading and was so gripped by the book that he stood there overnight, unable to put it down. "The railway officials and the police were obviously so fascinated by the sight of this young African getting so engrossed in what he was reading that trains passed and arrived without him moving an earlobe," he told his biographer.

> They refrained from interrupting a genius in ecstasy. He had never read anything like it. He was convinced that the book was placed at that railway station specifically for him to see it. Its words took him back to Barewa College where he had been taught by British teachers; and to relationships he had witnessed between British colonial officials and traditional rulers in northern Nigeria, including his own father. As he

FIGURE 2.1. Flight Lieutenant Jerry Rawlings of Ghana, seated, after his second coup, 1982. Photo by A. Abbas.

read the book, a deep fury began to swell and swirl in his mind and soul. His British teachers and colonial officials had related to him and his father's class *with a big lie.*[42]

Intellectuals like Usman were not the only ones entranced by Fanon. Soldiers shared his fascination—not only because Fanon was describing a reality they recognized, but because they found him useful. In a 1960 speech in Accra, Fanon laid out "why we use violence" to an audience of Ghanaians that included much of the country's political and military elite. In rousing language, Fanon warned that the violence "of the muscles, of the blood" that the anticolonial struggle required might not go away after the Europeans were gone. "This violence that wills itself to be violent, which becomes more and more boundless, irreparably provokes the birth of an internal violence in the colonized people and a just anger is born that seeks to express itself." Speaking "as a biologist," he argued that in "certain enslaved regions the violence of the colonized becomes quite simply a manifestation of his strictly animal existence."[43] It is meaningful that Fanon gave this speech in Ghana—one of the few he ever gave in West Africa. These words struck a chord there. Soldiers and their allies in the judiciary took them not as a warning, but as a *license.*

Fanon could be used to justify all kinds of means, so long as the ends were "freedom." In 1989, for example, Justice Chukwudifu Oputa cited a letter Fanon wrote on his deathbed to square the necessity of indefinite detention with the military's larger talk of liberty: "We are nothing on earth if we are not first of all slaves of a cause—the cause of people, the cause of justice, the cause of freedom, the cause of liberty." Indefinite detention was a "necessary evil in developing countries," Oputa argued, and being a "slave" to the cause of freedom sometimes meant depriving others of it.[44] What people like Oputa took from Fanon was that violence and repression could be reparative as long as it bent in a longer arc toward liberty. One can cavil about how faithful this interpretation was to Fanon's thought; it probably owed something to Jean-Paul Sartre's gloss on *The Wretched of the Earth*, which defended violence in stronger terms than Fanon himself did. But Oputa wasn't stupid, and neither were the soldiers he served—disciplinarians were right to find a kindred spirit in Fanon.

When military ideologues wanted to praise an officer, they compared him to Fanon. "In many respects," wrote a military governor's official biographer, "his vision and action is on the same philosophical level as that of Frantz Fanon."[45] Fanon's talk of destiny was useful too. A famous line from *The Wretched of the Earth* was the epigraph to both General Sani Abacha's authorized biography and the ideological charter of the Revolutionary United Front in Sierra Leone: "Each generation must out of relative obscurity, discover its mission, fulfill it or betray it."[46] In an admiring book about Ibrahim Babangida, Ikenna Nzimiro cited Fanon on the necessity of national struggle: "It is that fight for national existence which sets culture moving and opens to it the doors of creation. Later on, it is the nation which will ensure the conditions and framework necessary to culture."[47] Babangida had been committed to this project, Nzimiro wrote, and his neoliberal economic commitments didn't preclude him from being a Fanonian revolutionary. The problem, he argued, echoing many apologists for revolutions that don't succeed, was that the civilians surrounding him hadn't been committed enough. "Most of them had very little or no experience in the anti-colonial struggle," he wrote, implying incorrectly that most soldiers *did*. Civilians in the government "could not understand that their recruitment into the system meant struggle, first, to decolonize the minds of people they interacted with."[48] What is this radical language doing in a seemingly right-wing military dictatorship?

"I would say there are two things about Fanon that his many American readers have largely failed to really grasp," Paul Gilroy observed. One was that Fanon was a doctor whose political commitments always had something to do with healing. The other was that he was a soldier. Gilroy argued that Fanon's "revolutionary imagination" cannot be understood without this "agonistic pairing of the healer and the soldier."[49] Not all Nigerian militarists read Fanon, but those who did read him in exactly this way (unlike the Americans Gilroy shaded).[50] They shared a belief that violence was necessary to "heal" society—to fix a broken bone, you first have to endure the pain of setting it. Babangida's 1985 takeover, for example, was necessary because Nigeria was "gravely sick and dying." "The surgery to save [it] would be painful," wrote a supporter, but "there really was no alternative."[51] "Nigeria is sick," Major General Hassan Katsina declared in 1973, and "everybody needs to be whipped and thoroughly shaken to awaken from slumber."[52] Judges in military regimes also described themselves as healers. "We are the surgeons of society, the physicians of the body politic," Oputa declaimed. It was their job to lop off the damaged tissue of bad morals or bad laws "before dangerous putrefaction sets in."[53] Gilroy embraced Fanon and spurned military regimes like Nigeria's, but the soldiers who took up the mantle of decolonization were, in many ways, *Fanonians*. Intellectuals still use Fanon to diagnose the ills of countries like Nigeria—its capture by predatory elites, its fissures, its neocolonial entanglements.[54] Almost no one entertains the possibility that the physician himself might bear some fault for the sickness.

At the end of his life, Fanon seemed aware that his revolutions might end not in a humanist utopia, but in theocracy or permanent militarism. "Fanon himself had seen that anticolonial violence was driven not only by a noble desire for justice," writes Adam Shatz, "but by darker impulses, including the dream of 'becoming the persecutor.'" Shatz argues that Fanon anticipated "the 'big men' who would drape themselves in African garb, promote a folkloric form of black culture, and cynically exploit the rhetoric of anticolonialism—even, in the bitterest of ironies, Fanon's own words."[55] This gives rather a lot of credit to Fanon, and not very much to the "big men" who used those words. Were men like Babangida and Oputa "cynically exploiting" Fanon, or were they the logical terminus of his thought?

The decolonization of the mind, the righteous deployment of violence, the need to awaken a national consciousness—these were all things that both Fanon and soldiers like Murtala Muhammed, Rawlings, and Babangida espoused. Like Fanon, they were products of the empire, and like him they hadn't escaped the culture they ostensibly sought to overthrow. "He was calling for a revolutionary vanguard," Shatz continues, coming closer to the mark, "but his rhetoric of conquest was not far from that of colonialism."[56] Politics was not a clean fight between committed revolutionaries and toady colonial apologists, but a clumsy brawl in a thick haze. Everyone was turning the same weapons against one another, and it was hard to tell who was on whose side.

Although he falls outside the Commonwealth focus of this book, we might also consider Captain Thomas Sankara of Burkina Faso, the beloved young revolutionary remembered for his political creativity and his anticolonial posture. "Our revolution," he proclaimed, "is a revolution in a country that, because of imperialism's domination and exploitation of our people, has evolved from a colony into a neocolony." Sankara spoke constantly of the sacred bond between the army and the people, and he often called for them to join forces against their common enemies. Those "enemies" included the French, civilian politicians, and the educated elite (among them one of Africa's most celebrated intellectuals, the "inventor-historian-inquisitor-reactionary, Joseph Ki-Zerbo").[57] The uncomfortable truth is that Sankara's Nigerian counterpart, the much less beloved General Ibrahim Babangida, made many of the same arguments. For all his inspiring platitudes, Sankara's "revolutionary" project was not so different from those of Nigeria's centrist military regimes or even those further to the right.[58] Military "revolutions" had a consistent set of demands: an end to pernicious European influences (like miniskirts, an obsession of African authoritarians of many stripes); a vaguely elaborated reorganization of the state, including its legal system; the return of "discipline" and "honor"; and financial propriety.[59]

Like other military leaders, Sankara found law useful, even though he also preached the need to decolonize it. "The world trembles" before Burkina Faso, Sankara announced at the first sitting of the People's Revolutionary Court, "and all those who profit from the neocolonial system are trembling because [the people] have now become masters of their destiny and want to render their own justice."[60] He condemned the "bourgeois," "reactionary" form of law Burkina Faso had inherited from Europe. "They're all formalists," he spat at the country's judges, "obsessed by procedures and protocol, which they have not yet understood are aimed at tricking the people, turning the judge—draped in his robe, decked out with his sash, and sometimes even a wig—into a clown for whom we revolutionaries feel compassion."[61] Like his counterparts elsewhere, Sankara rejected the colonial trappings of the legal system, but he also hoped to use law to transform his society.[62] The People's Revolutionary Court proved to be a farce, and the "clown"-like judges Sankara disdained outlived him to serve under the next man in uniform. This was Blaise Compaoré, who overthrew Sankara in 1987 and ruled until 2014, during which time he moved Burkina Faso back into the orbit of France. Like other long-ruling soldiers, Compaoré successfully reinvented himself as a civilian statesman, but he never lost his martial edge.

Africa's long dalliance with militarism persuaded all kinds of people that independence had been a failure. In 1961 Fanon died in an American military hospital (his loyalties were complicated), and a few months later Algeria won its independence. In 1965 it became a military dictatorship—a fate it shared, of course, with many other African countries. Some sold off their hard-won sovereignty to foreign interests. Others were strangled by their elites. These facts have led a strange coalition of observers, including hard-nosed American diplomats, aging African radicals, and melancholy historians from all over to tell the story of decolonization as a tragedy.[63] In some ways they're right—half a century on, the high hopes of independence still haven't come to pass, at least if we measure them against Fanon's ambitions.

But this is not the only way to tell the story. In some ways decolonization was a *success*, even if what came out of it looked nothing like Fanon's vision. Military rule was not a betrayal of some more radical independence that was supposed to happen. Nor can it be understood as revanchism or counterrevolution. Soldiers did not sell out the anticolonial revolution; they *were* the revolution, and virtually all of them saw themselves that way. So did many of the people they governed. Independence only looks like a failure if we assume that its goal was to blunt imperialism's martial edge. In fact, many wanted to *sharpen* it, and then use it to carve Africa into a new shape. In accepting his lament that the "revolution" of independence was sold out, we have allowed Fanon, *the revolution's greatest loser,* to obscure what actually happened.[64]

* * *

What is the best adjective to describe military rule in Nigeria? Was it *conservative,* like the South American military regimes of the same era? Was it *revolutionary,* as soldiers themselves described it? Was it *neocolonial?* None of these labels adhere very firmly. The military's ambition to transform society meant that it was not conservative in any conventional sense. Nor were most soldiers determinedly right-wing; they opposed communism and vaguely favored the free market, but Nigeria was a nonaligned country where the ideological tremors of the wider world registered faintly. Nearly all military leaders spoke of what they were doing as a "revolution," but few of them actually changed much about how the state operated.

In the end, terms like *right* and *left* meant little in Nigeria, where soldiers took surprising stands and embraced unexpected causes. For example, in a speech to a group of visiting African American dignitaries, Babangida made a stirring case for reparations for slavery. Black people around the world, he argued, had been reduced to "economic serfdom in their own countries." "We demand full equality with all men for Africans at home and in the diaspora. We call on all the countries of Europe and North America to compensate Africa for the untold hardship and exploitation that the continent had been subjected to in the past."[65] Reparations activists were surprised to find an ally in Babangida—he followed the neoliberal economic line, and he was a friend of the Reagan administration. But this kind of unpredictability was key to soldiers' political strategy. Caprice was part of their genius.

The term that Nigerian soldiers and their allies most often used to describe their thinking was *liberal.* "It is by considered opinion that we enjoy the most liberal military democracy in modern history," wrote Justice Mohammed Bello of the Nigerian Supreme Court in 1973.[66] This boast came from a judge who was a close ally of the army, and it should be taken with a large grain of salt. To call Nigeria a "democracy" was a hard case to make; there were no elections or political parties, and all rulemaking flowed from the executive. But the fact that it was undemocratic didn't preclude it from being "liberal" in some important ways, and military autocrats made good use of the tensions and ambiguities in liberalism to argue that they, not civilians, were the true defenders of freedom.[67] The military disliked journalists, but the press was surprisingly free during most military regimes—and when soldiers *did* try to clamp down on it, such as Buhari's 1984 decree prohibiting criticism of the military or the 1987 ban of the dissident magazine *Newswatch*, they were met with waves of lawsuits and protests.[68] They let a fair number of them happen. Liberalism also extended to economics; although the state haphazardly regulated some aspects of the economy, free trade was one of the "freedoms" the military valued most.

This isn't to say that militarism was liberal toward everyone. Soldiers had different rules for the civilians they trusted and those they didn't. They gave the most leeway to their friends, including their families, the chiefs, and the rural peasantry from which they came. They tolerated some professionals, including engineers and doctors, whose technical bent they liked, along with judges, policemen, and other "natural" disciplinarians. They showed a different face to their enemies—journalists, activists, artists, scholars, politicians, and criminals. For these people, there was not much liberal or judicious about militarism. Soldiers turned their most draconian tools against them, including martial law, public humiliation, and, if all else failed, death.

Nigeria's officers thought of themselves as a vanguard whose sacrifice, self-restraint, and adaptability would liberate their country. "For their tomorrow, we gave our today," Babangida was fond of saying.[69] They saw themselves as rigid but not sclerotic. They saw no contradiction in the notion that a disciplined leader could be a dynamo. Their model was a kind of comic-book hero—a leader who could face any challenge that came his way with ingenuity and daring. General Gnassingbé Eyadéma of Togo even commissioned an actual comic book about himself, retelling his bloody takeover as a series of cheerful pows and bangs.[70] When asked about their ideology, generals were liable to cite the influence of cowboy movies or H. Rider Haggard books, to the eternal embarrassment of the intelligentsia.[71] Was it strange that their views were shaped by boys' adventure stories? Perhaps—but after all, many of them were only barely adults. An adolescent fantasy gripped Africa while they ruled it: *total freedom*. They had a peculiar view of what it meant.

Freedom and Discipline

Freedom had many meanings in postcolonial Africa. Emancipation from colonialism was only one of them, and once that struggle had been won there was no consensus about what being "free" entailed. As Frederick Cooper argued, "what gets lost in narrating history as the triumph of freedom followed by failure to use that freedom is a sense of *process*."[72] The diversity of opinion about what freedom *was* has gotten lost too. Its most obvious meaning was self-determination: the right for African states to exercise their sovereignty, and for Africans—whether as individuals, families, or "peoples"—to make their own choices about how to organize their lives. Soldiers had a different view of what freedom meant. They made a cliché of military life into a political philosophy: *discipline makes you free.*

In training, soldiers are told that it is only through strict constraints—in how to dress, move, speak, and interact with others—that a space of genuine freedom opens up. This freedom, which is a freedom *from the tyranny of one's own instincts*, is worth more than the petty choices that military life disallows (what to wear, who to talk to, when to wake up). Discipline allows the soldier to unshackle himself from doubt, fear, and egotism. This, he comes to see, is true freedom, and it can only be won by giving up the trivial liberties that *pass* for freedom in civilian society. To soldiers, there was nothing counterintuitive about the notion that true freedom came from self-control. When military dictators spoke of themselves as "liberators" (the junta that overthrew Nkrumah called itself the National Liberation Council, for example), they meant liberation from three things: neocolonialism, civilian maladministration, and, somewhat less obviously, one's own psychology. "Alexander the Great set out to conquer the world and he did a pretty good job of it," wrote the authors of an etiquette guide for Nigerian civilians. "There was just one thing wrong—he could not conquer Alexander himself. Self Discipline and Self Control are the beginning of practical wisdom."[73] Before they could conquer the world, the logic went, Nigerians had to conquer their own instincts.

The soldier's creed promises that sacrifice and self-control today will buy freedom tomorrow. This is a bargain that mirrors everyday life in the armed forces; it is only by diligently following the rules that soldiers or sailors can take the small liberties they're allowed—shore leave only comes after swabbing many decks. Most modern militaries, including Nigeria's, offer a contract to enlisted men (and now women): an unfree and maybe dangerous stint during your youth is rewarded with financial and personal freedoms later in life—those offered by a pension, for example, or help from the state in starting a family. Even though they were career soldiers for whom military service was not just a stage of life, officers put much stock in this idea that discipline today earns rewards that can be cashed in tomorrow. For civilians living under military rule, however, there was no freer tomorrow that their self-control would earn them. Militarism promised no pensions or medals for nonsoldiers—just bondage.

At a 1986 event organized by the Nigerian Bar Association, Chukwudifu Oputa described what "freedom" meant to disciplinarians:

> It is only when we divest ourselves of the impediments to freedom—
> that is, when we become disciplined—that we become free; otherwise
> in our desperate effort to snatch at unbridled freedom, we may end
> up splendid slaves to our passions, reasoning savages vacillating be-
> tween the dignity of an intelligence derived from God and the degrada-
> tion of passions of brutes. . . . Obedience to law is not a diminution of
> man's freedom, rather that true obedience is an act of freedom which
> springs from the love of both the law and the law giver. Real freedom
> implies that we are masters of our judgments; that we make the correct
> choices; that we act responsibly in order to attain our desirable goals.
> In short, we are searching for a society that accepts that *we are really
> free only when we are not free from the law*.[74]

This was how soldiers saw their political mandate. A military leader, one Nigerian officer declared, "has a mission to free the people from the tyranny of the social forces and objective conditions that have enslaved them to the vicious circle of poverty, ignorance and disease." "Like the revolutionary which he truly is," a good military leader had to make "bold, albeit painful, attempt[s] to alter the course of history by tackling the conditions that have been inhibiting the capacity of the people to realise their potential."[75] This was how soldiers liked to see themselves, not how they actually were, but it tells us something important about their view of the world.

It wasn't easy to reconcile the military's idea of freedom with how most people wanted to live, and this became the subject of a continent-wide debate. Weighing individual freedoms against those of collectives (families, classes, "tribes") became the most urgent problem in African philosophy, and it wasn't coincidental that Africa's best-known theorists of freedom, Kwasi Wiredu and Paulin J. Hountondji, knew military rule at home. The freedoms they described—to chart the course of one's own life, to vote, to speak openly and in your native tongue—were retorts to the austere illiberalism of army rule (however much soldiers bragged about how "liberal" they were).[76] But the rub lies in the fact that not everyone *wanted* the freedoms that people like Wiredu theorized. To some, those freedoms brought not pleasure, but anxiety and agoraphobia. Militarism, in contrast, hugged people in a comforting embrace. It had this in common with many authoritarian ideologies. "The person who gives up his individual self and becomes an automaton," Erich Fromm wrote of Nazism, "need not feel alone and anxious any more."[77] Militarism gave direction to the rudderless, comradeship to the lonely, and a balm to those whose pride had been wounded by colonialism. These things came at a high price.

People will put up with a lot if they think they're building something for their children. In the twentieth century, citizens of the Soviet Union accepted deprivations in the name of building *communism*, and Americans justified lives and money expended in foreign wars by telling themselves they were building *democracy*. Nigerians endured the strictures and censures of military rule because, their leaders told them, they were building *discipline*. This helps explain why they tolerated the military's punishments for so long. Walter Benjamin described militarism as "the compulsory, universal use of violence as a means to the ends of the state."[78] This is wrong; to see violence as the cardinal quality of militarism obscures its subtler means. Militarism does not require constant violence to work, and while soldiers sometimes used physical force to make and preserve laws, as Benjamin described, that was not the only way they governed. They also used enticement, conditioning, and the manipulation of feeling. Politics was a complicated game of shifting coalitions that only sometimes involved violence.[79] It was seldom *mass* violence. Palace coups might end with an assassination, but they rarely meant bloodshed in the streets. On the contrary, soldiers justified their coups, endlessly deferred elections, and annulments of those elections by arguing that *civilians* were the ones who ruled through violence, while they were men of peace.

Soldiers promised to tame people who had been made feral by colonialism, poverty, and an unruly form of democracy. In describing civilians, the comparison they reached for most often was to beasts. "Man is animalistic," General Olusegun Obasanjo wrote, because he is driven by the "basic instincts of most animals—aggression, fear, hunger and reproduction."[80] Any public policy, he argued, had to proceed from that fact. In the military view, public administration was like a mass form of obedience training. In return for their good behavior, Nigerians would get to live in a peaceful and orderly society. All this required was *discipline*, which was the political touchstone of every military regime. Soldiers' sense of discipline flowed from the same barracks culture that gave them their unusual ideas about freedom. Oputa described it as the rejection of individuality:

> The greatest obstacle to true discipleship and thus to discipline is the affirmation of the self. It is the self that stands in the way. We have to empty ourselves of *self*. When we have elated and exaggerated notions

of our own importance we tend to flout rules and regulations. The negation of the self is simply the recognition of our own littleness in comparison to what we ought to be. Unfortunately the modern tendency is towards the affirmation of the age, the exultation of selfishness riding roughshod over others, in order to satisfy our self-centeredness. Selfishness, egotism, pride, vanity—these strike at the very root of discipline.[81]

Officers believed this fervently. "Let us strive for a Nigeria *where no one is oppressed*," wrote military governor of Lagos State Colonel Mobolaji Johnson in a confidential note to his counterpart in the North-Central State. Johnson berated him for using their friendship to angle for a prime plot of land for his office in Lagos. This kind of corruption was "exactly what was done by the previous Civilian Government," he wrote, "and yet we still refer to ourselves as a CORRECTIVE MILITARY REGIME!! I can smell [a] rat, and I can hear the bells of further troubles in Nigeria if at our level we still think like this."[82] The discipline they imposed on themselves would trickle down to the rest of Nigerian society, and soon enough everyone would be marching in step. At least, that was the plan.

The most urgent question of military rule was a psychological one: How do you condition people to behave as you want them to? Externally imposed discipline is hard and expensive; it has to be enacted constantly, and making it stick requires keeping tabs on everyone, all the time. It is much more efficient to convince people to police themselves—to inculcate discipline as a value so the state doesn't have to stand over everyone with a whip. Militaries operate through the same logic. Training internalizes discipline in every soldier so he'll do his duty even when a drill sergeant isn't around. Nigeria's military rulers took this truism of military life into their politics. Soldiers wanted obedience to live in the minds of the Nigerian people. They wanted discipline to become a national trait—an "in-built mechanism of social correction," as Babangida called it.[83]

But this was easier said than done. In Nigeria, public education was not robust enough to shape how everyone thought and acted. The colonial legacy of underinvestment meant that schools, hospitals, asylums, and other public institutions reached only a small part of the population. Hasty attempts to expand them in the years after the Second World War (an era of state-led developmentalism that some call a "second colonial occupation") had only been partial.[84] Although African governments made enormous strides in the first years of independence, a European-style disciplinary state couldn't be built in a day. The military did not have the institutions it needed to educate consent—to internalize "good" behavior as soldiers defined it.

What soldiers *did* have were loud voices and strong arms, and so their disciplinary project took the form of scolding and thrashing, enacted up close and personally. Over many years of military rule, they never invested in the institutions that might have transformed Nigeria in deeper ways. There are many reasons for this. One is frugality: building a biopolitical state is expensive, but whips are cheap.[85] Another is the fact that most military regimes thought of themselves as temporary or "provisional," even when they weren't. Since they expected to be out of power in a year or two, they preferred quick, bright-burning interventions over long-term investments.

But the main reason is that they had an unshakable confidence in the military way of doing things. For thirty years, officers continued to believe that the military could transform Nigerian society in its own image—the last regime simply hadn't gone far enough. Each was convinced that the same discipline that had transformed him *personally* from an unruly boy into a sharp private could be scaled up into a political philosophy for everyone, and each acted like he had come up with the idea himself.[86]

Discipline was an ethos of perpetual self-improvement. In military regimes, it was a civic duty to better yourself—to become healthier, wealthier, and more productive with every passing year. Civilians should show respect, both for soldiers and for fellow civilians who deserved deference, like the elderly. There were rules about how to act in public: civilians shouldn't litter or relieve themselves in the street, they should form orderly queues, and they should call one another by their proper titles. These included not only "Sergeant" and "Lieutenant," but "Chief," "Pastor," "Prince," "Dr. Mrs.," or "Engineer" (Nigeria's grandiose honorifics are legendary). Women should "respect themselves" by dressing modestly, and men should remain fit for the nation by not smoking or drinking to excess. Some of these rules were enshrined in decrees, and others were unwritten. The penalties for violating them were often corporal. Some, like floggings, were injurious, but other punishments served the function of self-improvement. On-the-spot exercise was imposed for minor infractions, and it wasn't unusual to see a soldier standing over somebody doing push-ups for skipping a queue or talking too loudly.[87] In practice, "discipline" meant whatever soldiers wanted it to mean. At the higher levels of the state, it could mean cracking down on bribery, breaking up protests, or shutting down dissident newspapers.[88]

All officers preached the gospel of discipline, but General Murtala Muhammed was a particularly fervent believer. After taking power in 1975, he purged the government of thousands of employees (including judges) for being late to work, which effectively brought the state to a standstill. This inaugurated the only time in living memory when civil servants could reliably be found at their desks during business hours. Muhammad was assassinated six months later in an abortive coup by Buka Suka Dimka, cementing his status as a martyr. His successor, General Olusegun Obasanjo, vowed to continue his disciplinary mission. When Obasanjo handed over power to an elected civilian, Shehu Shagari, the rhetoric of discipline briefly disappeared from politics. Shagari's administration was plagued by intense corruption, communal violence (notably the Maitatsine uprising in the north), and crime. It gave credence to soldiers' insistence that civilians were unfit to govern, and people began to call for the army to come back. "Military Administration is known in Nigeria to be better in terms of doing justice and fairness to all," wrote one civilian petitioner, "for Nigerian Military rulers were known to be devoid of any vested interest in one faction or the other. They were always neutral and non-partisan."[89] When General Muhammadu Buhari deposed Shagari in 1984, many were happy to see him go.

Once he was in power, Buhari and his fellow officers saw bad behavior all around them—from corruption, to street crime, to the fact that people didn't queue to get on the bus. Indiscipline, as a sycophantic army poet wrote, was "the monstrous beast with human flesh and blood[,] the poisonous venom in mankind's abode, the sickle cell in sicklers' fragile veins."[90] The cure soldiers offered for it was a harsh one.

The War against Indiscipline

If all you have is a hammer, everything looks like a nail. To soldiers, every political challenge looked like a war. The most famous of the military's "wars" was the War Against Indiscipline (wai, pronounced like a plaintive *why?*), which was first "declared" during Buhari's dictatorship.[91] "One of the dangers and challenges of our time here in Nigeria seems to be that hydra-headed, devilish monster called *indiscipline*," Oputa declared at its height. "The menaces of this monster and its capacity for evil are so terrifying that the Federal Government of Nigeria had thought it fit to declare an open and all-out *War Against Indiscipline*."[92] During the three years it was in force, the wai shaped every aspect of public life. "We hear and talk of War Against Indiscipline at least every 30 minutes for 18 hours every day in this country," complained a civilian in Lagos.[93] Although it only officially lasted from 1984 to 1986, the wai was emblematic of military rule as a whole. It was a distilled version of the disciplinary tonic that all military leaders prescribed to their publics. The WAI was militarism in action. Better than anything, it shows how the ideology translated into street-level administration.[94]

The War Against Indiscipline was a national-level initiative to change how Nigerians behaved in the street, the workplace, and the home. It was to have five stages: instilling "orderliness," improving the national work ethic, promoting national unity, fighting corruption, and "sanitizing" the cities. The WAI's front line consisted of civilian "brigades," of which there were three categories—"Vanguards," "Crusaders," and "Patriots"—organized by the age of the "cadets" recruited into them. These brigades, which included children as young as twelve, were empowered to "restore discipline to our national life," "inculcate the spirit of nationalism and patriotism," "restore respect for our revered traditions and cultures," "foster respect for constituted authority," and "instill in the populace a sense of absolute loyalty to their fatherland." Brigade members did things like directing traffic and leading the public in displays of physical fitness. They were also tasked with improving "national consciousness" by "correcting and checking any citizen committing any act of indiscipline," which included "jumping queues, crossing the road under a flyover, cheating, hoarding, leaking official secrets, [and] committing environmental indecency."[95] As Wole Soyinka recalled, it mandated "flying the national flag even on roadside shacks that sold nothing but oranges and peanuts; sanitation, cleaning up the environment; fiscal control (you went to jail if you forgot some loose foreign coins in your pocket and failed to declare them at the airport) . . . and so on."[96] "Simply put," one administrator put it, "the war is expected to change the average Nigerian," to make him "patriotic," and to turn him into someone who "always takes the other man into consideration."[97] A handbook from the mid-1980s enumerated hundreds of rules for civilians to follow in the workplace ("Do not keep 'African time'"), the street ("Do not laugh boisterously"), and the home ("Do not leave your bedroom with your hair in curlers, or in any other state of dishabille").[98] The Supreme Military Council was vague about the war's duration, to say nothing of what it would mean to "win" it.

The leaders of the brigades interpreted their mandate widely. "War Against Indiscipline is [a] War Against Injustice," wrote one, "and it is also [a] War Against Indecency of any kind."[99] The WAI's official slogan was "Queue, queue, one by one. Turn by turn. Do not rush. Let us bring a little order into our lives."[100] Getting Nigerians to form queues at bus stops became the military's obsession. The custom, then as now, was to board buses not in a line, but in a rush of pushing. The military found this unseemly, inefficient, and

FIGURE 2.2. War Against Indiscipline stamp series, 1984.

dangerous. To force people to queue, WAI brigade members were posted at major bus stops in Lagos around the clock. Armed with whips, they would beat anyone who tried to rush aboard—man, woman, or child. More than anything, it is these whips that the WAI would be remembered for.[101] The fact that most WAI brigadiers were young made corporal punishment particularly shocking. Nigeria is a gerontocratic society, and it can't be overstated how radical it was to give teenagers the right to beat their elders in public.

Even so, the WAI was popular, at least among some segments of Nigerian society. "No more huddles at the bank counters, and passing checks through numerous hands before reaching the teller," one woman wrote after coming back to Nigeria after a stint abroad. "No more five arms at once pushing coins to buy one stamp at the post office. No more jumping out of cars, waving fists and shouting abuses at intersections in an attempt to decide who goes first. No more knocking heads and bruising elbows to obtain a boarding pass at the airport."[102] Others found the WAI's methods disturbing. Displays of violence were everywhere, making everyday life feel like a battlefield. The journalist Adewale Maja-Pearce, one of the most astute chroniclers of the era, recalled a scene from the WAI that, he wrote, "will remain with me forever." On a busy street in Lagos, a man caused a small commotion by shouting. "Suddenly, from somewhere in the crowd, a policeman appeared brandishing a whip. Without bothering to find out what had happened he set about the man" and whipped him until he was "covered in blood" and had to be hospitalized. "Perhaps they thought he had been shoplifting; perhaps they just felt like flexing their muscles."[103] Everyone who lived through the WAI has a story like this. Some tell it approvingly, others with shame or regret.

Other critiques of the WAI focused not on its excesses but on the fact that the higher-ups seemed untouched by it. It didn't stop the corruption that was making Nigeria internationally infamous, and some of the people slipping change from the till were soldiers. Every day, the press reported on soldiers who jumped the queues they were supposed to enforce, bureaucrats who continued to demand bribes, or public servants who were still neglecting their duties. "While the great mass of the Nigerian people welcomed the WAI exercise as long overdue, and were quite willing to pay the necessary price if it meant the restoration of civil order," Maja-Pearce observed, "they were not prepared to subsidize their leaders in the process."[104] Wole Soyinka argued that the WAI was not really about "discipline" at all, but an excuse to harass the military's enemies (including Soyinka himself).[105]

Brigade members could justify almost anything by saying that they were enforcing discipline, and some WAI units became violent and extortive. In Oyingbo, a busy market area in Lagos, the WAI became a kind of protection racket. This prompted a crackdown to "redeem the dwindling image" of the war, but by this point it was too late.[106] Eventually, even the leaders of the brigades felt things were going too far—they were civilian volunteers, after all, not a military occupation. A WAI commander in Oyingbo wrote to the Lagos State governor with concerns about how the boys in his brigade were acting. It was, he feared, becoming a "War Against the Innocent." He appealed to the military governor, "the last hope of the oppressed, the father of the godfatherless, the champion of justice, honesty, and fairplay," to scale back the WAI's activities.[107] He got no response.

The military's disciplinary edge was sharpest in neighborhoods like Oyingbo. Soldiers mistrusted urban areas. The hustle and din of cities Lagos and Ibadan was astounding, and soldiers, humble country boys that most of them were, found them dizzying. Everything was for sale, everyone wanted to cheat you, and spectacles of vice and abjection lurked down every alley. The most basic norms of human decency seemed not to apply. "A human corpse would remain in the middle of the street for weeks on end since it didn't pay anybody to take it away," Maja-Pearce wrote.[108] To remedy this situation, the Buhari junta declared a "War on Filth," which was theoretically a sanitation measure. Every household was required to spend a day each month cleaning the streets, and traffic was eased by allowing only cars bearing odd-numbered license plates one day and even the next. The War on Filth was an attempt to manage Nigeria's constant, seemingly unstoppable urbanization, and it brought the emerging global conversation about ecology into local politics. The military cared about environmentalism more than one might think, but it cherry-picked which environments it cared about. There was much concern about refuse and air pollution in Lagos, for example, and the army made decrees doing things like protecting endangered species and funding ecological research.[109] But conservation stopped where the oil industry started—making large swaths of the Niger Delta uninhabitable could be tolerated in the name of keeping the oil flowing.

The War on Filth was fiercest in Lagos, where the state government upped the ante with an initiative it called the Total War on Filthy Environment. The governor gave a task force free rein to do whatever they deemed necessary to clean up the capital city. Their directive was to make Lagos "the pride of the black race."[110] In his address announcing the "total war," Lagos State Military Governor Gbolahan Mudasiru went off script, leaving no doubt about the initiative's true objectives. It wasn't really about cleanliness at all. "In the first place, Government wants to get rid of all undesirable elements," he began. These "elements" included not only the abandoned cars and piles of trash that clogged streets and blocked waterways but also the squatters, itinerant traders, prostitutes, and pickpockets he blamed for "polluting" the capital city. The builders of "shantytowns" were singled out as Nigeria's "biggest public enemies." In his speech, Mudasiru looked wistfully on the time before colonialism, when "any person who [made] a nuisance of himself, or [dirtied] his surroundings was regarded as an enemy of society." Lagos's filth, he argued, "has been fueled largely by the indiscipline which, like a cancerous growth, has over the past few years spread its tentacles to all segments of the Nigerian society."[111]

Fundamentally, the War on Filth was an assault on the urban poor. Soldiers saw the *rural* poor as honorable—this was the class most of them came from, after all—and their status anxiety gave them a begrudging respect for the urban bourgeoisie. But poor city-dwellers, with their seemingly unruly ways of life, were the people they most reviled, and so they declared "war" on them. In Lagos, the most obvious effect of the war was the displacement of garbage from rich neighborhoods into poor ones.[112] Soldiers treated the thronged markets of Onitsha and Umuahia and the mazelike streets of Kano as if they were battlefields. The civilians who lived in those places experienced military rule as a long, brutal occupation.

"Discipline" was not just a principle for the street corner. It also shaped policymaking at high levels. In the military's long correspondence with the International Monetary Fund (IMF), for example, "fiscal discipline" was a constant refrain. Nigeria's military leaders had a complicated relationship with the World Bank and the IMF in the era of "structural adjustment"—the brutal liberalization and austerity measures forced on developing countries in return for assistance.[113] On the one hand, soldiers didn't like being dictated to.

In the lean years of the mid-1980s, the IMF offered Nigeria a multi-billion-dollar loan that would allow it to pay off its short-term debts. As with all IMF help in this period, it came with strings attached. The "adjustments" the IMF mandated were extensive—privatizing state-owned utilities, cutting public services, devaluing the local currency, and removing protectionist tariffs. These were restraints that Buhari wasn't willing to accept, and he rejected the IMF's offer even as debts piled up all around him.

But at the same time, the IMF spoke a language the military understood. The rhetoric of good stewardship, stabilization, and personal responsibility appealed to soldiers, and it mirrored their own vision for society. Behind closed doors, military regimes were more than happy to take advice from its economists, and both Babangida and Abacha would later accept IMF loans, along with all the conditionalities that came with them.[114] Many military leaders were seduced by the promise of autarky—that economic self-reliance would translate into political independence. When Babangida defended his ruthless structural adjustment policy, he did so in the name of self-sufficiency, not free trade. "A country that cannot feed herself cannot be truly independent," he told *Ebony* magazine.[115] In the end, the militarists and the economists were two sides of the same coin. Like military regimes, the IMF was top-down and undemocratic. Like the military, it saw itself as nonpolitical, and it insisted that it knew people better than they knew themselves. Both soldiers and IMF economists preached the need to "build a culture of discipline"— one political and the other fiscal.[116] To ordinary Nigerians, both forms of discipline felt more like punishment.

* * *

Besides force, the most important thing that soldiers had at their disposal was law. Military rulers believed law was a tool of social engineering, and they saw judges as their civilian proxies. Some judges were happy to play that role. In 1978, Chief Justice Sir Darnley Alexander boasted that Nigeria's judiciary was "one of the most disciplined and stable institutions" in the country.[117] Discipline was a legal value as well as a military one, he promised, and the English common-law tradition could help whip the country into shape. Justice Chukwudifu Oputa, ever a friend to the army, pledged that

the legal profession in Nigeria has come out boldly on the side of the Federal Government to go all out *in search of a disciplined society through law*. . . . The discipline we are looking for must be a discipline through law, a discipline dictated by law and the rule of law—not a discipline which forces the subordination of the individual to the State as in fascism, or the subordination of the human person to the race, as in Nazism, or the subordination of the individual to the class as in Communism. What we are searching for and should be fighting for is the subordination of *the State, the class, the race, and the individual* to the *ordinary laws of the land*. In other words, we are fighting for a disciplined society through law.[118]

Judges, Oputa wrote, were "social engineers." They did not want a "permissive society, which seems to be in vogue thanks to Fletcher and Freud. Instead, we are searching for a society that knows how to use freedom rightly; a society that understands the rather intimate connection between law and freedom and the difference between freedom and license; a society that knows freedom is a moral power, that laws and prohibitions are merely danger signals warning us against the wrong use or abuse of freedom."[119] "Law has been used as an instrument of social engineering to prevent anarchy and the disintegration of the Nigerian nation," wrote a military jurist. "Law is a means to an end, that end being an orderly and stable society, and not an end in itself."[120]

Soldiers promised that a better society was possible, and judges like Oputa made them think law could help them build it. What soldiers seldom understood about law was that it cut both ways. It could be a useful tool for keeping the gears of society turning, but it could also jam the machine.[121] Sooner or later, all military rulers learned that law could work against them. Not all judges were enthusiastic about their project, and courts didn't prove very useful in making the world soldiers envisioned.

At the lower levels of the legal system, the military's disciplinary vision sometimes gave way to pragmatism. A good (albeit unusual) example of this could be found in the courtroom of the English-born Judge Dulcie Oguntoye. In the 1950s Oguntoye married a fellow law student from Nigeria and moved to Lagos with him, where she became a magistrate in a working-class neighborhood. When Nigeria won independence in 1960, she gave up her British citizenship, becoming one of the first foreigners to be naturalized as a Nigerian. She served as chief magistrate of Lagos, and in 1976 she was appointed to the Lagos State High Court, becoming the second female judge appointed in Nigeria (the first was Modupe Omo-Eboh, appointed the year before). When she retired she wrote a tell-all memoir, which gives a rare picture of a judicial philosophy from the lower end of the legal system.

Oguntoye served under a series of law-and-order military regimes, but her soft-touch approach put her at odds with soldiers. She was ambivalent about drug use, for example. Cannabis was one of the junta's favorite social problems—the specter of "Indian Hemp" could be used to warrant just about any crackdown soldiers wanted to stage. As chief magistrate, Oguntoye was on the frontline of the army's antidrug policies, but she was hesitant about implementing them.[122] The long jail sentences for drug possession were excessive, she argued, and she refrained from imposing them when she could. The same was true of vice offenses, which crossed her bench every day. She and her fellow magistrates took a pragmatic approach toward homosexuality and prostitution, both of which were prohibited in theory but more or less tolerated in practice.[123] In her courtroom and many others, there was a gap between the laws the military made and how those laws were interpreted on the ground.

Does it matter that magistrates made little stands while soldiers cannibalized society? Whatever defense judges can mount against a military regime is usually a weak one. The rule of law only works when the executive accepts that the judiciary is a legitimate counterweight to its power. If it doesn't—if soldiers regard judges as fools, crooks, or clowns—it's easy for them to swat legal challenges away. If soldiers can convince the *public* that judges are those things, it's even easier to ignore them. This all presumes, moreover, that judges *want* to check authoritarianism. There is no reason to believe they all do. History offers a long list of judges who collaborated with dictators, and militarism appealed to at least as many judges as it put off.

The career of Fatou Bensouda, a Gambian judge who became the chief prosecutor of the International Criminal Court (ICC), is a good illustration of the bargains that judges make in authoritarian regimes. Bensouda studied law at the University of Ife in Nigeria during the Buhari administration. She returned to Gambia in the late 1980s, and after the 1994 putsch of Lieutenant Yahya Jammeh she became his legal adviser and eventually the country's minister of justice. Jammeh was a despot, known for his fierce repression of ethnic and sexual minorities. Bensouda was initially an ally of the regime; "We all rallied to support this new force . . . because we believed this was the change that we needed," she recalled.[124] She eventually crossed Jammeh, and he fired her. This catapulted her into the world of international institutions, where she made her name in the International Criminal Tribunal for Rwanda and as a critic of American war crimes in Afghanistan.[125] But her time in Jammeh's government always hung over her. The irony that an international civil servant who made her career pursuing tyrants got her start working for one was not lost on her enemies (Americans most of all). But what else could Fatou Bensouda do? Pursuing a career as a judge in a military regime meant legitimizing it by her very presence. Judges like Bensouda, Oputa, and Ogun-toye walked a moral tightrope throughout their careers. Their legal reasoning always reflected that balancing act.

The soul of African politics in this era was not *liberation*, as historians with a rosier bent than I have argued—it was *discipline*. But discipline guaranteed neither order nor peace. Soldiers' disciplinary ideology gave cover for chaotic, unchanneled violence, which was precisely what they had promised to prevent when they took the reins from civilians. This begs a question: What is the relationship between legalism and violence? The function of law is not necessarily to diminish violence—law *enacts* many forms of violence, literal and metaphorical, structural and personal. But what law *doesn't* do is give license to those in power to destroy whomever they want. Rather, law *categorizes* violence, labeling some acts of force permissible and others not; some lives inviolable and others disposable. It schedules the times when a person is sovereign over her body and when she isn't. It channels violence, but this doesn't necessarily make for less of it. Those who speak in law's name argue that this is a better approach than allowing violence to spray around freely, and they're probably right. But the belief that a lawful society is a gentle or peaceable one doesn't stand up to even casual scrutiny. In Nigeria, militarism's violence gushed out from barracks and bases, washing over anyone who stood in its way. In episodes like the WAI, soldiers tried to beat the bad habits out of people—quite literally. To them, this kind of violence was redemptive. But to those who didn't share their vision, it was alien and cruel.

Conclusion

Lawyers and soldiers both speak the language of history. Historical consciousness is embedded in law; in common-law countries, the importance of precedent compels lawyers to turn over the mulch of the past constantly.[126] Judges weigh whether a problem presented to them is comparable to one taken up in an older case, or they trace chains of causation to understand why something happened. Military officers obsess over history too, arguably more than other kinds of leaders. Cadets around the world still read about the Peloponnesian Wars when they study strategy, and generals consult Clausewitz or Sun Tzu when they're facing modern operational dilemmas. Military history reaches the public in a way that no other kind of history does, and soldiers are among its most voracious readers. As Vagts wrote in 1937, militarism and its corollary, imperialism, "are tendencies largely 'justified' by history—that is, they cover their new demands with a cloak of tradition, the one invoking the images of emperors long dead, the other recalling past glories of action."[127] Nigeria's military regimes funded historical research, convened conferences about it, and put the books that came out of them in their barracks libraries.[128] They used those books to justify the disciplinary dogma they preached.

The history soldiers liked best was history that celebrated heroism, adulated tradition, and rejected the corrupting influence of foreign ideas. African history was being written and rewritten while they were in charge. Up to this point, Nigeria's main contribution to the study of the past had been the Ibadan School, a group of British-trained historians who took a Rankean "just the facts" approach to their storytelling. This had little appeal to the military elite. If the Ibadan historians had a politics, it was that of civilian republicanism—the philosophy that soldiers insisted had steered Nigeria wrong. They disliked the school's individual members too. Jacob Ajayi, their leader, had served in the First Republic, which they found disgraceful. Kenneth Dike, who had founded the Nigerian National Archives, had sided with Biafra during the civil war, which was unforgivable.

Soldiers preferred historians like Yusufu Bala Usman, the young firebrand who was so spellbound by Fanon in a London train station. Usman grew up to be a historian at Ahmadu Bello University, and his work reached millions of people through columns he published in the newspaper. Even though he often criticized the military, the way he told Nigeria's story appealed to soldiers. Usman showed that the ethnic identities most Nigerians took for granted were of colonial manufacture, and he offered a plan for how to dismantle them.[129] He depicted precolonial West Africa as a land of honor and valor, which captured soldiers' imaginations. He gave them a language of revolution they could use and enemies they could prop up as straw men— decadent colonial administrators, nefarious foreigners, and corrupt Nigerian civilians who had sold out independence to fatten their wallets. When he called checks and balances an "inane notion of Anglo-Saxon liberalism" and said that the "elaborate machinery of the English judicial system" was a ruse for foreign domination, soldiers nodded along. They didn't follow Usman to the end of his argument—they liked his black-and-white vision of the past and his revolutionary spirit, but the point where he started to talk about *Marxist* revolution was the point where they put down the book.[130] Nonetheless, Usman's account of the past shaped how his readers thought about the future. Without intending to, radical historians like Usman gave soldiers a language for politics.

Not everyone dreams of liberty. To soldiers, the appeal of returning to a political and ethical world that had been destroyed by colonialism was not about building an unfettered type of freedom (whether individual or collective). Rather, it was about *tightening the constraints* they believed were necessary for a harmonious society and that colonialism had loosened. Decolonization, they argued, was about rebuilding a lost world of traditional authority—one that was ascetic, masculine, and in many ways very unfree, except perhaps by their own peculiar definition of "freedom." It meant handing power back to the chiefs, who had lost standing when civilians had been in charge. It meant restoring a gerontocratic system of rules that louche young women and ludic young men had broken. It meant maintaining "law and order." To soldiers, the problem with colonialism was not that it had been too violent, or too disciplinary. It was that it had *not been disciplined enough*. Their vision for decolonization, therefore, was one that embraced *penance*.

3

THE PORTABLE COUP

The Jurisprudence of Military "Revolution"

In January 1961, nearly two hundred African judges met in Lagos for the First African Conference on the Rule of Law. The question before them was a hard one: how to adapt colonial legal systems to the needs of independent nation-states. Nigeria was a fitting place for the conference. It had won independence from Britain the previous year, and there were, as president Nnamdi Azikiwe told the assembled jurists, "nearly as many lawyers within its borders as there are to be found in the rest of indigenous Africa." Nigeria's mature judicial institutions gave moral authority to his government, and they made it a model for the rest of the continent. "It is commonly agreed," Azikiwe said, "that Nigeria offers to Africa and to the world probably the best example of a country that is noted for orderly advance."[1]

Delegates to the 1961 conference couldn't agree on very much. They sparred over language, ideology, and what to do about the parts of the continent still under colonial rule. They were all in the same mind about one thing, however: the danger of tyranny. The Committee on Executive Powers, chaired by Abdoulaye Wade of Senegal and Herbert Chitepo of Southern Rhodesia, warned that Africa's new states were vulnerable—not only to external forces, but to threats from within. Military takeovers threatened to end democracy before it could begin, and emergency measures like martial law endangered hard-won freedoms.[2] Colonial despotism, they feared, might give way to locally made dictatorship. Ten years later, these fears had come to pass, and military rule was the order of the day for most of the next forty years.

When a prominent Nigerian civil rights lawyer was asked to describe how politics worked in his country, he cited neither a constitution nor a statute, but Mao Zedong's *Little Red Book*. "Power flows from the barrel of the gun," Mike Ozekhome wrote of military regimes. "Power is an aphrodisiac, a potent catalyst, and a ready tool in the hands of dictators, tyrants, fascists, and autocrats," "a bemusing liquor" which generals imbibed "again and again, with stupendous and insatiable Bacchanalian propensity."[3] What explains this turn to dictatorship, and how did it spread from one place to another? For former British colonies in Africa, a small group of judges who traversed the continent in the name of pan-African cooperation are an important part of the answer.

Soldiers and despots across the continent got "drunk" on power beginning in the mid-1960s, as Ozekhome wrote. But, to extend his metaphor, it was judges who passed the bottle between them. The jurisprudence that underpinned authoritarianism was portable, and judges conveyed it from one former British colony to another as they moved between jurisdictions. These judges were indispensable in authorizing executive power and converting the commands of military leaders into formal administrative structures. This chapter traces the itinerary of one judge, the Nigerian Sir Egbert Udo Udoma, whose rulings were foundational in two African countries with long experiences of military rule—Uganda, where he served as the first African chief justice, and Nigeria, where he sat on the supreme court and advised several military governments. His influence was much wider than these two countries, however. Udoma developed a jurisprudence that aspiring dictators worldwide found useful. His rulings were cited to sanction coups and constitutional suspensions across the common-law world, including in South Asia, the Pacific, and the Caribbean. Udoma is largely unknown today, but he lurks in the background of the global history of militarism in the late twentieth century.

The Traffic in Judges

Walk into a law library anywhere in Anglophone Africa and you'll find law reports from India, Pakistan, the United States, and a smattering of other countries once ruled by Britain. These well-thumbed books from faraway places were an important part of African legal culture. Britain's former colonies continued to use the English common law after independence, which meant that precedent from other common-law jurisdictions was usually admissible in their courts. British ex-colonies in Africa shared this ever-evolving body of law based on judicial precedent not only with one another, but with the sixty or so countries that had once been part of the British Empire. British imperial law had been a global phenomenon; judges had been interchangeable across the empire, even though the content of the law varied from one British colony to another.[4] Codes and cases were portable too. The path of appeal might pass from a rural magistrate, to a High Court in Lagos, to the West Africa Court of Appeal in Freetown, Sierra Leone. From there, it might end up before the Judicial Committee of the Privy Council in London. After independence, this globally connected legal culture didn't disappear, but it no longer worked under the sign of British imperialism.

Beginning in the early 1960s, African administrators in former British colonies devised an informal system for sharing legal expertise across their borders. Countries that had many African judges, like Nigeria, would assist those that did not, like Uganda. Former British colonies in the Caribbean would contribute personnel as well, all under the banner of Pan-African solidarity. This cooperation proceeded from an imbalance; some former British dependencies were better equipped to create their own legal systems than others. In West Africa, Africans had been deeply involved in colonial law since the mid-nineteenth century. In cities like Freetown, Accra, and Lagos, Africans and Europeans had coproduced feisty legal cultures to structure commerce and resolve disputes, which colonial administrators belatedly learned could be turned against them.[5] By the time British rule came to East Africa, administrators were warier of African involvement in law. In Uganda, Kenya, and Tanganyika, the British made a concerted effort to keep legal education beyond the reach of the African majority.[6]

This meant that at independence there were very few African lawyers in Commonwealth East Africa, and nearly all judges were European or Asian.[7] In contrast, in Ghana, Nigeria, and Sierra Leone (and to a lesser extent Gambia and British Cameroon), there was a large pool of experienced lawyers eligible for appointment to the judiciary by the mid-twentieth century. Some of them became judges by joining the bench in places like rural Botswana or the distant Seychelles, with the understanding that when they returned home it would be to take up prestigious positions in their national judiciaries. In this way, the administrative pathways that had once carried British judges between British colonies were repurposed to appoint West African judges to the rest of the continent, where they were welcomed in the name of solidarity.[8] As politicians saw it, sharing personnel not only fixed a staffing problem—it helped knit together Africa's now independent states through the legal tradition they shared as former British colonies.[9] "African judges," predicted the last colonial governor of Eastern Nigeria, "are not, I imagine, disposed to regard themselves as units in a world wide service in quite the same way as their English colleagues."[10] African judges *did* in fact come to see themselves as interchangeable units, but the network they moved within was not the British Empire. Rather, it was the circuit of Pan-African cooperation that emerged among Britain's former colonies.

In eastern and southern Africa, West African and Caribbean judges replaced the Europeans and Asians who had staffed the colonial courts.[11] This was part of a broader effort to replace the British administrators who still lingered on in independent African countries. "An ex-patriot is a man with dual loyalties," remarked a Nigerian minister to a visiting American academic.[12] There was a real fear that British or other European administrators retained by African governments would secretly work in the interests of their home countries. Leaders like Julius Nyerere in Tanzania and Milton Obote in Uganda hoped that African and Caribbean judges would be trustworthy, and palatable to the public, in a way that other foreigners were not. Politicians could gesture to the new judges as proof they had fulfilled their promises to "indigenise" the judiciary, even though they were not citizens of the countries they served. A network began to emerge, and a series of unusual firsts followed: The first African chief justices of Uganda and Botswana were Nigerians, and the first black chief justice of Tanzania was from the tiny Caribbean state of Dominica. Kenya and the Seychelles would both have Ghanaian chief justices, and high courts across eastern and southern Africa were presided over by Sierra Leoneans and Gambians. In their new postings, West Africans joined colonial-era appointees from South Asia, Britain, Ireland, and Cyprus, some of whom were quietly kept on after independence despite politicians' promises that African judiciaries would be composed of Africans.[13]

Intra-African judicial appointments took place at various levels.[14] Those who were posted at high ranks—to supreme courts, for example—were elites who had already served as high court judges in their home countries. Most had been educated in England, although a sizable minority studied at Irish universities. In the 1960s and 1970s all of them were male (women would join the African judicial circuit in the 1980s).[15] All had been lawyers before being called to the bench, and most had moved up through the ranks of the colonial courts. None were radicals, although many were nationalists. They believed in the common-law tradition their countries had inherited from Britain, even though some also wanted to reform, modify, or indigenize it. They were generally more accomplished than the Europeans they replaced, whose level of birth was often higher than their aptitude (the colonial judiciary promised a comfortable life, but few British judges chose it if they could have a career at home). Some of those judges took early retirements, and others continued their careers in Britain's dwindling overseas dependencies. Judges of South Asian descent were in the trickiest position, since many had been born in East Africa and had no other "home" to return to.[16] Some entered the world of international institutions or academia, while others gave up law entirely.

In lower courts, the foreign appointees to the bench were usually inexperienced. In Tanzania, the Nigerian Judicial Technical Assistance Program staffed rural magistrates' courts with Nigerian lawyers who had never had judicial appointments. Nigeria did not export its best graduates for these positions (the diplomat who facilitated the program could come up with no adjective to describe them besides "unemployed"), and there were regular complaints about their ignorance of local affairs.[17] One local official noted that the Nigerian magistrates openly disdained the "backwardness and low standard of living" of Tanzania and angled for appointments in urban areas, "where they cling to the hope they may find some of the High-Life to which they are accustomed back home."[18] They were widely disliked, and the hope that they might have more public credibility than Europeans and Asians quickly dissipated. Nonetheless, the fact that they were alienated from the communities they served wasn't a problem to the governments that hired them. In fact, it made them more valuable. If a judge began to rule against the state too often, it was easy to remove him if he was a foreigner. It was even easier if he was unpopular. Removing a respected judge might cause a scandal, but one with no local allies could be sent packing at any time.

How did the political fortunes of so many African states fall into militarism, and how did this happen so quickly? Some have blamed authoritarian personalities, others Cold War geopolitics. Ideology and psychology explain something about where Africa's authoritarians came from, but they don't explain how coup plotters and impetuous soldiers became "legitimate" heads of state. It was judges who translated their vaguely conceived promises of "order" into tangible policies. These judges carried a heavy burden in their adopted countries. In the era of military rule and "big man" politics that followed independence, the task of interpreting the rules made by heavy-handed executives fell to them. Most gave them the go-ahead. For Nigeria and Uganda, the story of how that happened starts in a Dublin lecture hall.

Sir Egbert Udo Udoma

The colonial barracks was not the only place militarism grew from. It had roots in law schools too. Starting in the late nineteenth century, a small trickle of West Africans studied law in English and Irish universities, supported by their families, towns, and churches. One of these students was Egbert Udo Udoma, an academically gifted trader's son from the Ibibio town of Ikot Abasi in southeastern Nigeria. Udoma studied law at Trinity College Dublin in the 1930s, where he became a prominent student leader. He then went to Oxford to read for a doctorate in law with Margery Perham, after which he was called to the bar at Gray's Inn.[19] The ideas that African students like Udoma encountered in their training shaped how they later interpreted the law. They studied law in order to practice it, but they were also exposed to debates in legal philosophy.[20] They read British philosophers like H. L. A. Hart and J. L. Austin, who would leave a deep mark on African law by way of them. They were also exposed to continental theorists like Carl Schmitt and Hans Kelsen, who were starting to appear in British university curricula.[21] Udoma would remember his lessons about legal positivism particularly well.

After completing his education, Udoma returned to Nigeria in 1945, where he became a successful lawyer.[22] In 1961, a year after independence, he was appointed to the High Court of the Federal Territory of Lagos, which was the main feeder to the Nigerian Supreme Court. In his telling, his appointment was a ploy by his rival Nnamdi Azikiwe, who "would have preferred to see me as a judge than a politician in Parliament in the opposition."[23] In his decisions, Udoma showed himself to be a staunch disciplinarian with little patience for civil liberties.[24] Executive power was the guiding light of his judicial philosophy, and ethnic patriotism lay at the center of his politics.[25] Throughout his career, Udoma would speak of the need to indigenize the practice of law, and he often claimed that his legal thought was influenced as much by the moral world of his upbringing as by his formal education.[26] Udoma saw the Ibibio people as an embattled minority caught between the larger groups that swayed national politics. For that reason, a concern for the interests of minorities—ethnic and otherwise—ran through his jurisprudence.[27] He was a Nigerian nationalist, but when forced to choose between the interests of the country and those of the Ibibio Union, he often chose the latter.

In 1962, Ugandan Prime Minister Milton Obote approached the Nigerian government to request an African judge who could serve as chief justice of Uganda. Udoma's name came up as a possible candidate, and after some deliberation Nigeria's chief justice, Sir Adetokunbo Ademola, offered him the opportunity. Udoma had reservations about it. The pay was not high enough, and although the prestige of being chief justice (and the knighthood that came with it) was attractive, Udoma's ambitions lay in Nigeria, not on the other side of the continent.[28] Ademola assured him that a spot on the Nigerian Supreme Court would await him after his sojourn to Uganda. Reassured by this promise, Udoma packed his bags and moved to Kampala with his family. One of the first people he met was the wife of the British high commissioner, who embarrassed him by remarking on how many Nigerians were serving in East African judiciaries. "Darling, this is a complete takeover!" she noted candidly.[29] She wasn't entirely wrong. Several Nigerian judges were already on the bench in Kenya, and more were being planned for Tanganyika— although none ranked as high as Udoma.

Uganda's president needed someone like Udoma. Milton Obote had many enemies, and he presided over a political system where his authority was tightly constrained.[30] He was not a populist, and he could not count on the mass support of the Ugandan people; he had been borne to power by a trickle of tepid political compromises, not a wave of public approval. He was hamstrung by the 1962 constitution that Uganda adopted at independence—a document drafted, like many African constitutions, around a negotiating table in London. This constitution gave outsized power to Buganda, the rich and politically savvy kingdom at the center of the country, and its king served as Uganda's president. This was a ceremonial position, but that made Obote no less wary of Kabaka Muteesa II, whom he saw as a rival. The legislature, dominated by Buganda, was beyond his control. He commanded the military, but soldiers like Idi Amin clearly had minds of their own (and Amin's coup would eventually be Obote's undoing). He had few friends, at home or abroad, and his political position was tenuous. His best hope was to capture the judiciary, but to do that he needed someone pliable at its top. Udoma, a respected judge with no local entanglements, and no protector but Obote himself, was the perfect candidate. Udoma knew little about Ugandan politics, which made him all the more useful. His technical approach to the law, and his accommodating stance toward executive power (which he had already demonstrated in Nigeria), meant Obote could count on his chief justice's support as long as he framed the facts in the right way. Obote controlled what Udoma saw and whom he met, which allowed him to do just that.

As soon as he arrived in Uganda, Udoma set about reforming the legal system. His first step was to abolish the terminological distinction between the High Court system, which was used mostly by Asians and Europeans, and the "African courts" that heard village-level disputes and handled most civil matters, most of which used local customary laws. "All the courts in the country were African courts," he contended, "since Uganda was an African country." The "African" courts that used custom were converted into magistrate's courts, making their structure of appeal to the High Courts more straightforward, and many customary offenses were abolished. Seeing that there was "not a single African judge" and only two African magistrates in Uganda, he promoted the magistrates to judges, and appointed others from the small but growing bar. He also saw to it that Uganda "no longer looked towards India for inspiration" in legal matters. This entailed replacing the penal code (derived from Calcutta's) with one modeled on Nigeria's.[31] Udoma did all this because he felt it was his mandate to create a legal system "unbesmirched by colonial folly or imperial impudence," as Justice James Ogoola wrote of his tenure.[32] He got on "congenially with Obote, whose major objective was to give Udoma maximum comfort," as one of his biographers wrote.[33] He was also the president of the constitutional court, which would soon make him a very important person in his new country.

Three years into his appointment as chief justice, Udoma took the Christmas holiday in Nigeria. While he was there, he witnessed the January 1966 coup that toppled the Nigerian First Republic and installed a military regime. He returned to Uganda the following month, which, to his astonishment, was also in turmoil. On 22 February, Obote suspended the constitution, seized all powers of government, and dismissed the president, Kabaka Muteesa II, on the grounds that he was plotting a coup. On 15 April, Obote announced a new constitution, giving himself wide, dictatorial powers. He dissolved Buganda and destroyed its palace, including the chamber holding the drums of state, which were the kingdom's primary political and spiritual symbols.[34] Obote defended this as an act of "decolonization"; it was, as Oloka-Onyango wrote, "an attempt at *autochthony*, in other words the indigenization of the constitutional regime seeing that the 1962 instrument was basically an arrangement with Britain."[35] It was also imperious and undemocratic. Udoma was blindsided by these back-to-back crises, and he began taking benzodiazepines to relieve his anxiety.[36] Several months later, Uganda's new constitution would be put to a legal test, and Udoma would be the one to judge it.

Uganda v. Commissioner of Prisons ex parte Matovu

The legal challenge to the new constitution came in the form of Michael Matovu, a provincial chief of Buganda who had been arrested under emergency regulations instituted during the constitutional transition. Matovu's lawyer filed a writ of habeas corpus for his client's release, which led to a suit before the supreme court, *Uganda v. Commissioner of Prisons ex parte Matovu*.[37] The state's case was made by Godfrey Binaisa, Uganda's attorney general and most accomplished lawyer. At this time Binaisa was an ally of Obote, although their relationship would later sour.[38] Matovu's lawyer was Abubaker Kakyama Mayanja, a member of Parliament for Kabaka Yekka, a Catholic party affiliated with Buganda. Udoma had a low opinion of Mayanja. He found the lawyer's filing defective for several procedural reasons, and he might have declined to consider it for any one of them.[39] But the court went ahead with the hearing: "We decided, in the interests of justice, to jettison formalism to the winds and to overlook the several deficiencies in the application."[40] Citing the American cases *Marbury v. Madison* and *Baker v. Carr* on the political doctrine question, and the Pakistani case *State v. Dosso* on what constituted a legitimate coup, Udoma ruled in favor of the state. In a lengthy decision, he concluded that the new constitution was legal because it was the product of a "revolution." For years to come, the legitimacy of many African governments would turn on Udoma's use of this term.

Udoma's understanding of what constituted a revolution came from the Austrian jurist Hans Kelsen, whose *Pure Theory of Law*, first published in 1934, had a strange career in the postcolonial world.[41] Udoma's interpretation of Kelsen went as follows: If a regime had taken power suddenly, and it was able to rule "effectively," then it was "revolutionary," which, in the custom of international law, made it "legitimate." A system was "effective" if its commands were obeyed, and infractions of them were punished according to its own precepts.[42] Udoma found Kelsen's positivism useful for several reasons, but especially for its emphasis on "effectiveness" as a tool to measure the validity of regimes born of coups.[43] In *Matovu*, the state presented a mere eight affidavits as evidence of this effectiveness, all by members of Obote's inner circle. One of them was by Binaisa himself in his capacity as attorney general. These sworn statements were scant evidence of the new constitution's broad acceptability in government, but they were proof enough for Udoma. A low bar for "effectiveness" had been set.

This was a crude kind of positivism, and it didn't do much justice to the theorist cited to prop it up.[44] Kelsen's "pure theory" of law was just that— a theory—and the jurist himself did not condone how military regimes used his postulate. The fact that Kelsen meant his work to be descriptive rather than prescriptive didn't stop judges from making Kelsen's theory into a political mandate, however. To politicians like Obote and their judicial enablers, Kelsen was helpful in transmogrifying power grabs into revolutions. As Tayyab Mahmud wrote, Kelsen's theoretical work "furnished the primary doctrinal vehicle" to validate usurper regimes. Kelsen was used to corroborate the claim any sudden, systemic political change counted as a coup, and any coup was legitimate so long as it was successful.[45]

The putsches, constitutional annulments, and sham declarations of independence that judges called "revolutions" were not revolutionary in any sense outside of the Kelsenian one (and not always even that). These "revolutions" made little attempt to destroy the existing structures of governance and build new ones in their place, and few of them were ideological transformations. Some, like Obote's constitutional "coup," didn't even involve a change in leadership. Soldiers and other authoritarians who took power through coups usually presented themselves as forces of stability and continuity—except in the courtroom, where it was in their interests to argue the opposite.

In Uganda, the effect of the *Matovu* decision was to sanitize the new constitution, and with it Obote's autocratic administration. The constitution eliminated Obote's most persistent rival—Buganda—and it allowed him to make Uganda "a police state in a real sense," as a British diplomat observed. It gave him the "physical and legal apparatus to enforce his will by whatever degree of persuasion or compulsion may be expedient—provided that he can keep the army in its corner."[46] Obote could not in fact keep the military on his side, but until that time came, the new constitution was a powerfully repressive tool at his disposal. The *Matovu* decision gave it a legal imprimatur.[47]

Matovu had a larger effect, which radiated outward across the continent in the wake of the trial. *Matovu* established that Uganda's *grundnorm*—the spirit that animated its law—was not to be found in a constitution, a monarchy, or an abstraction like "the people," but in Obote's "revolution" *as an event*. In so doing, it established the coup as a legitimate form of political succession, making it easy for plotters to cloak their actions in legality. As Oloka-Onyango writes, "it marked the first real test of the post-colonial judiciary, and it also commenced the transition from a parliamentary system of governance to a presidential regime, buttressed by a framework of military and autocratic central authority."[48] In Uganda itself, General Idi Amin would use this precedent when he overthrew Obote, his former ally, in 1971.[49] "Since I came into power," he proclaimed in a 1974 interview, "automatically

Uganda became revolutionary. Not only the armed forces, but the whole police, prisons, the whole public."[50] Amin was neither the first nor the last to find this positivist doctrine useful. By giving upstart soldiers a path to legitimacy, it emboldened them to overthrow civilian governments (and one another). Commonwealth judges cited one another in these cases, building up a self-supporting structure of jurisprudence for military rule as they went. *Matovu*, along with the *Dosso* case from Pakistan, served as its foundation.

After the *Matovu* decision had been handed down, Obote showered Udoma with respect. A driver and car with a special "Chief Justice" license plate was provided for him ("the car was a Mercedes Benz," he recalled wistfully in his memoirs), as were "soft furnishings of my residence" and an "increased emolument for myself" that allowed him to host elaborate garden parties.[51] In late 1968, Obote abruptly turned on his chief justice, firing him while he was on leave in Nigeria through a press release. Udoma believed he was dismissed because his Nigerian rivals had bribed Obote to dismiss him in a complex (and probably fictitious) plot to derail his career. The more likely explanation is that Udoma had simply run the course of his usefulness. Obote had gotten what he wanted out of him, and so he was sent home. Obote explained the dismissal by saying that the next step in the development of the Ugandan judiciary was to appoint a Ugandan as chief justice. In the next breath, he instead appointed Dermot Sheridan, an Irishman who had been Udoma's subordinate.

Udoma was embittered that his close relationship with Obote had ended, but he was proud of what he had done. "I left Uganda a happy man," he wrote, "satisfied that I had served Uganda honestly and sincerely to the best of my ability and which had won for me the admiration of the people and respect and affection for me in their hearts."[52] One biographer contends that Udoma had private misgivings about his role in enabling Uganda's authoritarian path, but his commitment to the "correct" interpretation of the law led him to rule as he did despite his reservations.[53] If Udoma did have qualms, he left no record of them. The fact that precedent was portable between common-law jurisdictions meant that judges far beyond Uganda would read his decision, cite it, and use it as a guide for how to suspend constitutions or sanitize coups. It cropped up in contexts ranging from Rhodesia's illegal independence to preserve white minority rule, to the flurry of military coups in the Seychelles, and to Suriname and Fiji in their eras of dictatorship. One of the most important stops on the *Matovu* decision's itinerary was closer to home, however—Nigeria, where Udoma returned in 1969 to take up the position on the Nigerian Supreme Court he had long coveted.

Lakanmi and Another v. the Attorney General of the Western Region of Nigeria and Others

Much had changed in Nigeria while Udoma was gone. The federal government had fought and won a war of "unity," and military rule was in full swing. Once the civil war was over, Nigerians started to ask questions about why soldiers were still in power. What gave the military the right to rule, and what was the regime's foundational force? Did it lie in the constitution, even though it had been suspended by decree? In the will of the executive? In some general public mandate? Did civilians have *any* rights that soldiers couldn't take away? These questions, which had been asked in Uganda in 1963, were now recapitulated in Nigeria.

The court case that raised them was *Lakanmi and Another v. the Attorney General of the Western Region of Nigeria and Others* of 1970. *Lakanmi* considered three linked questions: what constituted a coup d'etat; whether the sitting military government had seized power "legally"; and whether the Nigerian constitution remained in force under military rule.[54] The case arose over a convoluted dispute about which entity was allowed to investigate the assets of public servants in the Western Region who had been accused of corruption. This jurisdictional quibble was the product of a flurry of contradictory decrees and edicts by the federal and regional governments.

Decrees were the main lawmaking apparatus of military administrations, and most were broad, sweeping, and virtually incomprehensible to the general public. At issue in *Lakanmi* was one such decree, Decree No. 45 of 1968, which declared that "the validity of any order, notice or document made or given or purported to be made or given or of any other thing whatsoever done or purported to be done under the provisions of any enactment of law repealed . . . shall not be enquired into in any court of law." In effect, it declared that no civilian court could hear a case on an issue arising from the abandoned Nigerian constitution. Nor could courts adjudicate the validity of the decrees that the state and federal governments issued. Judges objected to this curtailment of their authority, and the Supreme Court took on *Lakanmi* in order to measure how far the power of judicial review extended now that Nigeria was ruled by decree.

Lakanmi also considered whether or not the Federal Military Government was a revolutionary government, and therefore whether it was legitimate. The court, under Chief Justice Ademola, ruled that the new government was not "revolutionary" and was therefore illegitimate.[55] From this, it followed that the constitution of 1963 was still in force, and the contents of decrees were justiciable by civilian courts. In support of this interpretation, Ademola cited the fact that power had been handed over to an "interim" military government after the July 1966 coup that brought Yakubu Gowon to power. If the "interim" government had been intended as temporary, as that term implied, then it did not meet the standard of permanence to be considered a "revolution." Although Decree No. 1 of 1966 had formally nullified the civilian constitution, he reasoned, the fact that much of the state apparatus had continued to operate as if it was still in place meant that the new regime was not "effective." This was further evidence that the events of 1966 did *not* constitute a revolution. Udoma disagreed, using the *Matovu* case from Uganda to argue that the 1966 coup in Nigeria had been legitimate, just as Obote's "coup" had been.

Ademola's ruling was narrow and technical, but it amounted to a defense of civilian democracy. It established that the military cabal that had ruled Nigeria for the last four years was an illegal regime. The civilian constitution had been in force all that time, albeit in the shadow of the junta. Ademola's decision was a brave and quixotic defense of the old civilian order, which he knew would provoke a backlash from the military.[56] The ruling was scorned by the press, who cared little about the theoretical and, as one journalist called it, "metaphysical" tone of the debate about *grundnorm*—a Kelsenian term of art that became an unlikely political buzzword in 1970s Nigeria. The public was more agitated by the decision's most immediate consequence: a group of corrupt bureaucrats had been let off the hook.[57] Nonetheless, *Lakanmi* was "a grave challenge" to the ruling soldier class, as Ben Nwabueze remarked, and there was no doubt in anyone's mind that it would provoke them.[58]

Their reaction was swift and decisive. The court delivered its judgment on 24 April 1970, and two weeks later the Supreme Military Council promulgated the Federal Military Government (Supremacy and Enforcement of Powers) Decree No. 78. The decree nullified Ademola's ruling by executive order, and its drafters leaned heavily on Udoma's ideas.[59] In language derived from Kelsen, the decree insisted that the military government was a "legal" regime. It proclaimed that the 1966 coups that toppled the First Republic and installed General Yakubu Gowon as head of state had been "revolutions," and were therefore legitimate transfers of power. "Both revolutions," moreover, "effectively abrogated the whole pre-existing legal order in Nigeria except what has been preserved under the Constitution (Suspension and Modification) Decree 1966, that is, Decree No. 1."[60] Courts, including the Supreme Court, could make no more judgments about the contents or validity of decrees, and they were to make no mention of the constitution.

At the heart of the *Lakanmi* case was a disagreement about law's purpose. To soldiers like Gowon, law was a tool of social control. It was useful because it could foster "discipline"—their ideological touchstone—but using it for anything beyond that might bind the military's hands. To Ademola, law's most important function was not to make order but to protect people against their leaders. The military's annulment of Ademola's ruling was a threat to lawyers not to meddle in the military's affairs. Many took it to heart, and jurists fell over themselves showing how the Supreme Court had erred in deciding the case. "The Supreme Court took its stand on a banana skin," one law lecturer wrote, "and not surprisingly, it has been helped to slip."[61] "It is to the credit of the military administrators that the judiciaries were left severely alone" during the civil war, wrote another, "but it is regrettable that it took them some time to appreciate the reality of the new political situation."[62] After this point, courts did not adjudicate the military's edicts and decrees so much as referee them against one another. The legal foundation for the next three decades of military dictatorship had been laid.[63]

Eventually, the Kelsen doctrine that military regimes found so useful ceased to be good law. In 1972, the Pakistani case *State v. Dosso*, which *Matovu* had cited, was overturned by *Asma Jilani v. Government of the Punjab*. In one fell swoop, this decision ended martial law in Pakistan, declared the former military head of state an illegal usurper, and renounced the language of "revolution" that validated military coups as legitimate state-making events.[64] Kelsen, the Pakistani court ruled, had been stretched to the breaking point: his definition of "revolution" was "by no means a universally accepted theory, nor was it a theory which could claim to have become a basic doctrine of modern jurisprudence."[65] Judges who were friendly to the military had willfully misinterpreted Kelsen's theory, making an academic abstraction into a concrete, empirical rule. Finally, it was recognized for what it was: a fig leaf for tyranny. *Asma Jilani* greatly diminished the validity of the Kelsen doctrine among international lawyers, but it would take a long time for Nigeria and Uganda to purge it from their legal systems. Even critics of the military accepted its basic validity. "Military revolution we now know from experience is a factual reality," wrote a rebellious lawyer in 1988, during Gen. Ibrahim Babangida's dictatorship, "as postulated by the renowned jurist Hans Kelsen."[66]

As for Udoma himself, he ended his career embittered that he had never been made chief justice of Nigeria. When Ademola retired, Udoma was passed over in favor of Attorney General Taslim Elias. Ademola made it clear that he did not want Udoma to be his successor; he considered his dissent in

Lakanmi a betrayal. Gowon, who was still in power when Ademola retired, respected the chief justice's opinion in spite of the stand he had taken against the military. He appointed Elias at Ademola's recommendation, whom he felt would be better equipped to preside over the eventual return to civilian rule. In 1975 Udoma was passed over again, this time for a foreign judge, Sir Darnley Alexander of St. Lucia. "It should be noted," observed one of Udoma's hagiographers, "that army officers at the highest echelon of government had preferred Udoma for the job because of his brilliance and seniority at the Bench."[67] It is no surprise that the army angled for Udoma, but it was not because of his "brilliance." It was because he had been an ally of executive power in every judicial appointment he had held.

In February 1975, Gowon made a speech to law ministers from thirty-four Commonwealth countries who had gathered in Lagos for their annual conference. He assured them that his government both "operates with a constitutional framework" and "maintains a deep respect for the rule of law and constitutional legality." Neither of these things was true. Nigeria's constitution had been abandoned for nearly a decade, and the "rule of law" meant little after *Lakanmi*'s nullification. But most of the ministers listening to him were in no position to point out this hypocrisy. Dictatorship was spreading rapidly across the former British Empire, and only a few months later Indira Gandhi would declare a state of emergency in the largest common-law country of them all, India.[68] Her law minister, H. R. Gokhale, who would draft some of the harshest measures of the Indian emergency, was probably in the audience for Gowon's address (members of his delegation certainly were). Perhaps they were emboldened by what they saw in Lagos, watching their fellow ministers politely assent as Gowon insisted that Nigeria's emergency measures "need not be construed as an aberration from the over-riding premise of the rule of law." To my knowledge Indira Gandhi did not cite African precedent to justify India's state of emergency, but her lawyers certainly knew what was going on in Nigeria.

Over time, judiciaries throughout Africa would see their ability to constrain executive power diminish even further. "The tempo by which our country is governed," wrote Nigerian law professor Olu Onagoruwa in 1990, "places more emphasis on power rather than right, on force rather than morality, on executive rascality and deceit rather than decorum and humane consideration." By the 1990s, the Nigerian military had so fully captured the state that judges could simply be commanded. General Ibrahim Babangida, he wrote, legitimized his power "by the sheer force of his own metamorphosis—a legal Frankenstein capable of consuming its creator."[69] Some observers came to doubt whether law had any real meaning in postcolonial Africa. As the Kenyan jurist Yash Ghai wrote, "Public consciousness is relatively unmarked by the discourse of rights, democracy or justice. The rule of law is a quixotic idea, although there are certainly ministers and lawyers who will pay lip service to it on suitably ceremonial occasions. More prevalent is the discourse of power."[70] Indeed, it was raw struggles for executive power, not sober debates between judges, that characterized most African politics in the late twentieth century.

Nonetheless, autocrats like Babangida, Amin, or Obote (who returned to power in 1981) continued to seek the approval of judges, both for their coups and for the decisions they made once they were in charge. What usurper regimes sought in law was legitimacy—both to their own people and to the wider community of nation-states. "The legitimizing effect of judicial recognition seems to fulfill a psychological-*cum*-political need of a regime which is obviously seeking to promote its own stability," wrote Farooq Hassan. "Clearly, acquiescence or acceptance by the courts of the previous government provides a uniquely valuable source of credibility for the revolutionary government."[71] They also sought tools to help them "discipline" society, such as the suspension of habeas corpus, which some judges were willing to give them. In the end, authoritarians usually got their way whether they had the support of their judiciaries or not. If a judge refused to be pliant, he could be overruled, removed, or, if all else failed, assassinated. Even so, it was better to have a judge's stamp of approval than not. The judges most likely to give it were foreigners.

Legal Challenges to Military Rule

As Ademola's ruling in *Lakanmi* shows, not all judges in military regimes accommodated authoritarianism. There were judges who moved in the same circles as Udoma who worked doggedly to keep soldiers out of politics. Some critiqued executive power from the bench, and several paid a high price for it.[72] We might consider Frederick Kwasi Apaloo, the Ghanaian Supreme Court justice who tenaciously sat on the court from Kwame Nkrumah's administration through Jerry Rawlings's. His attempts to constrain executive power perturbed all eleven of the governments (civilian and military) he served, and both Nkrumah and Rawlings tried unsuccessfully to remove him. After retiring, he became chief justice of Kenya in 1993. There, just like at home, he provoked the dictatorship of Daniel arap Moi by crusading against the death penalty. But unlike in Ghana, in Kenya Moi could get rid of his mouthy chief justice because he was a foreigner. Apaloo returned home after less than two years.[73]

Another important critic of military rule was Akinola Aguda, the Nigerian judge who served as Botswana's first African chief justice and later as the pugnacious director of the Nigerian Institute of Advanced Legal Studies at the University of Lagos. Aguda cut through the flimsy legal and intellectual scaffolding that upheld military rule. Why were soldiers in charge? "The only reason is that they control our guns," he answered in 1986. "No more, no less. Is that a viable political arrangement? Why not a government formed entirely of the trade union leaders? Or the doctors? Or the architects? Or the engineers? Or the lawyers? The only reason is that these people have not got guns."[74] Aguda took great risks in saying this while a military regime was in power (even though, as a law professor, he was more insulated from the military than those who held current judicial appointments). He had taken similar risks while on the Botswana Court of Appeal, where he made a landmark ruling against corporal punishment.[75] The Nigerian Institute of Advanced Legal Studies carried on the activist tradition that Aguda started, becoming pushier with the military the more repressive it became.[76]

Aguda's critique of military rule included a rejection of the positivism that judges had used to accommodate usurper regimes. He was withering toward his fellow judges: "Legal justice is justice according to the law as it is. Most lawyers and judges are quite satisfied with this, but I think that they are wrong. They are satisfied because of their English common law education founded on Austinian positivism. The other members of the elitist professions: medicine, engineering, accountancy, etc., and even the armed forces (catapulted in this regard!) cannot care less because of their bulging bank accounts."[77] Aguda upbraided the Nigerian judiciary for allowing soldiers to annul constitutions, legitimizing their heavy-handedness and gilding the destruction of legal protections as acts of "decolonisation." Any judge who gave credence to a military regime "should resign his appointment," he wrote, naming those whose actions he found especially shameful. The argument that they derived from Kelsen—that the "effectiveness" of a military regime was also proof of its legality—was, in his view, a cowardly "face-saving formula."[78] It was a self-serving interpretation that allowed them to keep their comfortable positions while leaving civilians defenseless against the military.

It would perhaps be asking too much of Udoma and others like him to have acted differently. A judge in a usurper regime is caught between a rock and a hard place. By continuing to serve he gives the regime a measure of legitimacy, but there wouldn't be much point in quitting. As Carlson Anyangwe writes, "no revolutionary regime has ever surrendered its newly won power for the sake of a judge's unhappy conscience."[79] This is a defeatist view, but it reflects the calculations judges have to make when faced with a case like *Matovu* or *Lakanmi*. The victories courts won against militaries were usually Pyrrhic—a judge might find his decision simply annulled, as in Nigeria, or he might face an even worse fate. In Amin's Uganda, there was no need to cultivate a judiciary that would support the executive's decisions. If a judge stood in his way, Amin simply had him killed.[80] Civilian courts were gelded by military dictators, who preferred tribunals (for soldiers and civilians alike), commissions of inquiry, or their own commands as instruments of law. Decisions like *Matovu* opened the door to dictatorship, but soldiers might have forced it open anyway.

It is significant that the *Matovu* decision, which profoundly shaped Uganda's postcolonial history, was not made by a Ugandan judge. Udoma's turn in Uganda illustrates a larger principle: it is easier for a judge to rule against the public good when she or he is not part of the "public" in question. He is not the only proof of this concept. We could look to any of the British judges who preceded him on the Ugandan bench who, to understate things, *also* made rulings that didn't benefit the Ugandan public. We might also consider James John Skinner, an Irish-born judge who became a fellow traveler to Zambia's nationalist movement. Skinner became a Zambian citizen at independence, and in 1969 he was appointed chief justice of his adopted country. In this position, he was a vocal defender of the independence of the judiciary, and he confronted Kenneth Kaunda several times over political matters.[81] Aware that he was wearing out his welcome, in 1970 Skinner accepted a position as chief justice of Malawi when the incumbent judge retired. In Malawi, where he had no status and no history, he would be less querulous. He would make no principled stands against executive power from the Malawian bench, and he settled into a copacetic relationship with the autocratic president who hired him, Hastings Banda. Up until his retirement in 1985, Skinner sided with the government on nearly everything, from banning miniskirts to allowing Banda to be president for life.

Another example is Philip Telford Georges, the Dominican judge who served as chief justice of Tanzania from 1965 to 1971. The Tanzanian Supreme Court heard few legal challenges to the ruling party's increasingly autocratic conduct during these eventful years, even as the country remade itself through villagization and implemented a radical new form of socialism— transformations that one would expect would keep the Supreme Court busy. The court was mostly silent on these transformations, partly because

Tanzania's chief justice was a foreigner from a small country who could be sent home if he rocked the boat. Georges developed a legal philosophy that largely accommodated *ujamaa*, the massive project of social and economic reorganization that the party implemented, rather than challenging it.[82] Skinner and Telford Georges were not necessarily bad judges, but they saw the sword hanging above them. Knowing they might be deported at any minute, they usually placated the governments they served. This could entail giving a legal gloss to a usurper, turning a blind eye to repression, or handing a civilian president a blank check. Putting their rhetorical commitments to indigenization aside, presidents and generals hired expatriate judges because they were pliable and disposable.

Conclusion

Udoma and others like him cast a long shadow in the places where they served. In Uganda, parts of *Matovu* remain in force today, and the form of military rule that *Lakanmi* enabled in Nigeria lasted for the next three decades. In Uganda, many jurists used the language of haunting to describe how *Matovu*'s legacy persisted.[83] Ghost metaphors are not to be trusted—saying that one thing "haunts" another is often a ploy to link phenomena that can't be connected concretely, and maybe don't connect at all. But here the ghost metaphor is apt; you can see the specter of these decisions in African politics. When Uganda's president detains dissidents, *Matovu* whispers in his ear. When Nigeria's president dismisses challenges by executive order, *Lakanmi* hovers just out of sight.

In the aftermath of colonialism, Pan-African cooperation forged paths across the continent, and imperial connections were remade as postcolonial solidarities. Once Africa's new states were connected by these circuits, there was no telling what would move along them. Sometimes they carried radical ideas about decolonization, new art forms, and new philosophies. At others, they carried absolutism and its legal contrivances. Cooperation made coups and the jurisprudence underpinning them portable, and judges like Udoma were the ones who carried it in their baggage. Behind the story of the portable coup is a larger point: independence had a dual spirit. One of those spirits was liberatory, but the choices soldiers and judges made did not always bend toward freedom. Its other spirit was martial. In many former British colonies, that was the one that prevailed.

Part II.

Militarism's Legal Forms

4

ORACLES AND AUTOCRATS

The Uses of Customary Law

Outside the village of Umuneoha, near Owerri in eastern Nigeria, is an over-grown house surrounded by police barriers. The house and the forested land that stretches out behind it is the home of an oracle named Igwekala. It has a checkered past. Like other oracles in the region, Igwekala played a role in feeding enslaved people into Atlantic slavery in the eighteenth and nineteenth centuries.[1] In the twentieth century it was banned, burned, and rebuilt multiple times. Igwekala was many things. Depending on what angle you viewed it from, it could look like an object, a spirit, a relationship, an institution, or a scam. In the first centuries of its existence it occupied a large piece of wood, which was destroyed by zealous Christian converts around 1900. Those who continued to believe in Igwekala's power argued that it needed no object to serve as its host; it became an invisible force that moved freely around the plot of thickly forested land it "owned." It was associated with fertility, and women struggling to conceive traveled from across the region to seek its assistance. Oracles also had judicial functions, and people consulted Igwekala to settle disputes over land, property, and family affairs.[2]

The shrine was also a business, and Igwekala's priests charged fees to render a decision. A series of rituals would be performed, the litigants were made to wait for a time, more fees were paid, and eventually the priests revealed the oracle's decision. How the oracle operated, and how the priests discerned its will, was a secret. To skeptics, this secrecy was proof that it was a fraud. Its only enforcement mechanism was fear; the parties were told that if they didn't follow through on the oracle's decision, it would "eat" them. A visitor in the 1960s described it as "a carefully organized affair with its own priesthood and a descending order of assistants." An "army of agents" served as middlemen between the priests and the public, and local people made money by renting rooms to visitors. The cost of a consultation depended on "the wealth of the individual and the cleverness of the agent in magnifying the client's future doom if the oracle is not consulted."[3]

The oracle was an instrument of "custom"—the assemblage of norms and institutions that constituted everyday law across much of rural Africa. Custom was a blanket term for the quotidian ways people resolved disputes, structured their families, transferred property, and punished misconduct. It was a sort of folk law.[4] Finding it cheap and effective, the British put custom (sometimes also called "native law") at the center of their rural administrative strategy throughout Africa. A century later, soldiers would do the same thing. To both British colonial officials and the soldiers who ruled in their stead, custom was useful because it could veil repression in "tradition."

Igwekala is an unusual motif to describe customary law. Unlike other implements of custom, it has been statutorily prohibited since 1897, and it remains illegal today under the Witchcraft and Juju Order of sections 207(2) and 210(f) of the Nigerian Criminal Code, which mentions it specifically. But in spite of its prohibition, people quietly consulted Igwekala throughout the twentieth century. After independence, the Nigerian government sometimes enforced the ban and sometimes didn't. The fact that it was technically illegal makes Igwekala distinct from other implements of custom that, far from being proscribed, were encouraged during colonialism and after.[5]

But Igwekala's checkered reputation also makes it a good index of how Nigerians, and the British before them, measured custom; for its "authenticity," on the one hand, and its "repugnance" to prevailing morals on the other. Like the colonial administration, military regimes found that custom was most useful when it found a balancing point: locally credible but not *so* credible that it might compete with their authority.[6] Many who lived under customary law saw the British hand hovering behind it; custom was a burden that had been foisted on them, not something that truly belonged to them. Some saw custom as an accurate reflection of their moral and cultural values, but they tended to be the people who benefited from it most—chiefs, men, and elders.

The oracle has no written records, which is not surprising given that it was pushed underground before the advent of literacy in the region. But even fully legal, officially recognized instruments of custom—those endowed with authority by the British and supported by military regimes after they left—kept sparse records. Few cases from customary courts were recorded in written form, and even fewer are still extant. Those that survive were typically recorded because they went up to magistrate's courts on appeal. Unlike the other legal forms described in this book (including tribunals, commissions of inquiry, and common-law courts), I cannot describe customary disputes in much detail. There are far more extant records from "secret" military tribunals than from customary courts, even though custom was the primary form of law used by tens of millions of rural people. There is a reason for this: the tracelessness of customary law was part of its appeal, first to the British and later to the military. Customary law itself could be useful as a tool of repression, but soldiers didn't use it against their most important enemies. When military prosecutors wanted to punish high-profile opponents, they tried them for treason in tribunals or wore them down through commissions of inquiry. In contrast, the people they turned customary law against were seldom well known or well connected. Custom was a law for commoners, and like most institutions designed for those at the bottom it gave powerful people a wide berth. They, in turn, usually avoided it.

Nigeria's military regimes valued customary law. They took its African characteristics at face value, believing that "traditional" laws could be the building blocks of a genuinely decolonized legal system. They relied heavily on customary courts to dispense justice and resolve disputes, and they tolerated judicial instruments like Igwekala that civilian governments had outlawed. To understand why military regimes embraced custom, this chapter traces the rise, fall, and rise of "customary law" in twentieth-century Nigeria. It begins with the advent of colonialism in Nigeria, when "custom"—how people resolved problems among themselves—became part of the colonial state's administrative repertoire. Projects to standardize and formalize customary law were abandoned after independence in 1960, and civilian jurists argued that there was no place for custom in modern jurisprudence. After the coups of 1966 that ushered in military rule, soldiers came to appreciate customary law for its frugality and for its sharpness; it was useful for disciplinary projects of all kinds.[7] Under military rule, custom moved back toward the center of the Nigerian legal system. Jurists began a long debate about whether "traditional" customs could replace the English common law as the basis for the law of independent countries.

Custom and Colonialism

Customary law's authority was predicated on the idea that it its origins lay in "time immemorial," as the boilerplate of customary statutes went.[8] In fact, these "timeless" customs often had fairly shallow histories. Historically, Igwekala was only the second-most powerful oracle in southeastern Nigeria. The first was Ibini Ukpabi, also known as the Arochukwu Long Juju, which, like Igwekala, had become prominent in the context of the transatlantic slave trade.[9] Ibini Ukpabi resided in a cave in the forest near Arochukwu, at the nexus between the coast and the densely populated Igbo-speaking inland regions. The oracle served a dual purpose. First, it was a source of justice. The oracle and the priests who maintained it used it to discern the will of Chukwu, a paramount god, in disputes and criminal proceedings. Matters of adultery, theft, and the violation of various taboos were all adjudicated before it. But as slave traders demanded larger and larger numbers of en-slaved people, the oracle also came to have an economic function.[10] When it imposed a penalty (which was often), the guilty party would be spirited away to the coast, where European traders waited with cash in hand to buy the person being punished. The priests who controlled the shrine benefited financially from this arrangement, and when the Atlantic system declined they adapted to the "legitimate" economy in palm oil by furnishing labor for it—again through punishment. As British rule expanded in the late nine-teenth century the oracle's influence shrunk, and a British expedition de-stroyed Ibini Ukpabi in 1901.

Several oracles survived the colonial conquest, however, and Igwekala was one of them. News of Ibini Ukpabi's destruction was brought to Umuneoha by an itinerant hunter. During the British occupation of Umuneoha, Igwekala was hidden, and the human sacrifice that allegedly "fed" it was driven under-ground. It survived surreptitiously, and the colonial administration resign-edly admitted that the shrines could not be "wiped out" from the maze of ravines and waterways in the area.[11] In the same breath that they banned Ig-wekala, the British deputized "traditional" authorities to administer villages on their behalf, and created a "customary" legal system to resolve disputes and punish crimes—tasks that the oracles had previously served. These courts were to be the sole arbiters of custom.[12] The first Native Court in the Igbo-speaking region of the east was established at Akwete in 1897, where the British charged the local judges "to apply Igbo customary law modified to agree with British sense of justice and natural law."[13]

Customary law took different forms from one place to another. Its most common expression was in village courts and councils of elders, although more metaphysical judicial implements like divination also had a place in it. In theory, customary law was limited to areas of personal law, chieftaincy, and low-level criminal matters. In practice, it embraced all areas of life. Matters like marriage, divorce, and probate were usually adjudicated by customary courts. So were disputes over land ownership, which swelled as the British crammed the region's vast array of land tenure systems into a singular model of ownership they could recognize. Customary courts also had jurisdiction over criminal matters, including trespass (which was important for land cases), assault, sanitation offenses, larceny, and dealing in diseased meat, but their scope waxed and waned over time.[14] The only matters that were fully off limits to customary courts were those involving Europeans. White skin was a jurisdictional bright line, and British administrators feared nothing more than the scene of a black judge casting judgment on a white merchant or bureaucrat.[15] That image would puncture the myth of British infallibility, they feared, and embolden the colonial government's critics.

Customary law was the legal logic of the administrative philosophy known as "indirect rule." This was the name given to the British policy of rule through existing authorities, which mobilized "natural" rulers like chiefs and kings to do the day-to-day business of colonial administration, especially in rural areas. Indirect rule was most closely associated with Lord Frederick Lugard, whose 1914 amalgamation of the northern and southern provinces made Nigeria into one colony. Lugard argued that colonial governors ought to leave in place the existing structures of governance that predated their arrival. A British administrator would be perched at the top of the hierarchy, but he was kept mostly out of sight, giving the appearance that the local chief, emir, or king was still the one in charge. Deputizing local authorities to rule on behalf of the British was cheaper, more efficient, and less likely to provoke dissent than the wholesale replacement of indigenous institutions with British ones. British administrators, the colonial theoretician Margery Perham described, were not like sculptors, trying to carve a new kind of person out of "human clay." Rather, "they were more like tailors trying to make the garments of their administration fit the restless, heterogeneous and swiftly growing shapes of their African wards."[16] The main appeal of this strategy was that it was cheap; it gave the maximum coercion for the minimum expenditure.

Decisions in customary courts were made on the basis of traditions and pseudotraditions, ranked against one another through a hazy logic of which ones were oldest. Practices that had "always" existed trumped those that had recent origins—unless they were inconvenient to a chief or village elder, in which cases the historical logic became blurry. In theory, customary law was a positivist form of law; it was what people did in a given place, and it was located "in the breasts of the judges" rather than in a code. Its purest form was in the memory of "the older generation, grey-haired African aristocrats, looking like Roman senators [in] locally made togas," as a young Udo Udoma argued. "They, and those African women who, arrayed in gaudy bubas [blouses], walk the street with naked feet, constitute the living link between the past and the present."[17] Custom was "the law prevailing in a particular locality among a particular ethnic group," as one jurist argued, "be it gerontocratic, acephalous, or chiefly."[18] "Customary law is an expression of the behaviouristic patterns among a people," described another.[19]

Custom was actually much less authentic than its defenders made it seem. The British had cherry-picked African traditions, preserving only the ones that served colonial interests. If a customary principle worked against those interests, there were ways to erase it from "tradition" and replace it with something more expedient. A "repugnancy clause" was written into British policy about custom, which ensured that any "indecent" practice could be stricken from a customary legal system, even if it was authentically "traditional."[20] Child marriage, trial by ordeal, and widow burning were the practices the British cited most often to defend the clause's necessity.[21] As for Igwekala, the oracle's connection to slavery was enough to deem it "repugnant." The prohibition of Igwekala made a mockery of the idea that customary law was actually about preserving local normative orders. Oracles were among the most important traditional judicial tools in the region, and yet the British banned them. Why?

They banned what they felt they couldn't control. If a custom seemed too powerful, dissident, arcane, or too spookily metaphysical, they called it "repugnant" and banished it from customary law.[22] At the end of the day, *custom* was whatever colonial administrators said it was. What resulted was a form of "decentralized despotism," as Mahmood Mamdani called it, which could be adapted to serve whatever ends the colonial state wanted.[23] The colonial government did nothing so much as tax people, and customary law was useful for collecting taxes because it allowed chiefs to punish defaulters harshly and swiftly. It was also useful in controlling migration to the cities; it tied people to their home villages through a web of obligations that kept them working on farms, where the British wanted them. It reinforced conservative ideas about gender and the family, which were forces of stability. Customary law fused political and judicial authority in one person—a chief, a king, or a *qadi*—which was convenient when a provocateur had to be silenced.[24] Colonial administrators liked customary law because they believed it was "naturally" authoritarian, even though they were the ones who had made it that way.

Opposition to Customary Law

Customary law had many detractors. African lawyers saw it as a backwater of the legal system. Critics argued that custom was a cudgel the British had handed to the chiefs, and colonial officials admitted it was susceptible to political manipulation (which was both what made it useful to them *and* what made it dangerous). Little customary law had been codified, and even when it was written down it was open to interpretation. Lord Hailey, the British social scientist much respected by colonial administrators, had warned that custom could not be expected to remain unchanged given how much colonization had altered African societies. Nigerian lawyers agreed. In 1956, one chastised the colonial government for ignoring the obvious: "If they are to play their part in the modern world, native institutions must undergo changes which may eventually make them unrecognizable."[25] But colonial jurists continued to believe that "indigenous tradition" could be preserved in modern law, like an ancient insect trapped in amber.

Customary courts were notorious for their corruption, disorganization, and excessive sentences. Corporal punishment was common.[26] There was a "bewildering" array of native courts, each with its rules about jurisdiction and appeal.[27] A schematic diagram of the eastern region's courts looked "like a map of the underground railways in London," as one lawyer complained. A colonial officer in the north observed that "the number of grades of court was unlimited, the permutations and combinations between the various grades of courts, the various classes of persons and the various classes of cases almost makes one's head reel."[28] The fact that many customary court judges were illiterate, which the British had once celebrated as proof of their authenticity, came to be embarrassing. Appointments to most customary courts required no education whatsoever, and poor character did not disqualify a candidate.[29] Judges could be petty—some were notorious for issuing fines on the spot to anyone who didn't rise when they entered a room. Others used their courts to enrich themselves, reward their friends, or punish their rivals.[30] Customary courts' rules of evidence relied on "boundary marks and the fragile memories of old men," as a teacher remarked in her memoirs. "They seemed so intensely local, concerned with this very stone and that very tree and with what the other old man had been heard to declare his father had once said. . . . Such fundamentals hardly seemed to have a place in the elegant legal edifice of enactments and precedents."[31]

In the leadup to independence, more and more people saw customary law as a relic of colonialism. Custom posited that Nigeria was made up of people with clear, singular ethnic identities who could be parceled out into jurisdictions on the basis of those identities. This was not easy to square with the ambition of creating a single country. Nationalists in the National Council of Nigeria and the Cameroons (the political party that took the most unitary view of Nigeria) argued that custom was inappropriate for a country where everyone was a citizen. All Nigerians, Nnamdi Azikiwe argued, ought to all be accountable to the same laws. After the Second World War, the colonial government "retreated from the undiluted Native Authority system," especially in the east, as Afigbo wrote. It adopted a more flexible system of appointments to native courts and administrations, allowing "the educated elements the opportunity to flood the local government councils," to the disappointment of the chiefs and the relief of most others.[32] The use of corporal punishment was banned (with one exception—whipping was still allowed for "male juveniles," who were thought to be irredeemable through other means).[33]

Some Nigerians defended customary law and the broader system of "native administration" it served. Unsurprisingly, its most ardent supporters were chiefs. "The argument that Chiefs tend to be unprogressive and autocratic does not hold water," wrote a group of eastern chiefs during the drafting of Nigeria's constitution, "because chiefs rule at the pleasure of the people and those in authority have less power than the people who place them there."[34] But the number of people who believed this diminished with every passing year. Among intellectuals, a consensus emerged that colonial administrators had played a kind of trick on Nigerians, convincing them that customary law was truly "traditional," and truly theirs.[35]

In the first flush of independence, those who were tasked with organizing Nigeria's legal system looked to many sources. They looked elsewhere in Africa, including to countries like Ghana and Sudan that were already independent, to the United States, India, and of course to the United Kingdom. This didn't mean that Nigeria could adopt other countries' structures wholesale. "Unlike a motor-car, political systems cannot be usefully imported in their *exact* patterns and forms," wrote Akpan. "For unlike the solid earth on which the motor-car can be operated in whatever country to which it may be imported, the people among whom political systems operate have peculiar feelings, peculiar needs, and a past which cannot be ignored."[36] No matter what they took as their model, however, they shared one conviction: "traditional" modes of governance and their corollaries in customary law were not the answer. Custom was not a resource—it was a *problem*.

During the Nigerian First Republic, jurists spoke as if custom was on its way out. As a law professor at the University of Nigeria–Nsukka explained to a group of visiting Americans in 1964, the importance of customary law in Nigeria was "diminishing as our legal system grows."[37] In some parts of the country, especially in the north, jurists defended custom. But even there, the consensus was that if it was to survive, it had to become more legible and more systematic. The old conviction that custom ought to be "authentic" began to fall away. "Customary courts are like a lady," wrote a federal administrator. "To keep her beauty, her dress should be trimmed and changed from time to time, to be kept up to date with fashions."[38] In the east, the jurisdiction of customary courts was reduced to just matters of family law and chiefly succession.[39] Elsewhere, Native Courts were reformed along the lines of English County Courts—with panels of citizens making decisions, rather than single chiefs, and members designated as justices of the peace. They also were given a clear structure of appeal (typically to magistrate's courts).[40] As F. A. Ajayi wrote, "contrary to certain fallacies that once held the field, but happily not now so widely accepted, that the Customary Law of simpler societies is, among other things, rigid and immutable, there is ample evidence that it has some inherent capacity for self-development."[41]

Strangely, it was British academics who had the greatest faith that African custom could be modernized. The push to reform custom was led by the legal scholar Antony Allott at the School of Oriental and African Studies in London, where his Restatement of African Law Project helped newly independent countries in Africa standardize, codify, and recalibrate their systems of customary law.[42] It was funded by a British charity, and it involved researchers from across the continent. Nigeria was one of its most important sites, and his Nigerian students were among the project's most prolific contributors.[43] Allott's goal was to systematize custom, and to provide the grounding for a "modern" customary law that would be robust and "nationally appropriate." A famous British judge who advised the project described it as a final gesture of goodwill for the colonies. Africa "will soon be on the march," Lord Denning declaimed. "Can we not help it [put] on its coat for the journey—it is a coat of many colours—the coat of African law?"[44] Allott sometimes talked about the project as the first step in unifying the continent's legal systems. "One may hope that the by-product of the conference," he said at one of the many international summits he hosted, "will be a coming together, or at least a harmonisation, of the different national legal systems in Africa in fields of mutual concern."[45]

Critics of the project argued that codifying customary law would void it of meaning. "The courts are not to by hypnotized by the authority of print," argued a skeptical Nigerian Supreme Court justice. "The crucial fact is that a book cannot be cross-examined, either as to the opinions expressed or as to the claims of the author to have special knowledge."[46] Others argued that codifying custom would obviate its greatest value—flexibility—which administrators liked because it gave them broad powers. Civil libertarians worried for a different reason: a rigid, codified version of custom would subject "modern life" to "a kind of mummified ancient law."[47] Those at the top of the Nigerian judiciary saw the project as folly. To Chief Justice Adetokunbo Ademola, custom was irredeemable, and the volumes that Allott's researchers produced were no more than ethnographic curiosities. Irony abounded: while European academics were busy making "African law" in London, African judges in Lagos were arguing that justice was best served by the English common law.

* * *

In independent Nigeria, Igwekala became a symbol of custom's backwardness and atavism. It was already formally banned, but in the first year of independence the federal government decided to enforce that ban. In 1960, the Nigerian Police Force opened an investigation, and two years later, on 22 April 1962, the shrine precinct was raided. Forty-eight people were charged with managing an illegal secret society, and most of them were found guilty. The head priest, Ndodo Nwosu, was sentenced to life in prison, the shrine's buildings were razed, and the forest was fenced in.

A cache of written solicitations to the oracle was seized, which gave a sense of how it worked and who consulted it. Some of the illicit appeals to the oracle were legalistic, concerning property disputes or family matters that the supplicants believed were better served by the oracle than the court. Others were simple requests. "Please try to help me to pass my standard six examination this year," went one. "Please further help me to marriy a good husband which can love me too much."[48] Igwekala was no longer an object of dread like it was in the time of Atlantic slavery, but Nigerian officials still saw it as a problem. Not only was it fraudulent, as an Owerri court ruled, it was an embarrassment to the modern judiciary.[49] In their minds, Igwekala was a totem of the superstition and antiquarianism that ruled customary law. Life should be governed by law, not superstition, and modern people should bring their problems to a magistrate, not an oracle. There was no place for mysticism in modern law, and Nigerians deserved something better than custom.

Custom under Military Rule

After the January 1966 coup toppled the Nigerian First Republic, the government made an about-face in its stance toward custom. The soldiers now running the country began to argue that custom had its uses. The customary court "is a poor man's court," wrote a military jurist, handy for providing cheap and speedy justice, while "preserving the custom, practices and usages of natives much harrowed by Western Law."[50] It could be used to enforce order in the countryside, keep unruly women in check, and silence opponents without the messiness of due process. Military rulers saw chiefs as allies in the their disciplinary "revolutions." Rural chiefs would help soldiers whip the country into shape. "Since our present pressing problem is Indiscipline, maybe a look at our old village society may put us on course," wrote Justice Chukwudifu Oputa.[51] Selfishness, alienation, greed, and irresponsibility had all crept into the Nigerian psyche through colonialism, Oputa argued. A return to "tradition" would purge those bad qualities. Soldiers found custom useful to this end, much to the dismay of modernizers like Akpan who had tried to minimize its place in Nigerian law. Under military rule, jurists gave credence to customary principles that their predecessors had fought tooth and nail.

Custom appealed to military governments not only because it was a tool for their disciplinary arsenal, but because it undermined the more liberal wing of the judiciary. Judges of the Supreme Court and the High Courts were among the few people who dared to criticize soldiers, as the military had learned in the *Lakanmi* case.[52] Soldiers were wary of going after judges directly. Their ideology of law and order gave them a begrudging respect for the courts, and jailing judges would be a bridge too far for most of them. What they could do, however, was empower the judiciary's most conservative and most easily manipulated members—the chiefs who presided over customary courts. Chiefs were often willing clients, and they were pliable in a way that legally trained judges, with all their high-minded rigidity, were not.

After the military takeover, the Federal Military Government increased the number of customary courts, expanded their powers, and rolled back attempts to "modernize" them. "Go deep into customary laws," the military governor of Plateau State told a Customary Courts Reform Committee in 1977. "You should try and feel the pulse of the people" and find "common aspects" of customary law that could be adopted nationally.[53] In a white paper, lawyers for the military government argued that every "distinct community" the length and width of the country should have its own customary court.[54] In the Mid-West State, military governor David Ejoor presided over a dramatic expansion of customary law while at the same time promising to reform the customary courts, standardize them, and prevent them from being politicized. "The hope was that in due course our nation's laws would be more definitively founded on the customary laws of our peoples," he wrote.[55] Chief Justice Taslim Elias, not typically an ally of the military, wrote approvingly of the return of customary law: "Although native or customary courts virtually disappeared in many states, they are now happily and suddenly re-emerging. This is a very commendable step, for all said and done these are the courts that have complete jurisdiction over you and I."[56]

In the north, some small-town emirs welcomed the return of customary law because they thought it would enhance their powers. They wanted to make sure, however, that Islamic law was given its own status, "separate from the Folk (Customary) legal traditions of the animist communities." "Since British occupation," wrote Ahmed Beita Yusuf, a law lecturer in Zaria, "both the Sharia and the legal tradition of the non-Moslem peoples, particularly in the north, have been erroneously lumped under a single vague label, 'native law and custom.'" This had been an error, he argued, but otherwise the reification of custom and Sharia under colonialism had been a good thing. After independence, the government had erred by failing to see custom's "wonderfully redeeming qualities." "Besides," he went on, "these redeeming qualities will no doubt rhyme well with the changing social and legal conditions in this country"—namely, military dictatorship.[57]

Some civilians welcomed customary law as a sign of decolonization. In 1975, an editorialist in a Lagos tabloid wrote that Nigerians didn't recognize English law as their own. "Perhaps the greatest injustice which the illiterate majority in Nigerian society is suffering, is the fact that they are being governed by bureaucrats and under laws alien to the traditional world, in the making of which they had never been consulted and the existence of which they were hardly aware." This alienation had created a crisis of credibility. "Little wonder that in exasperation—apart from the fact that he cannot afford the legal fees—the [common] man, believing that the matchet is better than the lawyer, administers instant justice; that the mob stones to death a self-confessing witch, or batters a thief on the spot, or beats to death unceremoniously a man believed to inflict impotence on a person by mere touching or handshake." All of these were preferred over "the imported white man's legal system."[58] The problem, a businessman in Imo State wrote, was "our lawyers, who are more British than the British." "The lawyers rigidly believe that justice is reached through a process, and therefore have so much regard for 'technicalities' . . . which baffle those who seek justice through the courts." Custom had no such technicalities, he argued, and it offered a purer, more "frictionless" form of justice. Customary law would give the "illiterate masses" a form of law that they could recognize.[59]

Law's rituals could be made more traditional too. Many believed that customary oaths were more effective at convincing people to tell the truth than oaths taken on Bibles or Korans. "'I swear by Ogun, the god of Iron . . .' How about that as an innovation?" asked a newspaper editorialist approvingly. "When people swear to juju," Chief Christopher Obumseli argued, "their conscience can prick for they will recall an instance where in the past someone has had to bear the brunt of invoking the name of the village juju in vain."[60] The convention of taking oaths on the Bible "remains British and derived and developed from the British way of life," observed a lawyer. "If one really wants to get the truth on oath from a Nigerian, one has to go down to his ethnic origin. . . . In my little clan, if a person swears with knife and mixed human blood (not more than the quantity mixed in some of the drugs one takes occasionally), the truth will be heard." These kinds of oaths, which custom's defenders believed Africans found more frightening and effective, ought to be integrated into *all* African courts. "I am not suggesting that we should go back to the primitive age entirely," he clarified. "But if something is good and effective, let's bring it from that gone-by age."[61]

Customary law had a veneer of popular legitimacy. Military regimes had learned from their colonial predecessors that custom was useful in exerting control while concealing where the exertion came from—making it seem like the village chief who handed down a judgment was calling the shots rather than the district officer (or soldier) standing behind him.[62] From a distance, custom looked like an organic legal system that had emerged from the grassroots. But this was just an illusion. Customary law's *grundnorm* was not to be found in any kind of consent to be governed. As Nwabueze wrote in the late 1970s, a customary court's "compulsory character derives from the fact that it is a *state* power, backed by the full authority and coercive sanction of the state, an attribute that distinguishes it from the authority of an arbitrator which is derived from the consent of the parties themselves."[63] It is this notion of custom—*völkisch* legal positivism given teeth by the state—that Nigeria's military regimes found useful. This may seem counterintuitive, given that the more common sense of "custom" is a system of rules that are *un*official, emerging from social consensus that emerges informally, beyond the reach of the state. But in twentieth-century Africa, customary law was inseparable from state power.

"A Genuinely African Body of Law": Custom and Legal Reform under Military Rule

There was a larger ideological force behind the return of customary law: "Tradition" was part of soldiers' vision for decolonization. They believed custom could be part of a reparative project to restore the ethical world colonialism had destroyed.[64] There was some historical irony in this—"custom" was at least partially a British invention, so a return to customary law was actually a return to colonial ways. Nonetheless, its defenders argued, custom was closer to the soul of African life than any other type of law. There was something genuinely African about custom, Oputa argued, riffing on Chinua Achebe: "Before the advent of colonialism and its devastating impact on our indigenous culture and our subsequent alienation, we lived in small village communities. In those communities, the influences surrounding the individual were relatively steady, uniform, harmonious and consistent. The village community was a society *strictly disciplined by cultural norms and mores. Things then fell apart.*" Colonialism had left Nigeria caught between the traditions of the past and a new society that had not yet been born. "We have been uprooted from our indigenous culture but not able wholly to assimilate the culture of our erstwhile colonial masters. We are on the trapeze between the death of an old civilization and the swing to the beginning of a new one."[65] The new society Oputa hoped to land in was one that was modern but had an ethical foundation of its own. It mattered less what this foundation *was* than what it was *not*—that is to say, British.

Soldiers and their friends in the judiciary argued that the common-law system Nigeria had inherited from Britain was deficient. They rued the fact that Nigerian law didn't have an African character. Nwabueze held the most damning view: "The present generation of African judges is handicapped by the fact that their education in England and in the techniques of English law has insulated them from the values and needs of their own people. Their minds have become imbued with ideas about the unquestionability of parliamentary legislation under English law and about the perfection and symmetry of the common law to render them almost incapable of performing effectively the more creative role demanded of them by constitutional adjudication under a written constitution."[66] The endurance of the English common law was a legacy of imperialism, and it was one of the factors keeping the country from coalescing as a true nation.

Military jurists found a remedy in a unified system of custom that they hoped could one day replace the English common law.[67] From being mere "village law," preoccupied with pilfered livestock and petty infidelities, custom could rise to the level of a national legal system—one that spoke to local realities and was self-consciously African in nature. They pointed out the fact that African customs were no more parochial than the medieval English rules that had become universalized as "law" through Europe's colonization of the rest of the world. After all, English law's origins *also* lay in rustic superstitions and countrified conservativism (i.e., feudalism). It was only with time that the English common law took on its dignified, ecumenical character, and the same would eventually happen with African custom. In the meantime, customary principles were more "appropriate" for Nigeria's needs, and they would better serve the task of decolonization.

Returning to those principles required filtering out colonialism's contamination. "At a time when the glamour of some of our indigenous laws seems to be dwindling to abysmal ignorance," a court administrator argued, customary law needed formal, statutory recognition if it was going to survive. Custom had been "mutilated" and "falsified" by "authors who were spoonfed with distorted opinions by ethnic groups who desired to be placed in positions of honour and advantage" by the British.[68] They believed that empiricism could solve this problem, and jurists who favored custom encouraged the collection and publication of customary statutes. This time the collecting would be done not by Allott and his army of research assistants in London but by the Federal Military Government itself.[69]

Jurists sympathetic to custom argued that Nigeria's hundreds of "native" legal systems could be harmonized.[70] There were nearly as many customary legal systems as there were villages, one law professor wrote, but the principles they shared were "so overwhelming that they overrule completely the advertised differences[,] which are either consciously or sub-consciously over-exaggerated to demonstrate the primitivity and incohesiveness of the black man."[71] With a few modest reforms, customary courts could be made the center of Nigeria's legal system. Omoniyi Adewoye argued that all African normative orders shared an ethos: "Always the objective was to seek a genuine settlement that would disperse all feelings of rancor and restore harmony to the whole community. This constant effort at peace-keeping is a distinguishing feature of African traditional jurisprudence."[72] There was a "measure of basic uniformity" across customary traditions, Nwabueze believed, which led him to argue that custom might serve as the foundation of "a genuinely African body of law."[73] A single system of African law that applied to everyone was possible, and it could be discovered by superimposing customs on top of one another to see which principles they shared. Once those principles were known, jurists could draw a line of best fit through them. That would become the basis of a general system of custom recognizable to all Nigerians.

What were those customary principles that inspired such faith? Nobody ever spelled out the specifics. When asked to describe what made custom valuable, soldiers usually mentioned efficiency. Customary courts meted out punishments quickly and cheaply, which was appealing in light of Nigeria's trenchant criminological problems. But "efficiency" didn't answer the question. Although they seldom said so explicitly, the customary principles they most valued were the ones that compelled people to work and kept them from moving around too much. These included the rights of men to keep women from leaving their homes and of older men to control the labor of younger men. Although soldiers were young men themselves, they differentiated themselves from the irrepressible migrants from the countryside (a *lumpenproletariat* known in Nigeria as "area boys"). They saw themselves as good sons who respected their elders and their chiefs, and a kind of filial piety was woven into the ideology of discipline they espoused.[74] Powerful customary prohibitions on vagrancy, for example, could keep young men on the farms rather than in the towns where they might abandon their duties to their families. In personal law, bride prices, which nearly all customary systems recognized, could keep young women under the thumb of their husbands and fathers. But aside from general values and a handful of shared principles, jurists like Oputa and Nwabueze were vague about what a universal system of customary law would look like.

They were clearer about which customary principles they did *not* want revived. They had no interest in principles that might deter investment, like strong entitlements to use land by the people who occupied it—Nigeria's military regimes courted foreign capital assiduously, and no one wanted to spook investors. Also off the table were customary rights that women had lost over the course of colonial rule. Military rulers had no nostalgia for the forms of power Nigerian women had wielded in the past, and they would not broker the views of feminists who argued that precolonial models of womanhood could empower Nigerian women in the present. Prominent intellectuals like Ifi Amadiume and Oyèrónkẹ́ Oyěwùmí made these arguments from exile in the 1980s and 1990s, when military rule was firmly entrenched. But the African "senses" they wanted to bring back—flexible notions of gender, a fluid logic of sexual difference, a meaningful place for women in politics—were not the ones that men like Babangida and Abacha wanted to resuscitate.[75]

Like their colonial predecessors, postcolonial jurists struggled with what custom should look like. How would a unified system of custom reconcile principles that were at odds with one another? Would Islamic law be considered "customary," and if so, how would it be squared with "pagan" regimes of personal law? How would this unified system of custom be implemented? As a code? Would it be imposed through decree, like everything else in military regimes? Even more fundamentally, how would jurists know what the scattered, mostly oral customary laws they wanted to implement *were*?[76] Military jurists fell back on vague bromides to argue that "native law" was all more or less the same. They cited proverbs as evidence of broadly shared principles, arguing that they could be the basis of laws.[77]

There were many problems with this approach. For one thing, the principles that were general enough that they applied everywhere were not very useful in founding a legal system. Folksy proverbs did not provide answers to the complex questions that came up in a vast, diverse, industrializing society like Nigeria. Moreover, there were real differences between different customary traditions, which general doctrines merely papered over. A certain spirit might be shared across African laws and modes of reasoning, but as soon as one drilled down into the details it became clear that they weren't all commensurable with each other. Custom also changed over time, which a codified system of custom could not account for. To historically minded jurists, this was a cardinal sin. "In retrospect," Omoniyi Adewoye wrote, "it was futile to embark upon a policy aimed at simply 'preserving' the traditional."[78] "Custom" was a moving target, and there was no reason to believe that it was going to stop moving once it had been written down. Moreover, its value to authoritarian governments (be they colonial or military) lay in its malleability—it was a blank that could be filled in with whatever was convenient. Standardizing and codifying it would make it less flexible, and therefore less useful as an administrative tool. It would become an "artificial dehydration of customary law," the jurist Alexander Nékám argued, which would be useful to nobody.[79]

Finally, it was hard to avoid ethnic chauvinism in arguments for custom. During military rule, philosophers like Sophie Olúwọlé led the charge in arguing that African ontologies made dormant by colonialism could be revived. Soldiers were receptive to this idea, and the notion that African customs and "traditional" systems of thought could serve as the basis of government appealed to Nigerians across the political spectrum. But not all traditions were equal. Revival could slip into jingoism: "Yoruba Philosophy is better than Western Philosophy," Olúwọlé said in a candid interview shortly before she died. "We are better than them."[80] Nearly every proponent of a unified system of custom had one *particular* customary tradition in mind as the basis for it—which was often the one he or she came from. One jurist wrote that he had "no doubt" that the normative order he had learned in his village "can be found in the hearts and minds of peoples of other tribes in Nigeria."[81] If this was true, it was only true in a very general sense.

A unified customary law never came to pass, but military regimes found Nigeria's bricolage of customs useful all the same.[82] Lawyers, for their part, continued to mistrust custom despite the military's embrace of it. "Any pedantic advocacy for exclusive adoption of our customary law as our sole source of law," wrote a civil rights lawyer during the Abacha regime, "will have the unfortunate tendency to hang traditions like fetters upon the hands of reformative enterprise."[83] This was exactly what soldiers liked about it.

Conclusion

For the Igwekala oracle, military rule was a heyday. Igwekala's grove was damaged during the Nigerian Civil War, first by the secessionist government of Biafra (which, like the Nigerian First Republic, was wary of custom) and subsequently by the Nigerian occupation. The town of Umuneoha was spared, however, which some local people took as a sign of Igwekala's power. After the war, it remained a "prohibited juju," but the shrine's business quietly boomed under military rule. The investigations and raids of the early 1960s were not repeated, and it operated relatively openly under several military administrations. Even though it was technically illegal, Igwekala was useful, both to the military government and to the people who consulted it. Nigerians went to Igwekala not because they saw it as "just" or even necessarily because they believed in its powers. Rather, they used it because it rendered cheap and speedy decisions. From commercial disputes to matters of the heart, sometimes it is less important where a decision comes from—be it a judge, a chief, or an oracle—than whether the parties accept it. If oracles, chiefs, and other "traditional" entities made rules that bent toward "discipline" and rendered decisions that fostered "harmony," as many soldiers believed they did, they let them flourish.

After the return of civilian rule in 1999, the prohibition of Igwekala—which had been on the books the whole time—was enforced again. The shrine has been raided several times since then, following accusations that its priests were engaged in human sacrifice, or meddling with electoral politics, or some jumbled combination of the two.[84] Igwekala is officially out of commission, but it isn't really gone. Today, it is rumored to play a role in many of Nigeria's criminal industries, including fraud and drug trading. Oracles are also used to explain human trafficking.[85] Towns in the region are part of a network that brings young women from southern Nigeria to Europe to engage in sex work, domestic labor, or jobs that are a little of both. Antitrafficking agencies maintain that women are "tricked" by "juju" oaths to convince them to go and to scare them away from absconding when they arrive in Palermo or Paris.[86] Urbane young women probably aren't duped by the theatrics of oracles, and their decisions are better explained by debt and a lack of local opportunity.[87] Nonetheless, oracles still have a grip on the public imagination. Today as in the past, those who want to control people's labor and movement find custom and its totems useful—whether they're formally recognized as law or not.

5

FELA KUTI GOES TO COURT

The Spectacle of Inquiry

For three weeks in March 1977, a crowd came to the National Theatre in Lagos to see Fela Anikulapo Kuti, Nigeria's most celebrated performer. They were not there for a show, but for a trial—or, more precisely, a "commission of inquiry." On 18 February, a month prior, soldiers had raided the Kalakuta Republic, the compound where Fela, as he was known, lived and performed with his large entourage. Over a hundred people were injured in the raid, and the building was burned to the ground. Nigeria's military government convened a commission to investigate the soldiers, but it was just as much an investigation of their victim—Fela. This would be Fela's first and only appearance on the National Theatre's stage, and he treated it like a performance. "I am the star of this show," he began his testimony. "Everybody who comes here must mention Fela's name, Fela's house and about Fela's house being burnt. So, it is important for you to hear me a little bit deeper."[1]

The commissioners heard not only from Fela but from nearly two hundred of his friends, neighbors, and enemies. The commission's records run over a thousand pages, which are full of details about Fela, his circle, and the workings of the Kalakuta Republic as a business. There are inventories of the personal effects of his band members, records of his financial dealings, and testimonies by his friends, lovers, and rivals.[2] Here, I examine Fela's legal ordeal for what it shows about law under military dictatorship, but a cultural historian would find something different in this archive. Militarism had its own modes of artistic expression, and soldiers were not philistines.[3] Nonetheless, the works of art that have endured from this era are the ones that critiqued them: Fela's music, the novels of Chinua Achebe and Buchi Emecheta, the plays of Wole Soyinka—all of whom were targets of the military at one point. Fela's music and his entanglements with the law were always related, but it is in the courtroom, not the nightclub, where his life most reveals the machinery of power.

The commission of inquiry at the National Theatre was a performance, but Fela wasn't the only one on stage. The commissioners were performing too, for both the Nigerian public and a wider international audience. Fela had devotees across Africa and the African diaspora, and his fans in Europe and North America (of whom he had more with every passing month) paid attention to how his government treated him. His fame was wide enough that the military feared the raid might reflect poorly on Nigeria abroad. General Olusegun Obasanjo staged the inquiry to perform his government's accountability, while also making sure that "justice" was rendered on his terms.[4] Obasanjo was not the first of Nigeria's leaders to find inquiry useful as a judicial tool, nor would he be the last. This chapter considers inquiry as a legal form under military rule. Where did it come from? What were its structures and objectives? What did it achieve, both for the state that convened it and for the people who testified before it? What kinds of justice could come out of a commission of inquiry? And just as importantly, what did it foreclose?

Inquiry as a Legal Form

The term *inquiry* sounds more inviting than *trial* or *tribunal*. This is by design. In the contemporary model of restorative justice, a commission of inquiry is usually a state's attempt to find a moral way that has been lost. A commission inquires, but it does not punish. It can forensically examine what happened during a given time period, lay bare structural inequalities, or suggest a framework for redress. The best-known example is South Africa's Truth and Reconciliation Commission, which examined the causes and consequences of white minority rule.[5] This vast endeavor was a form of "reconciliation without justice," as Mahmood Mamdani called it, which attempted to repair the psychic (but not economic) harm of apartheid without holding its perpetrators criminally responsible.[6] In the early 2000s, Nigeria itself had a "truth and reconciliation"–style inquiry into the abuses of military rule, the Human Rights Violations Investigation Commission.[7] These inquiries were not punitive. They had weak or nonexistent enforcement mechanisms, and if they made recommendations about redress they were just that— recommendations, not orders.[8] They had a mixed record of success, and some were vague about what "success" would look like. In theory, however, they all served a reparative purpose. They educated the public about the past, made a space for victims to enunciate their grief, and recorded that grief for the benefit of future generations. But not all inquiries aim for "repair" (how-ever partial or politicized). States also use inquiries to harass, repress, or cast doubt upon those they deem enemies. Just as any legal procedure can free or constrain people depending on how it is used, a commission of inquiry can heal, but it can also wound. It is this injurious model of inquiry, not the reparative one, that Nigeria's military regimes found useful. The mere act of inquiring could be a kind of punishment.

As a judicial form, the inquiry has a long history in Africa. Its genealogy is colonial.[9] A staggering number of inquiries took place during British rule, on every type of administrative problem imaginable. Colonial inquiries tack-led topics including corruption, government expenditures, and customary law. Some inquiries addressed colony-level political questions, such as the Willinck Commission on ethnic minorities in federal politics. Others exam-ined very local matters, such as the decades-long dispute over the chieftaincy of the House of Docemo in Lagos.[10] Some criminal matters, notably suicides, were dealt with through inquests, which bore a close resemblance to inqui-ries.[11] Episodes of civil unrest were often followed by inquiries, sometimes concurrently with criminal trials.[12] The best-known inquiry of the colonial period was the hearing on the *Ogu Umunwaanyi*, an anticolonial movement led by women in Aba in 1929 over taxes.[13] In Aba, the commissioners were less interested in figuring out what conditions had led to the uprising than they were in making sure it didn't happen again. This points to a fundamental quality of colonial commissions of inquiry: they did not aim to repair harm. Rather, they provided an outlet for dissent to keep it from getting out of hand. What was important was the *appearance* of justice, not justice in some substantive form (retributive, reparative, or any other).

After independence in 1960, Nigeria's governments continued to stage commissions of inquiry. Inquiries about chieftaincy appointments, land disputes, and the demarcation of borders between communities—all com-mon during colonialism—continued under the Nigerian First Republic.[14]

Commissions also began to investigate matters in the public interest, like the rate of school fees or the licensing requirements for doctors and engineers. There was a flurry of inquiries into the misuse of public funds, as politicians turned accusations of corruption against one another.[15] These were a new development. Inquiries that might undermine the colonial government had seldom taken place under British rule, and the notion that an inquiry might serve the public good—to protect consumers, for example, or to improve government efficiency—was an innovation of independence.

Under military rule, commissions of inquiry gained a new importance. Soldiers turned them into the centerpiece of administrative law. From 1966, when the first military coup took place, to 1999, when military rule came to an end, I count over seven hundred inquiries at the federal and state levels alone. Like the colonial model they followed, most were quasi-judicial investigative panels, convened for a set period of time to examine a particular issue. They were inquisitorial rather than adversarial, which put them at odds with the rest of Nigeria's common-law system.[16] Their members were appointed by the Supreme Military Council (the clique of officers who constituted the executive branch) or by a state administrator, depending on whether they were federal or state initiatives. They typically consisted of one or two military officers (some with legal training but most without) and a civilian judge (often retired). Most had the authority to issue subpoenas and summon witnesses.

The commission would meet, hear evidence, and deliberate about what course of action the government should take. The proceedings were dutifully recorded, transcribed, typeset, and published by the government printer. Some inquiries lasted only a day, resulting in a brief report. Others, like the 1977 Fela Kuti inquiry, ran for several weeks, and their reports ran into multiple volumes. Most of those reports were available for sale to the public. Some reproduced the entire testimony that had been collected, while others only outlined the matter at hand and issued terse recommendations. This report was advisory, but it was usually followed by a government white paper where the state publicly responded and laid out its intended actions. The state typically followed through on the commission's recommendations, which stood to reason given that the commissioners were appointed by the state military governor. He usually left no doubt about what outcome he wanted.

To military regimes, commissions of inquiry were preferable to other legal forms for several reasons. By virtue of the fact that they weren't trials, they gave the state a blank check. They were unconstrained by the normal rules of procedure, which made it easier to make accusations of wrongdoing stick.

They could interrogate witnesses and make pronouncements in whatever way they wanted, unencumbered by the conventions of regular legal proceedings. In a regular trial, there was always a chance that an independent-minded judge might deliver a ruling against the state. In an inquiry, the military could simply ignore the commissioners' final report if it wasn't to their liking. Commissions could not issue criminal convictions, but they could damage reputations. No one came out of one looking entirely innocent. The very act of inquiring suggested that the investigated party was somehow at fault. Although they presented themselves as objective and "truth-seeking," commissions of inquiry were blatantly political. The form also lent itself to spectacle. It encouraged grandstanding by witnesses and fiery statements from judges, and inquiries filled the galleries with journalists and spectators.[17] The more famous the person being investigated, the more sensational the inquiry—and there was no bigger showman in Nigeria than Fela.

The Events at 14A Agege Motor Road

The incident that would put Fela Kuti in the dock took place at 14A Agege Motor Road, a large house in a walled compound in an outlying area of Lagos. Fela had lived there since the early 1970s, accompanied by his mother and a large troupe of musicians, lovers, and hangers-on. The compound was home to a raucous nightclub called The Shrine (sometimes styled the Afrikan Shrine), where Fela performed with his band, Africa 70. It also housed a medical clinic run by his brother Beko, and there were stalls that sold food and drinks to the nightclub's patrons. Fela called the place Kalakuta—a reference to the infamous Black Hole of Calcutta, which he had meditated on during an earlier prison sentence. In a 1976 stunt, he declared independence from Nigeria and proclaimed himself president of the Kalakuta Republic. The borders of this micronation were the compound's walls. He also founded a radical youth organization called the Young African Pioneers, which he claimed had twenty-five thousand members. All of this was political theater, but it got under the army's skin.

The series of events that ended in the destruction of the Kalakuta Republic began with a traffic violation. Around noon on 18 February 1977, a member of Fela's entourage drove a Range Rover with the Africa 70 logo painted on the side the wrong way down a one-way street. He was stopped by a policeman, they argued, and the young man refused to surrender the car. Some soldiers loitering nearby got involved, and the situation escalated. At some point, a motorcycle belonging to one of the soldiers was set on fire

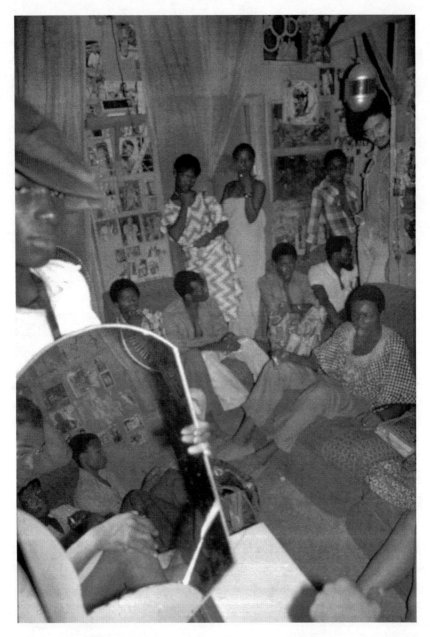

FIGURE 5.1. Scene at the Kalakuta Republic, Fela Anikulapo Kuti reflected in mirror at far left, 1977. Photo by B. Barbey.

(it was unclear how), and this became the pretext for a raid. The soldiers went to the Abalti Barracks, which was a short walk from The Shrine. They returned with over a hundred men in uniform, led by a Major Dawodu of the Nigerian Army. As the soldiers amassed outside the gate, Fela and his attendants gathered on a balcony looking down on them. One held a gaudy umbrella over him.[18] Fela rained down insults. "You stupid people," he addressed the soldiers, boasting that the only person who could touch him was a fellow president. "Go and call your Obasanjo himself to come and arrest me. You cannot do anything with us, you idiots!" A group of women began singing "Zombie," an antimilitary song Fela had released the year before. This whipped the soldiers up into a frenzy. The women's "provocation" became "an excuse to vent their spleen as would be expected," as the commission later concluded.[19] Soldiers from the nearby barracks testified that Fela and his followers had long treated them with disdain, calling them "beasts and robots" and taunting them in the streets around The Shrine. He routinely brought out the nightclub's loudspeakers and blared his music in the direction of the Abalti Barracks, they complained. One of Fela's confidants later blamed him for provoking the raid. "With tact and diplomacy, he would have gotten away with it," Lemi Ghariokwu recalled. "One of his boys burnt an army motorcycle. This should have been settled amicably."[20]

The compound was encircled by an electrified fence, so Major Dawodu sent an officer to a nearby substation to cut off the neighborhood's power supply. As soon as the power went off, one of Fela's men hooked up a mobile generator to the fence and turned it on. In the soldiers' account, the voltage of the fence was too high for the generator, and it exploded. It was this explosion, they claimed, that set fire to the compound. It spread quickly because the food kiosks ringing the perimeter had gas cylinders for cooking, which erupted in a chain reaction, surrounding the building with a wall of fire. Others gave a different version of how the fire started. An electrician testified that a generator couldn't explode in the way the soldiers described. Fela's business manager stated that he saw the soldiers douse it with petrol so it would blow up, and several women hiding in a cobbler's shop next door said that they had seen a soldier splashing kerosene over the compound wall. Complete chaos followed. The people who were inside the Kalakuta Republic scattered when it started burning, some into the arms of the soldiers waiting outside. Others climbed over the walls into the adjoining compounds, where they tried to barricade themselves in. Fela and several women took refuge in the house next door, which was owned by a Lebanese businessman. His maid, who was the only one at home at the time, became an important witness. Fela hid in a back room, and it was there that he was apprehended. A soldier claimed that he wrestled a rifle away from Fela during his arrest, although the gun was lost in the tumult (there may have never been one).[21]

By the end of the melee, 113 people had been hurt. The injuries were serious. Fela's road manager's intestines were exposed, at least two people lost eyes, and the nurses who treated the wounded expressed surprise that no one had died. Residents of the neighborhood reported that soldiers had looted cars and houses. The Shrine had been burned to the ground, and the adjoining buildings where people had taken refuge were heavily damaged. Those who were seriously hurt were taken to Lagos University Teaching Hospital for medical treatment, and everyone else was taken to the Abalti Barracks, where they were stripped naked and packed into a room together while the military figured out what to do with them. That evening, "anyone who could stand on his legs" was collected from the hospital and taken to a military base, where they were paraded before troops who "taunted us notwithstanding the fact that we were already half dead. They did all sorts of atrocities to us."[22] From there they were taken to a police station and then to Kirikiri Prison, where some were kept for a few days and others a few weeks. Several were still in jail by the time the inquiry began a month later.

The Commission of Inquiry at the National Theatre, March 1977

The inquiry was a field day for the press, and it was largely thanks to them that it took place at all. A new newspaper called *The Punch* (now one of Nigeria's largest) made its name reporting on the raid, and its articles made it difficult for the military government to sweep the matter under the carpet. It wasn't only the raid's visibility that made it hard to ignore but the type of people who were targeted. Fela and his associates weren't the only ones who suffered; the soldiers harassed everyone in the area, including people with no connection to him. Many of the victims were denizens of the down-at-heel neighborhood where the Kalakuta Republic stood, but some of them were well-connected people. The raid took place during the evening rush hour, and white-collar workers commuting home to the wealthy parts of Ikeja stopped to watch the commotion. Some stayed too long and became targets themselves. They included the wife of a federal civil servant, a professor of religion, and an official of the Ministry of Health. The fact that people with money and clout had gotten hurt made the possibility of a scandal greater. If all the complainants had been poor, the whole matter might have been more easily ignored. Instead, the Lagos State Ministry of Justice convened an inquiry, supported by the Federal Ministry of Justice and the Supreme Military Council.

The inquiry was chaired by a civilian judge, Kalu Okpan Anyah of the High Court of Imo State, and a military officer, Wing Commander Hamza Abdullahi of the Nigeria Air Force.[23] The proceedings lasted from 7 to 28 March 1977, after which the commissioners deliberated and issued a set of recommendations to the state government. Anyah emphasized that the inquiry was administrative, not judicial. Its purpose was not to mete out punishments—neither to Fela nor to any of the soldiers who had been involved in the events. Rather, the commission's purpose was to discern the truth. "It is the desire of the Lagos State Government," he declared "and, I am sure, that of every true Nigerian citizen that the facts must be truthfully stated for the good of our country and our friends abroad."[24] No one was on trial, and witnesses were not allowed to have legal representation for that reason. The Ransome-Kuti family's lawyer Tunji Braithwaite objected to the ban on lawyers, as did Aka Bashorun, who attended the hearings on behalf of the Nigerian Bar Association. They saw that the inquiry was about more than Fela Kuti's treatment. As Bashorun said, it was "not only investigating the incident of 18th February 1977, but also the rule of law."[25]

The proceedings were open to everyone, and any member of the public could testify by filing their name and address with the state government. The decision to hold it at the National Theatre in Lagos, which could accommodate some seven thousand people, made it especially spectacular. Inside the hall, the audience made their feelings known about what was being said on the stand. The greatest rancor came when victims displayed their wounds, or when Fela's friends made especially scandalous accusations. The transcript recorded the crowd's reactions—"uproar," "laughter," "hissing," and "jeering." There was a circus-like atmosphere in the theater, and itinerant vendors selling snacks had to be chased out more than once. For those watching the proceedings, they were equal parts spectacle of justice and entertaining day out.

The commission of inquiry was biased against Fela. From the order of witnesses to the nature of the questioning, the commissioners made clear whose side they were on. Nonetheless, the fact that the inquiry happened at all suggests that the military saw value in at least performing impartiality. Although the judges scolded witnesses who went on too long or strayed from the topic, no one who wanted to testify was turned away. When witnesses couldn't speak English or pidgin, translators were found to accommodate them. When they reported that soldiers were lurking outside the theater, hassling people who had testified against the military, civilian policemen were called in to patrol the area. The commissioners constantly reassured witnesses that they were not out to entrap anyone. Some of Fela's friends were facing charges of property destruction or drug possession in regular courts. They were told that the inquiry was unconnected to those charges, and the judges assured them that they could speak freely without fear of indicting themselves.[26] Most witnesses appear to have spoken candidly, although all (wisely) denied drug use.

Members of Fela's entourage testified that the soldiers treated them cruelly. "One of the things they did once they caught any of us," Fela's manager attested, "be he a man or a woman, was that they would strip him naked, take all his belongings, whatever he had on him before they started to beat him."[27] One woman after another described being sexually assaulted.[28] The commission treated all of them with incredulity. The government doctor who examined the women added insult to injury by testifying that any damage to their genitals had probably been caused by venereal disease, not assault.[29] The court gave much weight to the testimony of a female army nurse who treated them, reasoning that "as a woman," she was "the proper person to confirm" whether they had been sexually assaulted. She testified that they had merely been "rough handled."[30] One dancer closed her statement by angrily offering to "open my body for you to see" her injuries, to which the chairman responded by reprimanding her for "indecency."[31] Subsequent witnesses also tried to remove their clothes on the witness stand, which scandalized the judges. "Most of them threatened to strip themselves naked to expose their private parts but were restrained by us," Anyah carped. "By their style of dressing which leaves them half-nude and their movement and behavior in public as we see them, they have [come] perilously near to debasing the coinage of womanhood."[32] Their nakedness was probably a deliberate provocation—nudity has a deep history as a form of remonstration in West Africa.[33] But it was also a form of testimony. The women who removed their clothes on the witness stand were trying to show evidence that they had been raped, in the hopes that the commissioners would believe their own eyes instead of the doctor's statement. This strategy backfired. To the commissioners, the women's comportment voided their credibility, allowing them to dismiss their accusations out of hand.

Witnesses did not hold back in their criticism of the military. "That day was worse than the day I lost my father," recalled one neighbor who was beaten up by the soldiers. "I did not expect to see such from the people that govern us."[34] Another testified that she thought the soldiers "were from another planet because of the things they were doing on that day, which were inhuman."[35] Fela's Young African Pioneers, especially, did not mince words. "Their men are just like Nazi troops," swore one, which a commissioner warned him was going too far.[36] "As they were beating everybody, I said that is real Army power. They respected nobody."[37] A few took the opportunity of being on the witness stand to editorialize about recent history:

> The army came to power with hope of protecting the lives of the citizens of this country. This was as a result of the political situation in this country in 1966. Now, these people who are meant to protect the lives of the citizens of this country are now destroying the lives of the citizens. Now, how safe are we when members of the armed forces are looting and even robbing with arms, because they carry guns there and this portrayed them as armed robbers. There were policemen who could have arrested Fela if he had committed any offense. Your Lordship, the decision is yours, I hope the lives of innocent citizens of this country would be saved, because we hear of this attack every day all over the place.[38]

An American musician who played with Fela, Arthur James Moore of Indianapolis, gave a long account of the day. He testified that "I have been with Fela when there was an attack or confrontation with the military, but the incident of the 18th of February was quite different because it was full of violence. In the previous incidents there had never been shooting or looting or burning."[39] Moore testified that he was with Fela when the raid started, and he had been there when he finally surrendered to the soldiers. "Some had guns, some had handlebars of motorcycles, some had crow bars, and one had an axe. Our surrender meant nothing to them. The men appeared as if they wanted to kill Fela and us." The commissioners usually stopped witnesses if they wandered beyond the questioning, but they let Moore go on at length:

> I do not wish to stay in Nigeria and I do not wish to be forced back to America and I do not want to go back there looking like this, penniless. I did not leave there penniless and a pauper. My brother, you see most of the black people in the United States of America have no consciousness or any interest in Africa at all. When I left there as I did, it took me eight years of planning to come to Africa. Most of them derided me saying, "What do you want to go to Africa for? Those people do not want you." That is of course the same thing the white Americans

were telling us there. We were as brain-washed there as Africa is brain-washed about the plight of Africans anywhere else and all these things I had to take. . . . My wife has left me. She said that I am a mad man to stay here. But when I was leaving I told them that I was going to Africa even if I am alone. Now I want my body to be treated by people who I trust and I am afraid to have it done in this country.

In anguish on the witness stand, Moore warned of how bad the raid made Nigeria look to the rest of the world. It was only out of racial solidarity, Moore said, that he would "never publish certain things that happened to me in the past fifteen months, because I know that all those imperialist governments are interested to undermine any African government."[40] Fela practiced this solidarity, Moore insisted, but the Nigerian military did not. The judges didn't allow sermonizing like this from anyone else. Perhaps they let him speak because he was a foreigner, or maybe it was because his injuries, including a gruesome wound on his face, made him an especially pitiable witness. Moore was right to point out that the rest of the world was paying attention to Nigeria. The military government knew it too, and Obasanjo's sense that he was being watched was part of what spurred the inquiry in the first place.

The judges bent themselves into knots to excuse Major Dawodu and his men. A shopkeeper testified that a rowdy group of soldiers had purchased a large amount of kerosene from her that afternoon—the same accelerant that others testified was used to start the fire. The commissioners turned this seemingly damning piece of evidence inside out; "If the soldiers decided to set fire to 14A Agege Motor Road," they reasoned, "they would not have gone to a woman like Madam Elizabeth Efenarhua to beg for kerosine [sic] since to do so would be creating evidence against themselves for the offence of arson." Madam Efenarhua's account suggested that this was exactly what they had done, but the commissioners used her testimony to exonerate them.[41] "We hate to think," they observed, "that troops from Abalti Barracks under the orders of Major Daudu [sic] could have become so loose and gone on rampage."[42] Instead, a group of anonymous men in uniform—several hundred of them, if Fela's testimony could be trusted—were blamed for the destruction. Busloads of unknown soldiers "from Ikeja" arrived at the scene, and men also marched to the area from Yaba.[43] Off-duty soldiers who happened to be "passing by" joined in the operation. Some were dressed for combat. They were heavily armed, with weapons "of the sort they used in the Biafra War," as one witness noted, "not meant for ordinary civilians like us but for the war front."[44]

The worst of the violence—the assaults, the arson, and also the beating back of the firemen who arrived to put out the blaze—was pinned on these nameless men in uniform.[45] The board of inquiry could not (or would not) deduce who the "unknown soldiers" were.[46] The commissioners argued that since the buses carrying them were civilian charters, they could not have been on official military business. They wore no insignia on their uniforms, which meant they could not be tracked. In fact, the soldiers were hardly "unknown." Several were recognized as having come from the Abalti Barracks, which emptied out the afternoon of the raid. But the state preferred for their identities to remain a mystery. The commissioners concluded that they were free agents who had appeared out of thin air and vanished the same way.[47] They couldn't be prosecuted if they couldn't be identified.

In their final report, the commissioners withheld judgment even as they admitted that the soldiers had crossed a line in their treatment of Fela. They made no recommendation that the military should punish the soldiers. The band members facing criminal charges for destroying government property (namely the burned motorcycle that started it all) would have to answer for themselves in criminal court, but the commission made no conjectures about what would happen to them there. The commissioners saved their greatest scorn for the Young African Pioneers:

> The boys and girls of 14A Agege Motor Road strike us as abnormal in the way they behave. To watch them testify at the inquiry was pity provoking. They exhibited such boldness and shamelessness as were more consistent with or characteristic of persons affected by drugs than those in mere distress. We have no doubt left in our minds that these girls and boys drug themselves with Indian Hemp [cannabis] which they all call "Erinmoore Flakes."[48]

The commissioners asked nearly everyone about their drug habits. Drug use was becoming the government's obsession, and the next regime would make drug trafficking a capital offense. Ironically, soldiers were probably the Nigerians who used drugs most. Cannabis became popular when servicemen brought sativa seeds back from Burma during the Second World War, and ever since the army had tolerated it as a form of "Dutch courage."[49] Using it in combat was one thing, but using it for pleasure, as Fela and his followers did, was quite another.

* * *

Many people were hurt on 18 February, but one victim stood out from the rest. The raid's most famous casualty was Fela's elderly mother, Funmilayo

Ransome-Kuti. Ransome-Kuti was a teacher and activist who had spent her entire life at the center of Nigerian politics—first in the nationalist movement and, after the military takeover, as a dissident.[50] Her fame exceeded that of anyone in her famous family except perhaps Fela, and she had much influence over his work.[51] Her name adorns institutions across the country, and schoolchildren learn that she was the first Nigerian woman to drive a car. In death, she became a symbol of the military's despotism.

Funmilayo Ransome-Kuti's ordeal on the day the Kalakuta Republic burned became national folklore. She was in an upstairs bedroom when the raid began, and when the building caught fire, she was trapped. A group of soldiers barged into the room and threw (or, in their account, "lowered") her from a second story window, ostensibly to save her from the smoke. Later, she became ill and depressed. She went into a coma in February 1978, about a year after her fall, and died. Fela blamed the army for her death. He staged a mock procession of her coffin from the ruins of the Kalakuta Republic to the Dodan Barracks in Ikoyi, where the military dictatorship was headquartered. It was one of the most chilling acts of protest in twentieth-century Africa. Like most of Fela's performances, it was draped in legend. And like with everything else about him, it's hard to distinguish lore from fact.

During the inquiry, what happened to Funmilayo Ransome-Kuti was a minor concern. Her defenestration was treated as a botched attempt to remove her from the burning building, not an assassination, as Fela would later construe it. After all, she was still alive at this point, and she was well enough to appear before the commission in person. The doctor who treated her testified that her only injury was a sprained ankle, which he corroborated with X-rays. As far as the commissioners were concerned, this was one injury out of many, and it was hardly the most serious one. Nonetheless, out of deference to her age and fame, they devoted a few hours to it.

One important witness was Alhaji Ganiyu Ajala, an economics teacher who watched the raid from the rooftop of his brother's house.[52] Ajala's account was valuable because he was the closest thing there was to an impartial observer; he was neither a soldier, nor a resident of the neighborhood, nor an acolyte of Fela. From the roof he had a panoramic view of the scene, which no other witness did. He found the soldiers' behavior "barbaric," but he also declared that, as a Muslim, he found Fela and his friends' "paganism" repugnant. Ajala's statement broadly corroborated Fela's description of the violence. His accounts of sexual assault matched those given by several women, as did his testimony of the arson and the looting of the nearby houses. The judges cast aspersions on Ajala. "You saw quite a lot, you know," one of them wryly observed after he had finished speaking. But there was reason to believe that Ajala *had* seen a lot, and he had less reason to distort or exaggerate it than anyone else questioned.

Ajala gave a different account of how Funmilayo Ransome-Kuti was injured than the one Fela made famous. Fela would claim that she had been "thrown" out of the window by the soldiers. At the inquiry, the soldiers testified that they had "lowered" her from that window as the building burned because the stairs were filled with smoke. Ajala said he had seen the soldiers marching her roughly down an exterior staircase through thick smoke. As they reached the bottom either she or one of the men stumbled, causing them to lose their footing and fall down the last three or four steps, splaying Ransome-Kuti unconscious on the ground. The only people who testified that she had been lowered from the upper floor to save her were soldiers, and they gave inconsistent and implausible accounts of how this had been done. Ajala's testimony suggested that both accounts were embellished—by the soldiers to make it seem like they were saving her from the blaze, and by Fela to make it seem like they were trying to kill her. The heavy smoke ensured that those who had seen her on the ground couldn't be quite sure how she had gotten there.

Fela long insisted that his mother died from her injuries, but the fact that she lived a full year after the events suggests the line of causation wasn't quite so straight. In several interviews with journalists, Ransome-Kuti herself recalled that she had been pulled by the hair and thrown from the window— but these same lively volleys with the press cast doubt on Fela's insistence that it had destroyed her will to live.[53] This doesn't mean the military had no role in her death; even a fall of the type Ajala described could be fatal to a person of her age, and the psychological damage of the experience was real even though it didn't appear in the physician's report. Nonetheless, if Ajala's account was right, the circumstances of her injury were different from the story that became canonical. Being jostled and being thrown out of a window are different orders of harm. Given that Funmilayo Ransome-Kuti's death became one of the most often-repeated proofs of the military's violence, it is worth dwelling on the specifics. We may be inclined to accept the word of a dissident over the soldiers who started the brawl, but both parties had an interest in exaggerating what happened.

Class and Decolonization

The reverence Fela Kuti inspired after his death has overdrawn his stature in his own times. He was a public figure in Nigeria, but this didn't mean he was widely loved. The forces arrayed against Fela were larger than the Nigerian military, and this is clear from the records of the inquiry. His opponents included Christians and Muslims who took issue with his "paganism," traditionalists who did not recognize his impressionistic practice of African religion, and women who found something suspect in his treatment of the young girls in his entourage.[54] Others saw through his affected pidgin, hearing behind it the London-educated scion of an elite family. In his actions, they saw not the principled protest of a radical but the hijinks of a playboy, protected by his wealth and connections. Fela's work is full of what his most celebrated interpreter, Tejumola Olaniyan, called "antinomies"—contradictions or ironies that confound those looking for a clear message from his work. He was a "cosmopolitan nativist" who performed African authenticity with European instruments, an antiauthoritarian who ran his own household with despotic precision, and a feminist who, as Olaniyan wrote, "gave many boys of my generation a language for our sexism, and made that sexist language extremely musically pleasurable."[55] These points of intense friction structure every aspect of his work. They also confound simplistic readings of his life, and they're part of what makes him a figure of enduring interest. One antinomy, less obvious than these, is his class position in the military dictatorship.

Fela's working-class neighbors occupied the bottom rungs of Nigerian society, and those who testified against him had many reasons to dislike him. They had long complained about the noise, drug use, and general turpitude of the Kalakuta Republic, but even more frustrating was the air of untouchability that surrounded Fela. "He has a republic within the Republic of Nigeria," an elderly neighbor complained. "His men are a group of terror. They live by dope and drug. I usually go around correcting them. They do not yield." Fela's associates jeered at the neighborhood curmudgeon, but he continued his accusations: "Indian hemp and drugs. That is their business there, that is what they do there and I can bring somebody around here today whose mother and son they beat, too. They are terrors even to the Police. If a group of people can take the law into their own hands, I do not think there will be law and order in the country again."[56] Neighbors like the old man had complained about the Kalakuta Republic long before the raid, but the police had consistently declined to intervene. They claimed they didn't have the resources to respond to every call, but they also justified their inaction by noting that "a reasonable citizen of this country could not live around that area."[57] "Fela and his gang always treat people the way they like," claimed a young man who testified that the Young African Pioneers operated a racket in the neighborhood. "No police man will go to Fela's house because Fela will order his boys to beat him up."[58] The "prostitutes and hemp peddlers and smokers," who lived around the Kalakuta Republic, as well as the "general rudeness" of those who frequented it, made the area "the Soho of Lagos."[59] In their final report, the commissioners recommended that the entire area be razed.

Class differences jump off the page of the inquiry's transcript. Fela's statement does not survive in full, but it seems he was as charismatic on the witness stand as he was on stage. "He gave almost three hours of fun storytelling, creative art," complained an army officer who testified after him, "but almost 75% of what he said was utter falsehood."[60] There was a stark difference between how the soldiers and the artists expressed themselves. Fela and his family spoke in long statements in English, sharply reasoned and full of erudition. The Young African Pioneers were mostly teenagers, but even they were fluent during cross-examination, attesting to the fact that they had been to school.[61] In contrast, the soldiers, most of whom had no education at all, struggled to make themselves understood. The commissioners criticized their halting English and mocked their working-class argot—even though they were inclined to take the soldiers' side. For Fela, the pidgin he used onstage was a stylistic choice. But for the soldiers who testified against him, it was the only kind of English they spoke. Even the most junior members of Fela's entourage came from a higher social position than the soldiers who lived in the barracks down the street. Fela consistently presented himself as an underdog, but this wasn't quite the full story.

The controversy over Fela Kuti was one front in a much larger struggle over who would inherit power in postcolonial Africa. It was a contest between soldiers and the civilian professional elite—two factions of colonial society, still jockeying for position after decolonization. Fela came from a long line of people who had fought for independence and then lost the reins of power to upstart soldiers soon after it was won. The Ransome-Kuti family had nearly a century of political activism under their belts by the time Fela's compound was raided. Their critiques of colonialism had ranged from the Christian liberalism of his grandfather Josiah Ransome-Kuti, to Funmilayo Ransome-Kuti's dalliances with the international left in the 1930s, to the Black Consciousness of her son Fela. But for all their anti-imperialism, the family was tightly stitched into the empire. They had been educated in mission schools and British universities, which gave them the tools both to challenge imperialism and to thrive in it. They sat at the top of the colonial hierarchy, and their opposition to colonialism came from that elevated place. Even Fela had a British degree (from Trinity College of Music), and although he disavowed what he studied there, he never renounced the status it afforded him. In his initial confrontation with the soldiers, he bragged that "if he were in the Nigerian Army now he would have been a Brigadier or Colonel."[62] This was not an empty boast—Fela came from exactly the kind of family that produced leaders.[63] It counted elite politicians, doctors, intellectuals, and clergymen among its members. Military rule was profoundly frustrating to families like the Ransome-Kutis. It vexed them not only because they objected to it in principle, but because the unwashed grunts and hastily promoted generals leading the country were *not their kind of people.*

Most soldiers came from the bottom of the social order. As Ruth First observed, "No worthy Lagosian father, no successful lawyer or flourishing trader, would have dreamt of making his son a soldier."[64] The colonial military had recruited from rural areas, promising a leg up in the world to the sons of farmers and petty traders who otherwise had no hope of even a rudimentary education.[65] Military service appealed most to the poor; army pay was not high, but it was reliable, and soldiers were entitled to free clothing and housing. They didn't have to pay on buses or trains, and their children could enjoy barracks schools funded by the state. In most African countries, a soldier was "unlikely to find a job that would offer him comparable conditions," as one officer admitted.[66] After independence, the military continued to recruit from the bottom.

When those soldiers eventually seized power, they claimed their right to rule by arguing that civilian elites had fumbled the process of decolonization. The Ransome-Kuti family was emblematic of that elite class, and Fela's behavior added fuel to the fire. When he called soldiers "zombies," he meant that they continued performing colonialism's repressive tasks after the empire itself was dead. But he was at least as much a product of colonialism as they were. His surname had commanded respect since the advent of British rule. He moved in depraved European circles, and he embarrassed the new nation by proclaiming that his licentious, drug-fueled antics were an "authentic" mode of African expression. In contrast, soldiers saw themselves as true sons of the soil. Men in uniform hated Fela not only because he excoriated them as colonial stooges, but because *they* saw *him* as a symptom of colonialism—of its excesses, its pseudotraditions, and its disdain for subalterns. Rank-and-file soldiers knew they were at the bottom, and they lashed out when they felt someone was looking down on them. When Fela mocked them from his balcony, that was exactly what he was doing.

On the surface, what happened at Agege Motor Road was an attack on a freethinker and his circle by soldiers in the service of a neocolonial military regime. But to Fela's neighbors, to say nothing of the soldiers themselves, the day looked very different. Fela and his circle represented the undisciplined, bad-mannered civilian elite that had failed the country in its first years of independence. In their eyes, the half-clothed women and inebriated men who appeared before the board of inquiry were the dregs of a decadent, morally corrupt elite that military rule had swept from power. The raid was an assault on a bourgeoisie that had been allowed to go too far. From this angle, the animating spirit of military rule was neither neocolonialism nor sanctimony, but *the rage of a humiliated underclass.*

Truth and Justice in a Military Regime

The military government couldn't deny that the siege at Agege Motor Road had taken place, and the evidence of wrongdoing by soldiers was overwhelming. Hundreds of men had participated in the fracas. The military had staged a full-on assault in broad daylight, on a busy street in the capital city. Obasanjo faced criticism from many angles. Military hardliners argued that the state government had been too lenient toward what Fela's own supporters called a "secessionist movement." After all, a real act of secession had sparked Nigeria's Civil War only a few years ago, and the Kalakuta Republic's farcical "independence" mocked that tragedy. On the other side, many Nigerians were disturbed by the events; even those who found Fela distasteful didn't like the heavy-handed way he was treated. Some reckoning was bound to happen, but the military wanted to make sure it happened on their terms.

Making what might have been a trial into an *inquiry* served this purpose perfectly. This structure implied that *all* parties had done some wrong, including Fela himself, and it gave the commission license to pursue any avenue it wanted, whether that was cataloging the injuries the soldiers had inflicted or probing Fela's political activities in the years leading up to the raid. Unconstrained by rules of procedure, the commissioners could say whatever they wanted, blaming everyone and no one for what had happened. Since there was no verdict, the final report was hollow—people could fill it with whatever suited their politics. Those looking for a condemnation of the soldiers got one, but a reader looking for an indictment of Fela could find that too. Since the report was advisory, neither really mattered. No party was satisfied by this outcome, but all could feel vindicated by it. The thickly documented inquiry drowned objections in paper. When challenged, military administrators could point to the waist-high pile of evidence that had been collected. The commissioners' conclusions were not the point—rather, it was in the thousands of pages of documentation that "justice" was done. This justice was not very substantive, but the proof of it was there for anyone willing to purchase the nine volumes of the proceedings.[67]

Like any legal document, the commission's transcript is a record of how power could be deployed and resisted at a particular historical moment. In military Africa, commissions of inquiry functioned as tools of legitimation. They channeled grievances into places where they could be contained. They managed emotions, taming anger about events in the past so that they didn't threaten the order of things in the present. In this respect, they were like truth commissions anywhere. Commissions, as Adam Ashforth writes, "produce a rational and scientific administrative discourse out of the raw materials of political struggle and debate." The commission is "a theatre in which a central received 'truth' of modern State power is ritually played out before a public audience."[68] The Fela Kuti inquiry is a good example of this kind of performance. In the end, who started the fire, or what happened to Funmilayo Ransome-Kuti, is less important than what the inquiry reveals about the military junta's disposition toward justice. In it, we can see how soldiers reasoned, how they determined truth, and how they deployed "fair play"—the metaphor that soldier-statesmen used as their legal philosophy, flattening the vastly complicated calculus of law in a modern society into something like the rules of a football game.[69]

Olu Onagoruwa, a lawyer who attended the proceedings on behalf of the Nigerian Bar Association, argued that the inquiry had damaged the legal system's credibility. It had blurred the line between administrative and judicial inquiries, and the commissioners, in their "befogged and irredeemably facile analysis," had failed to see what had actually happened on the day in question. Justice Anya, especially, had "allowed Fela's irritating personality and life-style to weigh too heavily in his consideration of the facts." Most importantly, he argued, the inquiry had shown Nigerians that the law wouldn't protect them from aggression by the state—especially from the army. "For the first time in our history the whole weight of the coercive authority of the state as represented by the army had been brought against one unorthodox and eccentric individual." "Many people, particularly the common folks, are agonised by the sudden realisation that they live under a constitutional system in which their government is above the law and in which the interests and rights of the citizen can be damnified by the government or its agents, without any legal remedy."[70] Perhaps. But most Nigerians already knew that this was the case. Lawyers like Onagaruwa found this language useful in criticizing the state, but by 1977 the "common folks" had lived under military rule for over a decade—they knew how it worked. The only thing that made the military's pursuit of Fela unusual was that he was famous. Countless Nigerians were beaten by soldiers, and the military destroyed plenty of houses, not just Fela's. The slum clearances that punctuated Lagos life were also done in the name of cleaning up the streets, and the thousands they displaced never got their day in court. What made Fela's case different was that he was a public figure.

Nigerian civilians welcomed these commissions of inquiry—even demanded them—even though all they produced was paper. In the Fela Kuti inquiry, some witnesses appeared because the commission had subpoenaed them, but more came voluntarily. Why did they come, knowing that they might be humiliated, like the women the judges berated? It was because appearing before a commission of inquiry offered them something. Ordinary Nigerians had few avenues to stick up for themselves, and they had even fewer to complain about the everyday indignities doled out by men in uniform. They embraced commissions of inquiry because they had nowhere else to turn. There was no legislature that spoke for them and no constitution that enshrined their basic rights. Petitions usually fell on deaf ears. Publicly shaming soldiers sometimes worked, but that required some sort of platform. A commission of inquiry, which at least put their grievances on the record, was better than nothing. Nigerians called for these inquiries throughout military rule, despite the mounting evidence that not much came from them. Reading the transcripts of the Fela Kuti inquiry, one gets the sense that witnesses testified not only because they hoped for compensation or repair, but because speaking in public might bring some sort of catharsis. The state would listen to them and write down their names for posterity. For some, this was the only time in their lives when that would happen.

Those who were seeking a more tangible remedy (like financial restitution) weren't satisfied with getting it off the chest, but some still believed that a commission of inquiry might help. In the Fela inquiry, many witnesses concluded their statements by asking what the commission was going to do about their burned or looted belongings. The commissioners had them give detailed affidavits listing what they had lost, leading them to believe that they might be compensated. Dozens of inventories were collected, typeset, and published as part of the commission's final report. No one, to my knowledge, ever saw a kobo of reparation.[71] Fela and his family fought to be compensated for the destruction of the house for many years, to no avail. The family sued for damages several times over the next decade, and the state consistently responded that the Federal Military Government was immune on the basis of old common-law principle—"the King can do no wrong." Obasanjo was like a king, the court ruled, and the soldiers who staged the raid were like his servants.[72] Since the order for the raid had come from Obasanjo, the Nigerian state owed the family nothing for the harm it had caused them.

But sorting out compensation had never been the point of the commission, and for its *actual* purpose it was a complete success. It performed accountability by Nigeria's military regime, and it placated those who were concerned by how Fela had been treated (however they felt about him in general). It treated journalists to a spectacle, replete with salacious talk of sex and drugs, which distracted them from what the military was doing. Most importantly, it made it seem as if soldiers answered to someone. Whether they actually did was irrelevant.

Conclusion

After the military dictatorship was over, President Olusegun Obasanjo would testify about the raid before the Oputa Panel, the truth and reconciliation commission that he convened in 1999. Fela's brother Beko filed a petition to revisit the events at Agege Motor Road, which prompted the commission to subpoena Obasanjo himself about the raid. Having shed his military uniform and been democratically elected as a civilian president, Obasanjo was put in the unusual position of defending himself before an inquiry that he himself had convened, about a human rights violation that had transpired during his stint as a military ruler twenty-three years earlier.

When a lawyer challenged him about the impunity granted to the "unknown soldiers," Obasanjo rolled his eyes and answered with barely veiled contempt. "If that was the law, that was the law. I did not make the law, alright?" Pressed further, he vaguely blamed colonialism for the debacle (which he only dimly remembered). "I believe that law is dynamic. If in 1977 there were parts of our law that were colonial, then today maybe we need to amend them." At the end of his cross-examination, Obasanjo turned to the commissioners and addressed them directly. "Your purpose," he cautioned them, "is not to be an appellate court." Rather, it is "to establish truth, secure remorse, and forge reconciliation and forgiveness as the basis for peace and unity in our country."[73] It may come as a surprise that Nigeria's president would submit to cross-examination—or that he had allowed the Oputa Panel to happen in the first place. It is less surprising if we think back to the Fela Kuti inquiry, which had also happened under Obasanjo's watch. It had taught him the value of an inquiry. He knew that a "truth" commission could do him no real harm, and there was no danger for him to appear before it. Just like the Fela Kuti inquiry, Obasanjo staged the Oputa Panel because it was a way to vent hot tempers without any risk he might get burned.

Commissions of inquiry were very effective—not at dispensing justice, but at *simulating* it. This was Potemkin legalism; it was an imitation of law, with robes, gavels, and procedure, but no consequences. Commissions allowed people to register their complaints, put those complaints in print, and then closed the matter. Even if a commission of inquiry found evidence of wrongdoing, like the actions of the "unknown soldiers," it had no mandate to do anything about it. Commissions of inquiry served an important administrative purpose in Nigeria, as they did in many authoritarian states. They were a pressure valve, allowing public displays of accountability that in no way threatened the order of things. This was a truth known to both of twentieth-century Nigeria's varieties of despot—colonial governors on the one hand and military administrators on the other.

6

THE GIFT OF MARTIAL LAW

Military Tribunals for Civilians

Marie McBroom had found a good hustle. McBroom was a middle-aged American from New Jersey—a daughter of West Indian Garveyists with a deep affection for Africa. In the 1960s she had worked as a secretary at the United Nations, where she got to know some well-connected delegates from Nigeria. She leveraged these contacts to start a string of successful businesses in West Africa, including a travel agency and an outfit importing tomato paste from the United States. In the early 1980s, she began to take an interest in Nigeria's most valuable commodity: oil. "You see a black American woman to whom Africa was always the promised land," described an American journalist. "She looked around, and people were making money through business deals, so she decided to do it, too."[1] McBroom set herself up as a broker, facilitating oil transactions through the contacts she had made in her other ventures. She was a smart businesswoman. Soon, she had a good reputation in the oil trade and a Manhattan apartment filled with African art to show for it.

In 1983 McBroom was in Nigeria, brokering a sale of twenty thousand metric tons of unrefined oil from one speculator to another. On New Year's

Eve, Muhammadu Buhari staged a coup, and the new military government issued a decree cracking down on arbitrage of exactly the type McBroom was doing. She was caught off guard. A few days later, soldiers arrested her at her hotel and incarcerated her in Kirikiri Prison. After nine months in jail, she was charged with six counts of attempting to traffic oil without a license.[2] Arbitrage had long been a feature of Nigeria's oil industry, and transactions between brokers were not against the law (even though they were often shadowy).[3] But Buhari's decree made it illegal retroactively, and it was punishable by death.

McBroom was charged before the Miscellaneous Offences Tribunal. Despite its generic name this was Nigeria's most feared court, and it probably sent more people to the firing squad than any other. Illegally dealing in petroleum products came under its jurisdiction, along with currency counterfeiting and drug trading.[4] McBroom was a sympathetic figure. She had been treated badly in jail. She was a grandmother, and she was physically emaciated when she took the stand to testify. Her daughters in New Jersey appealed for help to everyone they could, and her plight was widely reported in the American press, including in *People* magazine and *Jet*.[5] Members of the US Congressional Black Caucus took an interest, and they pressured the Nigerian government to release her. Over a year after her arrest, with her tribunal still ongoing, the Nigerian government abruptly dropped the charges against her. She was acquitted of all counts on procedural grounds.[6] This was unusual—many who faced similar charges were sentenced to death.[7] In McBroom's case, it was her American passport that saved her from the firing squad.

Thousands of Nigerian civilians who got caught up in military law were not so lucky. Soldiers presented military-style tribunals as a way to streamline justice, but martial law was poorly suited to civilian society. This chapter describes how martial law was turned against the public, focusing on the military's deadliest legal implement—the tribunal. What about tribunals appealed as a tool to govern civilians? How did soldiers justify using martial law in peacetime? How did civilians adapt to life under a legal system that wasn't designed for them? Who among them liked it, and who felt strangled by it? Here, I examine these questions from the late 1960s, when the tribunals rose to prominence, to the early 1990s, when the Abacha regime turned to outright state terror. Martial law changed over those years, but the principles behind it didn't. Each regime put its own spin on it, but all of them agreed that martial law was useful for governing an unruly public. Debates about it were recapitulated over and over with each new military regime; one can find a newspaper editorialist nervously cautioning against allowing tribunals to execute civilians in the 1960s and then find him making the exact same argument thirty years later. Much changed over the course of military rule, but martial law remained exasperatingly the same. In law as in politics, military dictatorships had an uncanny ability to stop time.

In most political systems, law is a force of continuity. Staid and deliberate, the judicial branch is typically the arm of government most insulated from politics and least likely to change from one administration to the next. Martial law had a different logic. There was no fiction that tribunals were independent of executive power. The power of martial law lay in the element of surprise—it was agile, unpredictable, and perpetually new. But at the same time, some tribunals were in place for forty years. They developed their own rules and norms, and a legal culture built up around them (albeit a rickety one). This begs a question: Did martial law work by making *order* or *chaos*? It made both. It gave form and stability to military rule, but it was also volatile by design. This opposition, between stable authority and radical uncertainty, was its structuring tension. Martial law held people tightly, and there was a certain comfort in feeling the firm hand of a soldier. But there was always a chance he might impulsively crush you with it.

A Law for Strong Passions

Martial law is designed for an unusual kind of society—an army. As Georges Clemenceau may have quipped during the First World War, "military justice is to justice what military music is to music."[8] It is a stripped-down version of the art it imitates, serving first and foremost to keep men on the march. This is law for warlike young men, and it is designed to shock them with its caprice and awe them with its force. Martial law is a poor copy of the tools of redress available to civilians. That said, it serves a purpose. Every army, wrote David M. Jemibewon, Nigeria's most important military lawyer, "is an aggregation of men (mostly in the most criminally disposed age brackets) who had strong appetites, strong passions and ready access to deadly weapons." Military law's role was to keep them in line. There was no place for the niceties of civil liberties here: "The doctrine that it is better that ninety-nine guilty men go free than one innocent be convicted is not easily squared with the need to maintain efficiency, obedience and order in any army," he wrote.[9] Martial law doesn't prize nuance; the rules are simple, and the punishments for breaking them are harsh. To soldiers inducted into this system, martial law's starkness is threatening, but it is also *reassuring*. Since a soldier's duties can involve actions that civilian law abhors, up to and including killing people, it is in his interest to be crystal clear about what he is and is not allowed to do. Martial law provides that clarity.

In common usage, to say that a country is "under martial law" means that its government has started applying military law beyond the barracks. It can take many forms, but fundamentally it is what happens when the rules that soldiers make for *one another* are imposed on *society at large*.[10] In times of war or crisis, it attends the suspension of civilian constitutions or codes. It can follow coups, catastrophes, or revolutions. It is often imposed during wartime, when the drive to win trumps reverence for civil rights. Martial law is also associated with invasions and occupations; when a military occupies a foreign territory, the rules the occupying power uses for its own soldiers often become the law of the land. States also impose martial law during times of national crisis (real or imagined). Martial law is almost always presented as a provisional measure, even when it lasts a long time. In Syria it was in force for nearly fifty years, and in Taiwan for nearly forty, but the fiction was always that it was temporary. Martial law could be enacted on a single street or in an entire empire. It was an indispensable part of colonial rule, and it had been used to put down rebellions and mutinies in colonies as disparate as Ireland, New Zealand, India, and Nigeria.[11] Like many of the legal forms found in independent Africa, it had European roots.

Not everyone would agree that Nigeria was under martial law during military rule. Martial law is shorthand for a set of tools and norms, and as such it conceals certain subtleties. The military itself seldom used the term *martial law*, and one would struggle to find a singular document, decree, or legal decision that ushered it in.[12] There was no dramatic transition at the stroke of midnight. It crept in gradually, through little-publicized decrees and small jurisdictional tweaks. Every Nigerian had a different moment when she looked up and saw the riding crop looming over her. Some never noticed it at all.

Nor did martial law ever fully and formally come to an end, and some aspects of it have survived into the present. We might cavil about how "martial" it was; there was nothing particularly military about it, except that it was enacted by soldiers. It did not apply evenly throughout the country, nor to every kind of offense. Nonetheless, its technicalities were less important than its spirit. "In recent years, scarcely a day passes when one is not confronted with reports from all over Africa of convictions imposed by hastily convened tribunals," worried a Ghanaian law professor.[13] They left a deep mark on public life. Martial law brought many innovations, from mobile courts to beachside firing squads. Some of them outlived military rule.

Martial law thrives in low light. "Suspended laws," as Gyan Prakash wrote of India's emergency of 1975–1977, "let loose shadow powers and shadow laws." What makes martial law "insidious" is not that it explicitly gives powers to the executive but that it frees the state's hands from the ties that usually bind them.[14] Both martial law and emergency measures blur lines, and even lawyers get confused about their relationship to each other. They are right to be puzzled—both thrive on ambiguity. Martial law is most effective when it is opaque, so all the better if it isn't quite clear whether it's in force or not. "There is no occasion on which silence can be golden," complained an editorialist on the Gowon regime's refusal to clarify the scope of Nigeria's military-style courts. "Silence here can only lead to confusion." But confusion was useful to Gowon and the soldiers who followed him. An arcane structure with no clear rules could mean whatever a judge or military administrator wanted it to mean.[15] "The legal position of a soldier is an enigma," wrote Okay Achike, one of Nigeria's most prominent military jurists.[16] It may seem strange that Achike would throw up his hands and say the system he devoted his career to was a mystery—but the "enigma" of military law was part of what made it work.

Martial law established a third path in Nigeria's already plural legal system, running parallel to the common law and customary courts that Nigerians already knew well. It took the form of tribunals, which were panels of military officers and judges empowered to enforce the Supreme Military Council's decrees.[17] They could not overturn them, but they could interpret and occasionally referee them against each other. Those decrees, on everything from how much could be charged for a bag of rice to what constituted treason, were drafted by the lawyers of the Directorate of Army Legal Services. They also administered the tribunals. This small agency, headquartered in a decrepit complex on the outskirts of Lagos, therefore both made and interpreted a good portion of Nigeria's laws. The real decision makers were the head of state and the members of the Supreme Military Council, but it was the directorate's lawyers who worked out the details. They were not Nigeria's best legal minds, and their critics complained about how poorly written their doctrine was.[18]

Like most militaries, Nigeria's armed forces demanded unconditional obedience from its members. Discipline was strictly enforced, and infractions of the rules were severely punished. When a group of soldiers set fire to some cars in 1977, for example, the army convened a tribunal to determine who was responsible. But when the officer in charge started the proceedings, he saw no need to hear from witnesses or the accused—he had already made his decision. "Every one of you in this barrack is guilty of the offence of burning those vehicles. Every one of you will contribute compulsorily, towards making good all the vehicles that were lost in this incident. Is that clear!" The soldiers assented. "You should be ashamed of yourselves because that act of burning vehicles is primitive and barbaric. You as soldiers, uniformed men, are supposed to be disciplined men. You are supposed to be more disciplined than your brothers who are outside the uniform."[19] The tribunal was wrapped up in a matter of minutes. This was not how civilian courts worked. Even the strictest civilian judge would think twice about imposing collective punishment without any trial (however preordained). But this was normal for a military court.

What happens when this logic is applied to everyone? To civilians forced to live under it, martial law feels cruel and arbitrary. Even in an authoritarian civilian government there is usually some sense that law can be a tool of critique—a weapon of the weak or a megaphone to speak back to power. In military law, there is no such notion, even a contrarian one. Military and civilian law do not mix well. They have different mandates, and they operate under different rules. Each has its own logic and standard of truth. Soldiers and civilians are usually siloed off from one another in law, and the points where they overlap (when a soldier rapes a civilian, for example, or when a civilian reveals a military secret) often make for scandal.

But it isn't the case that civilian law is good and just while martial law is bad and unjust. Both are normatively empty, and what gives them shape is what is put into them. In some respects, military law is like any other kind of law. It is a body of rules subject to interpretation, and many factors determine which interpretation prevails in the courtroom. There is more to it than despotism, and like civilian law it instantiates a community as it works. Its harshness does not mean that it has no brakes or safeguards, and the officers who sit on tribunals strive for fairness more often than not. Martial law is not a black hole. It has norms and conventions, and there are limits to the punishments a tribunal can enact.

But the finer points of procedure in martial law didn't mean much to civilians like Marie McBroom. To civilians, it was a dark, foreboding void. It could be turned against anyone—soldier or civilian, rich or poor, male or female. Tribunals' rules were murky and inconsistent, and they seldom favored the defendant. Judge, jury, and prosecutor could be fused in one person. There was no presumption of innocence. The burden of proof lay with the defense rather than the prosecution, and the rules of evidence were hazy. Defendants were only sometimes allowed to have legal counsel, and it came from one of the military's own lawyers. Tribunals could impose long sentences. Many were empowered to issue the death penalty, including for offenses that did not incur it in civilian courts (like counterfeiting). They did not answer to the judiciary, and their place in the military power structure was unclear. Theoretically they had jurisdiction over everyone, including officers, but the higher a soldier's rank, the less likely he was to ever face one.

The decision to use the term *tribunal* itself is revealing. Military law often distinguishes between foreign enemies, who are subject to tribunals, and an army's own soldiers, who are subject to courts martial when they break the rules. In Nigeria, the military chose the term *tribunals*—which, again, typically are for the enemy—for the courts they used for their own citizens. This terminological choice reveals something important about soldiers: they were primed to see the civilians they governed as adversaries. They treated them like a conquered people.

Martial Law and Civilians

Soldiers spoke of martial law as a gift to civilians. They argued that tribunals were speedier, more efficient, and better at creating a harmonious society than civilian courts. They insisted not only that martial law was necessary given the challenges of the moment but that it was qualitatively *better* than other forms of law. This shouldn't be surprising—the form of law they liked best was the one they had built themselves. What should be "cherished" about law, Flight Lieutenant Jerry Rawlings told a meeting of the Ghana Bar Association in 1984, were its "principles as an instrument of social ordering." Tribunals, which grew during his administration, could preserve the principles of fairness and equity that lawyers liked, while also making law more efficient, and less colonial in its form. "It is not the intention of the PNDC [Provisional National Defence Council, i.e., the executive] to discredit the idea of positive Law or to hold Law in contempt," by establishing tribunals, he promised. "Rather, it is part of its response to the demands of a growing legal consciousness on the part of our people and to the need to simplify and speed up the dispensation of justice."[20] Rawlings was right that civilian law was inefficient. In Ghana, every court had a huge backlog, and once proceedings started they were rarely swift. Criminal defendants spent months or years in jail awaiting trial, and a civil suit could tie up a piece of land for decades as it shuffled through the court system. Judges became notorious for their obsession with procedural technicalities, and even a straightforward legal matter could ruin a claimant in fees and lost time.

Over and over again, military boosters argued that civilian law could not advance the good. Civilian judges' obsession with the rules of evidence allowed guilty men to walk free, their inefficiency stalled commerce, and their corruption damaged the state's credibility. Lawyers were no better. The military tarred the Nigerian Bar Association as a guild so enamored of itself that it had lost sight of the true purpose of law. Soldiers pointed to law's jargon as evidence that it was stacked against the common person (never mind that military justice had its own equally perplexing terms of art). They argued that civilian judges loved procedure merely for its own sake, treating law like a scholastic exercise—one more akin to debating how many angels could dance on the head of a pin than discovering "real" truths. They accused lawyers of greed, noting that the only people who benefited from lengthy proceedings and mountains of suits and countersuits were the people billing by the hour—attorneys.[21]

Martial law was offered as the solution to all these problems. It would be expressed in clear language that even the illiterate could understand. The rules of evidence would be those of "common sense." Proceedings would have a strict time limit to ensure a speedy trial (usually thirty days from start to finish), and there would be no appeals. Attorneys, whom the military saw as parasites, would simply not be allowed in the courtroom. Implementing martial law for everyone, military jurists argued, would cut civilians free from the hopelessly knotted legal system, saving time and money for both them and their government.

It would also make the public more obedient. Soldiers, Jemibewon observed, labor under two forms of law—the military regulations that apply to them as soldiers, and the civil rules that apply to everyone. This doubled set of rules was the essence of military discipline: "He religiously adheres to both almost to a fault to avoid the heavy sanctions of even the most minor breaches. This desire to keep to rules, coupled with the rigidity of the military hierarchy, tends to make a soldier a robot."[22] Jemibewon didn't mean this critically. It was good that soldiers were robots, and civilians ought to be more machinelike too. The hope was that martial law would make for a whole country of robots.

Even though soldiers saw martial law as a gift, they needed a justification for it. Nigeria was not at war, its military wasn't an "occupying" force (even though it sometimes acted like one), and there was no looming external threat, like a hostile neighbor. The alibi for martial law became *crime*. As long as there was crime, there was a reason for why tribunals were necessary. Armed robbery was easy to milk for dramatic effect. Poverty, inequality, and the circulation of countless unregistered guns ensured that there was always plenty of it. Whenever the public became squeamish, the military could point to the latest spate of home invasions or grisly highway robberies to explain why stern measures were necessary. "By imposing the ultimate penalty," namely death, "the idea was to scare fledgling armed robbers and to nip new initiates in the bud," wrote a sociologist critical of the military. "But 17 years after the imposition of the death penalty, the malaise has increased significantly. Robbers have become more vicious in response to the death penalty, believing that it is either their victims' lives or theirs. As a result, they do not hesitate to kill."[23]

The military saw things differently. The persistence of armed robbery was not a sign that tribunals were the wrong approach, but that they *hadn't gone far enough*. Each subsequent military regime doubled down on the severity of its predecessor. Armed robbery was a real problem, and the military didn't invent it. But it was also a pretext for officers to impose the summary form of justice they preferred. They were quiet about the fact that the perpetrators of armed robberies were often the people most likely to be armed—soldiers.[24]

The first decree establishing a tribunal was the Suppression of Disorder Decree No. 4 of 1966. It was followed by many others, notably the postwar Robbery and Firearms (Special Provisions) Decree No. 47 of 1970, and then a string of amendments that expanded martial law from its beachhead in suppressing crime into many areas of life. The boundary between political offenses (like treason) and criminal offenses (like theft) eroded. This was by design. Under militarism's disciplinary creed, *any* crime could be a crime against the state if it contravened the military's mission to establish "order." The use of tribunals rose and fell throughout the military period, but generally the trend was toward tougher rules and stiffer penalties.[25] Initially, sentences had to be confirmed by state governors, who could exercise the prerogative of mercy if they wished (though they rarely did).[26] As the importance of tribunals grew, this protection fell away, and death sentences could be imposed by progressively lower-ranked officers. In August 1974 the Armed Robbery Decree was amended to allow convicted armed robbers to appeal to the Supreme Court, creating an unusual situation where civilian judges could overrule men in uniform.[27] Murtala Muhammed annulled the decree a year later, and martial law's jurisdiction ballooned again. For every criminological problem there was a tribunal. The Counterfeit Currency (Special Provisions) Decree No. 22 of 1974, for example, created a tribunal that could impose the death penalty for forging Nigeria's new money (the naira, which replaced the pound in 1973), and the Exchange Control (Anti-Sabotage) Decree No. 57 of 1979 harshly penalized foreign exchange trading. (Military jurists used parenthet-icals extravagantly.)

During the brief civilian administration of Shehu Shagari in the early 1980s, martial law was, in effect, rebranded. The death penalty was suspended, and military officers were replaced with civilian judges. But the tribunals weren't closed. Not wanting to be perceived as "soft" on crime, Shagari kept martial law largely in place without calling it that.[28] It returned in full force after he was overthrown in the 1983 Buhari coup. In the mid-1980s the armed rob-bery tribunals returned, first emboldened by Buhari's War Against Indisci-pline and then dramatically expanded by Babangida. He had a convenient alibi in one man: Lawrence Anini, a highway robber who staged a series of terrifyingly efficient crimes in the Mid-West.[29] Anini became the bête noire of national politics, and Babangida used him to spook the public. In a 1986 address, after a particularly bloody bank robbery, he warned that Nigeria was losing the fight against armed crime. To win it, the civilian police would have to be purged of crooked officers (several had colluded with Anini). In the meantime, police duties would be handed to the army. A major antirobbery initiative would be launched in Bendel, Ondo, and Anambra states, includ-ing expanding the tribunals and imposing a dawn-to-dusk curfew. None of this was effective—by this point armed robberies were happening in broad daylight.

There were also tribunals set up to combat corruption and misconduct by civilian officials. Among the anticorruption decrees, the Public Property (Special Military) Tribunal Decree No. 3 of 1984 was the most severe. It en-couraged civilians to report misuse of public resources by bureaucrats, and the witch-hunt it set off necessitated the Public Officers (Protection Against False Accusation) Decree No. 4 a few weeks later. "The fang of these spe-cial tribunals has so-far stung 13 former civilian governors, who were sent to various jail terms," wrote Richard Akinnola in the *Vanguard*, reporting approvingly that there had been more than a hundred guilty verdicts for ci-vilian politicians of the Second Republic.[30] Sometimes soldiers got caught up in the anticorruption charges they leveled at civilians. In 1984, the colonel in charge of the National Youth Service Corps was found guilty of a "landslide" of fraud and embezzlement by a public property tribunal. Dispensing with formalities, the tribunal used the ruling to attack his character. "Col. Obasa suddenly and inexplicably lost all sense of patriotism[,] which we consider to be preposterous, mysterious, and mischievous," the chairman wrote. "He allowed himself to be carried away by insatiable ambition by joining the get-rich-quick by hook or by crook bandwagon."[31] Unlike the armed robbery tribunals, with their gruesome penalties, the anticorruption tribunals were popular with almost everyone (except, of course, public servants).

Jurists quibbled over whether all of these should be called "military" tribunals, given that they didn't pertain to soldiers. But a visit to one made their martial character clear. "The atmosphere at the tribunal is tense, charged, and unmistakably military," recalled a lawyer. "The areas surrounding the tribunal premises are cordoned off by heavily armed military and anti-riot police officers, all wrapped and stuffed up in war uniform, some with well-corked machine guns set and ready with several cannisters of tear gas on hand, ready to explode."[32] Nasty things went on inside.

Martial Law in Action

Tribunals are often associated with treason, sedition, and other serious crimes against the state, but in Nigeria they also tackled more everyday infractions. In 1973, the landlord of a building on the outskirts of Lagos accused one of his tenants, Boluwaji Ijadu, of breaking into his room, assaulting him, and taking a large sum of money.[33] The landlord, Kehinde Tokosi, called the police, who broke down Ijadu's door and arrested him. When they searched his room, the police found a radio belonging to the landlord and other valuables, including a large amount of cash. Ijadu spent the next two years in prison waiting for his court date. When it came, Ijadu was brought before a magistrate, but unluckily for him the magistrate decided his docket was too full that day to hear his case. Noting that Ijadu had allegedly wielded a rusted knife against his landlord, he shunted the case over to the Lagos State Armed Robbery Tribunal. This was against the letter of the law; the tribunal had been established in response to the specific problem of robberies committed with *firearms*, but the public prosecutor decided that Ijadu's knife was enough to bring a charge of armed robbery.[34] Ijadu's case went before the Armed Robbery Tribunal of T. S. Gomes. The prosecutor was Priscilla Fakeye, who was the first woman to occupy the role. She was known for her ruthlessness. Ijadu managed to secure a lawyer (which not all tribunals permitted), but he was no match for Fakeye.

Ijadu's defense was that he had been framed by his landlord. He testified that there was a long-standing dispute between them over a rent payment. The landlord had recently dragged Ijadu to a local oracle, hoping that the oracle would order Ijadu to pay up. When the oracle sided with Ijadu, Tokosi was furious. At this point, Ijadu claimed, Tokosi decided to frame his tenant for theft. This wasn't unusual; many people used law against their rivals, and accusations of the type Ijadu described were common. Ijadu explained that he ran the neighborhood's *esusu* (an informal savings and credit scheme common throughout Nigeria), which was why he had so much cash in his possession. The tribunal did not believe this defense. The priest who had allegedly interpreted the oracle was nowhere to be found, and Ijadu could not produce the receipts for the *esusu*. The tribunal decided that he had stolen the money. Ijadu was found guilty and sentenced to execution by firing squad.

Martial law had offered civilians a bargain: it guaranteed them fewer rights, but it would dispense justice more efficiently than civilian courts. But as Ijadu's case shows, tribunals were not as quick as soldiers promised they would be. Two years was a long time to await trial by any standard, and once it started, the hearing was slow. Ijadu's hearing dragged on for three months, over sixteen sessions of the tribunal. Every aspect of the crime was turned over by the military judge, and procedural conventions that the military had sworn would not be allowed to gum up the process were observed. Forensic evidence was presented, a medical expert was summoned to describe Tokosi's wounds, and irregularities in the photographs taken at the crime scene prompted a long digression about camera angles that the judge eventually decided was irrelevant. Military justice may have been harsh, but this didn't mean it was fast. After Ijadu's sentencing, it was another eight months before he was actually executed.[35]

Rather than cutting through the knot of jurisdictional complexity, martial law tied on another string. Ijadu died for what may have been a robbery but was probably more like a quarrel with his landlord. He should not have come before the tribunal at all, and had the magistrate been less busy on the day of his initial hearing he probably would have lived. "It is incredible that armed robbers are not subjected to a uniform system of trial," complained an editorialist in 1971. "While some are tried by special tribunals, others are sent to the High Court or even to magistrate's courts. The effect of this anomaly is that while an armed robber convicted at a special tribunal faces the firing squad, his fellow criminal tried [elsewhere] gets away with a mere jail sentence. This makes nonsense of the saying that 'all are equal before the law.'"[36] The morass became thicker with every new decree. If they were challenged about why a certain case went before a tribunal instead of a civilian court, bureaucrats could hide behind the thicket of countervailing rules. Confusion suited military judges—inscrutability meant that "the rule" was whatever they said it was.

What tribunals lacked in consistency they made up for in paperwork. The transcript of Ijadu's hearing was carefully typed up and bound, like many others. Over fifty pages of witness testimony were translated from Yoruba to English, which would have been costly and time consuming. A court usually goes to this trouble because there is a possibility of appeal, or because the principle of judicial precedent demands that detailed records be kept. But this wasn't technically a court, and there would be no revisiting the tribunal's decision. Appeals were forbidden, and Ijadu wouldn't be alive to make one anyway.[37] Since tribunals were not governed by precedent, it didn't need to be recorded for posterity either. Why, then, go to the trouble of documenting it in such detail?

These thick casefiles suggest that, even in its martial form, law couldn't shed its documentary impulse.[38] Moreover, the purpose of a tribunal was not just to liquidate those the military believed were "spoiling" the country. Tribunals also issued warnings. In keeping with the military's "revolutionary" project, they taught lessons about discipline to the public. For this reason, they needed to be written down. Journalists weren't allowed to watch the proceedings, but they could report on them through the transcripts that went on the public record.

Disloyal, larcenous, or violent *civilians* weren't the tribunals' only targets. They sometimes used martial law against the men it was designed for: soldiers. In 1975, three privates used a machine gun to rob a Dahomean named Blaize Adebayo Ajiborisha of his valuables. The victim was a migrant with no papers—a person whom the military was more likely to deport than help—but in this case it suited them to go after the soldiers who had robbed him.[39] The Lagos State Government was interested in the insalubrious area where the crime took place, "a nameless street in an obscure area of Mushin," as one police sergeant testified. The tribunal became the pretext to "clean it up." The tribunal left no stone unturned, and more than twenty witnesses were called to testify. From the actual robbery, the investigation fanned out into a survey of the neighborhood as a whole. The robbers' base was an overgrown wasteland where the suburbs gave way to the countryside. Lagos had many of these patches of forest hemmed in by the city's rapid growth, most of them abandoned farms now owned by land speculators waiting to sell to a developer. The people who squatted on them were poor, foreign, or new to the city. A tribunal member who visited as part of the investigation described it as "a place where any honest human being would dread to come even in the early hours of the evening," and he recommended that the entire area be cleared out. The bar the robbers frequented, the Right Time Spot, was ordered closed, and the shacks where the soldiers stored their booty were demolished. As for the accused men, the tribunal minced no words in describing them. One was "a coiled spring" who would "kill without batting an eye-lid. He is a trigger-happy robber that should be avoided." Another was a "vermin of the worst type" and a "thorn in the flesh of any decent citizen." All were hanged.

Tribunals' theoretically narrow mandates ballooned in the courtroom. Some of the crimes that came before the Armed Robbery Tribunal were not only not "armed," as in Ijadu's case, but not *robberies*. In 1974, a schizophrenia patient from the Yaba Psychiatric Centre in Lagos got into trouble during an outing from the asylum. His doctor had allowed him to go out by himself, and he traveled across town to visit his sister. At the end of the day, he began to worry that he was not going to be able to make it back to Yaba before his curfew. He became agitated when he couldn't find his bus in the rush-hour traffic, and when a taxi refused to take him he lost his temper, striking the driver in the head with a tire iron. The driver was injured but not badly. Nothing had been stolen, and although the psychiatric patient had wielded a weapon, it wasn't a gun. Nonetheless, he was charged before the Armed Robbery Tribunal under the Robbery and Firearms (Special Provisions) Decree of 1970. During questioning he became delusional, claiming to be "Head of the Army" and that he possessed "many aeroplanes." When the judge finally got him to talk about the taxi driver, he cartoonishly described seeing "many little birds on the driver's head[,] which he tried to drive away" with the iron. His doctor was summoned to describe his psychiatric condition. He insisted that his patient was not violent, and there must have been some misunderstanding.[40] At the end of the four-day hearing, the tribunal chairman concluded that he was "of unsound mind" and not fit to plead. He was returned to the hospital in Yaba, where he was to take no more outings on his own.[41] Tribunals could sometimes be merciful, but martial law was still poorly suited to civilian life.

Tribunals were not the only judicial innovation of martial law. One of the stranger legal forms the military implemented were "mobile courts," which brought law out from the courtroom and onto the roadway.[42] Nigeria's traffic problems were legendary (and still are today). Poor roads and horrific accidents frayed nerves, and daylong "go-slows" consumed vast amounts of time. The roads were places of "thrusting indiscipline," as Chinua Achebe described them. "Frenetic energy, rudeness, noisiness—they are all there in abundance."[43] Nigerians often used traffic as a metonym for politics. Crumbling infrastructure, reckless driving, and the disruptive convoys of the rich and powerful were symbols of everything wrong with the country. To soldiers, traffic was a perfect example of the sort of disorder they wanted to end.

The solution that Gowon and others after him offered was to create mobile "courts" that could be set up on busy street corners to try drivers for traffic violations as they happened. Benches and desks were welded onto open-back trucks, and an officer or magistrate would perch up at a busy intersection to adjudicate traffic offenses on the spot. Mobile courts didn't solve the traffic problem, but military governments liked what they represented. It may seem strange that these traffic courts were part of martial law, but that was where the idea came from. In wartime, courts martial have to be portable. They can be set up anywhere, even on the front lines, and they dispense justice immediately, on the spot. This was perfect, military jurists thought, for the chaotic conditions of Nigeria's roadways.[44] In the military imagination, every street corner was like a battlefield.

Public displays of punishment were also an important tool in the military's kit. Hangings and firing squads attracted huge crowds, especially on Bar Beach in Lagos, which became infamous as a venue for executions.[45] The soldiers who did the deed wore heavy jungle camouflage and covered their faces in boot black. Presumably this was for anonymity, but it also added to the horror of the spectacle. The bodies were taken away in garbage trucks.[46] The military defended public executions by arguing that they were a powerful deterrent. Those who had not broken the law had nothing to fear, the regime insisted, and law-abiding Nigerians should not look at the hanged and see some reflection of themselves. "There can be no comparison between the entire Nigerian populace and highly dangerous thieves," wrote an editorialist in a state newspaper. He compared the military's bloodlettings to the sacrifice of Christ; "if in 20th century Nigeria, the blood of the armed robbers will wash away the sins" of the people, "please may the government build the gallows higher."[47] "Execution by firing squad," the editors of the *Nigerian Herald* argued, was the only effective way "to check violence on the part of the men of the underworld." Executions might be unsavory, they argued, but the "unofficial" punishments that crowds imposed in their absence were even worse. During the Shagari administration's brief ban on capital punishment, Lagosians had started burning suspected armed robbers alive. The editors speculated that this grotesque vigilantism was happening because people thought the government had "gone soft."[48] Some were relieved when Buhari brought back the firing squad the following year.

But armed robberies continued no matter how many bodies crumpled at the stake, and there was cause for concern about what the executions were doing to the national psyche. Capital punishment was "abhorrent, and a retrogressive step in the onward movement towards more liberal penology," wrote a lawyer in 1971. The same year, a journalist described an execution in the main square of Benin City. The huge crowd gave him "quite a thrill," he wrote, and the carnivalesque atmosphere was "more sensational than all the cowboy movies ever shown in cinemascope." "My heart pounded as though it were being hit by 10,000 hammers." The journalist felt personally deterred from crime by the execution he witnessed, but it also made him queasy. "What I saw was enough to make the fruit of a highway robbery taste sour in my mouth," he concluded, "but what I am unable to understand is whether the exercise is really making sufficient impact on society, considering all the ballyhoo, time and energy being put into it."[49] Executions should be neither "days of national rejoicing" nor "carnivals," wrote a critic, alarmed by the party-like atmosphere of public killings.[50] They were becoming like "sporting spectacles," the editors of the *New Nigerian* warned. "What kind of people are we turning ourselves into?"[51] Twenty years later, a civil rights lawyer voiced the same worry. Public executions had no discernible effect on crime rates, but they "brutalized" those who watched them. "Human life means much less to our children now than it meant to our fathers."[52]

Critics and Supporters

"Probably one of the most criminal and stupid acts of the National Liberation Council to date has been the setting up of military tribunals," remarked Kwame Nkrumah from exile.[53] In Ghana itself, few could afford to be so openly critical of martial law. The people who lived under martial law found ways of navigating a legal system that wasn't designed for them, and a few even came to see its value. The judiciary was divided over martial law. Some judges embraced it, finding soldiers' disciplinary ambitions consistent with their own worldviews. Others wanted nothing to do with tribunals and criticized them publicly. Most judges fell somewhere in the middle; they disliked martial law, but they hoped their presence on tribunals alongside military officers might temper its force.

Being for or against martial law was not an abstract legal question—it was about who had power over life and death. Prince Bola Ajibola, Babangida's minister of justice, argued that judges who criticized tribunals were just bitter about losing clout. "It is like the case of the jealous wife unwilling to allow another woman to have a share of her spouse's love," he wrote. "In this case the spouse is the Law, to which the judiciary is wedded for better or for worse."[54] Dissenting judges argued that it wasn't about power but principle; tribunals were too harsh in their sentencing, and their rules of evidence weren't rigorous enough. Defendants had no access to legal aid, and the tribunal's atmosphere seemed designed to inspire dread. Comparing the armed robbery decree to a decree mandating better conditions in abattoirs, Justice Olu Ayoola of the Ibadan High Court wrote that "a society that is humane in slaughtering a cow must also be humane to its people."[55]

In the early 1970s, Chief Justice of the Nigerian Supreme Court Sir Adetokunbo Ademola encouraged the military government to require that High Court judges, not military officers, preside over armed robbery tribunals and that accused robbers be given legal counsel by the state.[56] He was troubled by the fact that someone could go from arrest to execution without ever speaking to a lawyer. General Yakubu Gowon agreed, admitting that summary justice might undermine the military government in the long run, a view "widely held in the legal profession."[57] The state military governors pushed back. The judiciary already had a huge backlog, the governor of Lagos State complained, and this would put it past the breaking point. Moreover, he wrote, the only people asking for reform were judges and lawyers.[58] "The generality of the public has found nothing lacking" in the tribunals.[59]

The governor wasn't wrong that people liked martial law, at least at first. Support for the military's peculiar form of justice could come from surprising places, and not all who endorsed it wore uniforms. "Summary justice may be good," wrote Tai Solarin in 1967, at the end of a long critical essay on Nigeria's "imperious, yet impotent" civilian criminal justice system. "If there is any institution in this country that breeds more debauched Nigerians than it cures, that institution is our laws." Solarin condemned the "gross indiscipline" on display in Nigerian society and criticized the courts for their dysfunction. Martial law, he thought, might be the answer.[60] If Solarin's name is unfamiliar, the reader might assume that he was a soldier, or one of the law-and-order ideologues who supported military rule. In fact, he was a left-leaning teacher and intellectual who had been a fierce critic of colonialism. Radicals like Solarin could find common cause with soldiers in criticizing the deficiencies of Nigeria's legal system, and soldiers were not the only people who found the harshness of martial law appealing. Thirty years later, with little to show for it besides a pile of bodies, fewer civilians would come to its defense.

Throughout these years, civilians made the best they could of a bad situation. The best guide to life under martial law was a little-known writer of self-help books named Nkem Liliwhite-Nwosu.[61] She owned a motel in Lagos, where she made a modest fortune by striking a deal with the Nigerian Football Association to accommodate visiting teams when they came to town. But her success didn't make her easygoing. She lived her life in a near-constant rage, doing battle with every authority figure who had the misfortune of crossing her path. Her books were nominally guides for how to be a better Christian woman, but her piety didn't mellow her—these are unrelentingly angry descriptions of life under military rule. Her writings are a reminder of how much fury civilians felt toward Obasanjo, Buhari, and other soldiers now remembered as moderates.

Liliwhite-Nwosu saw life in Nigeria as one long trial, and she spent a substantial chunk of hers in court. She was extremely litigious. She obtained her motel in shady circumstances, and she spent decades in court defending her claim to the property (and hashing out the details of her ever-contentious relationship with the football association). She did not suffer fools gladly. This put her at odds with her neighbors, her rivals, and, as she put it, the "fools in uniform" who ran the country. Law was valuable to people like Liliwhite-Nwosu—even the stripped-down version of it found in a tribunal. She fought in court because it was the arena she had access to; it was the only place where she could even *try* to corner the state. Martial law made it hard to win, but fighting under rules that were stacked against her was better than not fighting at all. She became an expert on the military's culture and structure, and she knew which gimmicks worked with a military judge and which ones didn't. For example, a smart critic might argue that some military policy was "dishonorable" or "cowardly" if she wanted to change it, because that was more likely to bring an officer over to her side than calling it "arbitrary" or "excessive" (even if that was what she really meant).

Lawyers were the tribunals' most persistent critics, and dissident civilians lionized them for it. Nigerians composed praise songs about lawyers who won money for them or kept their loved ones out of jail.[62] Some lawyers became folk heroes, and a few cast themselves as Davids against the Goliath that was the army. But even the most skillful lawyers struggled to help their clients on the unpredictable terrain of martial law. In law journals, international organizations, and at the meetings of the Nigerian Bar Association, they criticized the tribunals on both moral and professional grounds. "A situation where military officers who are part of the fused legislative and executive arm of government also participate in judicial activities is hardly commendable to fairness," wrote one of them about Babangida.[63] "The establishment of a parallel system of courts by successive military administrations to try ordinary criminal cases under refurbished nomenclature and stiffened penalties has been the single most effective subversion of the judiciary and ultimately the Rule of Law," wrote another in the *Constitutional Rights Journal*, a magazine edited by a group of progressive litigators.[64] "The effectiveness of the judiciary has been hampered by the creation of military tribunals and the promulgation of various decrees ousting the jurisdiction of courts," wrote Clement Nwankwo. The decrees "contradict universally accepted standards of human rights."[65]

Lawyers did not always speak with one voice, however. In 1984, there was a brutal internecine struggle in the bar association over a decision to boycott the tribunals the military had set up to try civilian politicians for corruption.[66] Most who supported the boycott did it to take a stand against the tribunals in principle. But the civil rights lawyer Gani Fawehinmi opposed the boycott, as did some of his colleagues. They argued that lawyers could not abandon the civilians on trial in the name of a gesture that the military would probably just ignore. His critics argued that his faction actually opposed the boycott for more selfish reasons—there was good money to be made representing wealthy civilians facing charges in tribunals. Lawyers, like everyone else, could find ways to prosper from militarism.

The lawyers who argued against martial law recognized that it wasn't going away anytime soon. "It does not require great clairvoyance to predict that so long as the military take part in government, for so long shall we continue to partake of all the peculiarities of 'military justice,'" wrote Akin Isidapo-Obe. In light of this, lawyers took a pragmatic approach to martial law. The best they could hope for was that the sharp edges of the tribunals could be blunted, and that the "wild men" in uniform could be domesticated. He hoped that soldiers could be injected with a "dose of mellowness" in governing the civilians under their thumbs.[67] "Military members of tribunals appear to proceed from the premise that as part of the executive arm of government, they have a mission to enforce military decrees promulgated by government[,] and often times a conviction means a victory or triumph for the government while an acquittal represents a government loss of face."[68] It was hard to defend a client in those circumstances.

Lawyers groped around in the dark for a weapon to use against the military, and what they found was "human rights."[69] Nigeria had no constitution in this period, and there was no charter or revolutionary declaration that civilians could point to as the basis of a civil right. The attraction of human rights was that its authority came from some indefinite place abroad, not from a national legal system that soldiers had bound and gagged. It wasn't a very effective weapon. Using it in a tribunal was like throwing darts at a brick wall—more damaging to the dart than the wall. Moreover, like other legal tools, it could be used by both sides. The military set up various "human rights" commissions in the 1980s and 1990s, and Babangida and Abacha found the language of human rights useful in sanitizing their policies. This was disingenuous, to be sure, but that language was loose enough that soldiers could stretch it to their purposes.

Some military jurists did worry that martial law might jeopardize human rights—but civilians weren't the humans they were worried about. In 1987, three former directors of legal services in the army and navy warned that "the present military courts left too many loopholes for the violation of the fundamental human rights *of the soldier*."[70] They called for the creation of a military court of appeal and a stricter division between prosecutors and judges. There was a cruel irony in the fact that the top brass fretted about the rights of soldiers under martial law—the people for whom it was designed—but gave no thought to the civilians who also struggled under its yoke.

Tellingly, the first martial law case to attract the attention of international human rights organizations was not about the rights of civilians, but *officers*. In 1990, sixty-nine officers were tried for treason following a failed coup attempt against General Ibrahim Babangida. Forty-two were executed immediately. A group of Nigerian lawyers publicized their plight abroad, and they found some allies. Amnesty International organized a letter-writing campaign, and the regime began to feel the eye of the outside world.[71] The remaining officers faced a chaotic series of retrials that the regime staged to appease the foreign press. Three separate tribunals tried the men again, some of them multiple times. Several were exonerated, only to have the decision reversed a few days later and be executed. Two had their sentences reduced to life in prison, and one was released (which Babangida's chief of staff held up as proof of the regime's magnanimity).[72] This was not much of a victory for the lawyers who had raised the alarm, but there wasn't much else they could do. Critics of the military had few successes during the Babangida years, and they would have even fewer in the final stretch of the dictatorship.

But a new dynamic had been introduced: the scrutiny of the wider world. Arguably, the most effective challenges to the military happened outside the courtroom. Just as anticolonial activists had once turned British rhetoric about "fair play" against their conquerors, dissidents in military regimes could turn bromides about "discipline" back on the officers who spouted them. Soldiers were narcissistic, and their savviest critics were the ones who played on their vanity. They bristled when civilians accused them of dishonor, and their anxiety about Nigeria's place in the world could be manipulated to rein them in.[73] As the Cold War came to an end, outsiders began paying attention to what was happening in Africa's military dictatorships. Soldiers' critics would jump at that opportunity.

Conclusion

After each coup, one of the first orders of business was to "clean up" the tribunals, which each coup-plotter accused his predecessor of having mismanaged. A special tribunal would be set up to try his deposed predecessor (provided he was still alive).[74] A new set of decrees would go out, dissolving the military courts of the old regime and creating new ones—even if they were indistinguishable from the ones they replaced. Days after Major General Ibrahim Babangida overthrew Buhari in 1985, a journalist found the military tribunals on Lagos Island, which usually buzzed with nervous activity, "completely deserted," "placed under lock and heavily guarded by law enforcement agents."[75] But they weren't silent for long. When Babangida reconvened the tribunals, he promised improvements. Retired judges, not military officers, would chair them, and a special appellate tribunal was established to hear appeals. His military tribunals would be "liberal and civilized," he told the All-Nigeria Judges Conference in 1988, and there was a basis for them in the Nigerian constitution.[76] The notion that a military tribunal might be "liberal" may sound strange, but martial law had settled into a staid institutionalism over the course of Nigeria's first six military administrations (though to critics it was more like rigor mortis). Nigeria's next and final military dictator would dispense with that notion. Under General Sani Abacha, "military liberalism" gave way to state-sponsored theft, terrorism, and murder.

Soldiers were subtler leaders than they've been given credit for. They gave civilians some breathing room, and over the years they found a balancing point between discipline and freedom (even though the freedom they offered took a peculiar form). Their "temporary" regimes came to seem stable and permanent. As a form of government, militarism was tolerable to enough people that there was no mass rebellion against it. Plenty of civilians liked its sharpness. There were true believers in the military's revolutionary project, and even for skeptics there were ways to turn it to personal advantage—to array martial law against your enemies, or to jockey for a better position when a coup shook things up. Soldiers begrudgingly consented to law's constraints because they understood that law came with disciplinary tools they could use.

Those subtleties vanished in the 1990s. In the last years of Nigeria's military dictatorship, the army's utopian vision crumbled. Soldiers lost their sense of purpose, withdrawing into their barracks and becoming, as more and more people saw them, a "cult."[1] Militarism lost its coherence as an ideology, and the vision of *discipline* gave way to a regimen of *punishment* that had no goal besides keeping the military in power. The army tried to strangle society, but it ended up asphyxiating itself.

Nigeria's government became a cult of personality for a person nobody liked. General Sani Abacha was a shamelessly corrupt usurper who made the country into a pariah state from 1993, when he came to power, until he died in 1998. This was militarism's denouement, and it would end with Abacha's death. Abacha was the outlier in Nigeria's parade of domineering but mostly well-intentioned soldier-kings. Every other soldier who ruled Nigeria had a plan for the country. These were not realistic plans, and all of them did more harm than good over the long term. But the men who had made them genuinely wanted to improve how Nigerians lived, worked, thought, and behaved. Abacha did not. Like all soldiers he spoke the language of order, but he offered no plan for how to achieve it. "Discipline" was just a veneer for vice—it didn't figure in his politics in any meaningful way. Unlike his predecessors, Abacha had a fundamentally pessimistic view of what Nigerians could achieve. In his speeches and writings, he almost never talked about the future. There were no platitudes about the essential qualities of the national character, no hopeful descriptions of the paradise to come. Nor did he give fiery warnings of what would happen if Nigerians didn't change their ways, like Murtala Muhammed and Buhari once had. Abacha was a nihilist.

The events that brought Abacha to power were more complicated than Nigeria's other coups.[2] In 1990, five years into his administration, Babangida announced that it was time to hand power back to civilians. This was not a change of heart but a strategy. Babangida had become unpopular; his austerity measures had pleased international bankers, but they alienated the public. His strategy of buying off some rivals and jailing others was beginning to flounder, and the long-promised transition to civilian rule couldn't be put off forever. He wanted to make sure that he could control it. The democratic process that followed was "an imbroglio of dinosaurian proportions," as Muhammed Kamil floridly put it.[3] Two political parties were created, one center-left and one center-right, and they spent the next few years campaigning. In June 1993 a national election was held, and a wealthy businessman from the south, Moshood Abiola, won. Many Nigerians had believed that Abiola was Babangida's favored candidate, but in an unexpected move, Babangida annulled the election. There was much speculation about why he did this, but the effect was to turn Abiola's reputation inside out—from the military's figurehead to its victim. The wealthy businessman who had been a friend of the dictatorship became an emblem of the democratic struggle against it.[4]

To justify the annulment, Babangida pointed to a high court decision that found evidence of corruption in the electoral process, inaugurating a tradition in Nigerian elections—nearly all of them are challenged in court by the losers. The United States, the European Union, and the Commonwealth all condemned the annulment, and protests broke out across the country. The rest of the military elite feared that the thread was coming off the spool, and they moved to isolate Babangida. He resigned, and the Armed Forces Ruling Council appointed a widely respected civilian businessman named Ernest Shonekan as interim president to organize a new election. Before this could happen, General Sani Abacha staged a coup, installing himself as head of state. Abiola still claimed to be the rightful president, which infuriated Abacha (they had once been personal friends). He retaliated by charging Abiola with treason and putting him in jail. More protests followed, including in the oil workers union, which threatened to tank Nigeria's already sinking economy. Abacha responded with a wave of repression. Labor unions and the press were his first targets, and scores of journalists and activists were detained on treason charges. Abacha also set his sights on prodemocracy organizations, especially the National Democratic Coalition (NADECO), which he called a terrorist group. A string of assassinations took place, and Abacha blamed them on NADECO.

Abacha claimed he had reluctantly taken power to save the state.[5] Throughout his administration, he insisted that he had a public mandate. The regime manufactured a "grassroots" movement called Youths Earnestly Ask for Abacha (YEAA). Its leader was a charismatic Nigerian American bodybuilder who organized a "Two Million Man March" (one-upping the American original) to demonstrate the public's support for Abacha. Abacha also claimed to be a democrat. He staged a transition to democracy in which there were five official political parties. All were created by the military, and all stood only one candidate for election—Abacha. Past military governments hadn't felt the need to do all this posturing. They had been open about the fact that they ruled by the gun, and although all claimed they were working in the public good, none pretended to be democrats.

But things had changed by the 1990s. As the Cold War ended, the international community became less tolerant of dictatorships like Nigeria's. Pressure for democratization was building from many directions. Nigeria watched several of its neighbors hold elections, which made the regime nervous. Abacha tried to forestall criticism by putting up a facade of public support. Traditional rulers were among his biggest backers, and Abacha mobilized them whenever he could. "The Obas, Ezes and Emirs cheered Abacha on," a critic wrote, "waving their royal fans in place of swastikas."[6] "Most Nigerians have come to loathe the military," the political scientist Julius Ihonvbere observed. In 1996, he reported that he "could not find a single supporter of military rule" among the people he interviewed. But "ironically, and this is one of the strange components of Nigerian politics, the very same people who loathe the military so much, welcome them to power with praises or dancing, or at least with some indifference, largely out of frustration with the character of Nigerian politicians."[7] Like his predecessors, Abacha constantly reminded people that, whatever the military's shortcomings, civilians were worse. But by the late 1990s, conditions had become so bad that this argument didn't hold water. Abacha had destroyed whatever credibility the military had, and Nigerians haven't trusted it ever since.

Like many soldiers, Abacha came from the bottom. He had grown up poor in a migrant quarter of Kano, followed by training at the Nigerian Military Training College in Kaduna and at Mons in England. He was ambitious and calculating, and he had the distinction of having been involved in all six of Nigeria's successful military coups—he had always chosen the right side. With each coup he rose in stature, such that by the time he took the saddle himself he was already minister of defense. The Nigerian public didn't know much about Abacha when he took the reins, but they knew his voice. During both the 1983 Buhari coup and the 1985 Babangida coup, Abacha had announced the takeover on the radio. His high, childlike voice was memorable, and Nigerians had nicknamed him "Kingmaker."[8]

Once he himself was in power, he ruled with an iron fist and sticky fingers. Abacha warped the ideology that the military had built over its years in power. Whatever good there had been in military rule—its genuine concern for the country's future, even if it led to dark places—was abandoned. Institutions soldiers had built to instill discipline were turned to outright repression. They used their weapons to cut open public assets and scoop out the flesh. Infrastructure was dismantled and stolen, without even the pretext of liberalization. The state sicced the police on anyone it deemed an enemy—which included more and more types of people, until virtually everyone had reason to fear it. "Totally lacking in vision, in perspectives, he is a mole trapped in a warren of tunnels," Wole Soyinka described. "Abacha is prepared to reduce Nigeria to rubble as long as he survives to preside over a name—and Abacha is a survivor."[9]

Abacha loved American westerns, which he studied with rapt attention. Christine Anyanwu argued that it was the cowboy archetype—the lone gunman who lives only by his own rules—that best described his leadership style.[10] He was suspicious of everyone, and more than one of his allies was sentenced to death for crossing him (most famously General Oladipo Diya, his loyal deputy). All officers were paranoid, but for Abacha distrust was the core of his political strategy. He was silent in public, and he avoided formal meetings almost entirely. Even his friends (and he did have a few) found him aloof. "His solemn posture, physical comportment and less talkative nature makes it impossible for anybody to permeate his mind and unravel what is there," wrote one, approvingly.[11] He rarely left the presidential villa in Abuja. "Abacha functioned only at night," recalled a British journalist who spent time with him. "In the early hours the anterooms of the garishly marbled statehouse would be lined with cabinet ministers, senior civil servants, foreign officials and businessmen all waiting nervously for an audience with the dictator, who would very often be drunk and occupied with his imported prostitutes."[12] Usually present for the revelry were his chief security officer, Major Hamza Al Mustapha, and national security adviser, Ismaila Gwarzo. These were the only people he appeared to trust. They parlayed Abacha's fears into personal gain, amassing wealth and power for themselves in the name of keeping him "safe" from his enemies. He rarely showed an interest in matters of state, except those that might make him some money, and his most constant companions were a group of Lebanese magnates with whom he did business.

His commercial dealings were patently criminal. One of his "businesses" was a form of currency fraud called "round tripping," where he and his conspirators bought foreign exchange at low official rates from the Central Bank of Nigeria and then sold it at the much higher market rate, pocketing the difference. Abacha was hardly the only soldier who stole from the state he claimed to protect. Graft, corruption, and fraud had taken place in all of Nigeria's regimes, and no military ruler could claim that everyone in his circle stayed above the fray even if he himself did. But no one came even close to Abacha's level of malfeasance. In the years Abacha was in power, he personally stole the equivalent of 2 to 3 percent of Nigeria's GDP *each year*.[13] He kept much of the money in cash; his widow would later get caught at Kano Airport trying to smuggle thirty-eight suitcases full of foreign currency out of the country. Four billion naira were found in the home of his closest friend, Lieutenant General Jeremiah Useni, stashed in beer cartons.[14] The billions he hid in tax shelters and Swiss bank accounts are still being traced today, and the economic harm his greed caused is immeasurable.[15]

Abacha's methods were not sophisticated, but in the absence of an independent judiciary they didn't have to be. He would have aides collect vast sums of money in cash from the Central Bank of Nigeria, ostensibly for some state purpose, and deposit it at his house by the truckload. He demanded enormous bribes (sometimes calling them "licenses") from foreign companies hoping to do business in Nigeria, and he made a fortune handing out government construction contracts to friends and family members, taking a cut for himself. They had no clue how to fulfill them, and so Nigeria's public infrastructure crumbled. Rumor had it that Abacha also made money from the drug trade. While it was true that Nigeria was an important stop on the international cocaine circuit in this era, I find no evidence that he was personally involved in it.[16] At any rate, his stolen fortune was so massive it seems unlikely to have come from drugs. It could only really have come from one thing.

Abacha lived and died by oil. Oil was the apotheosis of the Nigerian economy, and by the 1990s there was almost nothing left of that economy *aside* from oil. At times when crude prices were high, Nigeria's other exports (cocoa, palm products) had withered as the oil-inflated currency made them less price-competitive—a phenomenon economists call "Dutch disease." As oil eclipsed all other industries, the question of how oil revenues should be split between the states and the federal government became the most contentious issue of national politics. The oil companies that operated in the Niger Delta had an interest in maintaining good relations with the federal government. They used whatever means they had (typically, suitcases of cash) to channel the flow of oil into the international market—and profits into their hands. Oil executives influenced Abacha, but it is hard to get a clear view of his relationship with them. Companies like Royal Dutch Shell were secretive, and their archives are among the world's most tightly controlled. Little can be said confidently about how they operated, but rumor had it that Abacha's most infamous crimes were done with their support.

Abacha and the Judiciary

Abacha saw judges as the enemy. He found them haughty and dreary, and they were never invited to the drunken late-night gatherings where he conducted the affairs of state. Nigeria's previous military regimes had tended to see the judiciary as an ally, even if it wasn't always a loyal one. They appreciated law's dual nature; they understood that it could limit their powers, which made them wary of it. But they also knew that law could be useful in achieving the political ends they wanted. Over the course of military rule, soldiers and judges had duked it out over which metaphor better described their societies: Were they more like organisms that had to be "healed" or machines that had to be "fixed"? Soldiers were more inclined to see them like machines; their military training taught them to think mechanistically about social relationships. Many described politics as a form of "engineering," and the judges allied with them were the mechanics. Abacha brought this debate to an end. His political ends, such as they were, would be reached by culling, not by healing. He had no ambition to transform the country, so the engineering metaphor held no appeal either. Now that there was no design for Nigerian society, there was no need for engineers. He set about liquidating the judiciary.

In the first months of his administration, Abacha faced a series of challenges from the courts. The Supreme Court ruled that Abiola's detention was unlawful and demanded that he be released. While this was happening, Wole Soyinka sued the government. Soyinka and his lawyers took a technical strategy, deciding not to focus on the regime's shortcomings or on the annulled election. Rather, Soyinka reached for the Kelsen doctrine again; he argued that Abacha's "coup" had been *negotiated* with Shonekan rather than seized by force. This meant it wasn't a "revolution," and therefore the government it produced was "illegal." This put Abacha's lawyers in the awkward position of having to admit that his meetings with Shonekan, where the details of the military takeover were hashed out, were an explicit power grab where Shonekan would have been killed if he hadn't acquiesced. This clashed with Abacha's portrayal of himself as the reluctant savior of the nation. The chief justice of the Federal High Court, Mamoud Babatunde Belgore, sided with the government, holding that Abacha's seizure of power constituted a coup and was therefore legitimate. Belgore also ruled, however, that private citizens like Soyinka had a right to sue the state. There was such a thing as legitimate dissent, he argued, and it was better that it be raised in the courts, since "a system that denies people a legal path invites people to follow an illegal alley."[17] The regime disagreed. Abacha wanted there to be no avenue for dissent, legal or otherwise. Soyinka quietly left the country, and he was found guilty of treason in absentia. Nigeria was "retreating into the Dark Ages," he warned from exile in Paris, and an increasingly large part of the international community agreed with him.[18]

Abacha ignored both rulings, and Abiola remained in jail. He faced no consequences for snubbing the courts. This laid bare something that had been true in all military regimes, even though it was seldom said out loud: the balance of power slanted toward the men with guns. A court's capacity to check soldiers lay, at least in part, in their *willingness* to be checked. Abacha was much less willing than his predecessors. The fiction that there were limits on executive power disappeared as soon as the executive stopped acknowledging the rulings he disliked.

Nonetheless, these legal challenges made an impression on Abacha. Even though he had gotten his way, the very fact of being questioned had made the military government lose face. Abacha had the unusual advantage of having served in all of Nigeria's military governments up to that point, and over that time he had seen how this could happen, from *Lakanmi* to the flurry of election trials that preceded his own putsch. He decided to make sure that no one would ever challenge him again. He convened a panel to "sanitise" the judiciary, which was "in dire need of redemption." "In the public eye, the Judiciary was neck-deep in the cross-current which sounded the death knell of the emerging Third Republic," he remarked in a typically garbled speech. "The judiciary seemed to have embarked on an odyssey of self-ridicule which abridged its integrity and cast aspersion on its credibility."[19]

On 5 September 1994, Abacha announced a sweep of decrees targeting his enemies. The Nigerian Labor Congress and the oil workers' unions that had challenged him were dissolved, and dissident newspapers including the

Concord, the *Guardian,* and the *Punch* were banned outright. To leave no doubt about who was in charge, Abacha issued a series of decrees targeting the judiciary. The State Security Detention of Persons (Amendment) Decree No. 11 allowed the government to detain without charge anyone it deemed a security risk for three months, with no limit on how many times the detention could be renewed. This was the end of habeas corpus. The Supremacy and Enforcement of Powers Decree No. 12 proclaimed that the military government was a "revolution" and was therefore legal under international law. Further, it prohibited anyone from bringing any civil charge against any government decree. This was the end of the rule of law.

The prohibition was so broad that even the government's own lawyers were surprised by it. The following day, Minister of Justice Olu Onagoruwa called a press conference where he condemned the new decrees, which "sweep away all our liberties."[20] He claimed that they had been drafted and promulgated without his knowledge, and the crudely worded decrees suggest he was telling the truth—whoever wrote Decree No. 12 was probably not a lawyer. Onagoruwa was promptly fired, and the regime began to harass his family.[21] The chief justice of the Supreme Court at the time of Abacha's putsch was Mohammed Bello, a civil-servant-turned-judge who was more accommodating of militarism than some of his predecessors. He accepted the military's prerogative to issue decrees, and he made no protest when it effectively ended judicial review. His official biographer explains that he "had no inclination to throw the judiciary into a battle with the soldiers that the former was bound to lose, a loss that would be to the detriment of all Nigerians. For Mohammed Bello firmly believed that the judiciary should never seem to be playing a destabilizing role vis a vis government and the state."[22] This was the only kind of judge Abacha liked—one who kept his mouth shut.

No part of the legal system was safe. Even the judicial tools that soldiers had built themselves, like the tribunals, came under attack. In 1993, Abacha decreed that military officers had unlimited power to punish their subordinates, without having to follow the due process of martial law. In 1994, he turned on the Army Legal Services Corps and arrested Colonel Bello Fadile, along with several other prominent military lawyers. Abacha had come to believe, rightly or wrongly, that he had enemies among the army's lawyers, and from here out all tribunals would answer to him, not the army bureaucracy.[23] In 1995 he convened a Special Military Tribunal to investigate an alleged coup plot. The event it investigated came to be known as the "Phantom Coup"— phantom because no one could agree on whether it had really happened. It probably hadn't. "I did not know that someone could just stand up without evidence and fake a coup," an army intelligence officer later recalled. "Even when you were told there was no coup you went ahead with fake investigation, fake trial and on the basis of that, condemned innocent people and sent innocent people to prison."[24]

Dissident army officers, journalists, and bystanders were caught in the dragnet. Its most prominent victim was General Olusegun Obasanjo, who was sentenced to thirty years in prison. Another was Christine Anyanwu, the editor-in-chief of the *Sunday Magazine*, whose reporting displeased Abacha. Anyanwu left perhaps the most vivid account of what passed for law in Abacha's Nigeria:

> Fifteen men in uniforms sat on cushioned chairs on a raised platform. Ten uniformed men stood at strategic corners of the hall, automatic weapons in their arms. I sat on a bench facing the high table. Leg irons removed, I could at least cross my legs. In 30 minutes flat, Patrick Aziza, chairman of the tribunal, said he was giving me life imprisonment for being an "accessory after the fact of treason." It was the first time I ever heard of such a crime. . . . Before and during this sham, I was denied contact with the outside and not permitted to invite my lawyer. A military man just out of law school was imposed on me. He was not permitted to contact my staff, relatives or anyone who could help my case. No witnesses were allowed. He was not permitted to visit me. We met at the tribunal. In the first few minutes of his presentation, the judge advocate threatened him with a court marshal [*sic*]. He crawled into his shell and let his superior officers have their way.[25]

The officers, Anyanwu later recalled, were like aliens doing a bad pantomime of people:

> There I was, sitting before a judge and jury of military men, supposedly waiting for justice under military law. I might as well have sat before a group of thugs from Mars. They and I did not belong to the same world. Their perception and indeed understanding of trial and Justice and judgment was so perverse, so cock-eyed that it did not even remotely resemble the real court of justice for ordinary earthlings. I simply sat back and watched them do their thing.
>
> The tribunal comprised a bunch of puppets, puffy men posturing, pompous intellectual dwarfs trying too hard to mimic learned court justices; trying so hard to look serious, seeking desperately to be taken seriously, fixated on impressing with their fakery and illusion

of thoroughness. All that was a smoke screen, for the undercurrent of tension and fear was unmistakable. The tribunal was tense, hesitant, and tentative. Soldiers carried automatic weapons inside the court. Armed men and armoured cars took combat positions outside doors. Behind each member of the tribunal stood an armed man to watch his back. . . . The accused, broken men and women that they were, waddled into court like a chain gang, sometimes legs chained, and always hands cuffed. . . . Was it justice they hoped for? What manner of justice? Not even the "judges" were in a position to grant justice. It was not theirs to give. Someone else called the shots. Someone else beat the drums. They were dancing to his music, moving to the strings in his hands. They knew there would be no justice; that it was all a show. And as they played their roles, they looked to the cameras standing in the two corners of the hall. Big Daddy's eyes were watching.[26]

Anyanwu spent the first phase of her detention in a building called Security Group, near the headquarters of the Directorate of Military Intelligence in Apapa. It was the first place where many detainees were held. "The dominant impression one got of the place was that of a dark alley that opened out into a maze," she recalled. "This ugly complex housed the think-tank of Nigeria's military intelligence. In a way, the unbecoming structure reflected the quality of leadership of the whole military establishment. Nothing about the place showed long-term thinking or strategic planning. The environment had a stamp of transience and the behaviour of its managers showed a system operated more on whim and caprice rather than thorough planning and rational thinking."[27]

Once the judiciary had been stripped of its powers, the army's ugliest impulses came out. "Government is a science with laws like those of physics and chemistry," wrote Peter Bassey, a rebellious judge who had been removed from the High Court as part of a purge of the judiciary. "You cannot violate them and go scot-free. Nigeria has started suffering from the violations of these laws of government. Perhaps it is futile already to say the truth in Nigeria, but let us record it for history: with the judiciary virtually gone, Nigeria is moving into anarchy."[28] Nigeria had many problems before Abacha, but until the 1990s it would have been hard to say that anarchy was one of them. While other soldiers had used law to sanitize their power grabs, discipline society, and wear down their rivals, Abacha had no interest in putting law to those ends. Unlike other officers, he cared very little for what the world thought about him. He had none of the revolutionary fervor of his predecessors, which might have led him to use law as an instrument of change. As for dealing with his rivals, Abacha preferred a more direct approach.

"Find, Fix, and Finish"

On 11 January 2000, a year into Nigeria's return to democracy, a sergeant named Barnabas Mshelia Jaliba took the stand in the Lagos High Court. Clutching his Bible, Jaliba began to confess. He had been the Abacha regime's hit man, and he claimed responsibility for seemingly every death of a high-profile political figure between 1994 and 1998. He had been born again as a Christian, and he had come to believe he would only be saved if he confessed everything.[29] Operating under the orders of Abacha's security adviser, Jaliba, under the pseudonym Sergeant Rogers, had staged a spree of killings. He admitted to a range of crimes that seemed impossible for one person to have committed—murder, rape, torture, and arson among them. If Sergeant Rogers could be believed, everything that Abacha had blamed on NADECO and other prodemocracy activists was actually his doing. It seemed improbable that one man had committed so many murders, but Sergeant Rogers gave enough details about them that he seemed to be telling the truth. He had some accomplices from Abacha's personal security squad, and the police had often given him cover (though there was debate about how much they knew about what they were covering him for). He had been paid a small bonus for each of them, which raised the question of how to understand his motivations: Was he a soldier carrying out orders or a paid assassin who happened to be employed by the state?[30]

Sani Abacha was not the first soldier to use killing as a political tool, but he was the first to institutionalize it. Aside from coups and coup attempts, the first obviously political murder in Nigeria during the military era was the assassination of the journalist Dele Giwa by parcel bomb on 19 October 1986, during the Babangida administration. Military intelligence officers killed Giwa, the editor of the muckraking newspaper *Newswatch*, for his role in exposing a scandal that threatened to implicate high-ranking officers in the cocaine trade. This was a departure for the military, but Giwa's killing set a new precedent.

Abacha believed, with some justification, that his most powerful rival was the army itself. Taking a page from Muammar Gaddafi (one of his few allies abroad), he created two military units that he controlled directly. The first was his personal guard, consisting of soldiers he had vetted. The second unit was the Strike Force, a seventy-five-member special force that drew from all branches of the armed forces but answered only to him.[31] It was led by Hamza Al Mustapha, his ruthless and loyal aide-de-camp. Over the course of Abacha's administration, Al Mustapha set up a network of spies and informants across the country. When news of a plot reached him, he would deploy the Strike Force to quietly end it. When he believed a political opponent couldn't be silenced through a jail sentence, Sergeant Rogers would be tasked with killing them. Murders were staged to look like carjackings, home invasions, and muggings, all of which were common in Nigeria in these years. It was easy for the military to claim that these were property crimes gone wrong— and some of them may well have been. Crime was so rampant it was hard to be confident.

The military didn't try very hard to hide what it was doing. Brigadier General Samuel Ogbemudia promised that the "Find, Fix, and Finish" strategy, as the murder policy was apparently known in official circles, would be turned against anyone who tried to cross the government, and it became an open secret that Abacha had started to kill his rivals.[32] The list of his victims is long, and it includes Nigerians from many walks of life. The best known are the wealthy or powerful people: Chief Alfred Rewane, a nationalist politician who had served as the chairman of the national Democratic Coalition; Femi Oyewo, a doctor employed by the drug company Pfizer, who had interfered in Abacha's financial dealings; Iyalode Bisoye Tejuoso, the powerful head of the market women in Abeokuta; Alhaja Suliat Adedeji, a wealthy Ibadan businesswoman; and Toyin Onagoruwa, the son of the attorney general, who was murdered after his father criticized Abacha's decrees against the judiciary. Onagoruwa's tearful account of his son's abduction in the white Mercedes-Benz of a well-known brigadier would be one of the most damning testimonies in the truth commission that came later.[33]

Sergeant Rogers would also assassinate Alhaja Kudirat Abiola, the second wife of president-elect Moshood Abiola. Kudirat Abiola was a prominent political figure in her own right, whose Hausa language skills and extensive campaigning in the north had been instrumental in her husband's electoral victory. After he was imprisoned, she used her wealth and connections to tarnish the regime's reputation internationally. On 4 June 1996, she was on her way to meet the Canadian ambassador when six assassins blocked the road and shot her. One of them was Sergeant Rogers. But the Abacha regime's most famous victim would not die at his hands.

* * *

Ken Saro-Wiwa had been a rock in the army's boot for a long time. Saro-Wiwa was a novelist, poet, television writer, and political activist who had taken on many causes over the course of his thirty years in the public eye.[34] He had many friends abroad. His political commitments—environmentalism, democracy—were legible beyond Nigeria, and there was speculation that he was a contender for a Nobel Peace Prize. During the Nigerian Civil War, he sided with the federal government against Biafra, and some of the most stirring statements of the Nigerian cause came from his pen. But when the war ended and the dictatorship didn't, he became a critic of the government. Saro-Wiwa's politics were kindled by his ethnic patriotism. He was a member of the Ogoni ethnic group, a small community in the oil-rich region of the south that, like many minorities in Nigeria, tended to get overlooked in federal affairs. Their marginalization meant they saw none of the profits of oil production, but they felt its externalities acutely—especially pollution. Drilling had destroyed the rural landscape where they lived, and they got nothing in return. Oil had poisoned land and waterways, sickened a generation of people, and ruined the local fishing economy without replacing it with something else. Gas flaring turned swaths of the Niger Delta into biblical hellscapes, and slicks of spilled oil made creeks and wells into toxic fire hazards. Saro-Wiwa became the spokesman of the environmental movement, both in Nigeria and abroad. The oil companies came to see him as a threat—and a threat to the oil industry was a threat to the regime.

Saro-Wiwa's organization, the Movement for the Survival of the Ogoni People (MOSOP), gained strength in the early 1990s, and they began to disrupt oil drilling in the Niger Delta. The Nigerian military responded by burning Ogoni villages to the ground. The military blamed the destruction on the Ogoni's neighbors ("ethnic conflict"), but this was transparently false; the only ones using terror tactics at this time were soldiers. Meanwhile, a rift opened up in the leadership of the environmental movement. A group of moderate Ogoni chiefs, supported by the Rivers State government, announced that they were willing to negotiate with the federal government. Saro-Wiwa's faction had no interest in coming to the table. On 21 May 1994, four of the moderate chiefs were murdered, and a debate ensued about who killed them. Was it an opposing Ogoni faction? One of their neighbors? The most likely perpetrator was the military itself, where Abacha and his advisers had no interest in compromise, even with the moderates. The regime decided to pin the murders on Ken Saro-Wiwa. With record speed, a tribunal was set up to try MOSOP's members. Saro-Wiwa was the most famous of them, but eight other activists were tried alongside him.

The Ogoni activists faced a legal process, but it had a predetermined outcome. The Civil Disturbances Special Tribunal was convened to try the "Ogoni nine," as Saro-Wiwa and his supporters were called, for the "disturbances" in the delta. Like most tribunals it was secretive, and the charges were opaque. But even by the standards of the military, Saro-Wiwa's trial was unfair. His lawyer, Gani Fawehinmi, was prevented from meeting with him. Witnesses whose testimony might have exonerated the activists were barred from the courtroom, and almost no evidence was presented connecting Saro-Wiwa to the chiefs' murders. The tribunal was transparently a sham, and very little effort was put into making it seem otherwise. It ended the way everyone knew it would. Saro-Wiwa and his codefendants were found guilty, and they were executed in Port Harcourt on 10 November 1995. The gallows broke when the soldiers tried to hang him, which his supporters took as proof of his innocence. It took several tries before they succeeded, making for a gruesome spectacle.[35]

It might seem strange that Ken Saro-Wiwa's trial happened at all. Abacha dispatched most of his enemies extrajudicially, with no pretext of a guilty verdict. He had shown his contempt for the legal system through his decrees against it, and the first years of his administration had taught him that it was easier to quietly eliminate rivals through a staged car accident or a "robbery" gone awry than through law. Why commit the time, resources, and risk of public scrutiny to a trial, even one completely on the military's own terms? The outcome would be the same—Ken Saro-Wiwa would be dead, whether death came in the form of a hanging or something quicker, like a letter bomb. A trial was just murder with extra steps.

But a trial made a point in a way an assassination didn't. It mocked the principles that lawyers had tried to protect over the long course of military rule, and it announced that soldiers no longer consented to law's constraints— even the light and breakable ones they had fitted for themselves. By staging a legal process that everyone knew would end in an execution, Abacha showed how empty law's protections were. Saro-Wiwa's fame ensured there would be an audience for it. It was not so much a warning to the Nigerian *public*—there were plenty of those already, like the grisly firing squads on Bar Beach. Nor was a trial a concession to international pressure; it did nothing to convince the wider world that Nigeria was a lawful country (and in fact it did the opposite). Rather, the Ken Saro-Wiwa trial was a warning *to the law*—a rebuke to the lawyers and judges who naively thought law books could stop bullets. In the long contest between the military and the judiciary over who made Nigeria's rules, the soldiers seemed to have won. Ken Saro-Wiwa's trial was their victory lap.

"My father and eight Ogonis were judicially murdered," wrote Saro-Wiwa's son after the execution. "Redress is arduous, and in the long run possibly futile," he went on. But if "civilized behavior" was to survive, people had to keep their faith in law. "Anything else can only lead us back to a darker age."[36] He and the widows of the Ogoni Nine would spend the next two decades in court suing the Nigerian government and Royal Dutch Shell, which they accused of having colluded with Abacha. It might seem strange that they would keep such faith in law, but they weren't alone. Even at the nadir of the Abacha regime, many Nigerians believed that law could offer them something.

Critics of the military made legal forays against it, knowing full well they would lose. But their purpose wasn't really to win. Rather, it was to push out the boundaries of what was possible—to aim high, in the hope that the arrow might land somewhere in the middle. The few successes that they won were partial, Pyrrhic, and "broken," as John Fabian Witt calls the concessions activists can eke out of the courts, but few Nigerians concluded that law was worthless.[37] Law, as Lauren Benton argues, may seem to be "stacked against" subalterns, dissidents, or the poor, but the fact that an appeal may nonetheless provide a remedy—that justice might be won in *spite* of the law—keeps people going back to court even when they know the deck is stacked against them.[38] Saro-Wiwa's son eventually got his day in court, but it wasn't in Nigeria. His legal reckoning happened in the Southern District of New York, where the Alien Tort Statute allowed him to bring a claim against Shell on the grounds that the oil company was *hostis humani generis*—an enemy of all mankind.[39]

Condemnation of the Ogoni Nine's execution was almost universal. The UN Human Rights Commission criticized the Nigerian government, and the General Assembly passed a resolution against it. Nigeria was kicked out of the Commonwealth of Nations—a group that had no shortage of dictatorships. Protests took place all over the world, and governments that had paid no attention to Nigeria for the past forty years suddenly took an interest in its internal affairs. Demonstrations roiled outside Nigerian embassies, and activists like the American civil rights lawyer Randall Robinson pledged to "oppose the Nigerian government with as much tenacity as we opposed the former white South African government."[40] Abacha himself seemed unaffected by all this, but other senior officers felt the sting of the world's scorn. To be lumped in with apartheid South Africa, a government they universally reviled, was especially humiliating. International derision was not the only thing that brought military rule to an end, but it convinced some soldiers that their time was up.

Nigeria's four-decade experiment in militarism would end with a whimper, not a bang. On 8 June 1998, Abacha died suddenly. The circumstances of his death were murky. An autopsy conducted in Germany ruled the cause of death a heart attack, but national lore holds that he was poisoned. A group of junior officers allegedly decided that Abacha had gone too far and killed him with a glass of tainted apple juice (the lore also goes that he died in the company of two Indian prostitutes). It was certainly true that younger officers were on edge—the paranoia that had become endemic in the armed forces made the assassination story plausible. But no one ever stepped forward to take responsibility for it, and given how Abacha lived, an unexpected heart attack wasn't hard to believe.

Abacha's death was a deus-ex-machina moment of African history. He died at the rock bottom of the military's credibility. Whether his death was intentional or not, it caught the army establishment by surprise. His successor was General Abdulsalami Abubakar, the defense chief of staff. Abubakar was a member of Abacha's inner circle, and many saw him as complicit in Abacha's tyranny. He had avoided the purges of the 1990s by staying in the background, and he insisted that he had no desire for political power. Abacha had said this too, as had many soldiers before him, but for Abubakar it turned out to be true. One of his first orders was to create the Independent National Electoral Commission, which organized a democratic election within the year. That election brought to power Olusegun Obasanjo, the military dictator of the 1970s. Obasanjo had won goodwill by voluntarily handing power over to civilians, which no other soldier until Abubakar had done. Since stepping down, Obasanjo had retired from the army, done a stint in prison, made a fortune, and been born again (millions of other Nigerians found evangelical Christianity in this era too).

Unlike the Second and Third Republics, this one stuck, and the Fourth Republic has now survived a quarter century. But for over half of that time, Nigeria has been ruled by ex-soldiers; first Obasanjo, who ruled from 1999 to 2007, and later Muhammadu Buhari, from 2015 to 2023. Nigeria's young generals, now old men, reinvented themselves as civilian statesmen. They shed their uniforms in favor of expensive suits or *agbadas*, the flashy robes favored by the northern political elite. But they never quite gave up their martial affect. Obasanjo always wears matte black aviators in public, and Buhari still has the stiff, clipped manner of someone who spent most of his life on the march. This helps explain why the military stayed out of politics. Soldiers saw Obasanjo and Buhari as one of their own, even if they no longer wore uniforms.

Since the return of democracy, the fortunes of Nigeria's military have fallen sharply. After the disaster of the Abacha years, the army retreated from politics, leaving government to civilians. The regime's most egregious crimes were tried in the courts, where the Abacha family was represented by a slate of famous lawyers (including, briefly, the American attorney Johnnie Cochran, fresh from victory in the O. J. Simpson trial).[41] From 1999 to 2002, a truth and reconciliation commission called the Human Rights Violations Investigation Commission investigated the events of military rule, producing thousands of pages of documentation.[42] Obasanjo decided to bury the commission's report, and it only came to light when an activist leaked a copy on the internet.

In the past twenty years, Nigerians have learned to live with the soldiers who once ruled them. The military, which once tried to tame the country, has turned out to be tamable itself. Soldiers keep a low profile, and none of them are household names. Few command the respect they once did, and they no longer speak of themselves as the nation's saviors. But they haven't lost their old ways. People in uniform, now women as well as men, still harass civilians at checkpoints, and the army's deployments against the Boko Haram insurgency have been inept and destructive. I'm not privy to the military's inner life—maybe Nigerian soldiers dream of power in their bunks. Their comrades elsewhere in Africa certainly do, as the string of recent coups attests. The age of military rule in Nigeria has ended for now, but the martial spirit is still there.

* * *

Who do soldiers fight for? They fight for each other. Those who have commanded or observed armies agree about this: a soldier does the superhuman things that battle demands—including sacrificing himself—to protect his buddies. The politics that constitute what a war is "about" mean little in these moments. But this is a truism about *combat*, not about militarism in general. If soldiers fight for one another, for whom do they *govern*? When they're in charge they turn on each other, making politics into a kind of pie fight that civilians watch with bemused anxiety. The slapstick quickly gives way to real violence.

"The fastest way to destroy an army," a military analyst told me during a stint moonlighting in my own country's foreign service, "is to let it govern." Soldiers who take power invariably find that running a city is harder than commanding a unit. Fighting a war is one thing, but managing a sewer system is another. Rare is the army that can do both well. All militaries are designed to fight, and when they aren't fighting they face a crisis of purpose. Some go on the offensive to justify their existence, inventing enemies where there are none, or picking fights with neighbors to bring the country onto a war footing that feels more natural to them. Others turn their energies against civilians. These are bad ways to run a country, but sitting in judgment of military regimes doesn't tell us where they come from or why they last. The visions that soldiers had for their societies may not have been good ones, but no account of the twentieth century is complete without them.

The lessons of this history, such as they are, are mostly warnings. I have tried to treat military regimes with an even hand—they had light and shade, and most soldiers were trying to do good even when they blundered. But I have no interest in rehabilitating militarism in the name of nuancing it. The soldiers who ruled Nigeria, Ghana, Uganda, Sierra Leone, Sudan, and other countries this book touches were tyrants, including the ones who are fondly remembered. History is not populated by villains and victims, and the moral questions of this period are not black and white. Nonetheless, we shouldn't allow its shades to become a gray area. Military rule was a tragedy.

What made it tragic was not that it was colonialism by another name. Soldiers dreamed big, and they tried to transform their societies. In Nigeria, they believed they would see their country surpass Britain in their lifetimes—not only in population, in which they bounded ahead easily, but in *rectitude.* They would be lawful and moral in ways the British hadn't been. Traditions erased or warped by colonialism would be rediscovered and turned to the task of development. They saw a future when two hundred million Nigerians would march together to a martial rhythm, buoyed by self-esteem and flush with the cash a "disciplined" economy would earn them. Soldiers insisted they were the only ones who could bring about this future. The fact that they believed all this doesn't mean they were *right*, and they fell far short of the goals they set for themselves. Nonetheless, soldiers had a plan for decolonization, and that plan was consequential even in failure.

Decolonization is still an axiom of politics today, but its meaning has changed since the 1960s. It has ballooned from a term for a process—the end of empires, the reformation of minds—to something more like an article of faith. Puncturing overinflated concepts has long been a service that scholars of Africa provide, although not everyone sees it quite as a "service." In recent years we've taken pins to *modernity, globalization, sex, agency*, and others. *Decolonization* is next.[43] Worn out by overuse, this term that meant something in mid-twentieth-century Africa (though certainly not just *one* thing) has been stretched out to the point of being meaningless. The further we get from decolonization's historical context, the blurrier it becomes.[44] Its subtleties vanish when corporations, governments, and universities talk about decolonizing themselves as if this was (a) possible and (b) a straightforwardly good thing. It's only a matter of time before the call to "decolonize" turns up in a beer ad.

Looking at decolonization as a historical process reveals something important about decolonization as a slogan: It is an empty vessel, and you can put all kinds of things into it. The rejection of European imperialism took a dizzying array of forms, and decolonization promised many different futures, not all of which could be reconciled with one another. Africa's literal decolonizers—the people who made colonies into something else—can't be neatly divvyed up into rebels and bootlickers. Not all acts of decolonization were acts of liberation. There were decolonizations of the left and the right. Some united peoples cleaved apart by colonialism. Others split them up further. Some rejected "tribe" and tried to make nations that weren't defined by ethnicity. A few took ethnonationalist turns, with bloody ends. Many decolonizers wore uniforms.

If *decolonization* could be all these things, what was it? It had no singular normative meaning, good or bad. This might seem like an obvious point, but it has been lost in decolonization's turn from historical term of art (and a clunky one at that) to rallying cry. The adverb I have used most in this book is *sometimes*. Sometimes, weapons of colonial domination could be bent into shields. Sometimes, they could only be sharpened. Sometimes, the people most committed to freedom were soldiers. Sometimes, their "freedom" felt more like tyranny. Sometimes, soldiers deposed civilians because they wanted to build a better society. Sometimes, they just wanted to get rid of whoever was standing in their way. Telling the story of decolonization as *always* a triumph, or *always* a failure, hides all this conditionality—all this *sometimes*. What shows it is history. We can find that history in the large type of ideology and the small voice of everyday life.[45]

Decolonization's cognates, especially *decoloniality*, muddle the waters further.[46] The decolonial paradigm that emerged from Latin America at the end of the twentieth century rejected the hidebound empiricism of conventional history to try to access the intangible—sometimes metaphysical—aspects of Europe's conquest of the world.[47] In dismantling modernity, its proponents argued, we might find something valuable in the rubble: a plan for some better society, or a magic spell hidden in a gesture or a ritual. Decoloniality has traveled widely from its beachheads in the Americas (including this press), and it has now reached Africa. Some see liberation in it, others see romanticism or chauvinism. I admit I'm among the latter. When turned on twentieth-century Africa, the decolonial lens distorts more than it reveals. The people who opposed imperialism (anticolonialists) or affirmatively wanted nation-states (nationalists) go blurry. What snaps into focus is something de-colonial theorists call an "otherwise"—a way of being that wasn't constrained by the welter of ideas, feelings, and institutions that Europe forced on the rest of the world. A way out.

The soldier's paradise was one of those worlds imagined *otherwise*. The disciplined utopias that African armies imagined never came to pass, and they looked suspiciously British from some angles. But decolonial thinkers and military ideologues had more in common than either would have liked to admit. Both were looking for ways out of the tight corners that Europe had backed them into.[48] Both wanted to strip away colonialism's epistemological hoarding to find something better preserved underneath. In their writings, they took the same incantatory, messianic tone.[49] Soldiers and radicals offered visions of the world as it once was, or the world yet to come, or some confusing and mysterious thing that was both at once. They performed rhetorical sleight of hand, conjuring complexity to draw the eye away from the vagueness of their ideas. The reverie of planning paradises and thinking *otherwise* inspires some people. I don't begrudge that inspiration, even though I don't share it. The problem is that many other ideas, not all benign, could be smuggled in under decolonization's cloak. In twentieth-century Africa, it could serve as cover for militarism. What does it camouflage today?

If someone's boot is on your neck, does it feel lighter if he's your country-man? African history suggests it might. To most of the people in this book, it was worse to be ruled by foreigners than to be lorded over by a soldier who might be kin. But this didn't mean the moral calculus was simple once the British were gone. There was a long struggle between the executive and the judiciary over what kind of society was to come. Soldiers and judges fed one another one day and tried to starve each other the next. All the while, they were building a new civilization—one that held everyone in a tight, disciplinary embrace. Their Spartan vision was new, and it had no clear analogue in the colonialism that came before them, nor in the brand-name ideologies on offer in their own times. Soldiers made a form of government that broke the British mold, starting from the fact that the army had a political role at all. Their culture lasted long after they gave up power. The problem with Africa's postcolonial leaders wasn't that they were uncreative; it was that *it was hard to like what they made.* Looking back at Africa's military revolutions, it's obvious that this *otherwise* incarcerated the people it promised to free. But the bitter truth is that one person's paradise is always someone else's prison.

ACKNOWLEDGMENTS

1 Nigerian Institute of International Affairs (hereafter NIIA), Nigeria-Law General, "Execution of an Armed Robber," 2 May 1971.

2 First, *Barrel of a Gun*, chapter 3.

3 We've arguably been at this impasse for a long time. In 2003, the historian Luise White argued that the impulse to describe African societies sympathetically led some to make apologies for tyranny or to paper over the ugly things people did to each other in hard times. The flip side of this well-intentioned naivete was *fatalism*. Cynics portrayed Africa as a dystopia, in a style of high dudgeon that came to be known as the "new barbarism." White, review of *Mask of Anarchy*, 632; see also Glassman, *War of Words*, x. For a critique of the "new barbarism" thesis, see Wai, *Epistemologies of African Conflicts*.

INTRODUCTION

1 This application of "nondomination" comes by way of Getachew, *Worldmaking after Empire*.

2 Hutchful and Bathily, *Military and Militarism*; Assensoh and Alex-Assensoh, *African Military History and Politics*; Decalo, *Psychoses of Power* and *Coups and Army Rule in Africa*; Mwakikagile, *Military Coups in West Africa*; Ogueri, *African Nationalism*; Souare, *Civil Wars and Coups d'Etat*; Luckham, *Nigerian Military* and "Military, Militarization and Democratization."

3 One study counted 80 successful coups, 108 failed ones, and 139 plots between 1956 and 2001 across forty-eight independent states in Africa (excluding countries north of the Sahara). McGowan, "African Military Coups d'État."

4 First was a communist and anti-apartheid activist who was assassinated by the South African police in 1982. First, *Barrel of a Gun*, 4.

5 Mahama, *My First Coup d'Etat*.

6 Kamil, *Africa Has Come of Age*, 103.

7 Jemibewon, *Military, Law and Society*, 241.

8 Britain's ex-colonies in Africa include Nigeria, Ghana, Gambia, Sierra Leone, and parts of Cameroon and Togo in West Africa; Kenya, Uganda, Sudan, Somaliland, and Tanzania in East Africa; South Africa, Zimbabwe, Zambia, Malawi, Botswana, Lesotho, and Eswatini in southern Africa; and parts of

Mauritius and the Seychelles in the Indian Ocean. The map of colonial power shifted constantly, which makes it difficult to define what exactly counts as a former British colony. Back-and-forth conquest between Britain and France, the ambiguities of the League of Nations mandate system, and the recombination of colonial territories after independence makes for complicated legal systems across the continent. In general, Britain's ex-colonies in Africa share the English common law as the basis of their legal systems, but some mix that tradition with civil structures from France, Italy, Germany, and the Netherlands depending on the colonial history. Since precedent was portable between common law jurisdictions, a principle that soldiers found useful in one place could turn up on the other side of the continent—or the other side of the world. African jurists were in touch with their counterparts across the former British Empire, especially in South Asia and the Caribbean. They argued, shared expertise, and followed one another's examples regularly. Military officers, who had all trained together in Britain and India, did the same thing.

9   I define a military regime as one in which members of the armed forces openly took control of the state. This definition excludes certain places where militarism was nonetheless important. Zimbabwe and apartheid South Africa, for example, both had characteristics of military regimes—the former was a liberation movement that kept its martial character after it won, the latter a bellicose government where the armed forces had a large presence in public life. Neither is typically counted among Africa's military regimes, however.

10   For an overview of what inequality looks like in Nigeria, see Archibong, "Historical Origins of Persistent Inequality."

11   See Barber, "Popular Reactions to the Petro-Naira"; Adunbi, *Enclaves of Exception*.

12   See Smith, "Why Is Donald Trump," 149–61.

13   *Daily Times* (Lagos), 19 September 1968, NIIA, Nigeria-Law. The witness was the radical teacher Tai Solarin.

14   Quoted in Nigerian Institute of Advanced Legal Studies (hereafter NIALS), *Why Army Rule?*, 3.

15   "Notebook, Gold Coast Trip (Ghana's independence)," March 1957, box 282, Papers of Ralph J. Bunche, UCLA Special Collections.

16   Welch, *Soldier and State in Africa*, 12–13.

17   I place less importance on these pacts than do other historians, such as Whitaker, *Built on the Ruins*.

18   Rodney, *How Europe Underdeveloped Africa*; Amin, *L'Afrique de l'Ouest bloquée*; Shivji, *Class Struggles in Tanzania*.

19   First, *Barrel of a Gun*, 65–67.

20   "Enquiry," 16 March 1977, Lagos State Research and Archives Board (hereafter LASRAB), LCE.A12c, 12 (emphasis added). All emphases are in the original unless otherwise noted.

21   Soyinka, *Open Sore*, 139.

22   Kandeh, *Coups from Below*, 143–78.

23 Mazrui, "Lumpen Proletariat," 1–12. There were some exceptions to this. A few officers came from wealthy or well-connected families, most notably Chukwuemeka Odumegwu Ojukwu. But more came from humble backgrounds, and nearly all members of the rank and file came from the peasantry. The military was one of few social elevators available to all Nigerian men.

24 Though he also predicted that soldiers would become just as extractive as the civilians they replaced—in the lingo of Mazrui's times, a process of "embourgeoisement."

25 Patricia Lockwood, "America Is a Baby," *London Review of Books*, 3 December 2020.

26 Huntington summarized this mindset as "conservative realism." Huntington, *Soldier and the State*, 59–79.

27 A comparison can be made to the early modern Europe of Perry Anderson's description, where absolutist states were "machines built overwhelmingly for the battlefield." Many hallmarks of the modern state—bureaucracy, taxation—were refined for the purpose of building armies. Africa's leaders hoped militarism might give flesh to their new states in a similar way. Anderson, *Lineages of the Absolutist State*, 32. Another useful comparison is to Yugoslavia, where soldiers also believed they could build a martial utopia out of many different peoples. See Petrović, *Utopia of the Uniform*.

28 Ocran, *Politics of the Sword*, 94.

29 Their commitment to public welfare was usually skin-deep. In Sierra Leone, for example, it took the form of an annual event called the "Pauper's Treat"—a sort of party where soldiers doled out food and household goods to the poor. "The Way Forward—Reflections: Two Years Under the NPRC," Sierra Leone Department of Information, Broadcasting, and Culture, 1994.

30 It is telling that Olusegun Obasanjo entitled his memoir-*cum*-political-treatise *This Animal Called Man*.

31 Liliwhite-Nwosu, *Divine Restoration of Nigeria*.

32 See Schmidt, *Foreign Intervention in Africa*; Abrahamsen, "Return of the Generals?"

33 Venter, *War Dog*, 15.

34 Stanley Crouch, "Into Africa," *Village Voice* (New York), 17 December 1985.

35 Some decisions did both at once. In 1971, a cannabis dealer in Nigeria appealed his conviction for drug possession on the grounds that he had been given an excessive sentence. Justice Chukwudifu Oputa agreed with him, ruling that "it will be an absurd law that leaves the maximum sentence on conviction to the unpredictable whims and caprices of a trial Magistrate, or to the state of his digestion." In so doing, he both acquitted the appellant and established a sentencing limit for drug offenses. The military subsequently overturned that limit by decree, but the fact that a judge could take this kind of stand is worth noting. *Cletus Okeke and Commissioner of Police*, High Court of the East Central State, Nnewi, 11 May 1971, Enugu State High Court, uncataloged collection.

The names of defendants in unreported criminal trials have been changed to protect their privacy.

36 NIALS, *Why Army Rule?*, 248.

37 See Kureshi, *Seeking Supremacy*; Hilbink, *Judges Beyond Politics*; Ghias, "Miscarriage of Chief Justice"; Karekwaivanane, *State Power in Zimbabwe*; Tushnet and Khosla, *Unstable Constitutionalism*.

38 Shapiro, "Courts in Authoritarian Regimes."

39 Massoud, *Law's Fragile State*, 218.

40 Authoritarian leaders found value in the language of radical intellectuals, but this didn't stop them from silencing those intellectuals if they became inconvenient. In Kenya, Ngũgĩ wa Thiong'o was hounded into exile by Daniel arap Moi, only to watch soldiers like Babangida start adopting his language of "decolonising the mind." See Ngũgĩ wa Thiong'o, *Decolonising the Mind*; "Address by General Ibrahim Badamasi Babangida," 1989, NIALS uncataloged collection.

41 "Address by General Ibrahim Badamasi [*sic*] Babangida," 1989, NIALS uncataloged collection.

42 Not that only civilians are eligible for this honor. General Murtala Muhammed graces the twenty. On Zik's legacy, see Adebanwi, "Burying 'Zik of Africa.'"

43 Azikiwe, *Democracy with Military Vigilance*, 19.

44 Azikiwe, *Democracy with Military Vigilance*, 26–27.

45 This was a form of "positive action," not unlike the strategy Kwame Nkrumah pursued in Ghana. See Njoku, "Zikism."

46 The success of the Zikist movement was mixed. Fewer people took up the cause than he hoped, and a botched assassination attempt of a British official prompted a crackdown that landed him and his followers in jail. Nigeria's independence would ultimately be won by other means—namely tepid negotiation with the British, which Zik helped orchestrate.

47 On this war, see Daly, *History of Biafra*.

48 On the ins and outs of that drama, see Max Siollun's detailed books on Nigeria since independence, *Oil, Politics and Violence* and *Nigeria's Soldiers of Fortune*.

49 Comparatively, see Peterson et al., "Unseen Archive of Idi Amin."

50 See generally Stapleton, *West African Soldiers*.

51 Soyinka, *Open Sore*, 79.

52 Amuta, *Prince of the Niger*, 21.

53 Janowitz, *Military in Political Development*, 64.

54 General Ibrahim Babangida to Margaret Thatcher, 15 May 1990, National Archives of the United Kingdom, Kew (hereafter NAUK), PREM 19/3103.

55 Babangida, *Home Front*, 14.

56 A further note on terminology: I and many of my sources sometimes use the term *army* as a metonym for the armed forces as a whole. This is slightly misleading. Nigeria, for example, had an army, a navy, and an air force, all of which played a part in military administration. The army dwarfed the

other service branches, however, and most military rulers were army officers (Ghana's Flight Lieutenant Jerry Rawlings was a notable exception).

57 The "worm's eye view of war" is most associated with the journalist Ernie Pyle. See Chrisinger, *Soldier's Truth*. The best example of that view in Nigeria is Ken Saro-Wiwa's classic *Sozaboy: A Novel in Rotten English*.

58 Enonchong, *I Know Who Killed Major Nzeogwu!*, 29.

59 Quoted in Hutchful and Bathily, *Military and Militarism*, xiii.

60 On ethnicity and national politics in Ghana, see Allman, *Quills of the Porcupine*.

61 NIALS, *Why Army Rule?*, 86.

62 Kamil, *Africa Has Come of Age*, 240–42.

63 Afowowe, *Onward Soldier*, 14.

64 "Honor" has a long and equivocal history in Africa. See Iliffe, *Honour in African History*, 345–49.

65 Ogueri, *African Nationalism*, 46.

66 *Secular* is an imperfect term to describe their attitude toward religion, and the Nigerian state's official secularism was mostly honored in the breach. Nonetheless, it was an important idea under both colonialism and military rule. See Akande, *Entangled Domains*.

67 Jemibewon, *Combatant in Government*, 174.

68 Ochonu, *Colonialism by Proxy*; Osborne, *Ethnicity and Empire*.

69 This beats against the current of much scholarship in political science. See Harkness, *When Soldiers Rebel*; Dwyer, *Soldiers in Revolt*.

70 Amuta, *Prince of the Niger*, 98.

71 Ocran, *Politics of the Sword*, 126, 128.

72 Quoted in Kamil, *Africa Has Come of Age*, 243.

73 Quoted in Ocran, *Politics of the Sword*, 124.

74 Niki Tobi, "The Rule of Law Under the Current Military Regime in Nigeria: A Trial Judge's View Point," Beijing Conference on the Law of the World, 22–27 April 1990.

75 Keegan, *Mask of Command*, 11.

76 Amuta, *Prince of the Niger*, xx.

77 Oluleye, *Military Leadership*, 11–14, 16.

78 Olivia Y. Gaba, "Profile," Special Mails to Mobolaji Johnson, LASRAB.

79 Col. Mobolaji O. Johnson to Ukpabi Asika, 10 March 1972, Special Mails to Mobolaji Johnson, LASRAB.

80 "Call by Nigerian Minister of Justice and Attorney General, Prince Bola Ajibola on the Attorney General," 31 January 1986, United Kingdom Foreign and Commonwealth Office, FCO 58/4582, obtained by Freedom of Information Act 2000 Request, reference 0428–19.

81 Amuta, *Prince of the Niger*, 20.

82 This is a work of fiction, but Sankara was indeed the object of many crushes. Adichie, "Shivering," 166.

83 Babangida, *Home Front*, 34.

84 Militaries that enlist women often exclude them from combat, where the greatest risks and the greatest rewards of military service are found. For some rare exceptions to this rule, see Wilson, *Women and Eritrean Revolution*; Ly, "Promise and Betrayal"; and beyond Africa, see Alexievich, *Unwomanly Face of War*. See also Lindsay and Miescher, *Men and Masculinities*.

85 I never found archival trace of this, but it was given fictional treatment in David Caute's forgotten novel of decolonization, *At Fever Pitch*.

86 This argument was powerfully made in the early 2000s by Goldstein, *War and Gender*, but military historians never meaningfully took it up.

87 Mba, *Kaba and Khaki*, 4.

88 Mama notes that this labor became especially important in the context of structural adjustment, when formal employment withered away. Mama, "Bridging through Time," 89.

89 It was a different matter in bourgeois civilian governments, where the fiction that women exist only in the home could be maintained more easily.

90 Making families, making armies, and making states have long been linked processes in African history—arguably more than elsewhere. See Osborn, *Our New Husbands*; Burrill, *States of Marriage*.

91 Layonu, *Reflections on Leadership*, 150.

92 To some, this seemed to build on forms of influence women had exercised in African politics before colonialism. Jibrin, "First Lady Syndrome."

93 Aduku, *Maryam*, 39.

94 Aliyu, *Maryam Sani Abacha*.

95 Borno State Government, *Milestone*, 46.

96 Mama, "Khaki in the Family," 1–17.

97 Afowowe, *Onward Soldier*, 62–63.

98 On those scattered archives, see Daly, "Archival Research in Africa."

99 As Matthew Connelly writes of the United States in its own mute era, "the dark state can no more tell its own story than a man with dementia can write his own memoir." Connelly, *Declassification Engine*, 387.

100 "Soldier come, soldier go, but barrack remains" is a common expression in Nigeria. The implication: Militarism had institutional staying power in a way that no individual military regime did. Achebe, *Anthills of the Savannah*, 222.

101 In this respect they couldn't be more different from the soldiers of Luise White's *Fighting and Writing*, who chronicled themselves obsessively. Olusegun Obasanjo fully bucks this trend, however, having not only written several memoirs but built a presidential library in his hometown.

102 Jemibewon, *Combatant in Government*, 196.

103 Nigeria shares this predicament with many states where the military has dominated politics. Comparatively, see Mikhail, *My Egypt Archive*.

104 Mann, "Africanist's Apostasy," 117–27. Relatedly, see Hewage, "Event, Archive, Mediation," 186–217.

105 The places where these documents are held fly under the radar. They include the NIIA, LASRAB, NIALS, and the archives of various foreign governments

and international organizations. Some published materials ended up in the libraries of American universities like mine, where government-funded "area studies" programs boomed during the Cold War.

106 The best insights born of this approach include Chabal and Daloz, *Africa Works*; Hoffman, *War Machines*.

107 Wallace, *Infinite Jest*, 83.

108 Respectively, see Bayart, *State in Africa: Politics of the Belly*; Mbembe, "God's Phallus," in *On the Postcolony*.

109 Necropolitics is a form of government in which "weapons are deployed in the interest of maximally destroying persons and creating *death-worlds*, that is, new and unique forms of social existence in which vast populations are subjected to living conditions that confer upon them the status of the *living dead*." Mbembe, *Necropolitics*, 92.

110 Exemplars of this approach include Musila, *Death Retold*; Cohen and Odhi- ambo, *Burying SM*.

111 Eventually structural adjustment policies would force them to end those tar- iffs, flooding markets with cheap Thai rice and American grain, and under- cutting local agriculture.

112 Anyanwu, *Days of Terror*, 64.

113 Maja-Pearce, *In My Father's Country*, 82.

114 Chikendu, *Military Question*, 59.

115 Even the two who returned to power as civilians, Obasanjo and Buhari, spent years out in the cold before rehabilitating themselves.

116 Wilmot, *Seeing Double*, 15.

CHAPTER 1. THE MASTER'S TOOLS

1 See Anene, *International Boundaries of Nigeria*.

2 Chukwuemeka Odumegwu Ojukwu, the leader of the Biafran secessionist movement, was one of the few who did so explicitly, in *Ahiara Declaration*.

3 Amuta, *Prince of the Niger*, 196.

4 The novelist Chinua Achebe made this point most forcefully. On the origins of Achebe's thought, see Ochiagha, *Achebe and Friends*.

5 This goes against an increasingly wide consensus that it did. See especially Elkins, *Legacy of Violence*; Wagner, "Savage Warfare."

6 Young, *African Colonial State*; Berry, "Hegemony on a Shoestring."

7 Jasanoff, *Dawn Watch*.

8 This was the School of Oriental and African Studies, founded in 1916.

9 On these strategies, see Mamdani, *Citizen and Subject*; Ibhawoh, "Maxim Gun," 55–83.

10 The Maxim gun is an early machine gun that tipped the scale decisively in Europeans' favor in the wars of colonial conquest. Belloc, *Modern Traveller*, 41.

11 This approach is exemplified by the work of Frederick Cooper, especially *Citizenship between Empire and Nation*. See also Stoler, *Duress*.

12 This modifies Karl Marx's formulation "men make their own history, but they do not make it as they please." Marx, *Eighteenth Brumaire of Louis Bonaparte*.

13 *Daily Times* (Lagos), 19 September 1968, NIIA, Nigeria-Law.

14 A few used Nigeria as fodder for larger ideas about the state, most notably Peter Ekeh, whose conception of Africa's two publics—one "primordial" and the other "civic"—traveled far beyond Nigeria. Ekeh, "Colonialism and Two Publics." See also Adebanwi, "Africa's 'Two Publics'"; Osaghae, "Colonialism and Civil Society."

15 See Pierce, *Moral Economies of Corruption*; Joseph, *Democracy and Prebendal Politics*; Adebanwi, Obadare, and Diamond, *Democracy and Prebendalism*; Agbiboa, *They Eat Our Sweat*.

16 Outside Nigeria, opinions about their performance in Katanga were more mixed. See Lefever and Joshua, "United Nations Peacekeeping."

17 See Ademoyega, *Why We Struck*.

18 That condemnation is still voiced today. "It was startling to see Africans who'd claimed to champion independence take on the garb and manner of colonizers," writes Keguro Macharia, sounding not unlike the soldiers in this book. "Still-healing wounds from colonialism, briefly sutured by independence, split open. Rot set in." Macharia, "From Repair to Pessimism," 1.

19 Babangida, *For Their Tomorrow*, 174.

20 For example, General Sani Abacha: "We must all make maximum sacrifices to avoid another civil war. . . . We are a nation and we have to remain as one." Edet, *Abacha's Call to Duty*.

21 On the implications of this advice, see Mazrui, "Seek Ye First," 105.

22 Perhaps the only political commitment that virtually everyone in postcolonial Africa shared from the 1960s to the 1990s was the most explicitly anticolonial one—that white minority rule in southern Africa had to come to an end. Opposition to colonialism could be a great unifier.

23 Nkrumah, *Dark Days in Ghana*, 48, 45.

24 Not all of it was funded by public money. Institutions like Goodenough College (a student residence in London), the English Speaking Union, and a network of private charities and societies forged links to the former empire, creating a rapport between the British and their former colonial subjects that was cut with condescension. For an extensive description of these institutions, see Stockwell, *British End*.

25 American intelligence officers knew about this plan, but they do not appear to have been its makers. Memorandum of conversation, Washington, DC, 11 March 1965, *Foreign Relations of the United States*, vol. 24, *1964–1968, Africa*, ed. Nina Davis Howland (Washington, DC: Government Printing Office, 1999), document 251.

26 "Africa: Requests for Military Training," 6 June 1986, NAUK FCO 65/3706.

27 This changed with the United Kingdom's departure from the European Union, which brought with it a wave of imperial nostalgia. Priyamvada Gopal describes the "many apologists for colonial rule, still wheeled out on radio and

television programmes in Britain, for whom the blotted copy-book of many independent states is evidence of the inbuilt weaknesses of anticolonialism itself—proof that African countries, and not a few Asian ones, were not ready for independence." Gopal, *Insurgent Empire*, 448–49.

28　For a good statement of this case, see Siollun, *What Britain Did.*

29　Smith makes this comparison through a different institution (the police) and in a different setting (South Africa), but it is equally illuminating here. Smith, "State as Golem," 207–30.

30　Reid, *Warfare in African History*, 107–17.

31　"It is an historical fact that what is known today as the Nigerian Army has its antecedents in the colonial forces raised by the British," declares an authoritative book on the military. Achike, *Groundwork of Military Law*, 15.

32　Owusu, "Custom and Coups," 80. See also Wilfahrt, *Precolonial Legacies*; Mazrui, "Lumpen Proletariart."

33　Afowowe, *Onward Soldier*, 101.

34　Ocran, *Politics of the Sword*, 123.

35　See Clayton and Killingray, *Khaki and Blue*; Parsons, *African Rank-and-File.*

36　Ranger, "Invention of Tradition," 226.

37　Bhabha, "Of Mimicry and Man," 125–33.

38　See Korieh, *Nigeria and World War II*; Byfield et al., *Africa and World War II*; Coates, "Perspectives on West Africa," 5–39.

39　Quoted in Achike, *Groundwork of Military Law*, 21.

40　On the paths that Christianity could take in Africa, see Peterson, "Politics of Transcendence."

41　Ranger, "Invention of Tradition."

42　Afowowe, *Onward Soldier*, 25–26.

43　Other Nigerian officers trained at the Nigerian Military Training College, which was staffed primarily by Indian personnel until the 1970s. In addition to the Mons graduates, Johnson Aguiyi-Ironsi, Yakubu Gowon, and Murtala Muhammed trained at Sandhurst, Ibrahim Babangida at the Indian Military Academy in Dehradun, and Abdulsalami Abubakar in West Germany. Obasanjo did his basic training in Ghana, which later came in handy in navigating the delicate relationship between the two countries. Olusegun Obasanjo, "Ghana Is My Military Home," 25 May 1979, NIIA, Nigeria-Foreign Relations-Ghana. See also Obasanjo, *Nzeogwu*, 34–44.

44　Mons would be consolidated with Sandhurst in 1972. See Stockwell, *British End*, 235–82.

45　The twenty-week course being offered in 1968, for example, included basic military skills of drill, map reading, and physical fitness. By the end of the course they had progressed from how to handle their weapons to advanced points of strategy and leadership, all presented in the barest outline format. Twenty-nine of the forty-four cadets who graduated that year were from overseas. That year Sheikh Mohammed Bin Rashid, who would later become the ruler of the Emirate of Dubai, was among the graduates. "African Army

Cadets Pass Out from Mons Officer Cadet School," 16 October 1968, Reuters newsreel.

46 Stigger, "Military Minutiae," 147.

47 On this dynamic in the former French Empire, see Ginio, *French Army*.

48 On colonial rules of law in West Africa, see Thornberry, "Procedure as Politics"; Barnes and Whewell, "Judicial Biography"; Roberts and Mann, *Law in Colonial Africa*; Mann, *Slavery and the Birth*; Van Hulle, *Britain and International Law*; Date-Bah, *Supreme Court of Ghana*; Roberts, *Conflicts of Colonialism*; Moore, *Social Facts and Fabrications*; Chanock, *Law, Custom*.

49 On these bureaucratic tools, see Berda, *Colonial Bureaucracy*.

50 On the mechanics of how this happened, see Tobi, *Sources of Nigerian Law*.

51 Adetokunbo Ademola, who would go on to be Nigeria's first African chief justice, felt the sharp end of the law while studying in Cambridge, where he faced a racially motivated charge of assaulting a white woman in 1928. "Records of Solanke as Lawyer," 1928, box 28, Papers of Ladipo Solanke, Gandhi Library, University of Lagos. The papers of the director of the West African Students Union, Ladipo Solanke, are a remarkable source on the connections that African students made during their studies in Britain and Ireland. Solanke kept virtually every piece of paper that ever passed through his hands, making his papers a valuable source on nearly any topic in Nigerian history from the 1920s to the 1950s.

52 Adi, *West Africans in Britain*; Olusanya, *West African Students' Union*; Garigue, "West African Students' Union."

53 Even though they were exempt from military service, African civilians studying in Britain during the Second World War lived in a militarized society where soldiers commanded respect. Some of them continued to feel that respect long after the war ended.

54 Sir Udo Udoma, later a prominent judge, roomed with Kwame Nkrumah until he decided the future Ghanaian president was "rather too political" and asked him to find someplace else to live. "Naija Must Go!," *Daily Trust* (Lagos), 22 June 2019.

55 Taslim O. Elias, "Law and Justice in Independent Nigeria," *Sunday Observer* (Lagos), 1 January 1978.

56 "Editorial: How Free are the Judges?," *Sunday Sketch* (Lagos), 7 September 1975, 3.

57 Achike, *Groundwork of Military Law*, 149.

58 At the state level, military governors served as "the sole legislator of [his] state's legislature," allowing the fiction that state legislatures were still open. Achike, *Groundwork of Military Law*, 149.

59 This was true both during colonialism and under military rule. In some autocratic states, legislatures also played this role, at least to the extent that they could be used to secure the allegiances of elites and bring them into the task of governance. Since Nigeria's legislature was suspended for almost the entire period discussed here, it is not one of those states. On this function, see Opalo, *Legislative Development in Africa*.

60 Adewoye, *Judicial System*, 291. See also Oguamanam and Pue, "Lawyers' Professionalism."

61 Quoted in Adewoye, *Judicial System*, 285.

62 I also suspect colonial officials, not all of whom had elite educations, resented Africans who held degrees from more prestigious British universities than they did.

63 Adewoye, *Judicial System*, 288.

64 Oputa, *Conduct at the Bar*, 46–47.

65 Quoted in Widner, *Rule of Law*, 36.

66 Okonjo, *British Administration*, 338. Then as now, there is a gulf between what "rule of law" means as a legal term of art and what the public thinks it means. As judges use it, "rule of law" is not just the truism that law governs how people live. Rather, the rule of law describes a situation where an executive is constrained by a judiciary. In common usage, however, it means something vaguer—often, a general orderliness.

67 Tunji Abayomi, "Reforming the Nigerian Legal System," *Sunday Times* (Lagos), 19 April 1981, 5.

68 Later, military governments in Ghana would establish "People's Revolutionary Courts" and other implements of "revolutionary" justice, which were often just military tribunals gussied up with a new name so as not to alarm the public. Ghana's "experiment in revolutionary justice" was "part of a continent-wide trend to restructure legal systems inherited from the colonial past," as an American anthropologist observed at the time. Gocking, "Ghana's Public Tribunals," 201.

69 Feingold, *Colonial Justice*, 11.

70 Daniels and Woodman, *Essays in Ghanaian Law*, ix.

71 Taslim Elias, "The Law as an Instrument of National Unity," 20 January 1969, NIIA, Law-General.

72 Kuti, *Law and Policy*, 142.

73 "Workshop on Review of Colonial Laws Opens in Lagos," 27 October 1986, NIIA, Nigeria-Tribunals.

74 Oputa had a complicated relationship with militarism. He would preside over the post-1999 commission of inquiry into the crimes of the military era, and during this commission he ruthlessly pursued the soldiers whom he deemed responsible for Nigeria's decline. But he was also among the people who had given them license to take over in the first place. His son, the musician and activist CharlyBoy, is also a fascinating character. A gender-bending champion of the poor, CharlyBoy had a raunchy, puerile television program that mocked the military governments his father served. The military would almost certainly have shut it down if not for the fact that his father was on the Supreme Court.

75 Chukwudifu Oputa, "In Search of a Disciplined Society through Law: Being a Paper Presented during the Law Week, Marking the Centenary Celebrations of the Legal Profession in Nigeria," 22 February 1986, NIIA, Nigeria-Law (emphasis in original).

76 Chukwudifu Oputa, "Towards Justice with a Human Face," Plenary Session of the Law Week of the Nigerian Bar Association, February 1985, NIIA, Nigeria-Law.

77 Elias, "Law as an Instrument."

78 De, "Peripatetic World Court."

79 Ibhawoh, *Imperial Justice*, 150.

80 Opolot, *Just and Unjust Institutions*, 158–69; Gower, *Independent Africa*, 87–89.

81 *Federal Republic of Nigeria Official Gazette* 55, no. 59 (22 August 1968): 1136.

82 Elias, *Judicial Process*, 172–75.

83 *Daily Times* (Lagos), 19 September 1968.

84 Oputa, "Disciplined Society."

85 T. Akinola Aguda, "The Quintessence of Justice: A Lecture Delivered at the University of Maiduguri," 31 January 1985, NIALS uncataloged collection.

86 See Hussain, *Jurisprudence of Emergency*.

87 T. Akinola Aguda, "Law as an Instrument of National Unity: A Lecture Delivered to the Bendel State Civil Service," 24 April 1987, NIALS uncataloged collection.

88 *Sunday Sketch* (Lagos), 20 September 1970, NIIA, Nigeria-Law General.

89 The military planned to hand over power to civilians the following year, and they wanted whoever was elected to continue the project of "decolonising" the legal system. The commission created the administrative continuity to make sure they did.

90 *Sunday Standard* (Lagos), 16 September 1979, 12.

91 Satia, *Spies in Arabia*, 10.

92 Comparing laws to weapons, as I have done here, is a common rhetorical device. Both laws and guns have an inert violence that those who aren't familiar with them often find sinister. They can be wielded offensively or defensively, and they can maim their bearers as well as their targets. But this metaphor misses the mark; comparing law to an *object* like a gun conceals its discursive nature. Sticking to the martial theme, the better metaphor would be a spatial one. Law is not the weapon, it is the *battlefield*.

93 Throughout the colonial period Nigeria, Ghana, Gambia, Sierra Leone, and Southern Cameroon were administered by a skeleton crew of British administrators. Unlike in settler colonies (like Kenya), there was no permanent European population to speak of. The only non-African community of any significance were the Lebanese and Syrian merchants who had settled in West Africa in the first decades of the twentieth century. Although they were prominent in the commercial world, they were numerically insignificant.

94 Oputa, *Conduct at the Bar*, 1.

95 Mamdani, *Imperialism and Fascism*, 44.

96 A now canonical essay still says it best: "One should read the history of opposition to colonial domination neither as a victory won nor as an illusory moment in a protracted history of imperial domination." Cooper and Stoler, "Between Metropole and Colony," 36.

97 Shyllon and Obasanjo, *Rule of Law*, 16.
98 Shyllon and Obasanjo, *Rule of Law*, 27.
99 Lorde, *Sister Outsider*, 110–14.

CHAPTER 2. THE SOLDIER'S CREED

1 An exception is Pankaj Mishra, who attends to the ideological diversity of postcolonial dictatorships in a way that few others do in *From the Ruins of Empire*. Two exceptional works that convey the subtlety and depth of authoritarian thought in Africa are Cheeseman and Fisher, *Authoritarian Africa*; and Nugent, *Africa since Independence*, 204–59.

2 We might also consider "rebel" ideologies, which, even if they were never formally adopted by a state, shaped the lives of those who lived under them. These would include the voluminous ideological writings of the Shining Path, for example. See Starn and La Serna, *Shining Path*.

3 Their secretaries, however, sometimes distilled their ideas into manifestos and declared them isms. Even Murtala Ramat Muhammed, who ruled Nigeria for only two hundred days, received this treatment. Oshunkoya, *Wisdom of Ramatism*.

4 "A relevant point of convergence between Marxism and the Quran," Kamil wrote, "is the principle that internal contradictions are primary, external secondary." Kamil, *Africa Has Come of Age*, 9–10.

5 Aduku, *Maryam*, 77.

6 Quoted in Cheeseman and Fisher, *Authoritarian Africa*, xix; "Gambia's Yahya Jammeh Ready for 'Billion-Year' Rule," *BBC News*, 12 December 2011.

7 First, *Barrel of a Gun*, 430.

8 Successful coups almost always resulted in pay raises, both for officers and enlisted men. Soldiers might have learned what their labor entitled them to from another category of male workers the state depended on—rail workers, who had significant bargaining power. See Lindsay, *Working with Gender*.

9 Luanda, "Tanganyika Rifles."

10 Among the disgruntled officers was Gnassingbé Eyadéma, who would stage another coup four years later. He ruled the country for nearly forty years, during which he built an elaborate cult of personality.

11 See Janowitz, *Military in Political Development*, 1–12.

12 As Gowon declared in a 1970 broadcast to the nation, "As soldiers my colleagues and I are ready to go back to the barracks any day, but the work of national reconstruction must be completed." It would be nearly a decade before they went back—and then only for a few years. Quoted in Achike, *Groundwork of Military Law*, 186. See also Falola and Ihonvbere, *Rise and Fall*, 18–28.

13 Military regimes managed to put down many coups before they happened, some of which were publicized while others were not. Perhaps the most famous of them was Major General Mamman Vatsa's attempted coup against Babangida, an elaborate plot that would have involved bombing the military's headquarters in Lagos by air. Vatsa, who had been the minister of the Federal

Capital Territory in Abuja, was executed alongside eight coconspirators by firing squad in March 1986. Umoden, *Babangida Years*, 218.

14 See Livsey, *Nigeria's University Age*.

15 Parading was important to many military regimes. See Sow, "Military Parade in Mali."

16 Parts of it were demolished in 2023, over the objections of historic preservationists.

17 Though there are some notable exceptions, most notably the bitter, petty relationship between Buhari and Flight Lieutenant Jerry Rawlings of Ghana, which manifested most destructively as a mass expulsion of Ghanaians from Nigeria. See Daly, "Ghana Must Go."

18 Mugabe was not a soldier per se, but he was every inch a militant. Amuta, *Prince of the Niger*, 194.

19 In military rhetoric, even the most banal tasks were given the gravitas of battle. One officer made distributing some office furniture sound downright epic: "Colonel Eze, like the Artillery Officer and tactician which he is, first neutralized the tense situation with his charismatic aura, thus clearing the way for governance. His target, which he ostensibly achieved, was to carry the entire people of the then Anambra State along through equal distribution of key amenities"—i.e., filing cabinets. "1 Year In Office, Lt. Col. H.O. Eze, fss, psc (+), Military Governor, Enugu State of Nigeria," 1991, box 7, Nigerian Subject Collection XX787, Hoover Institution Archive, Stanford, CA.

20 Interstate wars that took place between military and civilian regimes would include the war between Tanzania and Uganda that led to Idi Amin's removal in 1979, and Senegal and Mauritania's border war from 1989–1991. Wars between military regimes were rare, but the Ogaden War between Ethiopia and Somalia in 1977–1978 and the Chadian-Libyan war of the 1980s would qualify. For a survey of these wars, see Reno, *Warfare in Independent Africa*.

21 See Ellis, *Mask of Anarchy*; Behrend, *Alice Lakwena*.

22 A war could be both a war of colonial liberation and a civil war, for example, as in Angola, or a border dispute and a domestic police action, as in Kenya's Shifta War. For a particularly knotty illustration of this category problem, see Drury, "Anticolonial Irredentism."

23 On the foreign policy of Nigeria's later military regimes, see Osayande, "Tortuous Trajectory."

24 First, *Barrel of a Gun*, 21.

25 Some posited a relationship between coups and boredom—especially the kind brought about by banning drinking or cardplaying, as many African militaries did. One observer convincingly argued that Sierra Leone's 1967 coups happened because the officers had too much leisure time. Bebler, *Military Rule in Africa*, 72.

26 Vagts, *History of Militarism*, 13, 15.

27 Like many of the soldiers in this book, Mobutu had a complicated relationship with "decolonization." See Monaville, *Students of the World*; Young and Turner, *Rise and Decline*. On Bokassa, see Smith and Faes, *Bokassa*.

28 Ben-Ghiat, *Strongmen*.

29 Finchelstein, *Ideological Origins*.

30 Obadare, *Pentecostal Republic*.

31 Babangida, *For Their Tomorrow*, 178–79.

32 Though only for Nigerians. Foreigners, especially Ghanaians and other non-Nigerian Africans, faced an obstacle course of restrictions. Moreover, the right of free movement that existed in principle did not always exist in practice. Igbos were not welcome in Port Harcourt after the war, for example, and Muslim northerners who tried to settle in the east only did so with great difficulty.

33 Quoted in Nnamdi Azikiwe to Col. Mobolaji O. Johnson, 24 October 1970, LASRAB CSG 1.4. This opinion was not universally shared, however. "Yes, Lagos is a land of Honey and butter free for all," Lagos State military governor Col. Mobolaji Johnson confided in a private letter to a friend in 1970, "so every Tom, Dick and Harry wants a bit of it to the detriment of the people born and bred there who have no claims to other places in Nigeria. Today, by the grace of God, Lagos is a State in membership with Eleven States forming the Federation of this Country. The Law does not show it as belonging to 'all of US.'" Col. Mobolaji O. Johnson to Col. Abba Kyari, 26 September 1970, LASRAB CSG 1.4.

34 Oluleye, *Military Leadership*, 228–29. This year of public service is still mandatory, and NYSC members can still be spotted in their sharply pressed khakis and olive drab caps. There are ways to shirk NYSC service, however, which breeds resentment among those who lack the connections to get out of it.

35 He feared that expanding access to guns would lead to greater instability. Training civilians "was intended to democratise violence [and] the use of the gun," Omara-Otunnu argued, but "its impact on Ugandan society has been lethal." Omara-Otunnu, "Currency of Militarism," 424.

36 Ocran insisted that in Ghana, "recruits from all over the country are considered for enlistment and provided they pass the necessary tests they are enlisted. From the very day a recruit enters barracks he loses his identity and becomes purely and simply a soldier of the State. His particular nationality [i.e., in this context, ethnicity] as a Ghanaian comes second. He learns comradeship; that is, to regard the case of one as the case of all; he is taught a variety of things, from civic education to personal hygiene and sanitation; to subject himself to military routine and discipline; to read and write; to be simple and considerate in living yet rough and hardy in the field. Apart from being taught his many professional skills as a fighting man he learns to live rough for the sake of the State." Ocran, *Myth Is Broken*, xvii. "More than any institution," Jemibewon wrote, the army was "uniquely representative of the whole country." Jemibewon, *Combatant in Government*, 168.

37 Babangida, *Home Front*, 13.

38 On the appellation *monstrous* in African politics, see Jörg Wiegratz and Leo Zeilig, "The West and Its African Monsters Syndrome," *The Elephant*, 18 June 2021.

39　Magaziner, *Law and the Prophets*, 5. The heroes' acre also includes a few non-Africans who were involved in the continent's politics, including W. E. B. Du Bois, Pauli Murray, and Aimé Césaire.

40　Mazrui, "Rise and Fall," 98–108. More recently, there has been a serious reckoning with their thought. See Wilder, *Freedom Time*; Getachew, *Worldmaking after Empire*; Tomás, *Amílcar Cabral*; Peterson, *Thomas Sankara*; Ahlman, *Living with Nkrumahism*.

41　"Decolonization, which sets out to change the order of the world, is, obviously, a program of complete disorder," he writes in *The Wretched of the Earth*. "But it cannot come as a result of magical practices, nor of a natural shock, nor of a friendly understanding. Decolonization, as we know, is a historical process: that is to say it cannot be understood, it cannot become intelligible nor clear to itself except in the exact measure that we can discern the movements which give it historical form and content." Fanon, *Wretched of the Earth*, 36.

42　Okello Oculi, "Whispers about Dr. Bala Usman," *University of Texas Bulletin*, no. 1192, n.d.

43　Fanon, "Why We Use Violence," 655.

44　Okeke, *Towards Functional Justice*, 165–66.

45　Afowowe, *Onward Soldier*, 97.

46　Edet, *Abacha's Call to Duty*, vii; Abdullah, "Bush Path to Destruction," 224.

47　Quoted in Nzimiro, *Babangida Men*, 5.

48　Nzimiro, *Babangida Men*, 77.

49　Gilroy et al., "A Diagnosis," 180–81.

50　On the Fanonian and Garveyist impulses in their thought, see Kamil, *Africa Has Come of Age*.

51　Umoden, *Babangida Years*, 70.

52　Quoted in Azikiwe, *Democracy with Military Vigilance*, vii.

53　Chukwudifu Oputa, "Towards Justice with a Human Face," Plenary Session of the Law Week of the Nigerian Bar Association, February 1985, NIIA, Nigeria-Law.

54　Hansen and Musa, "Fanon, the Wretched."

55　Shatz, "No Direction Home," 242–43.

56　Shatz, "No Direction Home," 240.

57　Prairie, *Thomas Sankara Speaks*, 90, 115.

58　The exception would be Sankara's ideas about gender, some of which were radical by any standard.

59　This was ironic given how profligate military regimes could be with public money, though Sankara was better than most. On the miniskirt panics, see Ivaska, *Cultured States*.

60　Shortly after this speech, Sankara renamed Upper Volta "Burkina Faso," meaning "the home of upright men" in Mossi and Dyula. Prairie, *Thomas Sankara Speaks*, 111.

61　Prairie, *Thomas Sankara Speaks*, 114.

62 Bayala, *Tribunaux populaires.*

63 The "emplotment of decolonization," Thomas Meaney writes, "was consistently tragic." Meaney, "Frantz Fanon," 993. For a good example of this kind of plotting, see Nwosu, "Nigeria's Decolonization Policy," 74–86. See also Quayson, *Tragedy and Postcolonial Literature.*

64 I borrow this admittedly mean sobriquet from Stephen Kotkin, who used it to describe how historians of the Soviet Union had allowed Leon Trotsky's critical writings to guide their understanding of Stalinism, thereby missing everything that gave it meaning. Kotkin, *Magnetic Mountain*, xx.

65 Ibrahim Babangida, "Address at Dodan Barracks," 31 October 1990, NIIA, Nigeria-Law.

66 Bello, "Fair Trial Is Guaranteed," 1–12.

67 In this respect they're much like the autocrats of the twenty-first century who use law to dismantle the structures of liberal democracy. See Scheppele, "Autocratic Legalism," 565.

68 "A journalist is a Nigerian, and all Nigerians worship money," remarked one major general, tautologically, "so they cannot be an exception." NIALS, *Why Army Rule?*, 120. On the press, see Onagoruwa, *Press Freedom in Crisis.* For an alternative interpretation, see Uko, *Romancing the Gun.*

69 Babangida, *For Their Tomorrow.*

70 Saint-Michel and Fages, *Histoire du Togo*; Wilder, "L'Homme de 13 Janvier."

71 To be fair to them, they also read books for grown-ups. Babangida regularly cited the influence of S. E. Finer's *The Man on Horseback*, which he seems to have used as a kind of how-to guide. "President Babangida's Views on Attempted Coup," 24 January 1986, NAUK FCO 65/3790.

72 Cooper, "Possibility and Constraint," 169.

73 Ipinyomi, Morbike, and Sani, *War Against Indiscipline*, 1. I thank Vincent Hiribarren for sharing this pamphlet with me.

74 Chukwudifu Oputa, "In Search of a Disciplined Society through Law: Being a Paper Presented during the Law Week, Marking the Centenary Celebrations of the Legal Profession in Nigeria," 22 February 1986, NIIA, Nigeria-Law.

75 Borno State Government, *Milestone*, 14.

76 Wiredu's "consensual democracy," for example, or Hountondji's "rooted freedom." See Wiredu, "Democracy by Consensus"; Hountondji, *Struggle for Meaning.*

77 Fromm, *Escape from Freedom*, 281.

78 Benjamin, *Reflections*, 285.

79 Dudley, *Instability and Political Order*, 15–18.

80 Obasanjo, *This Animal Called Man*, 131.

81 Oputa, "Disciplined Society through Law."

82 Col. Mobolaji O. Johnson to Col. Abba Kyari, 26 September 1970.

83 Babangida, *For Their Tomorrow*, 177.

84 Low and Lonsdale, "Introduction."

85 For a comparative account of how austerity made it difficult for an African state to implement its transformative vision, see Machava, "Reeducation Camps."

86　Some of the civilians who were deposed by their militaries ended up adopting the language of discipline themselves, which they hoped might allow them to wrestle back control from men in uniform. In exile in Conakry, Nkrumah wrote a kind of field guide for freedom fighters, inspired by the Black Power movement in the United States and various revolutionary movements in Africa and Asia. In it, he laid out how "true" African revolutionaries might take back power from the soldiers, "imperialist and neocolonial intelligence organizations," and "military and police traitors" who had come to dominate the continent. He enumerated rules including "obey orders in all your actions," "speak politely," "do not take liberties with women," and "know the enemy within." Nkrumah, *Handbook of Revolutionary Warfare*, author's note.

87　Some trace of this remains in the present. Once, when I was out after curfew in Kaduna, a soldier at a checkpoint gave me the choice of paying a fine or doing fifty push-ups. Neither penalty was officially sanctioned, but I did the push-ups, much to his amusement.

88　Even compared to other soldiers, Buhari went unusually hard against the press. Decree No. 4 essentially banned public criticism of the regime. When Babangida came to power in August 1985, one of his first actions was to repeal it. "Nigeria: The Young Turks?," *Africa Confidential* 26, no. 18 (1985): 1.

89　"Hypocrisy and Dis-Service to WAI Tenets and Objectives in Lagos State Public Service," 14 June 1985, LASRAB CSG 2.32.

90　Unoh, *War Against Indiscipline*, n.p.

91　Agbaje and Adisa, "Political Education."

92　Oputa, "Disciplined Society through Law."

93　"Hypocrisy and Dis-Service."

94　The WAI ended when Buhari was ousted in 1986, but this proved to be only a détente. A decade later, Sani Abacha launched a War Against Indiscipline and Corruption (WAIC), which recapitulated the WAI. The complaints of the regime were the same. The army chief of staff "affirmed the level of indiscipline and corruption in our society and how these have been an impediment to the progress of this country." Lt. General Oladipo Diya, "Report for the Awareness Campaign of War Against Indiscipline and Corruption," 2 December 1994, LASRAB CSG 2.32. When Buhari returned to office as a civilian politician thirty years later, he brought back the language of the War against Indiscipline—this time sans whips. Newell, *Histories of Dirt*, 150.

95　"The WAI Brigade of Nigeria," n.d., LASRAB CSG 2.32.

96　Soyinka, *Open Sore*, 76.

97　C. O. Agbe-Davies to S. A. S., 15 July 1985, LASRAB CSG 2.32.

98　Ipinyomi, Morbike, and Sani, *War Against Indiscipline*.

99　"Hypocrisy and Dis-Service."

100　Oputa, "Disciplined Society through Law."

101　Corporal punishment tends to stick in the memory. Comparatively, on Singapore, see Tushnet, "Authoritarian Constitutionalism."

102 "Memos from the Motherland: New Warring," *New Journal and Guide* (Norfolk), 9 May 1984.

103 Maja-Pearce, *In My Father's Country*, 7.

104 Maja-Pearce, *In My Father's Country*, 125.

105 Soyinka, *Open Sore*, 63.

106 "Activities of War Against Indiscipline (WAI) Brigade," 21 November 1986, LASRAB CSG 2.32.

107 "Why Is It that 'WAI' Is Not Applied in House Cleaning Exercise?," 5 October 1984, LASRAB CSG 2.32.

108 Maja-Pearce, *In My Father's Country*, 8.

109 Respectively, the Endangered Species (Control of International Trade and Traffic) Decree of 1985 and the International Institute of Tropical Agriculture Decree of 1967.

110 "Minutes of the Maiden Meeting of the Task Force Headquarters on Environmental Sanitation," 8 October 1984, LASRAB CSG 2.27.

111 "Address of the Military Governor of Lagos State Group Captain Gbolahan Mudasiru, at the Launching of the Total War Against Filthy Environment in Lagos State," 8 October 1984, LASRAB CSG 2.27.

112 Immerwahr, "Politics of Architecture," 179.

113 It wouldn't have struck most people as strange that economic development might be commanded by a military dictator. There were many varieties of executive-led development to choose from. There was of course the Soviet Union, and the state-planning model there was seductive even to states that did not embrace communism. In the nonaligned center and even on the right, the notion that economic policy might best be dictated from the top was not unusual. Comparatively, see Fakih, *Authoritarian Modernization*.

114 It is hard to imagine how these unpopular measures might have been pushed through if Nigeria were a democracy. It would not be correct to say that military rule paved the way for structural adjustment—some soldiers opposed it, and the IMF's mandates came for democrats and dictators alike. Nonetheless, the top-down nature of military administrations meant they could implement austerity measures without thinking much about the consequences for their popularity. One demand specific to Nigeria was the removal of the petrol subsidy. This subsidy, which guaranteed cheap petrol to the Nigerian consumer, was one of few public benefits available and arguably the only one accessible to everyone. The prospect of removing it was hugely unpopular. "Statement by Mr. El Kogali on Nigeria," Executive Board Meeting 89/11, 3 February 1989, IMF Archives; Davies, "IMF in Nigerian Economy." On structural adjustment generally, see Van de Walle, *African Economies*.

115 "Foreign Slavery?," *Ebony*, March 1990, 87.

116 "Statement by Mrs. Guti on Nigeria," Executive Board Meeting 98/63, 12 June 1998, IMF Archives.

117 Speech by Sir Darnley Alexander to the Judges Conference, 8 June 1978, NIIA, Nigeria-Tribunals.

118 Oputa, "Disciplined Society through Law."

119 Oputa, "Disciplined Society through Law."

120 Kuti, *Law and Policy*, 19.

121 The classic study of law's countervailing uses is Thompson, *Whigs and Hunters*. As Barbara Yngvesson wrote, modern law is "neither 'from above' nor 'from below' but simultaneously separate and immanent, imposed and participatory." Yngvesson, "Law at the Doorway," 412.

122 Other judges pushed back against the military's drug policies too. In one well-known case, a judge in Kaduna acquitted a man for selling cannabis—the drugs were found in a room he shared with another man, which muddled who owned them. State v. Nwaogwugwu, 1980 (2), *Nigerian Criminal Reports* 102.

123 Dulcie Oguntoye, "Your Estranged Faces," 2008, NIALS manuscripts.

124 David Pilling, "Fatou Bensouda: 'It's about the Law. It's Not about Power,'" *Financial Times* (New York), 25 September 2020.

125 She would also be criticized for sanitizing the image of the ICC, especially its tendency to prosecute African war criminals before others. On the ICC and Africa, see Ba, *States of Justice*; Clarke, *Affective Justice*.

126 See Steedman, *History and the Law*; Baxi, "Touch it Not."

127 Vagts, *History of Militarism*, 15. The better part of a century later, Priya Satia made a similar argument about how British imperialists used history to soothe the public conscience about colonialism's sins. Satia, *Time's Monster*.

128 See, for example, the extremely interesting book by Nwokedi and Daloz, *French Revolution: A Nigerian Perspective*, which compared that revolution's transformations to the one Nigeria was undergoing under military rule. Another political scientist measured Africa's military "revolution" against Bolshevism—and found the latter the weaker of the two. See Ogueri, *African Nationalism*, 18.

129 Usman and Abba, *Misrepresentation of Nigeria*. The British Empire had worked by defining ethnic communities and turning ethnographic abstractions like "tribe" into administrative categories. This was the subject of much of Usman's work. On Usman, see Mamdani, *Define and Rule*, 4.

130 Quoted in Mayer, *Naija Marxisms*, 117. Later, Usman would abandon Marxism and embrace the ethnic politics he had once condemned.

CHAPTER 3. THE PORTABLE COUP

A version of chapter 3 was published as "The Portable Coup: The Jurisprudence of 'Revolution' in Uganda and Nigeria," *Law and History Review* 39, no. 4 (November 2021): 737–64.

1 African Conference on the Rule of Law, *Report*, 175. There were approximately 540 African lawyers in Nigeria in 1960. This was a far greater number than any other former British colony in Africa. Several former French possessions could count the number of African lawyers on one hand, and the Belgian Congo had none at all. Adewoye, *Judicial System*, 286.

2 African Conference on the Rule of Law, *Report*, 56–81, 96–113. On the role of emergency measures in colonial administration, see Hussain, *Jurisprudence of Emergency*; Kolb, *Epidemic Empire*; McQuade, *Genealogy of Terrorism*.

3 Chief Mike A. A. Ozekhome, "The Recurring Battle for Supremacy between the Executive and the Judiciary in Nigeria: Who Wins," *Constitutional Rights Journal* (Lagos), July–September 1993, 26–28.

4 Initially most of these judges were British. Toward the end of the colonial period, they were joined by Indian and Caribbean judges, and a small number of west Africans. "Leave Passage Regulations in Respect of African Judges," 2 November 1949, NAUK CO 554/159/13; Adewoye, "Legal Profession," 355.

5 Among the most important of these African lawyers was John Mensah Sarbah in the Gold Coast. See Sharafi, "Colonial Lawyering."

6 The same was largely true in southern Africa, with the exception of South Africa. See Karekwaivanane, "Through the Narrow Door"; Gocking, "Colonial Rule"; Ross, "Rule of Law."

7 British law came to East Africa largely via India, as described by Bishara, *Sea of Debt*, chapter 5. South Asians had been present in East Africa since the nineteenth century, when the British had encouraged Indians to migrate to other British colonies. Laborers (to build railways) and clerks (to facilitate commerce) came to Uganda on a temporary basis, but many of them stayed. By independence, Uganda's Asian community had been there for several generations. See Mamdani, *From Citizen to Refugee*.

8 Old colonial institutions were turned to the task of facilitating their appointments. The Commonwealth Secretariat in London served as an informal clearinghouse for judicial placements, and governments could advertise judicial vacancies in the newsletter of the Commonwealth Magistrates and Judges Association. In this way, the web of administrators and institutions that had recently made justice in the British Empire was retooled as a network of African cooperation.

9 Col. Mobolaji Johnson to Sir Adetokunbo Ademola, 7 August 1971, Papers of T. Akinola Aguda, NIALS uncataloged collection.

10 Governor's Office, Eastern Region, Nigeria to Colonial Office, London, 26 September 1955, NAUK CO 554/1409.

11 East Africa's courts had been perpetually short-staffed before independence too. Judicial postings there were not seen as desirable, and personnel had to be brought from Malaya or Aden (an even greater "hardship" post) to cover gaps in service. "East Africa Court of Appeal," 30 March 1954, NAUK CO 822/644.

12 "Discussion with Mr. Saidu Garba," 12 March 1961, box 7, Charles R. Nixon Papers, UCLA Special Collections.

13 These judges were kept on after independence on a contract basis, but their presence embarrassed the now independent governments they served. They were, as one historian described Kenya's bench, "a mixed bag, ranging from talented jurists to racist eccentrics." Swanepoel, "Kenya's Colonial Judges,"

52. Some "British" judges were colonial subjects themselves. Sir Vahe Robert Bairamian, for example, was an Armenian Cypriot who became a prominent judge in Nigeria and later chief justice of Sierra Leone. All judges were paid the same salaries regardless of race, but Europeans and African judges who were "either of mixed European descent or had family ties in the United Kingdom" received more generous leave and more frequent passages to London than those who did not, which caused much resentment. See "Appointment of Judge to Supreme Court in Nigeria," NAUK DO 35/10485; "Leave Passages Regulations," 2 November 1949, and subsequent undated correspondence; Gower, *Independent Africa*, 40–41.

14 Later, West African judges served even more widely in the Commonwealth. A long-serving chief justice of Belize was from Sierra Leone, for example, and small states throughout the South Pacific hired West Africans as judges and magistrates long after they became sovereign. Some still do. On African jurists in Pacific constitution making, see Kirkby, "Commonwealth Constitution-Maker." See also Chappell, "'Africanization' in the Pacific."

15 Mabel Agyemang of Ghana, for example, would serve as chief justice of Gambia, and later as chief justice of Turks and Caicos. Nkemdilim Izuako of Nigeria was the first female judge in the Solomon Islands, and Mary Mam Yassin Sey was a powerful judge in Swaziland, Sierra Leone, and Vanuatu before taking a position on the supreme court of her home country, Gambia.

16 On the complex paths of Indian African lawyers in the region, see De, "Brown Lawyers, Black Robes."

17 Okwu, "Ahiara Declaration," 90. In East Africa, these Nigerians were usually the first magistrates in their posts to have legal training. Prior to independence, magistrates had been colonial officers, for whom dispensing justice was one small part of a portfolio of administrative duties. Hailey, *African Survey*, 614; Okwu, *Justice and Honor*, 198.

18 Quoted in Feingold, *Colonial Justice*, 206. Feingold notes that the Nigerian magistrates were abruptly called home in 1967, when Nyerere's support for Biafra's secession soured the relationship between Tanzania and Nigeria.

19 Udoma developed a reputation as a firebrand during his studies. In 1943 he delivered a speech entitled *The Lion and the Oil-Palm* criticizing British administrative policy in Nigeria, which caught the attention of Lord Frederick Lugard, who had been one of its main architects. When Lugard proposed to meet him, Udoma rebuffed him. His relationship with Perham, who was an influential theorist of colonial administration, was not a happy one; "she accused me of extreme nationalism that was likely to colour my work as a scholar," he recalled. "She felt that she was a liberal and I a nationalist and that the two were incompatible." "Sir Udo Udoma: My Life and Times," *Nigerian Law Times*, July–September 1993, 23; Udoma, *Eagle in Its Flight*, 64; Udoma, *Lion and the Oil-Palm*.

20 Correspondence with students, 1928–1940, Papers of Ladipo Solanke, West African Students Union, Gandhi Library, University of Lagos.

21 See Kletzer, "Work of Hans Kelsen," 133–67.

22 He was best known for his involvement in the trials of several chiefs accused of "leopard" murders. These trials, concerning a string of killings committed by people disguised as leopards, became famous across the empire. See Pratten, *Man-Leopard Murders.*

23 Udoma, *Eagle in Its Flight,* 119.

24 During Western Region Premier Obafemi Awolowo's 1962 treason trial, for example, a case came before Udoma challenging the federal government's decision to bar Awolowo's British lawyer from entering Nigeria in order to deprive him of counsel. Udoma sided with the federal government, upholding the state's right to make an immigration decision, even if it was clearly also a political matter. Chief Obafemi Awolowo v. The Hon. Mallam Usman Sarki (Federal Minister of Internal Affairs) and the Attorney-General of the Federation, 1 ANLR 1966, 178.

25 I borrow the term *ethnic patriotism* from Peterson, *Ethnic Patriotism.*

26 Udoma often recalled the fact that his mother had been shot by a British soldier during a 1929 tax protest—an event that marked him for life. The Ibibio Union had provided his scholarship to study in Ireland, and this initiated a lifelong involvement in the local politics of his ethnic community.

27 His great ambition was to secure a separate state for the Ibibio people, which he carried on even after becoming a judge. On Udoma's involvement in Ibibio politics, see the six-hundred-page book he wrote on the topic, *The Story of the Ibibio Union: Its Background, Emergence, Aims, Objectives and Achievements.* See also Udo-Inyang, *Sir Justice Udo Udoma.*

28 Chief justices of Commonwealth states typically received British knighthoods in this era. Udoka, *Sir Udo Udoma,* 174.

29 Udoma, *Eagle in Its Flight,* 132.

30 See generally Reid, *History of Modern Uganda,* xxv–xxvi.

31 Udoma, *Eagle in Its Flight,* 135–38.

32 Justice James Ogoola, "The Age of the Rule of Tear Gas: An Address to the Uganda Law Society," 8 October 2012.

33 Udoka, *Sir Udo Udoma,* 179.

34 The military officer assigned to this duty was Idi Amin. On Buganda's place in national politics, see Earle, *Colonial Buganda*; Makubuya, *Protection, Patronage, or Plunder?*; Low, *Buganda in Modern History.*

35 Joe Oloka-Onyango, "Ghosts and the Law: An Inaugural Lecture," 18, 12 November 2015, Makerere University, Kampala. See also Bradley, "Constitution-Making in Uganda," 25–31.

36 Udoma, *Eagle in Its Flight,* 155.

37 The British High Commission watched the case closely and collected many documents related to it. For this reason, an extensive record of the proceedings is available in "Validity of High Court Ruling under 1966 Constitution: Habeas Corpus Judgment re Michael Matovu," 1967, NAUK FCO 31/181.

38 Some evidence suggests that Binaisa was threatened into serving as Obote's counsel. British High Commission, Kampala to Commonwealth Office, 27 July 1967, NAUK FCO 31/185.

39 In deciding to hear *Matovu* at all, Udoma planted the seed of its demise. Joe Oloka-Onyango has argued that the decision to hear the case in spite of its defects established a precedent for public-interest lawyering; if a case was of sufficient importance from a constitutional perspective, formal or procedural irregularities could not be grounds to dismiss it. See Oloka-Onyango, *When Courts Do Politics*, 47.

40 Quoted in Oloka-Onyango, "Ghosts and the Law," 31.

41 The path of "pure theory" also passed through Latin America. See Medina, *Teoría impura del derecho*; Boucault, "Hans Kelsen."

42 Harris, "Grundnorm Change?," 120.

43 See Kirkby, "Exorcising *Matovu*'s Ghost."

44 See Osuntogun, "Pure Theory of Law," 233–61.

45 See Mahmud, "Jurisprudence of Successful Treason," 53.

46 "Uganda: A Stocktaking," 26 March 1968, NAUK FCO 31/184.

47 The following year, the 1966 constitution was itself replaced. The 1967 constitution was an amended version of Obote's 1966 document, with even greater authority earmarked for the executive. Kasfir, "Uganda Constituent Assembly Debate," 52–56.

48 Oloka-Onyango, "Ghosts and the Law," 2.

49 On Amin's legal strategy, see Allen, *Days of Judgment*; Decker, "'Karuma Falls.'"

50 Schroeder, dir., *General Idi Amin Dada*.

51 Udoma, *Eagle in Its Flight*, 169, 177.

52 Udoma, *Eagle in Its Flight*, 179.

53 Udoka, *Sir Udo Udoma*, 184.

54 Lakanmi and Another v. the Attorney General of the Western Region and Others (1970) LPELR-SC.58/69. See Nwabueze, *Judicialism in Commonwealth Africa*; Ojo, "Search for a Grundnorm"; Eweluka, "Military System of Administration."

55 Lakanmi and Another v. the Attorney General of the Western Region and Others (1970) LPELF-SC.58/69.

56 Ademola was about to retire, which perhaps explains why he was willing to speak back to executive power so stridently. Alao, *Statesmanship on the Bench*, 242–43.

57 Uzuokwu, *Grundnorm of Nigeria*, 2.

58 Nwabueze, *Judicialism in Commonwealth Africa*, 120.

59 Udoma, *Constitution of Nigeria*, 266–308.

60 Ojo, "Search for a Grundnorm," 238.

61 Quoted in Ojo, "Search for a Grundnorm," 135.

62 Ojo, "Constitutional Developments in Nigeria," 20; see also Aihe, "Nigerian Federal Military Government," 570–80.

63 There would be two brief interruptions to military rule: the civilian administration of Shehu Shagari from 1979 to 1983 and the aborted election of 1993.

64 Omar, *Emergency Powers*, 59.

65 Wolf-Phillips, "Legitimacy," 113. The full decision appears in PLD 1972 SC 183–204. For the 1958 case, see PLD 1958 SC 533–34, 537–38.

66 Adebayo Adejare, "Courts and Civil Liberties in a Military Revolution," *New Nigerian*, 21 September 1988, NIIA Press Collections, Nigeria-Courts.

67 Udoka, *Sir Udo Udoma*, 126.

68 On this episode, see Prakash, *Emergency Chronicles*.

69 Onagoruwa, "International Conventions," 1; Ozekhome, "Recurring Battle," 30.

70 Ghai, "Role of Law," 13.

71 Hassan, "Critique of Successful Treason," 234–35.

72 It was lawyers, however, who were arguably the most consistent critics of military regimes. Taking great risks to their professional standing (and indeed their lives), lawyers like Ben Nwabueze and Gani Fawehinmi in Nigeria, or more recently Sylvia Tamale and Nicholas Opiyo in Uganda, openly criticized autocratic leaders and the judges who authorized their actions. See Nwabueze, "Constitutional Problems," 31–43; Fawehinmi, *Ouster of Court Jurisdiction*; Tamale, *Hens Begin to Crow*.

73 Moi's most important judicial enabler had been the English judge Sir James Wicks, who was rumored to have rewritten his judgments to Moi's specifications. Moi rewarded him by raising the age limit for judges several times, allowing him to become Kenya's longest-serving chief justice to date. On Apaloo and his peers, see Cockar, *Doings, Non-Doings, and Mis-Doings*.

74 T. Akinola Aguda, "Re-Thinking Our Values: A Speech Made at Ikorodu," 6 April 1986, NIALS uncataloged collection.

75 Clover Petrus and Mokgamedi Selaolo v. The State, 1982, NIALS uncataloged collection.

76 See for example Azinge and Ani, *Freedom of Protest*. For a comprehensive overview of this period, see Ibhawoh, *Human Rights in Africa*, 173–220.

77 Aguda, *Crisis of Justice*, ix.

78 I. O. Agbede, "Hon. Dr. T. Akinola Aguda: The Man, His Works and Society," ca. 1987, NIALS uncataloged collection.

79 Anyangwe, *Revolutionary Overthrow*, 83.

80 In 1972, Amin famously ordered the murder of Uganda's chief justice, Benedicto Kiwanuka. Bade, *Benedicto Kiwanuka*; Kiwanuka, *Tragedy of Uganda*, 89–93; Carney, "Kiwanuka and Catholic Democracy." On Amin's other attacks on the judiciary, see Legum, "Behind the Clown's Mask," 250–58.

81 Gould, "Postcolonial Liberalism," 412–54.

82 This philosophy is articulated in Georges, *Law and its Administration*.

83 Among them Oloka-Onyango, "Ghosts and the Law"; Kirkby, "Exorcising *Matovu's* Ghost."

1   See Nwokeji, *Slave Trade and Culture*; Nwabara, *Iboland*, 27.

2   Ottenberg, "Ibo Oracles," 295–317; Ofoegbu, "Igbo National Dress," 209.

3   Ijere, "Economic Significance of Shrines."

4   See Fallers, *Law without Precedent*; see also Rathbone, "Laws, Polities, and Inference."

5   On custom, see Chanock, *Law, Custom*; Moore, *Social Facts and Fabrications*; Zips and Weilenmann, *Governance of Legal Pluralism*; Fenrich, Galizzi, and Higgins, *African Customary Law*.

6   On this tension, see Kaarsholm, "Inventions, Imaginings, Codifications"; Lawrance, "*Bankoe v. Dome*"; Morapedi, "Demise or Resilience?"; Ndlovu-Gatsheni, "Ruled by the Spear?"; Vaughan, "Chieftaincy Politics."

7   See Chanock, "Peculiar Sharpness."

8   This was not just an African phenomenon. See Yannakakis, *Since Time Immemorial*.

9   Ifemesia, *Southeastern Nigeria*, 59.

10 On the relationship between the Atlantic system and custom generally, see Balakrishnan, "Of Debt and Bondage."

11 Kalu, "Missionaries," 78. See also Chuku, "Igbo Historiography," 7.

12 Ekechi, "British Assault on Ogbunorie," 69.

13 Afigbo, *Ropes of Sand*, 315.

14 "Jurisdiction of Customary Courts, Criminal Code Laws Made by the Local Governments," 11 April 1964, Nigerian National Archives, Enugu (hereafter NNAE) MINJUST 6/1/1; Obilade, "Customary Law Matters."

15 See Crowder, *Flogging of Phinehas McIntosh*.

16 Perham was not the only one who found apparel a useful metaphor for British laws created for Africans. Kirk-Greene, *Principles of Native Administration*, xii.

17 Udoma, *Lion and the Oil-Palm*, 36.

18 *Nigerian Observer* (Lagos), 31 December 1973.

19 Quoted in Ibeziako, *Nigerian Customary Law*, 15.

20 On the repugnancy clause in general, see Ibhawoh, *Imperial Justice*, 62. See also Afigbo, "Eastern Provinces."

21 Widow burning was not an African phenomenon, however. It was a hold-over from nineteenth-century India, where the British had used its specter to formulate an early version of the repugnancy clause. Mani, *Contentious Traditions*.

22 This did not mean people stopped believing in the oracles. Their supplicants likely included those who thought the British-sponsored customary courts were corrupt or who could not afford their fees. Some probably were forum shopping, believing the oracle would give them a more favorable decision than an official customary court (especially if they had gripes with the local dignitaries who served as village judges). Ubah, "Religious Change," 71–91.

23 Mamdani, *Citizen and Subject*, 37.

24 Courts that used Islamic law were sometimes lumped in with animist chiefs under the banner of "custom." Most qadis resented this.

25 Ajayi, "British Territories in Africa," 47.

26 On the history of corporal punishment in colonial Nigeria, see Pierce, "Punishment," 186–214.

27 Jearey, "Structure, Composition and Jurisdiction," 409.

28 Quoted in Ajayi, "British Territories in Africa," 45.

29 D. N. Igara to Permanent Secretary, Ministry of Justice, 17May 1966, NNAE MINJUST 90/1/88.

30 Speech delivered by the Minister of Justice to the Association of Customary Court Judges at Abagana, 5 March 1960, NNAE MINJUST 112/1/2; Azumini Town and other villages to permanent secretary, Ministry of Justice, Enugu, 23 April 1964, NNAE MINJUST 21/1/24.

31 "Biafra, a World of Our Own," MS 6687, Private Papers of Mrs R Umelo, Imperial War Museum, London, 93.

32 Afigbo, "Eastern Provinces," 423.

33 Milner, Nigerian Penal System, 304.

34 Petition to the Nigeria Constitutional Conference by J. A.N. Orizu and other chiefs of Eastern Region of Nigeria, "Why we want a house of chiefs in the Eastern Region of Nigeria," 1957, GB 0162 Micr. Afr. 608, Papers of Adegoke Adelabu, Rhodes House Library, Oxford.

35 Adewoye, Judicial System, 287.

36 Akpan, Epitaph to Indirect Rule, 161.

37 Ibeziako, Nigerian Customary Law, 23.

38 J. O. Uchukwu, "Need to Eject Equitable Principles at an Early Stage," 1962, NNAE MINJUST 90/1/912.

39 Crown Counsel to the Divisional Officer, Brass, 13 April 1961, NNAE MINJUST 32/1/22.

40 Allott, Judicial and Legal Systems, 63.

41 Ajayi, "British Territories in Africa," 68.

42 Among many publications, see Allott, Essays in African Law. See also Harrington and Manji, "Emergence of African Law."

43 See especially Obi, Ibo Law of Property. One gets the sense that the project's rigor was not always as deep as its lengthy publications would suggest. "I told Tony [Allott] that this sounded all very exciting," recalled a researcher who was hired onto the project in 1959, "but I knew nothing about Africa or African law, let alone customary law. How could I begin to restate something of which I knew nothing? Tony was not deterred. He said that he had been in exactly the same position on taking a Lectureship in African law at SOAS a few years previously." Cotran, "Tony Allott," 15–17.

44 Allott, Future of Law in Africa, n.p.

45 Integration of Customary and Modern Legal Systems in Africa, 91.

46 Opening Address by Sir Lionel Brett, Justice of the Supreme Court of Nigeria, in Proceedings of the Conference of the Nigerian Association of Law Teachers.

47 Ajayi, "British Territories in Africa," 66.

48 "Igwe-Kala Juju Cult Is Dynamited, August 1963," in Dyson, *Nigeria*, 71.

49 State v. Ndodo Nwosu and Others, 1965, NNAE BCA.

50 Akpamgbo, "Customary Courts No. 2 Edict 1966," 27.

51 Chukwudifu Oputa, "In Search of a Disciplined Society through Law: Being a Paper Presented during the Law Week, Marking the Centenary Celebrations of the Legal Profession in Nigeria," 22 February 1986, NIIA, Nigeria-Law.

52 As discussed earlier, the judiciary's boldest stand came in the 1971 case *Lakanmi v. Attorney General of the Western Region*, where the Supreme Court ruled that the military regime could not legitimately issue decrees. Decrees were its main administrative implement, and the decision was tantamount to ruling that the military regime was illegal.

53 *Nigerian Standard* (Lagos), 3 March 1977, 7, NIIA, Nigeria-Law.

54 *White Paper on the Federal Military Government Views on the Report of the Customary Courts Reform Committee* (Lagos: Federal Ministry of Information, Printing Division, 1978), 16.

55 Ejoor, *Reminiscences*, 103.

56 Taslim O. Elias, "Law and Justice in Independent Nigeria," *Sunday Observer* (Lagos), 1 January 1978.

57 Ahmed Beita Yusuf, "National Stability: Legal Pluralism or Uniformity?," *New Nigerian* (Lagos), 5 June 1976, 5.

58 "Illusion of English Law in Blackman's Empire," *Sunday Sketch* (Lagos), 4 May 1975, 8.

59 "The Roads to Decongestion of Cases in Our Courts," *Nigerian Statesman* (Lagos), 25 August 1981, NIIA, Nigeria-Courts.

60 *The Punch* (Lagos), 12 April 1980, NIIA, Nigeria-Courts.

61 *New Nigerian* (Lagos), 21 June 1971, NIIA, Nigeria-Law.

62 As Ranajit Guha argued, law can "mystify" the relationship between the rulers and the ruled, rendering conquest as a rule of law and converting coercion into consent to be governed. The history of custom in Africa is a case study in how that can happen. Guha, *Subaltern Studies Reader*, 39.

63 Nwabueze, *Judicialism in Commonwealth Africa*, 4 (emphasis added).

64 See Ayittey, *Indigenous African Institutions*.

65 Oputa, "Disciplined Society through Law."

66 Nwabueze, *Judicialism in Commonwealth Africa*, 311.

67 Nigeria was not the only place where this conversation was taking place. The foreign minister of the Transkei Bantustan was also a believer in custom's viability. Koyana, *Customary Law*.

68 Patrick O. Okumagba, "Obstacles on Codification of Customary Laws," *Daily Times* (Lagos), 20 January 1976, 11.

69 *New Nigerian* (Lagos), 19 February 1981, 3. They had foreign allies in this endeavor, including some of the eminent Africanist historians and anthropologists of the day. See the contributions to Kuper and Kuper, *African Law*. See also Verhelst, "Safeguarding African Customary Law."

70 See Agbede, *Legal Pluralism*.

71 Anyebe, *Customary Law*, 19.

72 Adewoye, "Legal Profession," 2.

73 Quoted in Ibeziako, *Nigerian Customary Law*, 15.

74 Not *all* gerontocratic authority was respected, however. They paid deference to rural chiefs, but they often treated the "elders" of the First Republic and the broader nationalist movement with contempt. In the military itself, respect for the seniority of rank came to a screeching halt with every coup by an upstart junior officer.

75 Their now classic books on the historicity of sex and gender were published during the Babangida and Abacha regimes, respectively. Amadiume, *Male Daughters, Female Husbands*; Oyěwùmí, *Invention of Women*.

76 Allott's Restatement of African Law project was of some use in ascertaining what custom was, as was the work of academic anthropologists, whose books the Ministry of Justice collected assiduously. But with all their nuance, these academic studies tended to make the opposite point that military jurists wanted; their detailed descriptions emphasized what made individual customary traditions *distinct from each other*, making them seem impossible to harmonize.

77 On proverbs in the customary court, see Messenger, "Role of Proverbs," 64–73; Mensah-Brown, *Law in Contemporary Africa*, 35.

78 Adewoye, *Judicial System*, 287.

79 Nékám, "African Customary Law," 5.

80 The "them" of this claim is presumably both Western philosophy and Nigeria's other normative orders. The "we" is debatable—what "we" encompassed was a major question of her philosophy. Sophie Olúwọlé, "My Mum Never Believed I Could Become a Professor," *The Punch* (Lagos), 28 January 2017. See also Olúwọlé, *Witchcraft, Reincarnation* and *Socrates and Òrúnmìlà*.

81 Ekundayo, "Common Law of Nigeria," 208.

82 Some jurists continue to pursue the idea of a unified system of custom, though today it is mostly an academic exercise. See Azinge, *Restatement of Customary Law*; Azinge and Azoro, *NIALS Dictionary*; Onyango, *African Customary Law System*.

83 Quoted in Iheme, "Sources of Law," 45.

84 A similar crackdown on oracles took place during the short-lived civilian Second Republic (1979–1983), also on the grounds that oracles were being used to influence elections. In Ogbunike, a local chief was accused of using an oracle called Iyi Oji to force "Hordes of Ignoramuses" to vote for his candidate. The chief allegedly used it to "mortgage the conscience of the people under the threat of death if they disobey his despotic orders and exercise their freedom of choice of political party to which they would belong." When the Anambra State government sent a delegation to the town to investigate, the accused chief convened a "kangaroo masquerade court" to "try" the state officials for illegally entering his town without his permission. *Daily Star* (Lagos), 19 March 1981. See also Ellis, "Okija Shrine," 445–66.

85 Among many, see Dunkerley, "Use of Juju."
86 Lavaud-Legendre, *Prostitution nigériane*.
87 See Piot, "'Right' to Be Trafficked," 199–210.

CHAPTER 5. FELA KUTI GOES TO COURT

1 "Report of the Lagos State Government on the Administrative Board of
   Inquiry into the Disturbances at 14A Agege Motor Road, Idi-Oro," 1977, 15,
   LASRAB LCE.A13 (hereafter "Disturbances at 14A").
2 They are held at the Lagos State Research and Archives Board in the northern
   part of Lagos, not far from the overgrown lot where the Kalakuta Republic
   once stood. Unfortunately, the record is incomplete, and most of Fela's statement does not appear to survive.
3 One of the most celebrated artistic events of the era, the massive international
   festival of art from Africa and the African diaspora known as Festac '77, happened the same year as the Fela Kuti inquiry, under the same military regime.
   Poetry was the military's preferred mode of artistic expression, and the army
   had several poetry journals, including *Sojaman* and *Pedagogue*. They published some grand lines. Typical is Captain Loc Anene's ode to the National
   Theatre in Lagos, where the Fela Kuti inquiry was held: "Nigeria's Theatre, /
   tomb of petrogold, / there you sit a sphinx / as kings queue and go / like the endless wagons of time." *Pedagogue* 1, no. 1 (June 1979), box 6, Nigerian Subject Collection XX 787, Hoover Institution Library, Stanford University, CA. The army's
   most famous poet was General Mamman Jiya Vatsa, who was known for his
   verse and his gentle books for children, which he wrote in English, Hausa,
   and pidgin. He was popular with soldiers and civilians alike, until Babangida
   executed him for plotting a palace coup. On Festac, see Ose, *Festac '77*; Apter,
   Pan-African Nation. On Vatsa, see "Coup Plotters Verdict," February 1986,
   NAUK FCO 65/3790; "Death Penalty," 24 February 1986, NAUK FCO 65/3790;
   Vatsa, *Stinger the Scorpion*; *Tori for geti bow leg*; and *Voices from the Trench*.
4 Obasanjo was appointed head of state by the Supreme Military Council following the 1976 assassination of Murtala Muhammed by Buka Suka Dimka
   in an unsuccessful coup. Murtala Muhammed had come to power through a
   coup himself.
5 In former settler colonies, inquiries into the treatment of indigenous people
   have examined historical crimes of dispossession and mass violence, most
   extensively in Canada and New Zealand.
6 Mamdani, "Reconciliation without Justice," 3–5; and "Amnesty or Impunity?"
   33–59; Krog, "Research into Reconciliation," 203–17.
7 This was the *Human Rights Violations Investigation Commission Report*.
   For an unvarnished account of the panel's hearings, see Kukah, *Witness to
   Justice*.
8 This nonpunitive approach distinguishes commissions of inquiry from judicial
   reckonings with mass violence, such as those into war crimes or genocides.

9 In the nineteenth century, commissions of inquiry aimed to restore or defend the empire's moral authority. The most famous of these was the inquiry into Governor Edward Eyre's violent repression of the Morant Bay Rebellion in Jamaica in 1865. Balint, Evans, and McMillan, "Justice Claims."

10 Among hundreds, see *Report of the Commission of Inquiry into the Working of Port Harcourt Town Council* (Lagos: Government Printer, 1955); *Report of the Commission on Revenue Allocation* (Lagos: Government Printer, 1951); *Report of the Native Courts (Northern Provinces) Commission of Inquiry* (Lagos: Government Printer, 1952); *Problems of Nigerian Minorities* (Lagos: Pacific Printing Works, 1958); *The House of Docemo. Full Proceedings of an Inquiry into the Method of Selection of a Head to the House of Docemo before H.L. Ward-Price, Esq., Commissioner* (Lagos: Tika-Tore, 1933); *Commission of Inquiry into the Kalabari Chieftancy Dispute: Report of the Committee* (Lagos: Government Printer, 1959); *Report of the Commission of Inquiry into the Nembe Chieftaincy Dispute* (Enugu: Government Printer, 1960).

11 Vaughan, "Suicide."

12 *Report of a Commission of Inquiry Appointed to Inquire into Certain Incidents at Opobo, Abak and Utu-Etim-Ekpo* (Lagos: Government Printer, 1929).

13 Bastian, "Vultures of the Marketplace."

14 For example, *Report of the Inquiry into the Dispute over the Obiship of Onitsha* (Enugu: Government Printer, 1963); *Summary of the Report and Recommendations of the Commission of Inquiry into Outbreaks of Violence at Okrika* (Enugu: Government Printer, 1963).

15 *Report of Coker Commission of Inquiry into the Affairs on Certain Statutory Corporations in Western Nigeria* (Lagos: Federal Ministry of Information, 1962).

16 Lawyers disliked this model because they had no clear role in it. Some commissions did not allow witnesses to have legal counsel at all, which the Nigerian Bar Association opposed adamantly.

17 Commissions were also more efficient than trials. When civil unrest happened, a military governor could appoint a small panel to investigate a large number of people over a limited period, without having to worry about time-consuming appeals or countersuits. Comparatively, see Kaviraj, "Gandhi's Trial," 293–308.

18 The umbrella is a symbol of aristocratic authority in many parts of West Africa, and both Fela and the soldiers would have understood the symbolism of this gesture.

19 "Disturbances at 14A," 16.

20 Ghariokwu was known as the artist who designed Fela's album covers. Quoted in Olaniyan, *Arrest the Music!*, 134.

21 Incidentally, this soldier was a trumpet player like Fela. The military band he played in could hardly have been more different from Africa 70. "Enquiry," 10 March 1977, LASRAB LCE.A12a, 33.

22 "Enquiry," 10 March 1977, LASRAB LCE.A12a, 79.

23 Since it was a state rather than federal inquiry, they were appointed by the military governor of Lagos State, Commodore Adekunle S. Lawal.

24 "Disturbances at 14A," 8.

25 "Disturbances at 14A," 9.

26 Most of those criminal charges were dropped by the end of the year.

27 "Enquiry," 10 March 1977, LASRAB LCE.A12a, 78.

28 "Enquiry," 14 March 1977, LASRAB LCE.A12b, 4.

29 "Disturbances at 14A," 14.

30 "Enquiry," 10 March 1977, LASRAB LCE.A12a, 32.

31 "Enquiry," 10 March 1977, LASRAB LCE.A12a, 81.

32 "Disturbances at 14A," 18.

33 See Diabate, *Naked Agency*.

34 "Enquiry," 14 March 1977, LASRAB LCE.A12b, 16.

35 "Enquiry," 14 March 1977, LASRAB LCE.A12b, 46.

36 "Enquiry," 16 March 1977, LASRAB LCE.A12c, 45.

37 "Enquiry," 16 March 1977, LASRAB LCE.A12c, 14.

38 "Enquiry," 16 March 1977, LASRAB LCE.A12c, 20.

39 "Enquiry," 14 March 1977, LASRAB LCE.A12b, 37.

40 "Enquiry," 14 March 1977, LASRAB LCE.A12b, 39.

41 "Disturbances at 14A," 13.

42 "Disturbances at 14A," 13.

43 "Enquiry," 10 March 1977, LASRAB LCE.A12a, 33.

44 "Enquiry," 14 March 1977, LASRAB LCE.A12b, 56; "Enquiry," 10 March 1977, LASRAB LCE.A12a, 95.

45 One of them had threatened the firefighters dispatched to the scene that "if you love your lives, you should not put out the fire." "Enquiry," 14 March 1977, LASRAB LCE.A12b, 2.

46 They would inspire Fela's next album, *Unknown Soldier*, which related the events of the 1977 raid.

47 The final report also scapegoated the Lagos Police Command for the abuses, further erasing the "unknown soldiers" from the public record. It was not unusual that the military government blamed the police: the civilian police and the army were often at odds with one another.

48 "Disturbances at 14A," 18.

49 Cannabis also had an earlier Atlantic history. See Duvall, *African Roots of Marijuana*; Lasebikan and Ijomanta, "Cannabis Use and Disorders," 67–73.

50 Byfield, *Great Upheaval*, 160–61; "In Her Own Words"; Simola, "Nigerian Nationalist and Feminist"; Johnson-Odim and Mba, *For Women*.

51 Shonekan, "Fela's Foundation," 127–44.

52 "Enquiry," 14 March 1977, LASRAB LCE.A12b, 7–15.

53 Moreover, she had lost consciousness at some point, and it was not clear whether she had been awake during the ordeal.

54 He had relationships with many women, and by the early 1980s he had over two dozen wives. While polygamy was common in Nigeria, having that many was unusual. His critics found it suspicious.

55 Olaniyan, "Cosmopolitan Nativist," 76–89.

56 "Enquiry," 14 March 1977, LASRAB LCE.A12b, 62.

57 "Enquiry," 14 March 1977, LASRAB LCE.A12b, 87.

58 "Enquiry," 14 March 1977, LASRAB LCE.A12b, 71.

59 "Disturbances at 14A," 21.

60 "Enquiry," 16 March 1977, LASRAB LCE.A12c, 41.

61 It seems likely that their statements had been vetted by the Ransome-Kuti family's lawyers.

62 "Enquiry," 10 March 1977, LASRAB LCE.A12a, 43.

63 The family eventually produced a brigadier general. Fela's nephew Enitan Ransome-Kuti led the fight against the Boko Haram insurgency as commander of the Multinational Joint Task Force until 2015, when he was court-martialed for cowardice.

64 First, *Barrel of a Gun*, 84.

65 The first men commissioned as officers came from this pool of colonial-era enlistees. For this reason, African militaries developed a much more dynamic class character than their British model. In Britain, the armed forces reproduced and maintained the rigid class hierarchy—the rich became officers, the poor became their valets. In Africa, where nearly all soldiers came from the bottom, promotion through the ranks became a social elevator.

66 Ocran, *Politics of the Sword*, 110.

67 The volumes were priced well beyond the means of most people, and very few appear to have been printed. I have found no other extant copies besides the partial collection available at LASRAB. Again, however, the illusion of transparency was more important than any kind of actual accessibility.

68 Ashforth, "Reckoning Schemes of Legitimation," 3–9.

69 For a good summary of what "fair play" meant to soldiers, see Okonkwo, *Jeremiah Timbut Useni*, 93.

70 Olu Onagoruwa, "Is Government above the Law?," *Sunday Times* (Lagos), 26 March 1978, 17.

71 Their first attempt came immediately after the end of the inquiry, when Funmilayo Ransome-Kuti brought a claim against the government over the destruction of the house. Her suit was unsuccessful. Onagoruwa, "Is Government above the Law?," 17.

72 Chief Dr. (Mrs.) Olufunmilayo Ransome-Kuti and Others v. The Attorney-General of the Federation and Others, in the Supreme Court of Nigeria, 28 June 1985, SC.123/1984.

73 "Former President Olusegun Obasanjo Answers to Fela Kuti's Petition—Oputa Panel," Nigerian Television Authority recording, 2000.

CHAPTER 6. THE GIFT OF MARTIAL LAW

1 Quoted in Rekha Basu, "New Jersey Woman Faces Death Penalty in Nigeria," *New York Times*, 27 January 1985.

2 It emerged later that two of her Nigerian business partners felt she had shortchanged them and reported her to the military. This, as much as Buhari's crackdown, probably explains why she was arrested. *New York Amsterdam News*, 2 February 1985.

3 *Daily Star* (Lagos), 15 April 1985. See also Jian-Ye Wang, "Macroeconomic Policies and Smuggling: An Analysis of Illegal Oil Trade in Nigeria," September 1994, IMF Archives 414115.

4 It had jurisdiction over various offenses, including tampering with the post, damaging public property (e.g., siphoning oil from pipelines), and cheating on exams. But it was its jurisdiction over drug offenses that made the tribunal so lethal, and its profile rose as the traffic in cocaine accelerated in the 1980s. On the cocaine trade, see Oboh, *Cocaine Hoppers*.

5 *Jet*, 25 March 1985, 39; *People*, 14 January 1985.

6 *Guardian* (Lagos), 28 February 1985, 3.

7 Those sentences were sometimes commuted, especially in "white collar" cases where defendants were more likely to have political influence. "SMC Commutes Death Sentence Passed on Petroleum Products Dealers," 22 August 1985, NIIA, Nigeria-Tribunals.

8 Morris, *Military Justice*, 145. This is also sometimes attributed to Groucho Marx.

9 Jemibewon, *Military Law*, 16.

10 On martial law's Anglo-American genealogy, see Lieber et al., *To Save the Country*.

11 Halliday, *Habeas Corpus*, 293. On habeas corpus in the empire, see also Lobban, *Imperial Incarceration*.

12 A good example of this type of document would be Ferdinand Marcos's Proclamation 1081 in the Philippines.

13 Gyandoh, "Criminal Justice System," 1134.

14 Prakash, *Emergency Chronicles*, 167.

15 *Daily Sketch* (Lagos), 28 August 1968, 1.

16 Achike, *Groundwork of Military Law*, 42.

17 Confusingly, the term *tribunal* could also refer to several other things. The first tribunals in independent Nigeria were panels established to investigate the assets of public officials suspected of corruption. *Tribunal* and *inquiry* were used interchangeably to describe advisory commissions (like the Fela Kuti "tribunal" described earlier). Today there are electoral tribunals that examine irregularities in the democratic process. These are all separate from the military tribunals discussed here.

18 For example, Niyi Ademola, "Special Military Tribunals: Court Martials [*sic*] Revisited?," *Weekly Democrat*, 17 June 1984, 2.

19 "Address by the Chief of Army Staff, Lt. General T. Y. Danjuma to the 146 Third Brigade, First Division, Bukavu Barracks, Kano," 9 December 1977, NIIA, Nigeria-Tribunals.

20 Quoted in Gyandoh, "Criminal Justice System," 1165.

21 See, for example, the speeches of Prince Bola Ajibola, who would serve as federal minister of justice in the early 1990s. As president of the Nigerian Bar Association, Ajibola had led a prominent boycott of military tribunals in 1985. Once he became part of the government, he suddenly became a proponent of them. "For and Against Military Tribunals," *Constitutional Rights Journal* (Lagos), December 1990, 10.

22 Jemibewon, *Military, Law and Society*, 7.

23 Ekpenyong, "Social Inequalities," 25.

24 The armed robbery tribunal did pursue offenders in uniform, but their commanders advocated for them through unofficial channels. See, for example, "Request for Mercy, 65WA/24667 Lcpl Anthony Asu Quo," 9 August 1971, LASRAB CSG 2.55.

25 Dambazu, *Law and Criminality*, 85.

26 Commodore Adekunle S. Lawal, Military Governor of Lagos State, to Hon. Mr. Justice T. Gomes, High Court of Lagos State, 8 September 1976, LASRAB CSG 2.55.

27 "The Amendment of the Armed Robbery Decree," 19 July 1974, NIIA, Nigeria-Law.

28 Crime remained a problem, and armed robbery only became bolder. In 1982 a Lagos magistrate was robbed in his home in Ikeja by a group of men who "made sarcastic remarks about the Judge being one of those who made orders for the execution of armed robbers." The Lagos State Magistrates' Association wrote to the governor to request around-the-clock armed guards for its members. Justice J. A. Adefarasin to Alhaji Lateef K. Jakande, Governor of Lagos State, 27 May 1982; Secretary, Lagos State Magistrates' Association, to Governor of Lagos State, 16 July 1982, LASRAB LGS 2.89.

29 See Omeni, *Policing and Politics*, 187–93; Marenin, "Anini Saga," 259–81.

30 *Vanguard* (Lagos), 1 March 1985, 1.

31 *Daily Times* (Lagos), 20 October 1984, 2.

32 "The Militarization of Justice in Nigeria," *Constitutional Rights Journal* (Lagos), December 1990, 8.

33 In the Tribunal for the Trial of Offences under the Robbery and Firearms (Special Provisions) Decree, 1970, *The State v. Boluwaji Ijadu*, 30 September 1975, NIALS uncataloged collection.

34 The definition of what constituted an "arm" expanded from one year to the next. See *Morning Post* (Lagos), 25 October 1971, NIIA, Nigeria-Law General.

35 In Ghana, tribunals proved no more efficient, and no less corrupt, than the regular courts they supplanted. "There was always an *ad hoc* quality to how these bodies functioned," the American anthropologist Roger Gocking described his visit to a public tribunal in Accra in 1984, during the Rawlings administration. "On a superficial level, attire, the use of vernacular languages, and the participation of lay people on the judicial panel stamped this court as different from its 'traditional' counterparts. It was evident, however, that those panel members who were qualified lawyers dominated its proceedings.

Not surprisingly it had also become subject to delays and postponements that characterized the operations of the regular courts." Gocking, "Ghana's Public Tribunals," 201–16.

36 *Daily Times* (Lagos), 13 April 1971, NIIA, Nigeria-Law General.

37 Later, a structure of appeal from the Armed Robbery Tribunal would be established.

38 This was only true for some tribunals, however. Those dealing with anything like a "state secret" were not reported at all, and the most damning records were destroyed. For example, General Sani Abacha had the transcripts of an important tribunal about a 1995 coup attempt shredded. Tape recordings apparently survive somewhere. Anyanwu, *Days of Terror*, 76.

39 The State v. Thomas Osifo Edo, Osita Obi, and Festus Aigbe, 20 September 1974, LASRAB CSG 2.55.

40 "Ephraim Ariyo, Alias Buzugbe, Medical Report," 11 December 1974, LASRAB CSG 2.55.

41 The State v. Ephraim Ariyo alias Buzugbe, 12 December 1974, LASRAB CSG 2.55.

42 *Nigerian Observer* (Lagos), 20 December 1973.

43 Achebe, *Trouble with Nigeria*, 29. In his famous novel *The Famished Road*, Ben Okri also used Nigeria's traffic as a metaphor for how the country gobbles up its people.

44 They also collected fines, which was difficult to distinguish from bribery. Some Nigerian states continue to use mobile courts today. They found a new purpose during the COVID-19 pandemic, when state governments set them up in public squares to punish people for violating mask and social-distance mandates. Abraham Achirga, "Mobile Courts Target Nigeria's COVID-19 Rule-Breakers," *Reuters*, 11 March 2021.

45 *Daily Express* (London), 9 September 1971. See also Omeni, *Policing and Politics in Nigeria*, 178.

46 Tunde Obadina, "43 Convicted Armed Robbers Are Put to Death in Nigeria," *Los Angeles Times*, 23 July 1995.

47 C. Xrydz-Eyutchae, "Armed Robbery: Big Business or Boomerang," *Renaissance* (Enugu), 12 September 1971.

48 "Editorial: Restore Public Execution for Armed Robbers," *Nigerian Herald* (Lagos), 31 December 1982.

49 "Execution of an Armed Robber," 2 May 1971, NIIA, Nigeria-Law General. For a description of what these executions were like, see Okpewho, *Last Duty*, 15–22.

50 *Nigerian Observer* (Lagos), 2 May 1971, NIIA, Nigeria-Law General.

51 *New Nigerian* (Lagos), 28 April 1971, NIIA, Nigeria-Law General.

52 Akin Isidapo-Obe, "Dispensation of Criminal Justice under Nigerian Military Administrations," *Constitutional Rights Journal* (Lagos), December 1990, 34.

53 Nkrumah, *Dark Days in Ghana*, 109.

54 "In Justification of Military Tribunals," *Constitutional Rights Journal* (Lagos), December 1990, 14.

55 *Daily Times* (Lagos), 25 October 1971, NIIA, Nigeria-Law General.

56 *New Nigerian* (Lagos), 5 December 1971, 1.

57 General Yakubu Gowon to Colonel Mobolaji Johnson, 14 October 1971, LAS-RAB CSG 2.55.

58 Colonel Mobolaji Johnson to T. O. Elias, Federal Attorney-General, 7 May 1970, LASRAB CSG 2.55.

59 Colonel Mobolaji Johnson to T. O. Elias, Federal Attorney-General, 7 May 1970, LASRAB CSG 2.55.

60 *Daily Times* (Lagos), 20 April 1967, NIIA, Nigeria-Law.

61 Liliwhite-Nwosu, *Divine Restoration!* and *Divine Restoration of Nigeria*.

62 In 1973, the Nigerian Bar Association announced that it would take disciplinary measures "against any legal practitioner who allows musicians to wax records in praise of his professional skills." Lawyers, the association's president declared, "should disclaim the artistes and their songs of praise openly and take urgent steps to stop the continued circulation of such records." The military governor of Lagos State gave a speech endorsing the ban, and it seems likely that he was the one who had pressed for it in the first place. The military felt the songs sent a bad message; they celebrated lawyers for their ability to win money for their clients, which they feared would encourage frivolous litigation. Soldiers also didn't like civilians being revered in general—if there were going to be praise songs about anyone, they should be about them. Sadly, I have never found a copy of one of these recordings. *Daily Times* (Lagos), 17 August 1973, NIIA, Nigeria-Law General.

63 "For and Against Military Tribunals," *Constitutional Rights Journal* (Lagos), December 1990, 11.

64 "Military Tribunals," editorial, *Constitutional Rights Journal* (Lagos), January–May 1992, 26.

65 "Introduction," *Constitutional Rights Journal* (Lagos), December 1990, 4.

66 Mike Ozeokhome, "When a Hired Mob Failed to Stop Me from Defending Democracy in Nigeria," *Sun* (Lagos), 7 February 2018.

67 Isidapo-Obe, "Dispensation of Criminal Justice," 35.

68 "The Militarization of Justice in Nigeria," *Constitutional Rights Journal* (Lagos), December 1990, 9.

69 They weren't the only ones who found it—cause lawyers around the world began to make use of human rights language in the 1970s. See Eckel and Moyn, *Breakthrough*. On the idea's itinerary in Africa, see Mann, *From Empires to NGOs*; Ibhawoh, *Human Rights in Africa*.

70 "Military Court of Appeal Necessary—Experts," *New Nigerian*, 20 June 1987, NIIA, Nigeria-Courts (emphasis added).

71 Amnesty International, Further information on UA 163/90—Nigeria: death penalty/legal concern: 27 people executed, 19 September 1990, AFR 44/15/1990.

72 "Double Trial for Coup Suspects," *Constitutional Rights Journal* (Lagos), December 1990, 12.

73 A master of this approach was Amina Mama, a feminist academic who shamed the military at every turn. Mama, "Feminism or Femocracy?"

74 In Nigeria, those who survived the coups that deposed them were treated with a light hand. Their main punishment was public humiliation, typically in the form of a judicial inquiry. Babangida's treatment of Buhari was the harshest, but even he suffered nothing worse than a period of house arrest. Since Gowon had gone into exile in Britain, his inquiry took place in absentia. He used his stint in exile to complete a bachelor's degree at the University of Warwick (he was, after all, still young). There, Gowon had the unusual experience of studying political science after governing one of the world's largest countries. "The Ex-dictator and His Degree of Anonymity," *Times Higher Education*, 6 January 2006; "Buhari, Idiagbon to Go through Judicial Tribunals of Inquiry," 27 November 1985, NIIA, Nigeria-Tribunals.

75 *The Punch* (Lagos), 31 August 1985, 2.

76 This would have been a sign to every judge in the room that Babangida was punting. The constitution he invoked was the long-abandoned 1979 civilian constitution, which they had been barred from interpreting by decree. "Military Tribunals Defended by President Babangida," 7 September 1988, NIIA, Nigeria-Tribunals.

CODA

1 In the Nigerian context, *cult* has a complicated meaning. It refers to a sect or clique, but it also connotes a connection to the *occult* and, uniquely to Nigeria, to *organized crime*—something like a gang.

2 For a detailed account of this moment, see Diamond, Kirk-Green, and Oyediran, "Politics of Transition," xv–l.

3 Kamil, *Africa Has Come of Age*, 136.

4 See Usman, *Misrepresentation of Nigeria*, 1–30.

5 One of his supporters argued that it was the product of "an invitation made by concerned and prominent Nigerians demanding for an intervention primarily to end the ailing, convulsing, and drifting ship known as Nigeria." Edet, *Abacha's Call to Duty*, xvii.

6 Anyanwu, *Days of Terror*, 271.

7 Ihonvbere, "Military and Nigerian Society," 509–10.

8 Edet, *Abacha's Call to Duty*, 37.

9 Soyinka, *Open Sore*, 14–15.

10 Anyanwu, *Days of Terror*, 19.

11 Edet, *Abacha's Call to Duty*, 29.

12 Shawcross, *Deliver Us from Evil*, 307.

13 United Nations Office on Drugs and Crime, "Anti-Corruption Climate Change: It Started in Nigeria, 6th National Seminar on Economic Crime, Abuja," 13 November 2007.

14 Maja-Pearce, *Remembering Ken Saro-Wiwa*, 110.

15 See Monfrini, "Proceeds of Corruption."

16 On the beneficiaries of this trade in Nigeria, see Klantschnig, *Crime, Drugs and the State.*

17 Quoted in Edet, *Abacha's Call to Duty*, 89.

18 "Nobel-Winning Writer Flees Nigeria," *New York Times*, 22 November 1994, 11.

19 Abacha, *Abacha Speaks*, 29.

20 Quoted in Human Rights Watch, "Nigeria," 14.

21 Onagoruwa and his adversary Gani Fawehinmi had a vicious, public falling out over Onagoruwa's role in the Abacha administration. Both wrote memoirs about it: Onagoruwa, *A Rebel in General Abacha's Government*; and Fawehinmi, *The Lies and Lies of Dr. Olu Onagoruwa.*

22 Kamil, *Rendez-vous*, 144.

23 As was often the case, Abacha had personal gripes with the people he purged—here, over the allocation of some scholarships at the University of Nebraska. Anyanwu, *Days of Terror*, 50.

24 Anyanwu, *Days of Terror*, 337.

25 Anyanwu, "Rats on Two Legs," 21–24.

26 Anyanwu, *Days of Terror*, 65–67. Anyanwu was not the only one to use an extraterrestrial metaphor to describe soldiers. "Under a dictatorship, a nation ceases to exist," wrote Soyinka. "All that remains is a fiefdom, a planet of slaves regimented by aliens from outer space. The appropriate cinematic equivalent would be those grade B movies about alien body-snatchers." Soyinka, *Open Sore*, 139.

27 Anyanwu, *Days of Terror*, 50.

28 Bassey, *Nigerian Judiciary*, 44.

29 Albert, "When the State Kills," 210.

30 The court eventually decided he was the former. He was released, and he has lived out the rest of his life in obscurity.

31 The Strike Force was said to have been trained in North Korea, but it seems likely this was a myth the regime was happy to let circulate.

32 "Kudirat Abiola: A Martyr for Justice," Special publication of the Committee for the Defence of Human Rights, Nigeria, 1998, 7.

33 Osifodunrin, "Violent Crimes in Lagos," 234.

34 See generally Newell, "Introduction: Ken Saro-Wiwa"; Doron and Falola, *Ken Saro-Wiwa.*

35 Doron and Falola, *Ken Saro-Wiwa*, 143.

36 Wiwa, "Murder of Ken Saro-Wiwa," 107–8.

37 Witt, "Garland's Million," 123–47.

38 Benton, *Law and Colonial Cultures*, 256. See also Peterson, "Government Work," 632.

39 This case was *Wiwa v. Royal Dutch Shell Co.* of 1996, which was settled out of court. The Saro-Wiwa family were not the only activists to seek justice on American soil. *Kiobel v. Royal Dutch Petroleum Co.* went all the way to the

US Supreme Court, which ruled against the Nigerian appellants, citing the danger that a broad interpretation of the Alien Tort Statute could pose to American diplomacy. Nigerian activists would also make claims against Shell in the United Kingdom and the Netherlands.

40 Black Americans were among the most tenacious of Abacha's critics. Anyanwu, *Days of Terror*, lxvi; Sundiata, *Brothers and Strangers*, 336.

41 Devin Gordon, "Cochran Comes to the Rescue," *Newsweek*, 10 April 2000, 10.

42 The head of the commission was Justice Chukwudifu Oputa. Oputa had given juridical form to militarism's disciplinary spirit, so it was ironic that he would preside over its reckoning.

43 One historian has wielded the pin especially deftly—Frederick Cooper. On these and many other terms, see Desai and Masquelier, *Critical Terms*; Lawrance and Desai, "African Studies Keywords." The strongest, most polemical statement against treating decolonization as a theory of everything is Olúfẹ́mi Táíwò's. I do not follow Táíwò to the terminus of his argument, and I am ambivalent about the alternatives he offers, but he exposes the limits of the idea masterfully. Táíwò, *Against Decolonization*. See also Mokoena, "Who Owns 'Black'?"; Cooper, "Decolonizations."

44 On this narrower meaning, see Duara, *Decolonization*.

45 I borrow this phrasing from Guha, "Small Voice of History," 1–13.

46 Some would argue that *decolonization* and *decoloniality* are actually false cognates, which points to how difficult it is to pin these concepts down. There is precedent for this. In the 1990s, the historian Megan Vaughan published a takedown of the imperious theory of her time, postmodernism, and its offshoots in the study of the postcolonial world. Its arguments were "constructed in a language of theory which is at once enormously and deliberately ambiguous, she wrote, "and at the same time staggeringly ambitious and all-embracing (some would say 'imperialist')." It had "'hard' and 'soft' versions," and multiple veins and currents that ran against one another, "so that reference to the implications of 'it' immediately raises the question of which version of 'it' we are referring to." Something similar is happening with decoloniality today. Vaughan, "Colonial Discourse Theory," 4.

47 See Quijano and Ennis, "Coloniality of Power"; Mignolo, *Politics of Decolonial Investigations*; Escobar, *Designs for the Pluriverse*. For its legal guise, see Santos, *End of the Cognitive Empire*.

48 The "tight corner" is a metaphor that historians of Africa often find useful. Lonsdale, "Agency in Tight Corners," 5–16.

49 Compare, for example, the thundery proclamations of Chukwudifu Oputa to those of the decolonial legal scholar Roberto Unger, *False Necessity*.

Abacha, Sani. *Abacha Speaks*. Lagos: Blue-Haven Communication, 1997.

Abdullah, Ibrahim. "Bush Path to Destruction: The Origin and Character of the Revolutionary United Front/Sierra Leone." *Journal of Modern African Studies* 36, no. 2 (1998): 203–34.

Abrahamsen, Rita. "Return of the Generals? Global Militarism in Africa from the Cold War to the Present." *Security Dialogue* 49, no. 1–2 (2018): 19–31.

Achebe, Chinua. *Anthills of the Savannah*. New York: Anchor Books, 1988.

Achebe, Chinua. *The Trouble with Nigeria*. Oxford: Heinemann, 1984.

Achike, Okay. *Groundwork of Military Law and Military Rule in Nigeria*. Enugu: Fourth Dimension, 1980.

Adebanwi, Wale. "Africa's 'Two Publics': Colonialism and Governmentality." *Theory, Culture and Society* 34, no. 4 (2017): 65–87.

Adebanwi, Wale. "Burying 'Zik of Africa': The Politics of Death and Cultural Crisis." *Comparative Studies in Society and History* 63, no. 1 (2021): 41–71.

Adebanwi, Wale, Ebenezer Obadare, and Larry Jay Diamond. *Democracy and Prebendalism in Nigeria: Critical Interpretations*. New York: Palgrave Macmillan, 2013.

Ademoyega, Adewale. *Why We Struck: The Story of the First Nigerian Coup*. Ibadan: Evans Brothers, 1981.

Adewoye, Omoniyi. *The Judicial System in Southern Nigeria, 1854–1954*. London: Longman, 1977.

Adewoye, Omoniyi. "The Legal Profession in Southern Nigeria, 1863–1943." PhD diss., Columbia University, 1968.

Adi, Hakim. *West Africans in Britain, 1900–1960: Nationalism, Pan-Africanism, and Communism*. London: Lawrence and Wishart, 1998.

Adichie, Chimamanda Ngozi. "The Shivering." In *The Thing around Your Neck*, 142–66. New York: Knopf, 2009.

Aduku, Isaac. *Maryam: The Mirror of Motherhood*. Abuja: Family Support Programme News, 1998.

Adunbi, Omolade. *Enclaves of Exception: Special Economic Zones and Extractive Practices in Nigeria*. Bloomington: Indiana University Press, 2022.

Afigbo, A. E. "The Eastern Provinces under Colonial Rule." In *Groundwork of Nigerian History*, edited by Obaro Ikime, 410–28. Ibadan: Heinemann, 1980.

Afigbo, A. E. *Ropes of Sand: Studies in Igbo History and Culture*. Ibadan: University Press Limited, 1981.

Afowowe, Oluranti. *Onward Soldier Marches On: A Biography of Major-General Robert Adeyinka Adebayo*. Ibadan: Evans Brothers, 1998.

African Conference on the Rule of Law. *A Report on the Proceedings of the Conference: Lagos, Nigeria, January 3–7, 1961*. Geneva: International Commission of Jurists, 1961.

Agbaje, Adigun, and Jinmi Adisa. "Political Education and Public Policy in Nigeria: The War Against Indiscipline." *Journal of Commonwealth and Comparative Politics* 26, no. 1 (1988): 22–37.

Agbede, I. Oluwole. *Legal Pluralism*. Ibadan: Shaneson, 1991.

Agbiboa, Daniel. *They Eat Our Sweat: Transport Labor, Corruption, and Everyday Survival in Urban Nigeria*. Oxford: Oxford University Press, 2022.

Aguda, T. Akinola. *The Crisis of Justice*. Akure: Eresu Hills Publishers, 1986.

Ahlman, Jeffrey S. *Living with Nkrumahism: Nation, State, and Pan-Africanism in Ghana*. Athens: Ohio University Press, 2017.

Aihe, D. O. "Nigerian Federal Military Government and the Judiciary: A Reflection on *Lakanmi v. Attorney-General. Western State of Nigeria*." *Journal of the Indian Law Institute* 13, no. 4 (1971): 570–80.

Ajayi, F. A. "British Territories in Africa: The Future of Customary Law in Nigeria." In *The Future of Customary Law in Africa*, organized by the Afrika Instituut, Leiden, 42–69. Leiden: Leiden University Press, 1956.

Akande, Rabiat. *Entangled Domains: Empire, Law and Religion in Northern Nigeria*. Cambridge: Cambridge University Press, 2023.

Akpamgbo, C. Obi. "The Customary Courts. No. 2 Edict 1966." *Nigeria Lawyers' Quarterly* 3, no. 1–2 (1968): 27.

Akpan, Ntieyong U. *Epitaph to Indirect Rule: A Discourse on Local Government in Africa*. London: Cassell, 1956.

Alao, Akin. *Statesmanship on the Bench: The Judicial Career of Sir Adetokunbo Ademola, 1939–1977*. Trenton, NJ: Africa World Press, 2007.

Albert, Isaac Olawale. "When the State Kills: Political Assassinations in Abacha's Nigeria." In *Encountering the Nigerian State*, edited by Wale Adebanwi and Ebenezer Obadare, 199–215. London: Palgrave Macmillan, 2010.

Alexievich, Svetlana. *The Unwomanly Face of War: An Oral History of Women in World War II*. New York: Random House, 2017.

Aliyu, Abdullahi. *Dr. Mrs. Maryam Sani Abacha: A Visionary Mother with an Economic Mission for the Nigerian Family*. Wuse: Family Economic Advancement Programme, 1997.

Allen, Peter. *Days of Judgment: A Judge in Idi Amin's Uganda*. London: Kimber, 1987.

Allman, Jean M. *The Quills of the Porcupine: Asante Nationalism in an Emergent Ghana*. Madison: University of Wisconsin Press, 1993.

Allott, A. N., ed. *The Future of Law in Africa: Record of Proceedings of the London Conference, 28 December 1959–8 January 1960 under the Chairmanship of Lord Denning*. London: Butterworth, 1960.

Allott, Antony. *Judicial and Legal Systems in Africa*. London: Butterworths, 1962.

Allott, Antony. *New Essays in African Law*. London: Butterworths, 1970.

Amadiume, Ifi. *Male Daughters, Female Husbands: Gender and Sex in African Society*. London: Zed Books, 1987.

Amin, Samir. *L'Afrique de l'Ouest bloquée, l'économie politique de la colonisation, 1880–1970*. Paris: Éditions de Minuit, 1971.

Amuta, Chidi. *Prince of the Niger: The Babangida Years*. Lagos: Tanus Communications, 1992.

Anderson, Perry. *Lineages of the Absolutist State*. London: NLB, 1977.

Anene, Joseph C. *The International Boundaries of Nigeria, 1885–1960: The Framework of an Emergent African Nation*. New York: Humanities, 1970.

Anyangwe, Carlson. *Revolutionary Overthrow of Constitutional Orders in Africa*. Bamenda: Langaa Research and Publishing, 2012.

Anyanwu, Chris N. D. *The Days of Terror: A Journalist's Eye-Witness Account of Nigeria in the Hands of its Worst Tyrant*. Ibadan: Spectrum, 2002.

Anyanwu, Christine. "Rats on Two Legs." *Index on Censorship* 27, no. 5 (1998): 21–24.

Anyebe, A. P. *Customary Law: The War without Arms*. Enugu: Fourth Dimension, 1985.

Apter, Andrew H. *The Pan-African Nation: Oil and the Spectacle of Culture in Nigeria*. Chicago: University of Chicago Press, 2005.

Archibong, Belinda. "Historical Origins of Persistent Inequality in Nigeria." *Oxford Development Studies* 46, no. 3 (2018): 325–47.

Ashforth, Adam. "Reckoning Schemes of Legitimation: On Commissions of Inquiry as Power/Knowledge Forms." *Journal of Historical Sociology* 3, no. 1 (1990): 1–22.

Assensoh, A. B., and Yvette Alex-Assensoh. *African Military History and Politics: Coups and Ideological Incursions, 1900–Present*. New York: Palgrave, 2001.

Ayittey, George B. N. *Indigenous African Institutions*. 2nd ed. Ardsley, NY: Transnational Publishers, 2006.

Azikiwe, Nnamdi. *Democracy with Military Vigilance: The Samuel Jereton Mariere Inaugural Lecture Entitled Stability in Nigeria after Military Rule: An Analysis of Political Theory, Delivered in the College of Medicine Hall, University of Lagos*. Nsukka: African Book Company, 1974.

Azinge, Ephiphany, ed. *Restatement of Customary Law in Nigeria*. Lagos: Nigerian Institute of Advanced Legal Studies, 2013.

Azinge, Epiphany, and Laura Ani, eds. *Freedom of Protest*. Lagos: Nigerian Institute of Advanced Legal Studies, 2013.

Azinge, Epiphany, and Oluchi Nwakaego Azoro, eds. *NIALS Dictionary of African Customary Laws*. Lagos: Nigerian Institute of Advanced Legal Studies, 2013.

Ba, Oumar. *States of Justice: The Politics of the International Criminal Court*. Cambridge: Cambridge University Press, 2020.

Babangida, Ibrahim Badamosi. *For Their Tomorrow, We Gave Our Today: Selected Speeches of IBB, Volume II*. Ibadan: Safari Books, 1991.

Babangida, Maryam. *The Home Front: Nigerian Army Officers and Their Wives*. Ibadan: Fountain, 1998.

Bade, Albert. *Benedicto Kiwanuka: The Man and His Politics*. Kampala: Fountain, 1996.

Balakrishnan, Sarah. "Of Debt and Bondage: From Slavery to Prisons in the Gold Coast, c. 1807–1957." *Journal of African History* 61, no. 1 (2020): 3–21.

Balint, Jennifer, Julie Evans, and Nesam McMillan. "Justice Claims in Colonial Contexts: Commissions of Inquiry in Historical Perspective." *Australian Feminist Law Journal* 42, no. 1 (2016): 75–96.

Barber, Karin. "Popular Reactions to the Petro-Naira." *Journal of Modern African Studies* 20, no. 3 (1982): 431–50.

Barnes, Victoria, and Emily Whewell. "Judicial Biography in the British Empire." *Indiana Journal of Global Legal Studies* 28, no. 1 (2021): 1–28.

Bassey, Peter Odo Effiong. *The Nigerian Judiciary: The Departing Glory*. Lagos: Malthouse, 2000.

Bastian, Misty L. "'Vultures of the Marketplace': Southeastern Nigerian Women and Discourses of the Ogu Umunwaanyi (Women's War) of 1929." In *Women in African Colonial Histories*, edited by Jean Allman, Susan Geiger, and Nakanyike Musisi, 260–81. Bloomington: Indiana University Press, 2002.

Baxi, Upendra. "Touch It Not, if You Are Not a Historian." *Comparative Studies of South Asia, Africa, and the Middle East* 38, no. 3 (2018): 375–84.

Bayala, Blanchard Emmanuel. *Tribunaux populaires de la révolution et les droits de l'homme*. Ouagadougou: Editions L'Harmattan, 2018.

Bayart, Jean-François. *The State in Africa: The Politics of the Belly*. Cambridge: Polity, 2009.

Bebler, Anton. *Military Rule in Africa: Dahomey, Ghana, Sierra Leone, and Mali*. New York: Praeger, 1973.

Behrend, Heike. *Alice Lakwena and the Holy Spirits: War in Northern Uganda, 1985–97*. Oxford: James Currey, 1999.

Bello, Mohammed. "How Fair Trial Is Guaranteed in Our Judicial System: A Lecture Delivered on the 1st of March 1973 to the Law Students, ABU Zaria." *Law in Society: Journal of the Law Society, Ahmadu Bello University*, no. 1 (1974): 1–12.

Belloc, Hilaire. *The Modern Traveller*. London: E. Arnold, 1898.

Ben-Ghiat, Ruth. *Strongmen: Mussolini to the Present*. New York: W. W. Norton, 2020.

Benjamin, Walter. *Reflections: Essays, Aphorisms, Autobiographical Writings*. New York: Schocken Books, 1978.

Benton, Lauren. *Law and Colonial Cultures: Legal Regimes in World History, 1400–1900*. Cambridge: Cambridge University Press, 2002.

Berda, Yael. *Colonial Bureaucracy and Contemporary Citizenship*. Cambridge: Cambridge University Press, 2022.

Berry, Sara. "Hegemony on a Shoestring: Indirect Rule and Access to Agricultural Land." *Africa* 62, no. 3 (1992): 327–55.

Bhabha, Homi. "Of Mimicry and Man: The Ambivalence of Colonial Discourse." *October*, no. 28 (1984): 125–33.

Bishara, Fahad Ahmad. *A Sea of Debt: Law and Economic Life in the Western Indian Ocean, 1780–1950*. Cambridge: Cambridge University Press, 2017.

Borno State Government. *The Milestone: A Compendium of Achievements of Group Captain L. N. Haruna's Administration in Borno State*. Maiduguri: Borno State Government, 1999.

Boucault, Carlos Eduardo de Abreu. "Hans Kelsen: The Reception of 'Pure Theory' in South America, Particularly in Brazil." *Seqüência: Estudos Jurídicos e Políticos* 36, no. 71 (2015): 95–105.

Bradley, A. W. "Constitution-Making in Uganda." *Transition*, no. 32 (1967): 25–31.

Burrill, Emily. *States of Marriage: Gender, Justice, and Rights in Colonial Mali*. Athens: Ohio University Press, 2015.

Byfield, Judith A. *The Great Upheaval: Women and Nation in Postwar Nigeria*. Athens: Ohio University Press, 2021.

Byfield, Judith A. "In Her Own Words: Funmilayo Ransome-Kuti and the Auto/biography of an Archive." *Palimpsest* 5, no. 2 (2016): 107–27.

Byfield, Judith A., Carolyn A. Brown, Timothy Parsons, and Ahmad Alawad Sikainga, eds. *Africa and World War II*. New York: Cambridge University Press, 2015.

Carney, J. J. "Benedicto Kiwanuka and Catholic Democracy in Uganda." *Journal of Religious History* 44, no. 2 (2020): 212–29.

Caute, David. *At Fever Pitch*. New York: Pantheon, 1961.

Chabal, Patrick, and Jean-Pascal Daloz. *Africa Works: Disorder as Political Instrument*. London: James Currey, 1999.

Chanock, Martin. *Law, Custom and Social Order: The Colonial Experience in Malawi and Zambia*. Portsmouth, NH: Heinemann, 1998.

Chanock, Martin. "A Peculiar Sharpness: An Essay on Property in the History of Customary Law in Colonial Africa." *Journal of African History* 32, no. 1 (1991): 65–88.

Chappell, David. "'Africanization' in the Pacific: Blaming Others for Disorder in the Periphery?" *Comparative Studies in Society and History* 47, no. 2 (2005): 286–317.

Cheeseman, Nic, and Jonathan Fisher. *Authoritarian Africa: Repression, Resistance, and the Power of Ideas*. Oxford: Oxford University Press, 2021.

Chikendu, Patrick. *The Military Question: Path to a Pan-Nigerian Democratic Order*. Enugu: MaryDan, 1996.

Chrisinger, David. *The Soldier's Truth: Ernie Pyle and the Story of World War II*. New York: Penguin, 2023.

Chuku, Gloria. "Igbo Historiography: Part II." *History Compass* 16, no. 10 (2018): 1–12.

Clarke, Kamari. *Affective Justice: The International Criminal Court and the Pan-Africanist Pushback*. Durham, NC: Duke University Press, 2019.

Clayton, Anthony, and David Killingray. *Khaki and Blue: Military and Police in British Colonial Africa*. Athens: Ohio Monographs in International Studies, 1989.

Coates, Oliver. "New Perspectives on West Africa and World War Two." *Journal of African Military History* 4, no. 1–2 (2020): 5–39.

Cockar, Abdul Majid. *Doings, Non-Doings, and Mis-Doings by Kenya Chief Justices, 1963–1998*. Nairobi: Zand Graphics, 2012.

Cohen, David W., and E. S. Atieno Odhiambo. *Burying SM: The Politics of Knowledge and the Sociology of Power in Africa*. Portsmouth, NH: Heinemann, 1992.

Connelly, Matthew. *The Declassification Engine: What History Reveals about America's Top Secrets*. New York: Pantheon, 2023.

Cooper, Frederick. *Citizenship between Empire and Nation: Remaking France and French Africa, 1945–1960*. Princeton, NJ: Princeton University Press, 2014.

Cooper, Frederick. "Decolonizations, Colonizations, and More Decolonizations: The End of Empire in Time and Space." *Journal of World History* 33, no. 3 (2022): 491–526.

Cooper, Frederick. "Possibility and Constraint: African Independence in Historical Perspective." *Journal of African History* 49, no. 2 (2008): 167–96.

Cooper, Frederick, and Ann Laura Stoler. "Between Metropole and Colony: Rethinking a Research Agenda." In *Tensions of Empire: Colonial Cultures in a Bourgeois World*, edited by Frederick Cooper and Anna Laura Stoler, 1–86. Berkeley: University of California Press, 1997.

Cotran, Eugene. "Tony Allott, Pioneer of the Study of African Law: A Personal Memoir." *Journal of African Law* 31, no. 1/2 (1987): 15–17.

Crowder, Michael. *The Flogging of Phinehas McIntosh: A Tale of Colonial Folly and Injustice, Bechuanaland 1933*. New Haven, CT: Yale University Press, 1988.

Daly, Samuel Fury Childs. "Archival Research in Africa." *African Affairs* 116, no. 463 (2017): 311–20.

Daly, Samuel Fury Childs. "Ghana Must Go: Nativism and the Politics of Expulsion in West Africa, 1969–1985." *Past and Present* 259, no. 1 (2023): 229–61.

Daly, Samuel Fury Childs. *A History of the Republic of Biafra: Law, Crime, and the Nigerian Civil War*. Cambridge: Cambridge University Press, 2020.

Dambazu, A. B. *Law and Criminality in Nigeria: An Analytical Discourse*. Ibadan: University Press, 1994.

Daniels, W. C. Ekow, and G. R. Woodman, eds. *Essays in Ghanaian Law: Supreme Court Centenary Publication, 1876–1976*. Legon: Faculty of Law, University of Ghana, 1976.

Date-Bah, Samuel Kofi. *Reflections on the Supreme Court of Ghana*. London: Wildy, Simmonds, and Hill, 2015.

Davies, A. E. "The IMF in the Nigerian Economy: Pressures and Responses." *India Quarterly* 46, no. 4 (1990): 91–114.

De, Rohit. "Brown Lawyers, Black Robes: Decolonization, Diasporas and the Global History of Minority Rights." Paper presented at South Asia Unbound:

Artistic, Literary, Professional, and Business Entanglements across and beyond South Asia, King's College London, 19 March 2021.

De, Rohit. "'A Peripatetic World Court' Cosmopolitan Courts, Nationalist Judges and the Indian Appeal to the Privy Council." *Law and History Review* 32, no. 4 (2014): 821–51.

Decalo, Samuel. *Coups and Army Rule in Africa: Motivations and Constraints.* New Haven, CT: Yale University Press, 1990.

Decalo, Samuel. *Psychoses of Power: African Personal Dictatorships.* Gainesville: Florida Academic Press, 1998.

Decker, Alicia C. "'Sometimes You May Leave Your Husband in Karuma Falls or in the Forest There': A Gendered History of Disappearance in Idi Amin's Uganda, 1971–79." *Journal of Eastern African Studies* 7, no. 1 (2013): 125–42.

Desai, Gaurav, and Adeline Masquelier, eds. *Critical Terms for the Study of Africa.* Chicago: University of Chicago Press, 2018.

Diabate, Naminata. *Naked Agency: Genital Cursing and Biopolitics in Africa.* Durham, NC: Duke University Press, 2020.

Diamond, Larry, Anthony Kirk-Greene, and Oyeleye Oyediran. "The Politics of Transition without End." In *Transition without End: Nigerian Politics and Civil Society under Babangida,* 1–30. Boulder, CO: Lynne Rienner, 1997.

Doron, Roy, and Toyin Falola. *Ken Saro-Wiwa.* Athens: Ohio University Press, 2016.

Drury, Mark. "Anticolonial Irredentism: The Moroccan Liberation Army and Decolonisation in the Sahara." *Journal of North African Studies* (2022): 1–22.

Duara, Prasenjit, ed. *Decolonization: Perspectives from Now and Then.* London: Taylor and Francis, 2003.

Dudley, Billy J. *Instability and Political Order: Politics and Crisis in Nigeria.* Ibadan: Ibadan University Press, 1973.

Duke, Hajia Zainab. *The Revolutionary Potentials of the Nigerian Military 1886–1986.* Lagos: Self-published, 1987.

Dunkerley, Anthony W. "Exploring the Use of Juju in Nigerian Human Trafficking Networks: Considerations for Criminal Investigators." *Police Practice and Research* 19, no. 1 (2018): 83–100.

Duvall, Chris S. *The African Roots of Marijuana.* Durham, NC: Duke University Press, 2019.

Dwyer, Maggie. *Soldiers in Revolt: Army Mutinies in Africa.* Oxford: Oxford University Press, 2017.

Dyson, Sally, ed. *Nigeria: The Birth of Africa's Greatest Country, Volume Two.* Ibadan: Spectrum, 1998.

Earle, Jonathon L. *Colonial Buganda and the End of Empire: Political Thought and Historical Imagination in Africa.* Cambridge: Cambridge University Press, 2017.

Eckel, Jan, and Samuel Moyn, eds. *The Breakthrough: Human Rights in the 1970s.* Philadelphia: University of Pennsylvania Press, 2014.

Edet, Charles. *General Abacha's Call to Duty*. Enugu: Promat, 1994.

Ejoor, David Akpode. *Reminiscences*. Lagos: Malthouse, 1989.

Ekechi, F. K. "The British Assault on Ogbunorie Oracle in Eastern Nigeria." *Journal of African Studies* 14, no. 2 (1987): 69–78.

Ekeh, Peter P. "Colonialism and the Two Publics in Africa: A Theoretical Statement." *Comparative Studies in Society and History* 17, no. 1 (1975): 91–112.

Ekpenyong, Stephen. "Social Inequalities, Collusion, and Armed Robbery in Nigerian Cities." *British Journal of Criminology* 29, no. 1 (1989): 21–34.

Ekundayo, A. A. M. "The Common Law of Nigeria: A 'Stranger' or an Indigene in Nigeria?" In *Fundamentals of Nigerian Law*, edited by M. Ayo Ajomo, 200–209. Lagos: Nigerian Institute of Advanced Legal Studies, 1989.

Elias, Taslim O. *Judicial Process in the Newer Commonwealth*. Lagos: University of Lagos Press, 1990.

Elkins, Caroline. *Legacy of Violence: A History of the British Empire*. New York: Knopf, 2022.

Ellis, Stephen. *The Mask of Anarchy: The Destruction of Liberia and the Religious Dimension of an African Civil War*. New York: New York University Press, 2007.

Ellis, Stephen. "The Okija Shrine: Death and Life in Nigerian Politics." *Journal of African History* 49, no. 3 (2008): 445–66.

Enonchong, Charles. *I Know Who Killed Major Nzeogwu! Read Me! Envy Me! I Know!* Lagos: Century, 1991.

Escobar, Arturo. *Designs for the Pluriverse: Radical Interdependence, Autonomy, and the Making of Worlds*. Durham, NC: Duke University Press, 2018.

Eweluka, D. "The Military System of Administration in Nigeria." *African Law Studies* 10, no. 1 (1974): 67–125.

Fakih, Farabi. *Authoritarian Modernization in Indonesia's Early Independence Period*. Leiden: Brill, 2020.

Fallers, Lloyd A. *Law without Precedent: Legal Ideas in Action in the Courts of Colonial Busoga*. Chicago: University of Chicago Press, 1969.

Falola, Toyin, and Julius Omozuanvbo Ihonvbere. *The Rise and Fall of Nigeria's Second Republic, 1979–84*. London: Zed Books, 1985.

Fanon, Frantz. "'Why We Use Violence,' Address to the Accra Positive Action Conference, April 1960." In *Alienation and Freedom: Frantz Fanon*, edited by Jean Khalfa and Robert J. C. Young, 653–60. London: Bloomsbury Academic, 2018.

Fanon, Frantz. *The Wretched of the Earth*. 1963. New York: Grove, 2004.

Fawehinmi, Gani. *The Lies and Lies of Dr. Olu Onagoruwa, in His Book Titled "A Rebel in General Abacha's Government."* Lagos: Nigerian Law Publications, 2006.

Fawehinmi, Gani. *Ouster of Court Jurisdiction in Nigeria, 1914–2003*. Lagos: Nigerian Law Publications, 2004.

Feingold, Ellen R. *Colonial Justice and Decolonization in the High Court of Tanzania, 1920–1971*. London: Palgrave Macmillan, 2018.

Fenrich, Jeanmarie, Paolo Galizzi, and Tracy E. Higgins, eds. *The Future of African Customary Law*. Cambridge: Cambridge University Press, 2011.

Finchelstein, Federico. *The Ideological Origins of the Dirty War: Fascism, Populism, and Dictatorship in Twentieth Century Argentina*. Oxford: Oxford University Press, 2014.

Finer, S. E. *The Man on Horseback: The Role of the Military in Politics*. London: Pall Mall, 1962.

First, Ruth. *The Barrel of a Gun: Political Power in Africa and the Coup d'Etat*. 1970. London: Ruth First Papers Project, 2012.

Fromm, Erich. *Escape from Freedom*. 1941. New York: Henry Holt, 1994.

Garigue, Philip. "The West African Students' Union." *Africa* 23, no. 1 (1953): 55–70.

Georges, Telford. *Law and Its Administration in a One Party State: Selected Speeches*. Nairobi: East African Literature Bureau, 1973.

Getachew, Adom. *Worldmaking after Empire: The Rise and Fall of Self-Determination*. Princeton, NJ: Princeton University Press, 2019.

Ghai, Yash. "The Role of Law in the Transition of Societies: The African Experience." *Journal of African Law* 35, no. 1/2 (1991): 8–20.

Ghias, Shoaib A. "Miscarriage of Chief Justice: Judicial Power and the Legal Complex in Pakistan under Musharraf." *Law and Social Inquiry* 35, no. 4 (2010): 985–1022.

Gilroy, Paul, Tony Sandset, Sindre Bangstad, and Gard Ringen Høibjerg. "A Diagnosis of Contemporary Forms of Racism, Race and Nationalism: A Conversation with Professor Paul Gilroy." *Cultural Studies* 33, no. 2 (2019): 173–97.

Ginio, Ruth. *The French Army and Its African Soldiers: The Years of Decolonization*. Lincoln: University of Nebraska Press, 2017.

Glassman, Jonathon. *War of Words, War of Stones: Racial Thought and Violence in Colonial Zanzibar*. Bloomington: Indiana University Press, 2011.

Gocking, Roger. "Colonial Rule and the 'Legal Factor' in Ghana and Lesotho." *Africa* 67, no. 1 (1997): 61–85.

Gocking, Roger. "Ghana's Public Tribunals: An Experiment in Revolutionary Justice." *African Affairs* 95, no. 379 (1996): 197–223.

Goldstein, Joshua S. *War and Gender: How Gender Shapes the War System and Vice Versa*. Cambridge: Cambridge University Press, 2001.

Gopal, Priyamvada. *Insurgent Empire: Anticolonial Resistance and British Dissent*. London: Verso, 2020.

Gould, Jeremy. "Postcolonial Liberalism and the Legal Complex in Zambia." In *Fates of Political Liberalism in the British Post-Colony*, edited by Terence Halliday, Lucien Karpik, and Malcolm Feeley, 412–54. Cambridge: Cambridge University Press, 2012.

Gower, L. C. B. *Independent Africa: The Challenge to the Legal Profession*. Cambridge, MA: Harvard University Press, 1967.

Guha, Ranajit. "The Small Voice of History." In *Subaltern Studies IX: Writings on South Asian History and Society*, edited by Shahid Amin and Dipesh Chakrabarty, 1–13. Delhi: Oxford University Press, 1997.

Guha, Ranajit, ed. *A Subaltern Studies Reader, 1986–1995*. Minneapolis: University of Minnesota Press, 1997.

Gyandoh, Samuel. "Tinkering with the Criminal Justice System in Common Law Africa." *Temple Law Review* 62, no. 4 (1989): 1131–74.

Hailey, William Malcolm. *An African Survey*. Oxford: Oxford University Press, 1957.

Halliday, Paul D. *Habeas Corpus: From England to Empire*. Cambridge: Cambridge University Press, 2010.

Hansen, William W., and Umma Aliyu Musa. "Fanon, the Wretched and Boko Haram." *Journal of Asian and African Studies* 48, no. 3 (2013): 281–96.

Harkness, Kristen A. *When Soldiers Rebel: Ethnic Armies and Political Instability in Africa*. Cambridge: Cambridge University Press, 2018.

Harrington, John A., and Ambreena Manji. "The Emergence of African Law as an Academic Discipline in Britain." *African Affairs* 102, no. 406 (2003): 109–34.

Harris, J. W. "When and Why Does the Grundnorm Change?" *Cambridge Law Journal* 29, no. 1 (1971): 103–33.

Hassan, Farooq. "A Juridical Critique of Successful Treason: A Jurisprudential Analysis of the Constitutionality of a Coup d'Etat in the Common Law." *Stanford Journal of International Law* 20, no. 1 (1984): 191–258.

Hewage, Thushara. "Event, Archive, Mediation: Sri Lanka's 1971 Insurrection and the Political Stakes of Fieldwork." *Comparative Studies in Society and History* 62, no. 1 (2020): 186–217.

Hilbink, Lisa. *Judges beyond Politics in Democracy and Dictatorship: Lessons from Chile*. Cambridge: Cambridge University Press, 2007.

Hoffman, Danny. *The War Machines: Young Men and Violence in Sierra Leone and Liberia*. Durham, NC: Duke University Press, 2011.

Hountondji, Paulin J. *The Struggle for Meaning: Reflections on Philosophy, Culture, and Democracy in Africa*. Athens: Ohio University Press, 2002.

Human Rights Violations Investigation Commission Report. Washington, DC: Nigerian Democratic Movement, 2005.

Human Rights Watch. "Nigeria: The Dawn of a New Dark Age." *Human Rights Watch Report* 6, no. 8 (October 1994).

Huntington, Samuel P. *The Soldier and the State: The Theory and Politics of Civil-Military Relations*. Cambridge, MA: Harvard University Press, 1957.

Hussain, Nasser. *The Jurisprudence of Emergency: Colonialism and the Rule of Law*. Ann Arbor: University of Michigan Press, 2019.

Hutchful, Eboe, and Abdoulaye Bathily, eds. *The Military and Militarism in Africa*. Dakar: CODESRIA, 1998.

Ibeziako, S. Mb. *The Nigerian Customary Law*. Onitsha: Etudo, 1965.

Ibhawoh, Bonny. *Human Rights in Africa*. Cambridge: Cambridge University Press, 2018.

Ibhawoh, Bonny. *Imperial Justice: Africans in Empire's Court*. Oxford: Oxford University Press, 2013.

Ibhawoh, Bonny. "Stronger than the Maxim Gun: Law, Human Rights and British Colonial Hegemony in Nigeria." *Africa* 72, no. 1 (2002): 55–83.

Ifemesia, C. C. *Southeastern Nigeria in the Nineteenth Century: An Introductory Analysis*. New York: Nok, 1978.

Iheme, Babs A. "Sources of Law in Nigeria: The Question of Autochthony and Relevance." *Abia State University Law Journal*, no. 2 (1997): 45.

Ihonvbere, Julius O. "The Military and Nigerian Society: The Abacha Coup and the Crisis of Democratisation in Nigeria." In *The Military and Militarism in Africa*, edited by Eboe Hutchful and Abdoulaye Bathily, 503–40. Dakar: CODESRIA, 1998.

Ijere, M. O. "The Economic Significance of Shrines." Occasional paper, Department of Religion, University of Nigeria–Nsukka, 1964.

Iliffe, John. *Honour in African History*. Cambridge: Cambridge University Press, 2005.

Immerwahr, Daniel. "The Politics of Architecture and Urbanism in Postcolonial Lagos, 1960–1986." *Journal of African Cultural Studies* 19, no. 2 (2007): 165–86.

Integration of Customary and Modern Legal Systems in Africa, a Conference Held at Ibadan, 24th–29th August 1964. New York: Africana Publishing, 1971.

Ipinyomi, Kayode, Frank-Hill Morbike, and Ibrahim Sani. *How to Win the War Against Indiscipline*. 1984. Onitsha: Network Publishing, 1986.

Ivaska, Andrew. *Cultured States: Youth, Gender, and Modern Style in 1960s Dar es Salaam*. Durham, NC: Duke University Press, 2011.

Janowitz, Morris. *The Military in the Political Development of New Nations: An Essay in Comparative Analysis*. Chicago: University of Chicago Press, 1964.

Jasanoff, Maya. *The Dawn Watch: Joseph Conrad in a Global World*. London: Joseph Collins, 2017.

Jearey, J. H. "The Structure, Composition and Jurisdiction of Courts and Authorities Enforcing the Criminal Law in British African Territories." *International and Comparative Law Quarterly* 9, no. 3 (1960): 396–414.

Jemibewon, David M. *A Combatant in Government*. Ibadan: Heinemann, 1979.

Jemibewon, David M. *An Introduction to the Theory and Practice of Military Law in Nigeria*. Lagos: Friends Foundation, 1989.

Jemibewon, David M. *The Military, Law and Society: Reflections of a General*. Ibadan: Spectrum, 1998.

Jibrin, Ibrahim. "The First Lady Syndrome and the Marginalization of Women from Power: Opportunities or Compromises for Gender Equality?" *Feminist Africa*, no. 3 (2004): 1–14.

Johnson-Odim, Cheryl, and Nina Emma Mba. *For Women and the Nation: Funmilayo Ransome-Kuti of Nigeria*. Chicago: University of Illinois Press, 1997.

Joseph, Richard A. *Democracy and Prebendal Politics in Nigeria: The Rise and Fall of the Second Republic*. Cambridge: Cambridge University Press, 1987.

Kaarsholm, Preben. "Inventions, Imaginings, Codifications: Authorising Versions of Ndebele Cultural Tradition." *Journal of Southern African Studies* 23, no. 2 (1997): 243–58.

Kalu, Ogbu U. "Missionaries, Colonial Government and Secret Societies in South-Eastern Igboland, 1920–1950." *Journal of the Historical Society of Nigeria* 9, no. 1 (1977): 75–90.

Kamil, Muhammed. *Africa Has Come of Age: The Ideological Legacy of General Murtala Ramat Muhammed*. Lagos: Munascripts Noetic, 1996.

Kamil, Muhammed. *Rendez-vous . . . : An Authorized Biography of Chief Justice Mohammed Bello*. Lagos: Malthouse, 1995.

Kandeh, Jimmy D. *Coups from Below: Armed Subalterns and State Power in West Africa*. New York: Palgrave Macmillan, 2004.

Karekwaivanane, George H. *The Struggle over State Power in Zimbabwe: Law and Politics since 1950*. Cambridge: Cambridge University Press, 2017.

Karekwaivanane, George H. "'Through the Narrow Door': Narratives of the First Generation of African Lawyers in Zimbabwe." *Africa* 86, no. 1 (2016): 59–77.

Kasfir, Nelson. "The 1967 Uganda Constituent Assembly Debate." *Transition*, no. 33 (1967): 52–56.

Kaviraj, Sudipta. "Gandhi's Trial and India's Colonial State." In *Experiencing the State*, edited by Lloyd I. Rudolph and John Kurt Jacobsen, 293–308. New Delhi: Oxford University Press, 2006.

Keegan, John. *The Mask of Command*. New York: Viking, 1987.

Kirkby, Coel. "Commonwealth Constitution-Maker: The Life of Yash Ghai." In *Commonwealth History in the Twenty-First Century*, edited by Saul Dubow and R. Drayton, 61–80. Cham: Palgrave Macmillan, 2020.

Kirkby, Coel. "Exorcising *Matovu*'s Ghost: Legal Positivism, Pluralism and Ideology in Uganda's Appellate Courts." LLM thesis, McGill University, 2008.

Kirk-Greene, A. H. M., ed. *The Principles of Native Administration in Nigeria*. London: Oxford University Press, 1965.

Kiwanuka, Semakula. *Amin and the Tragedy of Uganda*. Munich: Weltforum Verlag, 1979.

Klantschnig, Gernot. *Crime, Drugs and the State in Africa*. Leiden: Brill, 2013.

Kletzer, Christoph. "The Role and Reception of the Work of Hans Kelsen in the United Kingdom." In *Hans Kelsen Abroad*, edited by Klaus Zeleny and Robert Waler, 133–67. Vienna: Manz, 2010.

Kolb, Anjuli Fatima Raza. *Epidemic Empire: Colonialism, Contagion, and Terror, 1817–2020*. Chicago: University of Chicago Press, 2021.

Korieh, Chima J. *Nigeria and World War II: Colonialism, Empire, and Global Conflict*. Cambridge: Cambridge University Press, 2020.

Kotkin, Stephen. *Magnetic Mountain: Stalinism as a Civilization*. Berkeley: University of California Press, 1997.

Koyana, Digby Sqhelo. *Customary Law in a Changing Society*. Cape Town: Juta, 1980.

Krog, Antjie. "Research into Reconciliation and Forgiveness at the South African Truth and Reconciliation Commission and Homi Bhabha's 'Architecture of the New.'" *Canadian Journal of Law and Society* 30, no. 2 (2015): 203–17.

Kukah, Matthew Hassan. *Witness to Justice: An Insider's Account of Nigeria's Truth Commission*. Ibadan: Bookcraft, 2011.

Kuper, Hilda, and Leo Kuper, eds. *African Law: Adaptation and Development*. Berkeley: University of California Press, 1965.

Kureshi, Yasser. *Seeking Supremacy: The Pursuit of Judicial Power in Pakistan*. Cambridge: Cambridge University Press, 2022.

Kuti, A. F. Demola. *Law and Policy: The Supreme Court Approach*. Lagos: Law Times, 1988.

Lasebikan, Victor O., and Ijomata N. Ijomanta. "Lifetime and 12 Months Cannabis Use and Disorders among Soldiers Residing in a Military Community in Nigeria." *Journal of Substance Use* 23, no. 1 (2018): 67–73.

Lavaud-Legendre, Bénédicte. *Prostitution nigériane: Entre rêves de migration et réalités de la traite*. Paris: Karthala, 2013.

Lawrance, Benjamin N. "*Bankoe v. Dome*: Traditions and Petitions in the Ho-Asogli Amalgamation, British Mandated Togoland, 1919–39." *Journal of African History* 46, no. 2 (2005): 243–67.

Lawrance, Benjamin N., and Gaurav Desai. "African Studies Keywords: An Introduction." *African Studies Review* 64, no. 1 (2021): 116–28.

Layonu, Taslim, ed. *Reflections on Leadership in Nigeria: Living Documents*. Ibadan: Lay-Tal Communications, 1992.

Lefever, Ernest W., and Wynfred Joshua. "United Nations Peacekeeping in the Congo, 1960–1964." Washington, DC: Brookings Institution, 1966.

Legum, Colin. "Behind the Clown's Mask." 1976. *Transition*, no. 75/76 (1997): 250–58.

Lieber, Francis G., Norman Lieber, Will Smiley, and John Fabian Witt. *To Save the Country: A Lost Treatise on Martial Law*. New Haven, CT: Yale University Press, 2019.

Liliwhite-Nwosu, Nkem. *Divine Restoration of Nigeria: Eyewitness Account of Her Trials and Triumphs*. Lagos: css Bookshops, 2004.

Liliwhite-Nwosu, Nkem. *Divine Restoration!: Testimonies of Our Motherland on Trial*. Lagos: Self-published, 2002.

Lindsay, Lisa. *Working with Gender: Wage Labor and Social Change in Southwestern Nigeria*. Portsmouth, NH: Heinemann, 2003.

Lindsay, Lisa, and Stephan Miescher, eds. *Men and Masculinities in Modern Africa*. Portsmouth, NH: Heinemann, 2003.

Livsey, Tim. *Nigeria's University Age: Reframing Decolonisation and Development*. London: Palgrave Macmillan, 2017.

Lobban, Michael. *Imperial Incarceration: Detention without Trial in the Making of British Colonial Africa*. Cambridge: Cambridge University Press, 2021.

Lonsdale, John. "Agency in Tight Corners: Narrative and Initiative in African History." *Journal of African Cultural Studies* 13, no. 1 (2000): 5–16.

Lorde, Audre. *Sister Outsider: Essays and Speeches*. 1984. Berkeley: Crossing Press, 2007.

Low, D. A. *Buganda in Modern History*. Berkeley: University of California Press, 1971.

Low, D. A., and John M. Lonsdale. "Introduction: Towards the New Order, 1945–63." In *History of East Africa, Vol. III*, edited by D. A. Low and Alison Smith, 1–63. Oxford: Clarendon Press, 1976.

Luanda, Nestor. "The Tanganyika Rifles and the Mutiny of January 1964." In *The Military and Militarism in Africa*, edited by Eboe Hutchful and Abdoulaye Bathily, 175–210. Dakar: CODESRIA, 1998.

Luckham, Robin. "The Military, Militarization and Democratization in Africa: A Survey of Literature and Issues." *African Studies Review* 37, no. 2 (1994): 13–75.

Luckham, Robin. *The Nigerian Military: A Sociological Analysis of Authority and Revolt 1960–1967*. Cambridge: Cambridge University Press, 1974.

Ly, Aliou. "Promise and Betrayal: Women Fighters and National Liberation in Guinea Bissau." *Feminist Africa*, no. 19 (2014): 24–42.

Macharia, Keguro. "From Repair to Pessimism." *Brick*, no. 106 (2021).

Machava, Benedito. "Reeducation Camps, Austerity, and the Carceral Regime in Socialist Mozambique, 1974–79." *Journal of African History* 60, no. 3 (2019): 429–55.

Magaziner, Daniel. *The Law and the Prophets: Black Consciousness in South Africa, 1968–1977*. Athens: Ohio University Press, 2010.

Mahama, John Dramani. *My First Coup d'Etat: And Other True Stories from the Lost Decades of Africa*. New York: Bloomsbury, 2012.

Mahmud, Tayyab. "Jurisprudence of Successful Treason: Coup d'Etat and Common Law." *Cornell International Law Journal* 27, no. 49 (1994): 50–140.

Maja-Pearce, Adewale. *In My Father's Country: A Nigerian Journey*. London: Heinemann, 1987.

Maja-Pearce, Adewale. *Remembering Ken Saro-Wiwa and Other Essays*. Self-published, CreateSpace, 2013.

Makubuya, Apollo N. *Protection, Patronage, or Plunder?: British Machinations and Buganda's Struggle for Independence*. Newcastle upon Tyne: Cambridge Scholars Publishing, 2018.

Mama, Amina. "Bridging through Time: Inhabiting the Interstices of Institutions and Power." In *Feminist Freedom Warriors*, edited by Chandra Talpade Mohanty and Linda E. Carty, 85–106. Chicago: Haymarket Books, 2018.

Mama, Amina. "Feminism or Femocracy? State Feminism and Democratisation in Nigeria." *Africa Development* 20, no. 1 (1995): 37–58.

Mama, Amina. "Khaki in the Family: Gender Discourses and Militarism in Nigeria." *African Studies Review* 41, no. 2 (1998): 1–17.

Mamdani, Mahmood. "Amnesty or Impunity? A Preliminary Critique of the Report of the Truth and Reconciliation Commission of South Africa." *Diacritics* 32, no. 3–4 (2002): 33–59.

Mamdani, Mahmood. *Citizen and Subject: Contemporary Africa and the Legacy of Late Colonialism*. Princeton, NJ: Princeton University Press, 1996.

Mamdani, Mahmood. *Define and Rule: Native as Political Identity*. Cambridge, MA: Harvard University Press, 2012.

Mamdani, Mahmood. *From Citizen to Refugee: Uganda Asians Come to Britain.* London: Frances Pinter, 1973.

Mamdani, Mahmood. *Imperialism and Fascism in Uganda.* London: Heinemann, 1983.

Mamdani, Mahmood. "Reconciliation without Justice." *Southern African Review of Books* 10, no. 6 (1997): 3–5.

Mani, Lata. *Contentious Traditions: The Debate on Sati in Colonial India.* Berkeley: University of California Press, 1998.

Mann, Gregory. "An Africanist's Apostasy: On Luise White's *Speaking with Vampires.*" *International Journal of African Historical Studies* 41, no. 1 (2008): 117–27.

Mann, Gregory. *From Empires to NGOs in the West African Sahel: The Road to Nongovernmentality.* Cambridge: Cambridge University Press, 2015.

Mann, Kristin. *Slavery and the Birth of an African City: Lagos, 1760–1900.* Bloomington: Indiana University Press, 2007.

Marenin, Otwin. "The Anini Saga: Armed Robbery and the Reproduction of Ideology in Nigeria." *Journal of Modern African Studies* 25, no. 2 (1987): 259–81.

Marx, Karl. *The Eighteenth Brumaire of Louis Bonaparte.* 1852. New York: International Publishers, 1926.

Massoud, Mark Fathi. *Law's Fragile State: Colonial, Authoritarian, and Humanitarian Legacies in Sudan.* Cambridge: Cambridge University Press, 2013.

Mayer, Adam. *Naija Marxisms: Revolutionary Thought in Nigeria.* London: Pluto, 2016.

Mazrui, Ali A. "The Lumpen Proletariat and the Lumpen Militariat: African Soldiers as a New Political Class." *Political Studies* 21, no. 1 (1973): 1–12.

Mazrui, Ali A. "The Rise and Fall of the Philosopher King in East Africa: The View from Uganda." *Ufahamu* 15, no. 3 (1987): 98–108.

Mazrui, Ali A. "Seek Ye First the Political Kingdom." In *General History of Africa, VIII: Africa since 1935*, edited by Ali A. Mazrui and C. Wondji, 105–26. Paris: UNESCO, 1999.

Mba, Nina. *Kaba and Khaki: Women and the Militarized State in Nigeria.* East Lansing: Michigan State University Women in International Development Program, 1988.

Mbembe, Achille. *Necropolitics.* Durham, NC: Duke University Press, 2019.

Mbembe, Achille. *On the Postcolony.* Berkeley: University of California Press, 2001.

McGowan, Patrick J. "African Military Coups d'État, 1956–2001: Frequency, Trends and Distribution." *Journal of Modern African Studies* 41, no. 3 (2003): 339–70.

McQuade, Joseph. *A Genealogy of Terrorism: Colonial Law and the Origins of an Idea.* Cambridge: Cambridge University Press, 2020.

Meaney, Thomas. "Frantz Fanon and the CIA Man." *American Historical Review* 124, no. 3 (2019): 983–95.

Medina, Diego E. L. *Teoría Impura del Derecho: la transformación de la cultura jurídica latino americana.* Bogotá: Legis, 2004.

Mensah-Brown, A. Kodwo. *Introduction to Law in Contemporary Africa.* Owerri: Conch, 1976.

Messenger, John C. "The Role of Proverbs in a Nigerian Judicial System." *Southwestern Journal of Anthropology* 15, no. 1 (1959): 64–73.

Mignolo, Walter D. *The Politics of Decolonial Investigations.* Durham, NC: Duke University Press, 2021.

Mikhail, Alan. *My Egypt Archive.* New Haven, CT: Yale University Press, 2023.

Milner, Alan. *The Nigerian Penal System.* London: Sweet and Maxwell, 1972.

Mishra, Pankaj. *From the Ruins of Empire: The Revolt against the West and the Remaking of Asia.* London: Allen Lane, 2012.

Mokoena, Hlonipha. "Who Owns 'Black'? Decolonization and Its Aporias." *Current History* 122, no. 844 (2023): 193–95.

Monaville, Pedro. *Students of the World: Global 1968 and Decolonization in the Congo.* Durham, NC: Duke University Press, 2022.

Monfrini, Enrico. "Recovering the Proceeds of Corruption: General Sani Abacha, a Nation's Thief." In *Recovering Stolen Assets*, edited by Mark Pieth, 63–78. New York: Peter Lang, 2008.

Moore, Sally Falk. *Social Facts and Fabrications: "Customary" Law on Kilimanjaro, 1880–1980.* Cambridge: Cambridge University Press, 1986.

Morapedi, Wazha G. "Demise or Resilience? Customary Law and Chieftaincy in Twenty-First Century Botswana." *Journal of Contemporary African Studies* 28, no. 2 (2005): 215–30.

Morris, Lawrence J. *Military Justice: A Guide to the Issues.* Santa Barbara, CA: Praeger, 2010.

Musila, Grace A. *A Death Retold in Truth and Rumour: Kenya, Britain and the Julie Ward Murder.* London: James Currey, 2015.

Mwakikagile, Godfrey. *Military Coups in West Africa since the Sixties.* Huntington, NY: Nova Science, 2001.

Ndlovu-Gatsheni, Sabelo J. "Who Ruled by the Spear? Rethinking the Form of Governance in the Ndebele State." *African Studies Quarterly* 10, nos. 2–3 (2008): 71–94.

Nékám, Alexander. *Experiences in African Customary Law.* Edinburgh: Centre of African Studies, 1966.

Newell, Stephanie. *Histories of Dirt: Media and Urban Life in Colonial and Postcolonial Lagos.* Durham, NC: Duke University Press, 2020.

Newell, Stephanie. "Introduction: Ken Saro-Wiwa as Public Intellectual." *Research in African Literatures* 48, no. 4 (2017): vii–xvi.

Ngũgĩ wa Thiong'o. *Decolonising the Mind: The Politics of Language in African Literature.* London: Heinemann, 1986.

Nigerian Institute of Advanced Legal Studies (NIALS). *Proceedings of the Colloquium on Why Army Rule?: 20–22 May 1986.* Lagos: Nigerian Institute of Advanced Legal Studies, 1986.

Njoku, Athananasius O. "Zikism: The Forgotten Philosophy of African Liberation." *Black World* 16, no. 8 (1967): 30.

Nkrumah, Kwame. *Dark Days in Ghana*. London: Lawrance and Wishart, 1968.

Nkrumah, Kwame. *Handbook of Revolutionary Warfare: A Guide to the Armed Phase of the African Revolution*. London: Panaf Books, 1968.

Nugent, Paul. *Africa since Independence: A Comparative History*. London: Palgrave Macmillan, 2004.

Nwabara, S. N. *Iboland: A Century of Contact with Britain, 1860–1960*. Atlantic Highlands, NJ: Humanities Press, 1978.

Nwabueze, Ben. "Constitutional Problems of Military Coups in Nigeria." *Legal Practitioners' Review* 2, no. 1 (1987): 31–43.

Nwabueze, Ben. *Judicialism in Commonwealth Africa*. London: Hurst, 1977.

Nwokedi, Emeka, and Jean-Pascal Daloz. *French Revolution: A Nigerian Perspective*. Ibadan: Macmillan Nigeria, 1990.

Nwokeji, Ugo. *The Slave Trade and Culture in the Bight of Biafra: An African Society in the Atlantic World*. Cambridge: Cambridge University Press, 2010.

Nwosu, Nereus I. "The Dynamics of Nigeria's Decolonization Policy in Africa." *Transafrican Journal of History* 22 (1993): 74–86.

Nzimiro, Ikenna. *The Babangida Men: The Making of Ministers*. Oguta: Zim Pan African, 1993.

Obadare, Ebenezer. *Pentecostal Republic: Religion and the Struggle for State Power in Nigeria*. London: Zed Books, 2018.

Obasanjo, Olusegun. *Nzeogwu: An Intimate Portrait of Major Chukwuma Kaduna Nzeogwu*. Ibadan: Spectrum, 1999.

Obasanjo, Olusegun. *This Animal Called Man*. Abeokuta: ALF, 1998.

Obi, S. N. Chinwuba. *The Ibo Law of Property*. London: Butterworths, 1963.

Obilade, Akintunde. "Jurisdiction in Customary Law Matters in Nigeria: A Critical Examination." *Journal of African Law* 17, no. 2 (1973): 227–40.

Oboh, Jude. *Cocaine Hoppers: Nigerian International Cocaine Trafficking*. Lanham, MD: Lexington Books, 2021.

Ochiagha, Terri. *Achebe and Friends at Umuahia: The Making of a Literary Elite*. Woodbridge, UK: James Currey, 2015.

Ochonu, Moses E. *Colonialism by Proxy: Hausa Imperial Agents and Middle Belt Consciousness in Nigeria*. Bloomington: Indiana University Press, 2014.

Ocran, A. K. *A Myth Is Broken: An Account of the Ghana Coup d'Etat of 24th February, 1966*. Harlow, UK: Longman, 1968.

Ocran, A. K. *Politics of the Sword: A Personal Memoir on Military Involvement in Ghana and of Problems of Military Government*. London: Rex Collings, 1977.

Ofoegbu, Mazi Ray. "Igbo National Dress and Acculturation." In *Igbo Language and Culture*, edited by F. Chidozie Ogbalu and E. Nolue Emenanjo, 205–16. Ibadan: Oxford University Press, 1975.

Oguamanam, Chidi, and W. Wesley Pue. "Lawyers' Professionalism, Colonialism, State Formation and National Life in Nigeria, 1900–1960: 'The Fighting Brigade of the People.'" Occasional paper, University of British Columbia, 2006.

Ogueri, Eze. *African Nationalism and Military Ascendancy*. Owerri: Conch, 1976.

Ojo, A. "Constitutional Developments in Nigeria since Independence." In *Law and Social Change in Nigeria*, edited by T. O. Elias, 1–20. Lagos: Evans Brothers, 1972.

Ojo, Abiola. "The Search for a Grundnorm in Nigeria—The Lakanmi Case." *Nigerian Journal of Contemporary Law* 1, no. 2 (1970): 117–36.

Ojukwu, Chukwuemeka Odumegwu. *The Ahiara Declaration: The Principles of the Biafran Revolution*. Geneva: Markpress, 1969.

Okeke, Chris, ed. *Towards Functional Justice: Seminar Papers of Justice Chukwudifu A. Oputa*. Ibadan: Gold, 2007.

Okonjo, I. M. *British Administration in Nigeria 1900–1950: A Nigerian View*. New York: Nok, 1974.

Okonkwo, Ikoku. *Jeremiah Timbut Useni: Portrait of a Gentleman General in Selfless Service*. Lagos: Self-published, 1995.

Okpewho, Isidore. *The Last Duty*. Harlow, UK: Longman, 1986.

Okri, Ben. *The Famished Road*. New York: Nan A. Talese/Doubleday, 1991.

Okwu, Austine S. O. "The Ahiara Declaration: Polemics and Politics." In *Writing the Nigeria-Biafra War*, edited by Toyin Falola and Ogechukwu Ezekwem, 81-108. Suffolk, UK: James Currey, 2016.

Okwu, Austine S. O. *In Truth for Justice and Honor: A Memoir of a Nigerian-Biafran Ambassador*. Princeton, NJ: Sungai, 2011.

Olaniyan, Tejumola. *Arrest the Music!: Fela and His Rebel Art and Politics*. Bloomington: Indiana University Press, 2004.

Olaniyan, Tejumola. "The Cosmopolitan Nativist: Fela Anikulapo-Kuti and the Antinomies of Postcolonial Modernity." *Research in African Literatures* 32, no. 2 (2001): 76–89.

Oloka-Onyango, J. *When Courts Do Politics: Public Interest Law and Litigation in East Africa*. Newcastle upon Tyne: Cambridge Scholars, 2017.

Oluleye, James J. *Military Leadership in Nigeria, 1966–1979*. Ibadan: University Press, 1985.

Olusanya, O. *The West African Students' Union and the Politics of Decolonisation, 1925–1958*. Ibadan: Daystar, 1982.

Olúwọlé, Sophie B. *Socrates and Òrúnmìlà: Two Patron Saints of Classical Philosophy*. Lagos: Ark, 2017.

Olúwọlé, Sophie B. *Witchcraft, Reincarnation and the God-Head: Issues in African Philosophy*. Lagos: Excel, 1995.

Omar, Imtiaz. *Emergency Powers and the Courts in India and Pakistan*. The Hague: Kluwer Law International, 2002.

Omara-Otunnu, Amii. "The Currency of Militarism in Uganda." In *The Military and Militarism in Africa*, edited by Eboe Hutchful and Abdoulaye Bathily, 399–426. Dakar: CODESRIA, 1998.

Omeni, Akali. *Policing and Politics in Nigeria: A Comprehensive History*. Boulder, CO: Lynne Rienner, 2022.

Onagoruwa, Olu. "International Conventions: The Constitution and Military Decrees in Nigeria." *Lord Justice: A Journal of the Law Students' Society, University of Ibadan* 3 (1990): 1.

Onagoruwa, Olu. *Press Freedom in Crisis: A Study of the Amakiri Case.* Lagos: Daily Times, 1978.

Onagoruwa, Olu. *A Rebel in General Abacha's Government.* Lagos: Inspired Communication, 2006.

Onyango, Peter. *African Customary Law System: An Introduction.* Nairobi: LawAfrica, 2013.

Opalo, Ken O. *Legislative Development in Africa: Politics and Postcolonial Legacies.* Cambridge: Cambridge University Press, 2019.

Opolot, Ejakait. *A Discourse on Just and Unjust Legal Institutions in African English-Speaking Countries.* Lewiston, NY: Edwin Mellon, 2002.

Oputa, C. A. *Conduct at the Bar and the Unwritten Laws of the Legal Profession.* Holmes Beach: Wm. W. Gaunt, 1982.

Osaghae, Eghosa. "Colonialism and Civil Society in Africa: The Perspective of Ekeh's Two Publics." *Voluntas* 17, no. 3 (2006): 233–45.

Osayande, Emmanuel. "A Tortuous Trajectory: Nigerian Foreign Policy under Military Rule, 1985–1999." *African Research Review* 14, no. 1 (2020): 143–54.

Osborn, Emily Lynn. *Our New Husbands Are Here: Households, Gender, and Politics in a West African State from the Slave Trade to Colonial Rule.* Athens: Ohio University Press, 2011.

Osborne, Myles. *Ethnicity and Empire in Kenya: Loyalty and Martial Race among the Kamba, c.1800 to the Present.* Cambridge: Cambridge University Press, 2014.

Ose, Elvira Dyangani, ed. *Festac '77.* Cologne: Walther König, 2019.

Oshunkoya, J. O. *Wisdom of Ramatism.* Ibadan: Hope Business Enterprises, 1976.

Osifodunrin, Paul. "Violent Crimes in Lagos, 1861–2000: Nature, Responses and Impact." PhD diss., University of Lagos, 2007.

Osuntogun, Abiodun Jacob. "Pure Theory of Law: Another Perspective." In *Jurisprudence and Legal Theory in Nigeria*, edited by Adewale Taiwo and Ifeolu John Koni, 233–61. Lagos: Princeton Associates, 2019.

Ottenberg, Simon. "Ibo Oracles and Intergroup Relations." *Southwestern Journal of Anthropology* 14, no. 3 (1958): 295–317.

Owusu, Maxwell. "Custom and Coups: A Juridical Interpretation of Civil Order and Disorder in Ghana." *Journal of Modern African Studies* 24, no. 1 (1986): 69–99.

Oyěwùmí, Oyèrónkẹ́. *The Invention of Women: Making an African Sense of Western Gender Discourses.* Minneapolis: University of Minnesota Press, 1997.

Parsons, Timothy H. *The African Rank-and-File: Social Implications of Colonial Military Service in the King's African Rifles, 1902–1964.* Portsmouth, NH: Heinemann, 1999.

Peterson, Brian J. *Thomas Sankara: A Revolutionary in Cold War Africa*. Bloomington: Indiana University Press, 2021.

Peterson, Derek R. *Ethnic Patriotism and the East African Revival: A
History of Dissent, c. 1935–1972*. Cambridge: Cambridge University Press,
2012.

Peterson, Derek R. "Government Work in Idi Amin's Uganda." *Africa* 91, no. 4
(2021): 620–40.

Peterson, Derek R. "The Politics of Transcendence in Colonial Uganda." *Past and
Present* 230, no. 1 (2016): 197–225.

Peterson, Derek R., Richard Vokes, Nelson Abiti, and Edgar C. Taylor. "The
Unseen Archive of Idi Amin: Making History in a Tight Corner." *Comparative
Studies in Society and History* 63, no. 1 (2021): 5–40.

Petrović, Tanja. *Utopia of the Uniform: Affective Afterlives of the Yugoslav
People's Army*. Durham, NC: Duke University Press, 2024.

Pierce, Steven. *Moral Economies of Corruption: State Formation and Political
Culture in Nigeria*. Durham, NC: Duke University Press, 2016.

Pierce, Steven. "Punishment and the Political Body: Flogging and Colonialism in
Northern Nigeria." In *Discipline and the Other Body: Correction, Corporeality,
Colonialism*, edited by Anupama Rao and Steven Pierce, 186–214. Durham,
NC: Duke University Press, 2006.

Piot, Charles. "The 'Right' to Be Trafficked." *Indiana Journal of Global Legal
Studies* 18, no. 1 (2011): 199–210.

Prairie, Michel, ed. *Thomas Sankara Speaks: The Burkina Faso Revolution,
1983–1987*. New York: Pathfinder, 2007.

Prakash, Gyan. *Emergency Chronicles: Indira Gandhi and Democracy's Turning
Point*. Princeton, NJ: Princeton University Press, 2019.

Pratten, David. *The Man-Leopard Murders: History and Society in Colonial Nigeria*. Edinburgh: Edinburgh University Press, 2007.

Proceedings of the Conference of the Nigerian Association of Law Teachers. Lagos:
University Press, 1967.

Quayson, Ato. *Tragedy and Postcolonial Literature*. Cambridge: Cambridge
University Press, 2021.

Quijano, Anibal, and Michael Ennis. "Coloniality of Power, Eurocentrism, and
Latin America." *Nepantla: Views from South* 1, no. 3 (2000): 533–80.

Ranger, Terence. "The Invention of Tradition in Colonial Africa." In *The Invention of Tradition*, edited by Eric Hobsbawm and Terence Ranger, 211–62.
Cambridge: Cambridge University Press, 1983.

Rathbone, Richard. "Laws, Polities, and Inference." In *Recasting the Past: History
Writing and Political Work in Modern Africa*, edited by Derek R. Peterson and
Giacomo Macola, 113–24. Athens: Ohio University Press, 2009.

Reid, Richard J. *A History of Modern Uganda*. Cambridge: Cambridge University
Press, 2017.

Reid, Richard J. *Warfare in African History*. Cambridge: Cambridge University
Press, 2012.

Reno, William. *Warfare in Independent Africa*. Cambridge: Cambridge University Press, 2011.

Roberts, Richard. *Conflicts of Colonialism: The Rule of Law, French Soudan, and Faama Mademba Sèye*. Cambridge: Cambridge University Press, 2022.

Roberts, Richard, and Kristin Mann, eds. *Law in Colonial Africa*. Portsmouth, NH: Heinemann, 1991.

Rodney, Walter. *How Europe Underdeveloped Africa*. Dar es Salaam: Tanzania Publishing House, 1972.

Ross, S. D. "Rule of Law and Lawyers in Kenya." *Journal of Modern African Studies* 30, no. 3 (1992): 421–42.

Saint-Michel, Serge, and Dominique Fages. *Histoire du Togo: Il était une fois—Eyadema*. Paris: Afrique Biblio Club, 1976.

Santos, Boaventura de Sousa. *The End of the Cognitive Empire: The Coming of Age of Epistemologies of the South*. Durham, NC: Duke University Press, 2018.

Saro-Wiwa, Ken. *Sozaboy: A Novel in Rotten English*. New York: Longman, 1994.

Satia, Priya. *Spies in Arabia: The Great War and the Cultural Foundations of Britain's Covert Empire In the Middle East*. Oxford: Oxford University Press, 2008.

Satia, Priya. *Time's Monster: How History Makes History*. Cambridge, MA: Harvard University Press, 2020.

Scheppele, Kim Lane. "Autocratic Legalism." *University of Chicago Law Review* 85, no. 2 (2018): 545–84.

Schmidt, Elizabeth. *Foreign Intervention in Africa: From the Cold War to the War on Terror*. Cambridge: Cambridge University Press, 2013.

Schroeder, Barbet, dir. *General Idi Amin Dada: A Self-Portrait*. 1974. Criterion Collection, 2008. DVD.

Shapiro, Martin. "Courts in Authoritarian Regimes." In *Rule by Law: The Politics of Courts in Authoritarian Regimes*, edited by Tom Ginsburg and Tamir Moustafa, 326–36. New York: Cambridge University Press, 2008.

Sharafi, Mitra. "A New History of Colonial Lawyering: Likhovski and Legal Identities in the British Empire." *Law and Social Inquiry* 32 (2007): 1059–94.

Shatz, Adam. "No Direction Home: The Journey of Frantz Fanon." In *The Best American Essays 2018*, edited by Hilton Als, 225–48. Boston: Houghton Mifflin, 2018.

Shawcross, William. *Deliver Us from Evil: Peacekeepers, Warlords, and a World of Endless Conflict*. New York: Simon and Schuster, 2000.

Shivji, Issa G. *Class Struggles in Tanzania*. New York: Monthly Review Press, 1976.

Shonekan, Stephanie. "Fela's Foundation: Examining the Revolutionary Songs of Funmilayo Ransome-Kuti and the Abeokuta Market Women's Movement in 1940s Western Nigeria." *Black Music Research Journal* 29, no. 1 (2009): 127–44.

Shyllon, Folarin, and General Olusegun Obasanjo. *The Demise of the Rule of Law in Nigeria under the Military: Two Points of View*. Occasional publication, no. 33. Ibadan: Institute of African Studies, University of Ibadan, 1980.

Simola, Raisa. "The Construction of a Nigerian Nationalist and Feminist, Funmilayo Ransome-Kuti." *Nordic Journal of African Studies* 8, no. 1 (1999): 94–114.

Siollun, Max. *Nigeria's Soldiers of Fortune: The Abacha and Obasanjo Years.* London: Hurst, 2019.

Siollun, Max. *Oil, Politics and Violence: Nigeria's Military Coup Culture. 1966–1976.* New York: Algora, 2009.

Siollun, Max. *What Britain Did to Nigeria: A Short History of Conquest and Rule.* London: Hurst, 2021.

Smith, Daniel Jordan. "Why Is Donald Trump so Popular in Southeastern Nigeria and What Can We Learn from It?" In *Corruption and Illiberal Politics in the Trump Era*, edited by Donna M. Goldstein and Kristen Drybread, 149–61. London: Routledge, 2022.

Smith, Nicholas Rush. "The State as Golem: Police Violence in Democratic South Africa." In *Everyday State and Democracy in Africa: Ethnographic Encounters*, edited by Wale Adebanwi, 207–29. Athens: Ohio University Press, 2022.

Smith, Stephen, and Géraldine Faes. *Bokassa: Un empereur Français.* Paris: Calmann-Lévy, 2000.

Souare, Issaka K. *Civil Wars and Coups d'Etat in West Africa: An Attempt to Understand the Roots and Prescribe Possible Solutions.* Lanham, MD: University Press of America, 2006.

Sow, Alioune. "Military Parade in Mali: Understanding Malian Politics through Spectacle." *Journal of Modern African Studies* 59, no. 2 (2021): 219–35.

Soyinka, Wole. *The Open Sore of a Continent: A Personal Narrative of the Nigerian Crisis.* Oxford: Oxford University Press, 1996.

Stapleton, Timothy. *West African Soldiers in Britain's Colonial Army, 1860–1960.* Martlesham: Boydell and Brewer, 2022.

Starn, Orin, and Miguel La Serna. *The Shining Path: Love, Madness, and Revolution in the Andes.* New York: Norton, 2019.

Steedman, Carolyn. *History and the Law: A Love Story.* Cambridge: Cambridge University Press, 2020.

Stigger, Philip. "Military Minutiae Part II, Preparing for National Service, 1946–1953: Recruit Training, the Potential Officers' Wing and Mons Officer Cadet School, 1953–1954." *Journal of the Society for Army Historical Research* 93, no. 374 (2015): 139–48.

Stockwell, Sarah. *The British End of the British Empire.* Cambridge: Cambridge University Press, 2018.

Stoler, Ann Laura. *Duress: Imperial Durabilities in Our Times.* Durham, NC: Duke University Press, 2016.

Sundiata, I. K. *Brothers and Strangers: Black Zion, Black Slavery, 1914–1940.* Durham, NC: Duke University Press, 2003.

Swanepoel, Paul. "Kenya's Colonial Judges: The Advocates' Perspective." *Journal of Asian and African Studies* 50, no. 1 (2015): 41–57.

Táíwò, Olúfẹ́mi. *Against Decolonization: Taking African Agency Seriously*. London: Hurst, 2022.

Takriti, Abdel Razzaq. "Colonial Coups and the War on Popular Sovereignty." *American Historical Review* 124, no. 3 (2019): 878–909.

Tamale, Sylvia. *When Hens Begin to Crow: Gender and Parliamentary Politics in Uganda*. Boulder, CO: Westview, 1999.

Thompson, E. P. *Whigs and Hunters: The Origin of the Black Act*. New York: Pantheon, 1976.

Thornberry, Elizabeth. "Procedure as Politics in the Cape Colony: The Career of Andrew Gontshi." *Journal of African History* 61, no. 3 (2020): 409–27.

Tobi, Niki. *Sources of Nigerian Law*. Lagos: MIJ Professional Publishers, 1996.

Tomás, António. *Amílcar Cabral: The Life of a Reluctant Nationalist*. Oxford: Oxford University Press, 2021.

Tushnet, Mark. "Authoritarian Constitutionalism." *Cornell Law Review* 100, no. 2 (2015): 391–462.

Tushnet, Mark, and Madhav Khosla, eds. *Unstable Constitutionalism: Law and Politics in South Asia*. New York: Cambridge University Press, 2015.

Ubah, C. N. "Religious Change among the Igbo during the Colonial Period." *Journal of Religion in Africa* 18, no. 1 (1988): 71–91.

Udo-Inyang, D. S. *The Man: Sir Justice Udo Udoma*. Calabar: Wusen, 1985.

Udoka, Ini Akpan. *Sir Udo Udoma: A Portrait of History*. Port Harcourt: Footsteps, 1996.

Udoma, Udo. *The Eagle in Its Flight: Being the Memoir of the Hon. Sir Udo Udoma, CFR*. Lagos: Grace and Son, 2008.

Udoma, Udo. *History and the Law of the Constitution of Nigeria*. Lagos: Malthouse, 1994.

Udoma, Udo. *The Lion and the Oil-Palm: A Study of British Rule in West Africa*. Dublin: University Press, 1943.

Udoma, Udo. *The Story of the Ibibio Union: Its Background, Emergence, Aims, Objectives and Achievements*. Ibadan: Spectrum, 1987.

Uko, Ndaeyo. *Romancing the Gun: The Press as a Promoter of Military Rule*. Trenton, NJ: Africa World Press, 2004.

Umoden, Gabriel E. *The Babangida Years*. Lagos: Gabumo, 1992.

Unger, Roberto M. *False Necessity: Anti-Necessitarian Social Theory in the Service of Radical Democracy: From Politics, a Work in Constructive Social Theory*. London: Verso, 2001.

Unoh, Solomon O. *War Against Indiscipline and Other Poems*. Ibadan: Evans Brothers, 1986.

Usman, Yusufu Bala, and Alkasum Abba. *The Misrepresentation of Nigeria: The Facts and the Figures*. Zaria: Centre for Democratic Development Research and Training, 2000.

Uzuokwu, Livy. *Grundnorm of Nigeria*. Lagos: Greg Groupe, 1991.

Vagts, Alfred. *A History of Militarism: Civilian and Military*. 1937. New York: Greenwich Editions, 1959.

Van de Walle, Nicholas. *African Economies and the Politics of Permanent Crisis, 1979–1999*. Cambridge: Cambridge University Press, 2001.

Van Hulle, Inge. *Britain and International Law in West Africa: The Practice of Empire*. Oxford: Oxford University Press, 2020.

Vatsa, Mamman Jiya. *Stinger the Scorpion*. Enugu: Fourth Dimension, 1979.

Vatsa, Mamman Jiya. *Tori for geti bow leg*. Lagos: Cross Continent, 1985.

Vatsa, Mamman Jiya, ed. *Voices from the Trench: An Anthology of Poems by Soldiers of the Nigerian Army*. Enugu: Fourth Dimension, 1978.

Vaughan, Megan. "Colonial Discourse Theory and African History, or Has Postmodernism Passed Us By?" *Social Dynamics* 20, no. 2 (1994): 1–23.

Vaughan, Megan. "Suicide in Late Colonial Africa: The Evidence of Inquests from Nyasaland." *American Historical Review* 115, no. 2 (2010): 385–404.

Vaughan, Olufemi. "Chieftaincy Politics and Communal Identity in Western Nigeria, 1893–1951." *Journal of African History* 44, no. 2 (2003): 283–302.

Venter, Al J. *War Dog: Fighting Other People's Wars: The Modern Mercenary in Combat*. Havertown, PA: Casemate, 2006.

Verhelst, Thierry. "Safeguarding African Customary Law: Judicial and Legislative Processes for Its Adaptation and Integration." Occasional paper, no. 7, African Studies Center, University of California, Los Angeles, 1968.

Wagner, Kim A. "Savage Warfare: Violence and the Rule of Colonial Difference in Early British Counterinsurgency." *History Workshop Journal* 85 (2018): 217–37.

Wai, Zubairu. *Epistemologies of African Conflicts: Violence, Evolutionism, and the War in Sierra Leone*. New York: Palgrave Macmillan, 2012.

Wallace, David Foster. *Infinite Jest*. 1996. New York: Back Bay Books, 2006.

Welch, Claude E., ed. *Soldier and State in Africa: A Comparative Analysis of Military Intervention and Political Change*. Evanston, IL: Northwestern University Press, 1970.

Whitaker, Blake. *Built on the Ruins of Empire: British Military Assistance and African Independence*. Lawrence: University Press of Kansas, 2022.

White, Luise. *Fighting and Writing: The Rhodesian Army at War and Postwar*. Durham, NC: Duke University Press, 2021.

White, Luise. Review of *The Mask of Anarchy: The Destruction of Liberia and the Religious Dimension of an African Civil War*, by Stephen Ellis, and *Expectations of Modernity: Myths and Meanings of Urban Life on the Zambian Copperbelt*, by James Ferguson. *Comparative Studies in Society and History* 45, no. 3 (2003): 632–39.

White, Luise. *Speaking with Vampires: Rumor and History in Colonial Africa*. Berkeley: University of California Press, 2000.

Widner, Jennifer A. *Building the Rule of Law: Francis Nyalali and the Road to Judicial Independence in Africa*. New York: W. W. Norton, 2001.

Wilder, Gary. *Freedom Time: Negritude, Decolonization, and the Future of the World*. Durham, NC: Duke University Press, 2015.

Wilder, Gary. "L'Homme de 13 Janvier: The Animation of Tradition and the Postcolonial Social Contract." *Columbia: A Journal of Literature and Art*, no. 15 (1990): 101–23.

Wilfahrt, Martha. *Precolonial Legacies in Postcolonial Politics: Representation and Redistribution in Decentralized West Africa.* Cambridge: Cambridge University Press, 2021.

Wilmot, Patrick F. *Seeing Double.* London: Jonathan Cape, 2005.

Wilson, Amrit. *Women and the Eritrean Revolution: The Challenge Road.* Trenton, NJ: Red Sea, 1991.

Wiredu, Kwasi. "Democracy by Consensus: Some Conceptual Considerations." *Philosophical Papers* 30, no. 3 (2001): 227–44.

Witt, John Fabian. "Garland's Million, or, the Tragedy and Triumph of Legal History." *Law and History Review* 40, no. 1 (2022): 123–47.

Wiwa, Ken. "The Murder of Ken Saro-Wiwa." 1996. *Soundings,* no. 78 (2021): 103–8.

Wolf-Phillips, Leslie. "Legitimacy: A Study of the Doctrine of Necessity." *Third World Quarterly* 1, no. 4 (1979): 97–133.

Yannakakis, Yanna. *Since Time Immemorial: Native Custom and Law in Colonial Mexico.* Durham, NC: Duke University Press, 2023.

Yngvesson, Barbara. "Making Law at the Doorway: The Clerk, the Court, and the Construction of Community in a New England Town." *Law and Society Review* 22, no. 3 (1988): 409–48.

Young, Crawford. *The African Colonial State in Comparative Perspective.* New Haven, CT: Yale University Press, 1994.

Young, Crawford, and Thomas Turner. *The Rise and Decline of the Zairian State.* Madison: University of Wisconsin Press, 1985.

Zips, Werner, and Markus Weilenmann, eds. *The Governance of Legal Pluralism: Empirical Studies from Africa and Beyond.* Berlin: Lit Verlag, 2011.

Balewa, Abubakar Tafawa, 16

Banda, Hastings, 118

Barre, Siad, 66–67

Bashorun, Aka, 151

Bassey, Peter, 198–99

Belgore, Mamoud Babatunde, 194–95

Bello, Mohammed, 82–83, 196

Ben-Ghiat, Ruth, 72

Benjamin, Walter, 86

Bensouda, Fatou, 96–97

Benton, Lauren, 203

Better Life for Rural Women, 27

Biafra, Republic of, 14, 16, 41–42, 71, 98, 140–41, 200–201, 215n2, 230n18. *See also* Nigeria

Biko, Steve, 75

Binaisa, Godfrey, 109

biopolitics, 88

Black Consciousness, 159–60

Bokassa, Jean-Bédel, 9–10, 72, 76

Boko Haram, 205

Botswana, 103–4, 117, 209n8

Braithwaite, Tunji, 151

Brazil, 7

bribery, 88–89, 91–92, 111, 193, 244n44

bride prices, 138

British Empire, 3–5, 37–40, 44–45, 47–48, 53–56, 62–63, 69–70, 102–5, 124–29, 209n8. *See also* colonialism

Buhari, Muhammadu, 16–18, 48–49, 69, 82–83, 88–94, 167–68, 176, 181–84, 189–90, 204, 246n74

Bunche, Ralph, 5

Burkina Faso, 1–2, 25–26, 80–81, 224n60; People's Revolutionary Court, 81

Butt Naked (Joshua Milton Blahyi), 70

Cabral, Amilcar, 75

cannabis, 95–96, 155, 211n35. *See also* drugs

capitalism, 7–8, 42. *See also* economy

capital punishment, 63–64, 116–17, 168, 172–82, 202–3

charisma, 21, 24–26, 159

CharlyBoy, 219n74

chieftaincy, 20–21, 46, 99, 124–25, 127–31, 133, 140–41, 145–46

child marriage, 60–61, 128

Chitepo, Herbert, 101–2

civilian: brigades, 90–92; colonialism and, 47, 50–51, 55; discipline and, 88, 226n86; governance by, 16–17, 40–42, 55, 84, 86–89, 98–99, 113, 125–26, 141, 159–61, 190–91, 204–5, 220n89; military rule and, 1–9, 14–16, 20–26, 47, 49–50, 66–67, 84, 86–94, 112–13, 117–18, 125–26, 167–87, 189, 191, 207

civil war. *See under* Nigeria; war

class: decolonization and, 158–61; education and, 159–60; military and, 6–9, 93, 211n23, 241n65

Clemenceau, Georges, 169–70

Cochran, Johnnie, 204–5

Cold War, 9–11, 66–67, 105–6, 186–87, 191

collective punishment, 171–72

collectivism, 19–20, 85–86

colonialism, 9–16, 206–8, 209n8, 216n27; anticolonialism, 10, 13, 14–16, 54–55, 75, 77–78, 80–82, 145, 186–87, 216n22; class and, 159–61; commissions of inquiry and, 145; culture and, 62–63; custom and, 125–30, 133–37; education and, 48–52; elitism and, 5–6, 55, 64, 79, 159–61, 218n59; end of, 1–3, 5–6, 13–16, 30–31, 37–40, 44–45, 83–84, 99; ethnicity and, 98, 228n129; executive power and, 53–54; governmentality and, 38–48; history and, 45–46; law and, 13–14, 51–64, 102–3, 125–30, 134–37, 164–65, 229nn7–8, 229n13; liberalism and, 53–54; as method, 39; militarism and, 47–51, 61–62, 74–75, 170; racism and, 76; religion and, 213n66; violence and, 37–39, 44. *See also* decolonization

commission of inquiry, 125, 143–45, 150–60, 238n8, 239n9, 239nn16–17, 242n17; class and, 158–61; justice and, 144–45, 161–65; legal counsel and, 239n16; legitimizing function of, 162–64; as performance, 162, 164–65; public good and, 145–46

common-law court, 33, 125

Commonwealth of Nations, 3, 10, 40–41, 43–45, 48–51, 110–11, 115, 203, 209n8. *See also* British Empire

communism, 7, 69–70, 75, 86

Comoros, 9–10

Compaoré, Blaise, 81

comradeship, 69–70, 85–86

conflict, 70–71

Connelly, Matthew, 214n99

Conrad, Joseph, 39

conservativism, 7, 82, 137

constitution, 13; democracy and, 113; after independence, 107–8; as repressive tool, 110–11, 117; revolution and, 109–13, 115

Cooper, Frederick, 83–84, 248n43

cooperation, 69–70, 102–3, 119

corporal punishment, 88, 90–91, 117, 129–30, 235n26

corruption, 5, 40–41, 50–51, 86–92, 98, 129–30, 174–77, 185, 189–94

council of elders, 127

counterfeiting, 168, 175–76

coup, 1–2, 66–67, 209n3; attempted, 221n13; legitimacy of, 109–19, 194–96; as neocolonial, 9–11; as precolonial political tradition, 46; as revolutionary, 6–7. *See also under* Nigeria

Crabbe, Samuel Azu, 58

crime, 88–89, 127, 174–76, 243n28; capital punishment and, 181–82; against state, 177

cronyism, 59–60

Crouch, Stanley, 11

custom, 124–26; authoritarianism and, 139–40; colonialism and, 126–30, 133–37; discipline and, 133, 140–41; ethnicity and, 140; gender and, 138–39; law and, 126–41, 234n22, 237n76; military and, 133–41; opposition to, 129–33; power and, 135–36; reforming, 130–32, 134, 136–40; repugnancy clause, 128–29, 234nn20–21

customary court, 133–34, 137–38

Danjuma, Theophilus, 48–49

Dawodu, Major, 147–50, 154

death penalty. *See* capital punishment

decoloniality and, 207–8, 248n43, 248n46

decolonization, 3, 5–7, 12–16, 42–43, 47–48, 81–82, 99, 206–7, 212n40, 219n68, 220n89; class and, 158–61; law and, 12–13, 51, 56–64, 80–81, 106–8, 117, 125–26, 134–37, 219n68, 220n89; as process, 42–43; violence and, 78–81

decree, 171, 236n52; Counterfeit Currency (Special Provisions) Decree No. 22, 175–76; Decree No. 45, 112–13; Decree No. 78, 113; Exchange Control (Anti-Sabotage) Decree No. 57, 175–76; Public Officers (Protection Against False Accusation) Decree No. 4, 176–77; Public Property (Special Military) Tribunal Decree No. 3, 176–77; Robbery and Firearms (Special Provisions) Decree No. 47, 175–76, 180; State Security Detention of Persons (Amendment) Decree No. 11, 195–96; Suppression of Disorder Decree No. 4, 175–76, 226n88; Supremacy and Enforcement of Powers Decree No. 12, 195–96, 243n24. *See also under* Nigeria

democracy, 21–22, 82–83, 86, 190; constitution and, 113; threats to, 101–2; transition to, 191

Democratic Republic of Congo, 9–10, 40–41; Katanga crisis, 70–71

Denard, Bob, 9–10

Denning, Tom, 131–32

detention, indefinite, 78

developmentalism, 87–88

dictatorship, 1–5, 9; class and, 158; colonialism and, 38, 42, 44–45; documentation and, 28–31; economy and, 227nn113–14; international

pressure and, 191; law and, 11–12, 39, 114–18; power and, 101–2

dignity, 69–70

Dike, Kenneth, 98

Dimka, Buka Suka, 16, 88–89, 238n4

discipline, 1, 7–8, 20, 58–59, 66, 69, 80–81, 83; decolonization and, 99; education and, 87–88; as ethos, 88–89; fiscal, 93–94; freedom and, 83–89, 99, 189; ideology of, 138, 140–41; indiscipline, 89–93; law and, 11–12, 94–97, 106–7, 114, 116, 125–26, 133, 174, 186–87; military and, 138, 171–72, 174, 179, 186–87, 192, 226n86; psychology of, 87–88; violence and, 86, 92–93

dissent, dissidence, 24–25, 32, 51, 88–89, 145, 155–56, 184–87, 194–96

divination, 127

Diya, Oladipo, 192–93

documentation, 28–31, 65–66, 146, 178–79, 214n101, 214n105

draft, public service, 73

drugs, 95–96; trafficking, 44–45, 141, 155, 158–59, 168, 193, 199, 211n35, 242n4

due process, 133, 196–97

Dutch disease, 193–94. *See also* economy

duty, 53, 66, 88

Economic Community of West African States Monitoring Group (ECOMOG), 71

economy: austerity and, 190; autarky and, 94; decolonization and, 40, 42; free trade and, 82–83; liberalism and, 53–54; military and, 227n113; oil and, 193–94; oracles and, 126; structural adjustments and, 93–94, 214n88, 215n111, 227n114

education, 41; class and, 159–60; discipline and, 87–88; legal, 51–52, 103, 106

egalitarianism, 20–22, 72

Ejoor, David, 134

election, 16–17, 82–83, 86, 190–91, 204, 233n63, 237n84

Elias, Taslim, 52–53, 58–59, 114–15, 134

elitism, 5–6, 55, 64, 79, 159–61, 218n59

emancipation, 15–16, 83–84

embezzlement, 176–77

Emecheta, Buchi, 143–44

empiricism, 137

environmentalism, 92–93, 200–201

Esugbayi Eleko v. Officer Administering the Government of Nigeria, 54

esusu (informal savings and credit scheme), 177–78

Ethiopia, 3–4, 222n20

law (*continued*)

 reforming, 56–62, 108, 130–32, 134, 136–40; repression and, 125; revolution and, 114, 194–96; romance and, 55; sexuality and, 60–61; stability and, 128–29; tribunals and, 168–69, 177–78, 180, 184; village, 137; violence and, 62, 97, 220n92. *See also* legalism; military

lawyers, 12, 51–63, 97–98, 103–5, 114, 140, 151, 174, 184–86, 201–2, 228n1, 230n16, 233n72

legalism, 11–12, 51–63; Potemkin, 165; violence and, 97. *See also* militarism

legal positivism, 106, 109–11, 117, 128, 135–36

legitimacy, 116–18, 135–36, 162–63, 194–96

Lesotho, 3, 209n8

liberalism, 39, 53–54, 82–83, 93–94; Christian, 159–60; free-market, 40; military, 187

liberation, 5–7, 51, 75, 78–79, 84, 97, 119, 207. *See also* decolonization

Liberia, 3, 30; "Every Car or Moving Object Gone" mission, 71

libertarianism, 132

Liliwhite-Nwosu, Nkem, 183–84

literacy, 6–7, 29, 129–30, 134–35, 174

Lockwood, Patricia, 7

Lorde, Audre, 64

"lost decades," 2–3

Lugard, Frederick, 38, 127–28, 230n19

Lumumba, Patrice, 9–10, 76

Machel, Samora, 21

Magaziner, Daniel, 76

Mahmud, Tayyab, 109–10

Maitatsine (Islamic revival movement), 71, 88–89

Maja-Pearce, Adewale, 91–93

Malawi, 118, 209n8

Mali, 1

Mama, Amina, 26–27, 214n88, 246n73

Mamdani, Mahmood, 63, 128–29, 144–45

Mandela, Nelson, 76

Mao Zedong, 65–66, 102

Marbury v. Madison, 109

marriage, 60–61, 127

Marxism, 66, 98

Massoud, Mark Fathi, 12

Matovu, Michael, 109

Mayanja, Abubaker Kakyama, 109

Mazrui, Ali, 6–7

Mba, Nina, 26–27

Mbembe, Achille, 31, 215n108. *See also* necropolitics

McBroom, Marie, 167–68, 172–73

Memmi, Albert, 75

migration, 128–29, 138, 229n7

militarism: artistic expressions of, 68–69, 143–44; charisma and, 24–26; colonialism and, 9–11, 13–16, 37–39, 42–51, 61–62, 74–75; decolonization and, 3, 5–7, 14–16, 42–43, 47–48, 63–64, 75, 79–82; as ideology, 1–22, 24–28, 30–34, 50–51, 65–67, 69–72, 89–90, 189; in Nigeria, 72–75; law and, 101–2, 105–6, 110–11; modernity and, 46; nationalism and, 20–21; philosophy of, 76–82; politics and, 82; psychology of, 7–8, 29, 87–88; relationality and, 69–70; revolution and, 6–8, 76–82; as sensibility, 31–33; strongman type, 72; time and, 28–29; violence and, 37–39, 86, 90–93, 97. *See also* ideology; legalism

military: civilians and, 1–9, 14–16, 20–26, 47, 49–50, 66–67, 84, 86–94, 112–13, 117–18, 125–26, 167–87, 189, 191, 207; class and, 93, 159–61, 211n23, 241n65; collectivism and, 19–20; commissions of inquiry and, 143–47, 150–57, 162–65, 239n17; corruption and, 91–92, 193–94; culture of, 19–20; custom and, 124–26, 133–41; decolonization and, 99, 159–61, 206–8, 212n40; discipline and, 83–89, 93–97, 99, 116, 133, 138, 171–72, 174, 179, 186–90, 192, 226n86; documentation by, 28–30, 214n101, 214n105; drug use and, 155; elitism and, 48–49; environmentalism and, 92–93; ethnicity and, 21, 23, 72–74; freedom and, 83–88, 99, 101–2, 189, 207; gender and, 26–27, 69, 214n84; governance by, 19, 21, 40–42, 72, 86–87, 189–90, 204–6, 208, 211n27, 218n59, 222n19; history and, 97–98; human rights and, 185–87; justice and, 161–65, 169–70, 178, 183–84, 219n68; law and, 11–14, 32–34, 53–55, 58–59, 61–64, 94–97, 101–2, 105–6, 109–11, 114–19, 133–40, 143–44, 146–47, 162–65, 168–87, 189, 194–99, 202–3; liberalism and, 82–83, 187; mobile courts and, 180–81; politics and, 1–3, 5–11, 19–24, 30–34, 89–90, 98; power and, 96, 102, 112–13, 116–18, 135–36, 162–64, 169, 172–73, 189–99, 204–6, 220n89; religion and, 21–22, 72–74, 213n66; revolution and, 189, 194–96; training and, 48–51; tribunals and, 168–69, 171–87, 196–98, 201–3; uniforms and, 28–29, 31–32, 69, 73–74; violence by, 150–57, 162–64, 199–202; war and, 70–72. *See also* law; militarism

mimicry, 47

Mishra, Pankaj, 221n1

mobile courts, 180–81, 244n44

Mobutu Sese Seko, 9–10, 66–67, 72, 76

modernity, 2–3, 46, 61, 207–8

Moi, Daniel arap, 116–17, 212n40, 233n73